Baudelaire and the
Art of Memory

Baudelaire and the Art of Memory

J. A. Hiddleston

CLARENDON PRESS · OXFORD

This book has been printed digitally and produced in a standard specification
in order to ensure its continuing availability

OXFORD
UNIVERSITY PRESS

Great Clarendon Street, Oxford OX2 6DP

Oxford University Press is a department of the University of Oxford.
It furthers the University's objective of excellence in research, scholarship,
and education by publishing worldwide in

Oxford New York

Auckland Bangkok Buenos Aires Cape Town Chennai
Dar es Salaam Delhi Hong Kong Istanbul Karachi Kolkata
Kuala Lumpur Madrid Melbourne Mexico City Mumbai Nairobi
São Paulo Shanghai Singapore Taipei Tokyo Toronto

with an associated company in Berlin

Oxford is a registered trade mark of Oxford University Press
in the UK and in certain other countries

Published in the United States
by Oxford University Press Inc., New York

© J. A. Hiddleston 1999

The moral rights of the author have been asserted
Database right Oxford University Press (maker)

Reprinted 2002

ISBN 0-19-815932-3

Cover illustration: Eugène Delacroix, Les Femmes d'Alger
(photo: AKG London)

Glorifier le culte des images (ma
grande, mon unique, ma primitive passion).

Preface

A COMPREHENSIVE study of Baudelaire's art criticism would be a vast and highly complex undertaking. His aesthetic ideas, his relationship with Delacroix, his theories on laughter and caricature, his understanding of Guys and choice of him as the painter of modern life, even his silences (about Courbet and Manet, for example), his rhetoric and critical method, would each require a separate volume, as the works of Horner, Moss, Hannoosh, and Kelley's edition of the *Salon de 1846* all eloquently demonstrate. In order to treat the subject in one volume, I have had accordingly to condense discussion of each of these principal aspects to a single chapter. 'In Search of an Aesthetic' seeks to analyse Baudelaire's ideas on the function of criticism, on *naïveté* and individualism, Romanticism, colourists and draughtsmen, memory, imagination, and his attitude towards individual painters such as Ingres and Courbet. The emphasis is principally on the *Salon de 1846*, the most seminal and controversial of his art-critical works, though I have tried at the same time to highlight the evolution of his thinking through the *Exposition universelle* of 1855 to the *Salon de 1859*. This first chapter is closely linked to the last one, 'Language and Rhetoric', in which, after a survey of his principal stylistic devices, the notorious *dédicace* 'Aux Bourgeois', the chapter 'Des écoles et des ouvriers', the notion of progress, and the contention that the 1846 *Salon* constitutes a *summum* of Baudelaire's aesthetic, social, and political thinking, are analysed in terms of his rhetorical strategy. I argue that commentators have been too ready to read into some of his pronouncements of the mid-1840s a political or social message, without taking sufficiently into account the specific context in which they are embedded and their function in the overall economy of the argument. The Baudelaire of 1848 is clearly another matter.

In the chapter on Delacroix, where I have concentrated on a relatively small number of key paintings (*La Madeleine dans le désert*, *La Mort de Sardanapale*, *La Lutte de Jacob avec l'ange*, *Pietà*, *Les Femmes d'Alger*, and *Ovide chez les Scythes*), and in Chapter 4, on caricature, I have tried above all to bring out the nature of his response, which is almost always very brief, and to develop in a 'Baudelairean' manner the suggestive quality of the works he admires. Wherever relevant, I have sought also to indicate the relationship of the art criticism to his other writings, in particular *Les Fleurs du Mal* and *Le Spleen de Paris*. In Chapter 3, a close analysis of his theory of laughter, I have tried to identify and tease out some of the contradictions in the argument, in which the doctrine of the Fall seems to sit badly with the joy which, as in Hoffmann, is said to characterize 'le comique absolu'. In Chapter 5, 'From Landscape to the Painting of Modern Life', Boudin is seen as a pivotal figure, inflecting the poet towards an aesthetic of the fleeting and the evanescent, which is eventually spelled out in *Le Peintre de la vie moderne* and exemplified in the works of Constantin Guys. Here again, as with Delacroix and caricature, I have concentrated on Guys's drawings and the sections of the essay in which their presence is most palpable. This has involved accentuating 'Les Annales de la guerre', 'Pompes et solennités', 'Le Militaire', and 'Les Femmes et les filles' at the expense of the chapters on 'Le Dandy' and make-up, which in any case have been the subject of much critical attention. Finally, Baudelaire's silence about Manet, whom he knew well and whose work has many parallels with that of the poet, seems such an important gap in the art criticism as to merit a separate chapter. Here, I argue that his silence and implied disapproval can be explained by what the poet, who believed in the inviolable specificity of art forms, must have identifed in Manet as a mismatch between medium (the oil on canvas) and an ironic or 'agnostic' content.

I have called this study *Baudelaire and the Art of Memory* because the idea that art, whether it is painting, poetry, or for that matter music, springs from the memory of the artist and speaks to the memory of the consumer of that art, is a fundamental truth which the poet emphasizes in relation to Delacroix, Daumier, Guys, and Wagner, and which is exemplified in his own creative writing. It is a fundamental tenet of his aesthetic that criticism is primarily a phenomenon of recognition; and it is that sense of recognition that I have sought to elucidate and develop throughout.

The secondary literature is so vast that for obvious reasons of space I have been constrained to limit the bibliography to the major contributors and to the works directly cited or crucial to the argument. Many 'canonical' studies and articles receive little or no mention. I trust that their omission will not be seen as laxity or arrogance; their presence is embedded in the text, and the work of Gilman, Ferran, Ruff, Sérullaz, and Moss, to name but a few, have made such a contribution that their ideas have become integrated into the corpus of acquired knowledge. In this subject, possibly more than in some others, we build upon the acquired knowledge of earlier generations. For all that, this study is aimed as much at the undergraduate as at the specialist reader.

I am grateful to the editors of *The Modern Language Review*, *Etudes baudelairiennes*, and *Romantisme*, for permission to use material previously published in articles on Baudelaire and Manet, Baudelaire and Guys, Baudelaire and Delacroix, and Baudelaire and caricature. My sincere thanks are also due to the Librarians of the Taylor Institution, the Ashmolean Museum, the Department of the History of Art at Oxford, to the Curators of the Musée Carnavalet and the Musée des Arts Décoratifs in Paris, to Monsieur Jérôme Dufilho for his ever-courteous help with reproductions of Guys, and to Bernard Howells for his painstaking reading, well beyond the call of duty or friendship, of Chapters 1, 2, and 7, and for his helpful suggestions and profound observations which have freed me from many an error and 'foolish notion'.

J. A. H.

Acknowledgements

I am grateful for the following permissions: to the British Museum for permission to reproduce Charlet's *L'Allocution*, Daumier's *Rue Transnonain* and *Les Nuits de Pénélope*, and Cruikshank's *The Comforts of a Cabriolet*; to the Ashmolean Museum for Hogarth's *The Reward of Cruelty*, Goya's *Quién lo creyera!* and *Y aún no se van*, and Meryon's *Le Petit Pont* and *Le Stryge*; to the Réunion des Musées nationaux for Delacroix's *Madeleine dans le désert*, and Guys's *La Loge de l'Empereur*; to Editions Arnaud Seydoux, Paris, for Guys's *Turks conveying the Sick to Balaclava, Lord Raglan's Headquarters at Balaclava, Captain Ponsonby riding in Alexandria*, and *Consecration of a Burial Ground at Scutari*; to AKG, London for Delacroix's, *La Mort de Sardanapale, La Lutte de Jacob avec l'ange, Les Femmes d'Alger* and *Ovide chez les Scythes*, and Manet's, *Le Balcon and Olympia*; to Bridgeman Art Library for Manet's, *Lola de Valence* and *La Musique aux Tuileries*; and to E. T. Archive for Delacroix's, Pietà.

Contents

List of Plates

List of Illustrations

List of Abbreviations

Corr.   Charles Baudelaire, *Correspondance*, ed. Claude Pichois, 2 vols. (Paris: Gallimard, 1973)

Oc.   Charles Baudelaire, *Œuvres complètes*, ed. Claude Pichois, 2 vols. (Paris: Gallimard, 1975, 1976)

Page references in the text are to volume ii of the *Œuvres complètes*.

I

In Search of an Aesthetic

BAUDELAIRE TWICE asks 'A quoi bon la critique?'; in the 'Envoi' to the *Salon de 1859* in a tone apparently of resignation and ennui, and tentatively yet confidently in the opening pages of the *Salon de 1846*. In 1859, when his aesthetic ideas have been clarified and established on permanent foundations, he affects to be as unsure of his audience as at the outset of his career, his only consolation being 'd'avoir peut-être su plaire, dans l'étalage de ces lieux communs, à deux ou trois personnes qui me devinent quand je pense à elles' (p. 682). Though in 1846 he concedes that many artists have owed their renown to critics, he is quick to deflate any pretentiousness by evoking a famous caricature by Gavarni showing, bent over his canvas, an artist behind whom a desiccated gentleman holds in his hand his latest article with the inscription 'Si l'art est noble, la critique est sainte' (p. 418).[1] In both *Salons* Baudelaire confesses that he has nothing to teach great artists, who, like the critic, believe nothing to be more tiresome than having to explain what everyone ought to know; in both *Salons* it is implied or stated that the bourgeois cannot or will not learn anything from the critic, nor indeed will the poor or mediocre artist. Who, then, is the critic addressing, and what benefit can come from his thankless labours? The question appears urgent in an initial chapter, poignant in a brief envoi, but in neither case is a clear answer given, and one is left with the impression of the critic in the posture of a shipwrecked captain casting on the seas his message in a bottle in the hope that somehow it will find a safe haven, or its ideal reader. One could object that the famous *dédicace* 'Aux Bourgeois' of 1846 gives a clear indication of the author's intended readership, but the intricate interplay of ironies in the text, betraying as it does a scepticism not far removed from the seeming disillusionment and modesty of the later *Salon*, prompts one to

[1] Reproduced in *Art in Paris 1845–1862: Salons and Other Exhibitions Reviewed by Charles Baudelaire*, ed. Jonathan Mayne (Oxford: Phaidon, 1965), plate II.

identify Baudelaire's ideal audience in both works as the small circle of artists and acquaintances, sympathetic to his views and susceptible to persuasion.[2]

At the outset Baudelaire relegates matters of technique to the studio, as being the concern of practitioners alone. As with Delacroix's magnificent cupola in the Luxembourg palace, what interests him is not the technical aspects, which he takes for granted, but the spirit of a painting: 'Je ne ferai pas à E. Delacroix l'injure d'un éloge exagéré pour avoir si bien vaincu la concavité de sa toile et y avoir placé des figures droites. Son talent est au-dessus de ces choses-là. Je m'attache surtout à l'esprit de cette peinture' (p. 438). With the obvious exception of colour, he very rarely makes as much as a passing reference to technique, even in respect of such works as *La Mort de Sardanapale*, where Delacroix was generally judged to be lacking in expertise. But this is not the only reason for his neglect of technique. From 1845, through all the stages of his development as a critic, Baudelaire complains that everyone paints better and better, and condemns what he calls the 'préoccupation excessive du métier' (p. 402). This might at first appear surprising in a poet contemptuous of the formal laxities of the earlier Romantics and the 'style coulant' of those who, like his *bête noire* George Sand, wrote as easily as they sewed.[3] One might have expected so conscious a craftsman in poetry to have welcomed a similar attention in the visual arts, but his point is that the 'pratique exclusive du métier' (p. 612), in sculpture as in painting (p. 402), is a contributing factor in the decline of contemporary art, since it leads to the exclusion of passion, temperament, and imagination: 'la passion frénétique de l'art est un chancre qui dévore le reste; et, comme l'absence nette du juste et du vrai dans l'art équivaut à l'absence d'art, l'homme entier s'évanouit; la spécialisation excessive d'une faculté aboutit au néant' (p. 48). Romanticism is devalued by too strict an adherence to craftsmanship, producing what he disparagingly calls 'le rococo du romantisme', the worst of all the forms it can take.[4]

Setting aside questions of technique, Baudelaire argues that, far from being cold and mathematical, the best criticism should be amus-

---

[2] Baudelaire's readership and the *dédicace* 'Aux Bourgeois' will figure in Ch. 7.

[3] George Sand, *Correspondance*, ed. Georges Lubin (Paris: Garnier, 1964–90), ii. 135: 'j'y suis tellement habituée à présent que j'écris avec autant de facilité que je ferais un ourlet'.

[4] Of *Les Oies du frère Philippe* by Baron he writes in the *Salon de 1845*: 'C'est d'un aspect fort attirant, mais c'est le rococo du romantisme. [. . .] Réfléchir devant ce tableau combien une peinture excessivement savante et brillante de couleur peut rester froide quand elle manque d'un tempérament particulier' (382).

ing and poetic, arising from the convictions and temperament of the critic. Just as the artist reflects nature in his painting, the critic should reflect that painting in a sensitive and intelligent mind, so that the best account of a picture might be a sonnet or elegy. Such transpositions abound in Baudelaire's own poetry, particularly *Les Fleurs du Mal*, the most famous being 'Sur *Le Tasse en prison*', and 'Don Juan aux enfers', both based upon Delacroix, with 'Le Masque' and 'Danse macabre' based on the statues of Ernest Christophe. Their proper place is, however, in anthologies of poetry and not in 'la critique proprement dite', by which he means primarily Salon writing and, by extension, articles and works of interpretation. If it is to justify itself at all, criticism proper must be 'partiale, passionnée, politique, c'est-à-dire faite à un point de vue exclusif, mais au point de vue qui ouvre le plus d'horizons' (p. 418). Two things stand out immediately from this often quoted statement. First, it is expressed, typically, as a paradox, since the exclusive point of view with its implications of restriction seems to be contradicted by the point of view which opens up horizons, the paradox of restriction opening on to abundance and expansion. Even those familiar with the poet's seemingly endless store of oxymorons is arrested by this enigmatic and suggestive formulation; they will also recognize in it the origin of his aesthetic of the verse and prose poem. Baudelaire's taste for short poems and stories and his distrust of the epic and novel are well documented. Long poems are the option of those who are incapable of writing short ones,[5] and short stories, Poe's for example, have this advantage over novels that their brevity adds to the intensity and totality of effect (p. 329), since the compactness and concision of the form are in inverse proportion to its expansion in the mind of the reader. Baudelaire equates creativity with notions of explosion, expansion, and suggestiveness, as is witnessed in his predilection for aphorisms which act like *fusées*, and for mysterious titles which have the explosive power of a *pétard*.[6] Like poetry, and indeed all art, the best criticism must also be a suggestive magic (p. 598), 'une sorcellerie évocatoire' (p. 118); it will have a similar restriction of reference and the same power to open up unexpected horizons in the mind of the reader. The idea of restriction and expansion lies at the heart of Baudelaire's aesthetic, in literature, in the visual arts, or in criticism. First clearly formulated in 1846, it is exemplified in the subsequent criticism, undergoing various reformulations, as in the

[5] *Corr.* i. 676.
[6] 'J'aime les titres mystérieux ou les titres pétards' (*Corr.* i. 378).

Exposition universelle of 1855, where he declares: 'Il m'arrivera souvent d'apprécier un tableau uniquement par la somme d'idées ou de rêveries qu'il apportera dans mon esprit' (p. 579).

There is no attempt, then, to make of criticism a scientific or impersonal discipline. The critic's own experiences and convictions are essential ingredients in the evaluation of any art—poetry, prose, music, or painting—and it is good to remind ourselves that Baudelaire is no academic or scholar, nor would he claim a place among what, after Heine, he disdainfully calls the 'professeurs-jurés' of contemporary academies (p. 577). He is essentially a poet and journalist, seeking to understand and above all to fashion contemporary taste in the arts, and committed to certain criteria of excellence. If his criticism is political, it is not because it is committed in any partisan manner, but because above all it seeks to confront the problems besetting the production and consumption of art in the particular circumstances of the historical moment; and if it is passionate, it is because he is passionately attached to those criteria through which he defined Romanticism and the modern sensibility.

The first criterion, and clearly the most important, since it justifies the critic's enterprise in his opening chapter in 1846, is what he calls 'l'individualisme bien entendu' (p. 419). The qualification is crucial, since throughout his career he considers individualism without some form of restraint or discipline to be pernicious. The aim of the critic must be to 'commander à l'artiste la naïveté et l'expression sincère de son tempérament, aidée par tous les moyens que lui fournit son métier'. It is important to avoid any misunderstanding over the word *naïveté*, which has nothing to do with the modern connotations of ingenuousness. It is rather to be understood in its etymological sense, from the Latin *nativus*, meaning what is native to or inherent in the nature and temperament of the artist. *Naïveté* requires the sincere expression of temperament, and more than that, 'la domination du tempérament dans la manière' (p. 491); that is to say that temperament should preside over the work, its style and techniques. *Naïveté* is consequently linked to notions of authenticity and originality, to what makes the artist *sui generis* (p. 596).[7] Here again, we must be careful not to associate it with any lax notions of sincerity. It is in no way related to emotionalism or its even more unbecoming companion sentimentality, and is far removed from the outpourings, powerful or otherwise, of

---

[7] The expression is among the most frequent to appear in Baudelaire's criticism.

a certain Romanticism. Sincerity is not a reflex but a conquest, based on self-knowledge. For any man it takes a long time to attain sincerity; how much more true is this of the artist who must learn to speak with his own voice and distinguish it from the cacophony of competing contemporary and ancestral voices. It is the virtue of Delacroix's paintings to be 'de grands poèmes naïvement conçus, exécutés avec l'insolence accoutumée du génie', and in a footnote Baudelaire explains that by the *naïveté* of genius one must understand 'la science du métier combinée avec le *gnôti séauton*, mais la science modeste laissant le beau rôle au tempérament' (p. 431). *Naïveté* is always associated with strength or *force* and a certain single-mindedness or faith which direct the creative energies of the man of genius into his art. Whatever modesty he may show in his social demeanour, the great artist is arrogant, insolent in the conception and execution of his works; for in the domain of artistic genius, might is right, 'car rien n'est vrai que la force, qui est la justice suprême' (p. 14). On its own, in a weak temperament, *naïveté* would lack direction and be dissipated; to that extent it bears some resemblance to Balzac's notion of willpower which, when chanelled into one obsession, can multiply the energy of an individual and raise him to great accomplishments, for good or for ill.

Armed with this one sure criterion drawn from nature itself,[8] the critic can proceed to do his critical duty with passion, which, he claims, in a logical leap which he takes as axiomatic, 'rapproche les tempéraments analogues et soulève la raison à des hauteurs nouvelles'. Passion here appears to have much the same galvanizing power as imagination in the *Salon de 1859*, driving the other faculties, in particular reason, into combat (p. 620). Also, it makes of criticism not so much a relationship between subject and object, but by bringing similar temperaments together between subject and subject. Nothing could be more characteristic of Baudelaire's own critical *démarche*, since he recognizes himself not just in Delacroix or Poe, who have become universal figures, but in such minor artists as Haussoullier in the *Salon de 1845* or Guys in *Le Peintre de la vie moderne*, whose elevation among the great still seems, some century and a half later, quirky and idiosyncratic.

Baudelaire's view of *naïveté* and temperament may at first appear incompatible with his disapproval of unbridled artistic individualism

[8] Baudelaire means that the criterion is not some abstract principle drawn from a philosophy of art but from what has been implanted in the artist by nature.

and the decline of the *écoles* of painting, in place of which there are now only 'des ouvriers émancipés'. Just as sincerity requires the rigour of self-knowledge, so freedom can be fruitful only when accompanied by discipline and restraint. In 'Des écoles et des ouvriers' he is at pains to distinguish freedom from licence, deploring that since nowadays everyone wants to reign, 'personne ne sait se gouverner'. The distinction is fundamental and is repeated thirteen years later in the *Salon de 1859* where he warns against *fantaisie*, which is all the more dangerous because it is more facile and unconstrained, '*dangereuse comme toute liberté absolue*'.[9] The associative discipline of the *école* under the leadership of a powerful genius is an antidote to chaos, an antidote unfortunately lacking in the world of contemporary painting, in which the republicans or anarchists of art have taken the place of the disciplined workers of previous ages. Only the genius has the right to reign, being endowed with a great passion and the kind of powerful temperament that makes his calling a 'fatality'. In this ideal tight-knit community in which the prerogative of the *ouvrier* is to preserve the purity of the master's doctrine through obedience and tradition, 'les individus vraiment dignes de ce nom absorbent les faibles; et c'est justice, car une large production n'est qu'une pensée à mille bras'. Some commentators have sensed here more than a whiff of 'cultural fascism',[10] while others have detected the presence of Fourier and the cohesive function of the *phalanstère*, as opposed to the anarchic tendencies of republicanism. But whatever Baudelaire's political views in 1846,[11] his main point is clearly the damaging effect on art of the decline of the *écoles*.

'Des écoles et des ouvriers' ends with an allusion to Hugo, to book 4 of *Notre-Dame de Paris*, 'Ceci tuera cela', in support of Baudelaire's contention that the painter has killed painting, just as, for Hugo, the printed word has killed the cathedral. But the reference is little more than a rhetorical flourish. The substantial intertext refers not to Hugo, nor for that matter to Fourier, but to the hero of modern life, whose name and prestige are fulsomely evoked in the stirring appeal for a new heroic art in the final paragraph of the *Salon*. In the concluding lines

---

[9] My emphasis. For the particular meaning Baudelaire gives to *fantaisie*, a genre of painting so free as to escape categorization, see *Salon de 1859*, 644–5.

[10] Bernard Howells, *Baudelaire, Individualism, Dandyism and the Philosophy of History* (Oxford: Legenda, 1996), 25.

[11] The grounds for questioning the presence of utopian views in the Baudelaire of 1846 are examined in Ch. 7.

of 'Des écoles et des ouvriers', too, it is the voice of the conservative Balzac which is more audible than that of any other contemporary figure: 'Cette glorification de l'individu a nécessité la division infinie du territoire de l'art. La liberté absolue et divergente de chacun, la division des efforts et le fractionnement de la volonté humaine ont amené cette faiblesse, ce doute et cette pauvreté d'invention' (p. 492). Balzac's admittedly ambiguous denunciation of individualism pervades La Comédie humaine, but what we have here, transposed from the context of politics to that of art, is the terminology and the philosophy of Louis Lambert concerning will-power: 'Le code, que l'on regarde comme la plus belle œuvre de Napoléon, est l'œuvre la plus draconienne que je sache. La divisibilité territoriale poussée à l'infini, dont le principe y est consacré par le partage égal des biens, doit engendrer l'abâtardissement de la nation, la mort des arts et celle des sciences.'[12] The thrust of Balzac's argument in this passage, which Baudelaire's vocabulary of territory and division seems deliberately to echo, is that the Napoleonic code, by abolishing 'le droit d'aînesse',[13] has brought about a debilitating division of land and property which has weakened the nation as a cohesive unit. The parallel with Baudelaire's thinking about the disappearance of the écoles is clear: the territory of art has been fragmented and enfeebled in the same way as the state, and with the same grievous consequences. From this division only a man of genius, 'un régent de classe', would be capable of uniting the nation and assuring its future, in much the same way as the painter of genius is the directing force in the school.

There were schools, Baudelaire declares, in the time of Louis XV and under the Empire. Of the latter, only David, Guérin, and Girodet have remained, 'débris inébranlables et invulnérables de cette grande école' (p. 411), while in the Salon de 1859 the Restoration seems to come near to forming a brief continuation.[14] In the same Salon the school of Rome is given ironic mention as one apparently in name only since its function, like that of the Comédie française in the domain of tragedy, is to snuff out originality and imagination in favour of dispiriting banalities (p. 649). In 1859 the emancipated worker has been replaced by the even more lamentable figure of the 'enfant gâté' (p. 611), brought up without discipline to produce a hotch-potch of

---

[12] Balzac, La Comédie humaine, vol. x (Paris: Gallimard, 1950), 414.

[13] The law of primogeniture whereby an estate passes from eldest son to eldest son.

[14] 'Rien, pour le moment, ne nous donne lieu d'espérer des floraisons spirituelles aussi abondantes que celles de la Restauration' (610).

derivative works, without conviction, orginality, or *naïveté*, but whose mediocrity and blandness, appealing as they do to an equally untutored popular taste, assure a handsome living and the accumulation of unmerited honours.

In 1846 the artist of genius is given due recognition, but his peculiar qualities are not defined until the later essays. Fittingly, it is in the *Exposition universelle* of 1855 that first mention is made of the requirement for the *critic* to have the openness of a cosmopolitan spirit, enabling him to free himself of Winckelmannian prejudices about absolute beauty and savour the diversity of artistic styles and subject matter from different times and cultures outside the European norm. Such adventurous spirits enjoy an intoxicating *disponibilité*: 'Aucun voile scolaire, aucun paradoxe universitaire, aucune utopie pédagogique, ne se sont interposés entre eux et la complexe vérité' (p. 576). The most gifted among such people are solitary travellers who have lived far from the prejudices of so-called civilized societies. They bear an unmistakable similarity to the missionaries and founders of colonies celebrated in the prose poem 'Les Foules', whose openness of spirit enables them, through a 'sainte prostitution de l'âme', to give themselves over entirely to the chance encounters of the unforeseen and unknown. In the *Salon de 1859* this openness is no longer required of the critic alone; in a brief passage on Legros it is said to be essential to the artist himself, and in *Le Peintre de la vie moderne* Constantin Guys's curiosity and cosmopolitanism are shown to be the point of departure of his genius (p. 689). For Baudelaire, then, the artist must be a man of the world, but '*homme du monde* dans un sens très étendu'; he must also be a man of erudition with a rich knowledge of the past like Lebrun, David, and the great contemporaries whom he admires— Daumier, and Delacroix himself.[15] These were no narrow specialists, but highly intelligent men of a wide and deep culture which informed every aspect of their work and life. Daumier is said to be endowed with a luminous good sense that coloured all his conversation, while that of Delacroix was 'un mélange admirable de solidité philosophique, de légèreté spirituelle et d'enthousiasme brûlant' (p. 611). Above all the artist must be well read and have a wide knowledge of the great poets of the past. Of Delacroix he claims that 'la lecture des poètes laissait en lui des images grandioses et rapidement définies, des tableaux tout

---

[15] 'Jadis, qu'était l'artiste (Lebrun ou David, par exemple)? Lebrun, érudition, imagination, connaissance du passé, amour du grand. David, ce colosse injurié par des mirmidons, n'était-il pas aussi l'amour du passé, l'amour du grand uni à l'érudition?' (610).

faits, pour ainsi dire', and that, like his republican and imperial ancestors, he was possessed by a desire to rival the written word: 'David,
Guérin et Girodet enflammaient leur esprit au contact d'Homère, de
Virgile, de Racine et d'Ossian. Delacroix fut le traducteur émouvant
de Shakespeare, de Dante, de Byron et d'Arioste. Ressemblance
importante et différence légère' (p. 746).

The final paragraphs of 'A quoi bon la critique?' appropriate an idea
from *Histoire de la peinture en Italie* where, in a footnote to 'Froideur
des arts avant Michel-Ange' (chapter clvi), Stendhal claims that painting 'n'est que de la morale construite'. It is important to place
this somewhat elliptic formulation in context to understand how
Baudelaire has adapted it to his needs. In the previous chapter
Stendhal had described an encounter with an Italian duke, who admired the understatement of ancient art and vigorously rejected the
overstatement of Michelangelo. Disagreeing with the duke, Stendhal
uses the distinction to drive home a fundamental truth about painting,
namely that it illustrates the moral maxim that 'la condition première
de toutes les vertus est la force'. It is to this sentence that he appends
the footnote, before developing his point; 'si les figures de Michel-
Ange n'ont pas ces qualités aimables qui nous font adorer le *Jupiter* et
l'*Apollon*, du moins on ne les oublie pas, et c'est ce qui fonde leur
immortalité. Elles ont assez de force pour que nous soyons obligés de
compter avec elles.' Stendhal's idea is clear, that painting is 'la morale
construite' to the extent that it represents the primary virtue of force.
Clearly, Baudelaire would have been attracted to such a view, but he
goes beyond Stendhal, implying, if not directly stating, that painting
springing from *naïveté* is 'la morale construite', because it represents
not the random feelings, however intense, arising from individual
experience, but a painterly, or poetic world which is *sui generis* and
embraces in the broadest terms a metaphysics or philosophy of life. He
interprets the idea of 'morale construite' liberally, extending it to all
the other arts, so that it becomes a fundamental and general aesthetic
truth. Since, Baudelaire continues, the arts are always the beautiful
'exprimé par le sentiment, la passion et la rêverie de chacun, c'est-à-
dire la variété dans l'unité, ou les faces diverses de l'absolu,—la critique touche à chaque instant à la métaphysique'. Further extending
the notion of 'morale construite' from the individual to different
peoples and ages, he equates it with the view of the world made up of
the various perceptions of the artists of any one age. By so doing
Baudelaire has endowed criticism with a philosophical function, which

is to understand and interpret the resultant *Weltanschauung* that characterizes each era, and which he defines two pages later as 'la morale du siècle' (p. 421). The logic of these final paragraphs of the chapter is clear: just as there is a *naïveté* of the individual artist, there is, so to speak, a corresponding *naïveté* or distinctive genius of a particular age. The conclusion provides an elegant transition to the next chapter: since each age and each people have given expression to their own beauty and ethos,[16] and since Romanticism is the most recent and modern expression of beauty, the great artist will be the one who combines *naïveté* with the greatest possible amount of Romanticism.

In defining Romanticism as the most recent expression of the beautiful, Baudelaire has come down vigorously on one side of the great aesthetic debate of the time, and established, less by argument than by a rapid series of uncompromising affirmations, the relativity of art as against the classical, absolutist view associated with Winckelmann and Quatremère de Quincy. The idea is inseparable from his view of *naïveté* and central to his art criticism, which is why he is at pains to set them out together as early in the *Salon* as possible, at the end of the first chapter. It is there also that we find another idea, less prominent, slipped into the argument by an explanatory 'c'est-à-dire', that of 'la variété dans l'unité, ou les faces diverses de l'absolu'. The phrase is revealing, since, like other parts of the *Salon*, it seems to show Baudelaire imbued with the notion of a unified beauty made up of the totality of all manifestations of the relative, a notion indeed of variety within unity. The idea is only one aspect of a wider overarching concept of the resolution of opposites in the fundamental harmony of the world, both physical and moral. According to this view, developed in 'De l'idéal et du modèle', the idea of contradiction is purely human and consequently illusory: 'la dualité qui est la contradiction de l'unité, en est aussi la conséquence', to which he appends the following note as explanation: 'Je dis la contradiction, et non pas le contraire; car la contradiction est une invention humaine' (p. 456). The fundamental law that governs the moral order and the physical order is one of complementary contrasts. Elements of this idea can be found in many sources, for example in illuminist thinkers of the time. A fragment of

---

[16] The idea is close to another of Stendhal's: 'Car voici la théorie romantique: il faut que chaque peuple ait une littérature particulière et modelée sur son caractère particulier, comme chacun de nous porte un habit modelé pour sa taille particulière' (*Racine et Shakespeare* (Paris: Le Divan, 1928), 194).

Louis Lambert states that 'L'Univers est donc la variété dans l'Unité. Le Mouvement est le moyen, le Nombre est le résultat. La fin est le retour de toutes choses à l'Unité, qui est Dieu.'[17] It also linked to the Fourierist view of a *harmonien* society as the necessary complement to the deeper harmonious structures of nature itself. Many commentators have stressed the importance of the idea for the *Salon de 1846* which they see as heavily influenced by Fourier, and David Kelley is at pains throughout his edition to point to its relevance to the central preoccupations of the poet's criticism. There is no doubt that a strong undercurrent carries the thought through his writings of the 1840s, but whenever it surfaces in the *Salon* it reveals strains and tensions in the coherency of the argument, in what Kelley calls Baudelaire's moral and aesthetic 'système'.[18] I shall try to treat these as they occur. In the present context of 'la morale du siècle', it may be sufficient for the time being to note that Baudelaire gives no indication of how exactly the unity emerges and how it is able to contain or synthesize so many strident and conflicting convictions.

In 'Qu'est-ce que le romantisme?',[19] Baudelaire's principal concern is one of definition. For greater emphasis, he is at pains to state what it is not, taking advantage of the strategy to mock some contemporary pretensions and misconceptions. Romanticism lies not in the subject matter, as some of its would-be practitioners have thought, not in religion and Catholic subjects, not in the kind of medievalism popularized by Walter Scott, not in realism or the depiction of local colour as advocated by Victor Hugo, not even in the rejection of Greek and Roman subjects, since one can paint Romantic Greeks and Romans if one is truly Romantic oneself. Here no doubt he is thinking of works such as Delacroix's *Dernières Paroles de Marc-Aurèle*, discussed in the *Salon de 1845*.[20] In four ringing single-sentence paragraphs, each one with the authority and memorability of a maxim, Baudelaire spells out his position:

Le romantisme n'est précisément ni dans le choix des sujets ni dans la vérité exacte, mais dans la manière de sentir.

[17] Balzac, *Comédie humaine*, 454.

[18] Baudelaire, *Salon de 1846*, ed. David Kelley (Oxford: Clarendon Press, 1975), 105.

[19] The title is borrowed from Stendhal, 'Ce que c'est que le romanticisme', *Racine et Shakespeare*, 175–203.

[20] For his attitude towards the Greeks and Romans, see below p. 47. *Ovide chez les Scythes* (1859) would be another example of a Roman subject treated in a Romantic manner, as would Gérome's *Jules César*, fulsomely praised, with, however, some reservations, in the *Salon de 1859* (641).

Ils ont cherché en dehors, et c'est en dedans qu'il était seulement possible de le trouver.

Pour moi, le romantisme est l'expression la plus récente, la plus actuelle du beau.

Il y a autant de beautés qu'il y a de manières habituelles de chercher le bonheur.

The first three sentences sum up the argument of the previous chapter, while the fourth adds an idea, again taken from Stendhal, linking beauty to the pursuit of happiness.[21] It appears in a slightly different form in *Le Peintre de la vie moderne* ('le Beau n'est que la promesse du bonheur' (p. 686)), and one suspects that it lies at the origin of Baudelaire's later definition of lyricism as 'les beaux jours de l'esprit' and 'l'*âme* dans ses belles heures'.[22] It appears to be linked to notions of heightened awareness or an intuition of happiness which appears beyond what can be afforded by the real world, the emphasis falling more upon its pursuit than on its realization. Then follows the famous definition: 'Qui dit romantisme dit art moderne,—c'est-à-dire intimité, spiritualité, couleur, aspiration vers l'infini, exprimés par tous les moyens que contiennent les arts.' Romanticism will be modern since it will lie 'dans une conception analogue à la morale du siècle'. As a consequence it is the duty of the artist to be acquainted with aspects of nature and the human experience which previous artists had spurned or not known. Such an art will be 'intimate', since it will come from inside,[23] from the *naïveté* and temperament of the artist. It will give expression not to a realist conception, but to a spiritual one, and will accordingly be linked to an aspiration towards the infinite. Although it is not spelled out in the *Salon*, such a view of art implies a dualist conception of humanity, a dissatisfaction with the here and now and a yearning for another reality, which lies at the heart of Baudelaire's thinking and is exemplified nowhere more clearly than in the binary (and telescoping) opposites of *Les Fleurs du Mal*. True, the problem of good and evil and the doctrine of original sin have no place in the *Salon*, but they are already present in his thinking and preside over the theory of laughter he was elaborating at the time.[24] The notion of duality is essential to Baudelaire's Romanticism;

---

[21] 'La beauté est l'expression d'une certaine manière habituelle de chercher le bonheur', *Histoire de la peinture en Italie* (Paris: Le Divan, 1929), vol. i, 131, ch. cx.

[22] See below p. 96.

[23] It is thus to be distinguished from 'le romantisme pittoresque'.

[24] See Ch. 3 for a fuller discussion.

for without it the spirituality and aspiration to the infinite would be meaningless. The problem is that this view of modernity does not sit well with the harmonious view of the resolution of opposites, of complementary contrasts, which is claimed to be fundamental to the poet's thinking of the time. What is worse, the philosophy of harmony is incompatible with the world of Baudelaire's hero, Delacroix, 'malade de génie' (p. 356), whose paintings are a poignant expression of 'douleur morale' and aspiration towards the infinite. He alone of modern painters knows how to paint religious subjects, and his talent is perfectly suited to the Christian religion, 'profondément triste, religion de la douleur universelle' (p. 436). Kelley is aware of this tension in the poet's thinking: 'Et même si la vision dramatique de Delacroix correspond à la conception d'un univers dont l'unité n'existerait que par l'opposition de deux principes complémentaires, elle met en valeur la lutte des forces opposées, au lieu de les réconcilier par la vue plus naturelle et plus synthétique des choses que recommande le poète.'[25] But it is not clear that the poet is ever recommending this natural and synthetic view in the case of specific painters, since it appears only in the most general contexts. That being the case, it must be considered of less importance than the dualist view which, in the *Salon*, informs the key notion of Romanticism.

Romanticism is equated with colour which receives its first mention in this part of the *Salon*. Drawing on Madame de Staël's famous distinction in *De la littérature* between north and south, Germanic and Mediterranean, Baudelaire characterizes the painters of northern countries, England, Flanders, and, stretching a point, Venice, because of its lagoon and its northerly position, as colourist, because dreams are born of their mists; whereas southern countries are naturalist. The south, where the light is clear and man has nothing to desire but what he sees, is brutal and positive; whereas 'le Nord souffrant et inquiet se console avec l'imagination'. Consequently, Raphael is an 'esprit matériel' constantly seeking out what is concrete, whereas Rembrandt is a powerful idealist who makes us dream and guess at what lies beyond. The one presents creatures in a new and virginal state, like Adam and Eve; the other 'secoue des haillons devant nos yeux et nous raconte les souffrances humaines'. It is now clear why colour is an essential ingredient in modern art; it is equated to imagination, dream, 'aspiration vers l'infini', and is, in a word, Romantic. The distinction

---

[25] *Salon de 1846*, 34.

between north and south leads inevitably to another, absolutely fundamental to Baudelaire's aesthetic theory, between draughtsmen and colourists which will be the subject of later chapters of the *Salon*.

The chapter on Romanticism ends with remarks which provide a natural bridge to one of the most important aspects of Baudelaire's aesthetics, the question of colour, which he had touched upon in the *Salon* of the previous year in his discussion of Delacroix's *Dernières Paroles de Marc-Aurèle*. His commentary in 1845 goes straight to the heart of the subject:

Cette couleur est d'une science incomparable, il n'y a pas une seule faute,— et, néanmoins, ce ne sont que tours de force—tours de force invisibles à l'œil inattentif, car l'harmonie est sourde et profonde; la couleur, loin de perdre son originalité cruelle dans cette science nouvelle et plus complète, est toujours sanguinaire et terrible.—Cette pondération du vert et du rouge plaît à notre âme. (p. 355)

He praises the painting fulsomely for its new science of colour and for the pleasing balance of red and green, but without defining what the science is or why and how it is pleasing. It is not until the second chapter of the 1846 *Salon* that he undertakes an explanation. Inviting the reader to imagine a fine expanse of nature in which 'tout verdoie, rougoie, poudroie et chatoie en pleine liberté' and in which poppies and pimpernels stand out against the green of the grass, trees and mosses (p. 422), he establishes that everywhere 'le rouge chante la gloire du vert.' His point is that the effect of red on its opposite and contrasting colour green is to enhance it.[26] There is nothing new in this kind of observation, except that it is developed at length in Chevreul's *De la loi du contraste simultané des couleurs* of 1839 into a general law of colour,[27] whereby the difference between contrasting colours is heightened when they are juxtaposed, red and green, orange and blue, violet and yellow. The passage casts light retrospectively on Delacroix's 'science nouvelle', whose painterly practice appears to be governed not just by observation but by a 'law' of colour, analogous to Chevreul's, with which Baudelaire may have had at least a second-hand acquaintance, since it was reviewed in *L'Artiste* in 1842 (p. 1296). Here is how

[26] The contrast is most intense at the point of division, which explains Baudelaire's mixed reaction to 'un cabaret mi-parti de vert et de rouge crus, qui étaient pour mes yeux une douleur délicieuse' (425).

[27] For a remarkable account of Baudelaire and Chevreul's theory, see Howells, *Baudelaire*, 175–99.

he defines the 'theory' in 'De la couleur': 'la couleur est donc l'accord de deux tons. Le ton chaud et le ton froid, dans l'opposition desquels consiste toute la théorie, ne peuvent se définir d'une manière absolue: ils n'existent que relativement' (p. 424). Whether the idea came from Chevreul or from his own observation of Delacroix, Baudelaire sees in the contrast of red and green a positive feature to which he returns time after time: the green and pink in Pensotti (p. 383) and 'l'ajustement vert et rose' of the negress in La Mort de Cléopatre by Lassalle-Bordes (p. 442), the 'couleur terrible' of Catlin whose works he admires not least for the use of red, 'cette couleur si obscure, si épaisse, plus difficile à pénétrer que les yeux d'un serpent', and green, 'cette couleur calme et gaie et souriante de la nature', the melodic contrast of which he finds on the tattooed faces of Catlin's Indians (p. 446). It is of course in Delacroix that the contrast is most expertly and dramatically brought out, in the magnificent Pietà with its turmoil of crimson garments and open wounds, 'cette sanglante et farouche désolation, à peine compensée par le vert sombre de l'espérance' (p. 436), the green being represented by the background which Baudelaire thinks resembles as much a pile of rocks as 'une mer bouleversée par l'orage'. The same phenomenon returns with the insistence of an obsession or a painterly hallmark. Baudelaire would assuredly have noticed it in the paintings he refers to: in the headgear and gown of Dante in La Barque de Dante, in the contrast between the violent reds and the smoky-green background of La Mort de Sardanapale, in the tapestries in L'Exécution du doge Marino Faliero, in the green flag with its red centre in Les Convulsionnaires de Tanger, in the patches of red clothing set against the green woodwork in Noce juive au Maroc, and perhaps most alluringly in the subtle, infinitely delicate interplay of green and red tones in Les Femmes d'Alger.

The natural scene described by Baudelaire is far from static, as is accentuated by the active verbs, 'verdoie, rougeoie, poudroie et chatoie'. On the contrary, under the influence of light, shade, and heat, all things are subject to perpetual vibration, causing outlines to tremble rather than be clear-cut, in accordance with the law of universal movement. Furthermore, all the colours exist in dynamic relationship to one another and cannot be perceived in isolation—even the non-colour black is intensified by the juxtaposition of blue and red. The result is that nature taken in its entirety resembles a spinning-top which, though it includes the whole gamut of colour, appears grey to our eyes. In the Salon de 1845 Baudelaire identifies this natural phenomenon observable in nature in Delacroix's *Le Sultan du Maroc*, which in spite of its brilliant tones is so harmonious that it appears grey, 'gris comme la nature—gris comme l'atmosphère de l'été, quand le soleil étend comme un crépuscule de poussière tremblante sur chaque objet' (p. 357).[28]

The second paragraph of this remarkable passage evokes the reflections from objects as they attract light and colours from near and far off, and the effect of shadows as the sun wheels towards the west, culminating in a lyrical evocation of sunset as fine as any in Baudelaire:

Quand le grand foyer descend dans les eaux, de rouges fanfares s'élancent de tous côtés; une sanglante harmonie éclate à l'horizon, et le vert s'empourpre richement. Mais bientôt de vastes ombres bleues chassent en cadence devant elles la foule des tons orangés et rose tendre qui sont comme l'écho lointain et affaibli de la lumière. Cette grande symphonie du jour, qui est l'éternelle variation de la symphonie d'hier, cette succession de mélodies, où la variété sort toujours de l'infini, cet hymne compliqué s'appelle la couleur.

To reinforce the argument, he demonstrates the same effect of colour on the infinitely smaller scale of a woman's hand with the green of the large veins and the red tones on the knuckles, the pink nails set against the grey and brown tones of the joints, and on the palm the pink and wine-coloured life-lines separated from one another by the system of green or blue veins running across them. To make the point even stronger, he imagines the same hand placed under a magnifying glass showing the same perfect harmony of 'tons gris, bleus, bruns, verts, orangés et blancs réchauffés par un peu de jaune' (p. 424). Though not spelled out, the implication is clear; the microcosm of the hand under the glass obeys the same laws as the macrocosm of sunset, both of them presenting to the eye a pure effect of colour in which outline and form have been swallowed up. If one were to push the vision of the colourist to its ultimate logical conclusion, one would be left with nothing but a formless harmony of colours from which outline would be completely expunged;[29] which is precisely why he reaches the dramatic definition expressed in the mnemonic form of a maxim: 'La loupe, c'est l'œil du coloriste.'

---

[28] In the same *Salon* he makes a similar point about greyness and harmony in *La Madeleine dans le désert*, whose colour is much more subdued: 'l'aspect en est presque gris, mais d'une harmonie parfaite' (354).

[29] It is likely that Baudelaire had this passage in mind when describing the magnificent skyscapes of Boudin (666). See p. 185.

In his description of the hand under the glass Baudelaire makes, almost as an aside, an important point to which he had alluded several times in the previous *Salon*: that the harmony of tones when combined with shadows produces the modelling characteristic of colourists, fundamentally different from that of draughtsmen, whose difficulties amount to little more than the copying of a plaster-cast model. Etex, who had made his reputation as a sculptor, had been criticized for not having mastered the science of colour and of modelling with it (p. 376), whereas Delacroix, in *Une Sibylle qui montre le rameau d'or*, and especially in *Dernières Paroles de Marc-Aurèle*, had proved himself incomparable in his mastery of modelling. To model with a single tone is, Baudelaire argues, to model with a stump;[30] whereas to model with colour is much more difficult. It means finding the logic of light and shade, and then the rightness and harmony of tone 'dans un travail subit, spontané, compliqué' (p. 355); if, for example, the shadow is green and the light red, it means finding a harmony of red and green, the one dark, the other luminous, to create the effect of a monochrome object in relief, in the triple dimensionality of space.[31] It is precisely this feature that was to impress Charles Blanc in the figure of the half-naked woman in the painting of *L'Elysée* in the Luxembourg palace. He admires 'la hardiesse qu'avait eue Delacroix de sabrer brutalement le torse nu de cette figure avec des hachures d'un vert décidé qui, neutralisé en partie par sa complémentaire le rose, forme avec ce rose, dans lequel il s'absorbe, un ton mixte et frais'.[32] Baudelaire could well have noticed the technique in this painting, or in the figure of the woman in white stockings,[33] or in Delacroix's pastel studies for his great paintings, where it is most noticeable. Baudelaire's exemplification of the law of contrasting colours seems to be limited to red and green, since, for example, he makes no mention of violet and yellow which had so impressed Delacroix;[34] but this passage shows he was aware of the way it had served to free painting from the limitations of

---

[30] A stump is a kind of pencil made of soft material, and used, among other things, for blending lines of shading.

[31] This is how we interpret Baudelaire's expression '*tournant*'. In addition to the sense of relief, it gives also that of movement, a feature which of course he also admired in Delacroix.

[32] Charles Blanc, *La Peinture* (Grammaire des arts du dessin) (Paris: Renouard, 1886), 177.

[33] *La Femme aux bas blancs* (1825–6), Louvre.

[34] Blanc recounts how Delacroix, having difficulty with a piece of yellow draping, decided to go to the Louvre to see how Rubens and Veronese had handled the problem. He called a cabriolet which turned out to be canary yellow, noticed that the shadows were violet, and cancelled his visit forthwith (*Peinture*, 168).

traditional, conservative chiaroscuro modelling. Perhaps it was his observation of the sombre, murky drama of *L'Evèque de Liège*[35] that led him to assert that the black coat of the modern age, 'le frac funèbre et convulsionné que nous endossons tous', does not present an insuperable obstacle to the modern painter, since 'les grands coloristes savent faire de la couleur avec un habit noir, une cravate blanche et un fond gris' (p. 495).

Baudelaire insists on harmony as the basis of colour theory. However, he expands the musical analogy by adding the notions of melody and counterpoint, finding justification in a passage from *Kreisleriana* in which Hoffmann establishes analogies between colours, sounds, and perfumes, similar to those of the second quatrain of the sonnet 'Correspondances'. Counterpoint may be thought to be subsumed in the harmony of contrasts; melody, however, concerns the ensemble of colours within a painting, which makes for its unity of effect; 'la mélodie est l'unité dans la couleur, ou la couleur générale'. If, he says, one looks at a work from sufficiently far off to see only the colour masses rather than the outline of specific objects, one will perceive its melody or unity, which will imprint itself on the memory in a way that would be impossible in a work made of disparate and fragmented colours. The appeal to memory, so important in Baudelaire's aesthetic, is in the first instance a question of the unity and melody of the constitutive colours. With draughtsmen the sense of unity comes from the structure provided by the various objects, groups, and lines, whereas in the work of a colourist the unity is not primarily to do with forms but with colour masses.[36]

Clearly, the poet is wedded to the analogy with music. Returning to it in the *Exposition universelle*, he declares that the admirable concord of colour in Delacroix causes one to dream of harmony and melody, so that the impression given by his paintings is often quasi-musical (p. 595). Analogy is fundamental to his aesthetic, because it is fundamen-

---

In his description of the setting sun, Baudelaire does however notice blue and orange: 'Mais bientôt de vastes ombres bleues chassent en cadence devant elles la foule des tons orangés et rose tendre qui sont comme l'écho lointain et affaibli de la lumière' (423).

[35] He makes no mention of *Boissy d'Anglas*, which is even more deeply black than *L'Evèque de Liège*.

[36] On pure draughtsmen Baudelaire makes the following disparaging comment: 'Ils commencent par délimiter les formes d'une manière cruelle et absolue, et veulent ensuite remplir ces espaces. Cette méthode double contrarie sans cesse leurs efforts, et donnent à toutes leurs productions je ne sais quoi d'amer, de pénible et de contentieux' (458).

tal to the operations of the mind, forming an integral part of its structure, to such an extent that he declares in the essay on Wagner that empirical evidence is scarcely necessary since a priori it would be quite astonishing if sound *could not* suggest colour, and that colours *could not* give the idea of melody.[37] Colour obeys analogous laws to music. It is one thing, however, to say that generally in Delacroix the harmony of colour evokes the music of Weber, and quite another to try to apply the temporal and successive notion of melody to the timeless spaciality of painting. The analogy cracks under the strain, as Baudelaire was no doubt aware when he argues that melody requires a conclusion, the equivalent of which is 'un ensemble où tous les effets *concourent*[38] à un effet genéral'. The analogy is plainly hazardous. Chevreul, we are told, would have no truck with it,[39] neither would Delacroix, who is at pains in the *Journal* to distinguish his art from poetry and music, and set it above them precisely because of its non-successive nature.[40] To speak of harmony and counterpoint in colour is merely to perpetuate well-worn metaphors, but to add melody is to bring the analogy dramatically to life in a rhetorical flourish, both daring and problematic.

Whatever reservations one may have about the music–painting analogy, there can be no doubt that for Baudelaire colour is not merely documentary, but a language of signs which, far from being arbitrary and idiosyncratic, is essential to the meaning of a work. The sense of colour is an integral part of the *naïveté* of the artist and of his peculiar mental universe, so that there are tones which are 'gais et folâtres, folâtres et tristes, riches et gais, riches et tristes'; Veronese's colour is calm and gay, Delacroix's often plaintive, and Catlin's awesome. In the *Salon de 1859* it is imagination that teaches 'le sens moral des couleurs', it being universally understood that, for example, yellow, orange, and red convey ideas of joy, richness, glory, and love (p. 625). The language of colour, like that of flowers 'et des choses muettes',[41] is

[37] 'D'ailleurs, il ne serait pas ridicule ici de raisonner a priori, sans analyse et sans comparaisons; car ce qui serait vraiment surprenant, c'est que le son *ne pût pas* suggérer la couleur, que les couleurs *ne pussent pas* donner l'idée d'une mélodie, et que le son et la couleur fussent impropres à traduire des idées' (784).
[38] My emphasis; it is clear that there is a kind of play on words as Baudelaire is using 'concourir' in an almost literal and 'spatial' sense, the concurrence being circular, so to speak.
[39] See Howells, *Baudelaire*, 187: 'The possibility of significant succession confers upon sound what Chevreul calls a "special existence", that is, *the power to signify independently of things*. Colour on the other hand has no "special existence".'
[40] Eugène Delacroix, *Journal 1822–1863* (Paris: Plon, 1981), 373, 20 Oct. 1853.
[41] See 'Elévation', *Les Fleurs du Mal*.

of course only one illustration of the general theory of correspondence and analogy that presides over the world of the poet who,
like Delacroix, conceived of the visible universe (at least in his moments of optimism or lyricism) as a dictionary upon which the
artist draws for his creation, as 'un magasin d'images et de signes
auxquels l'imagination donnera une place et une valeur relative; c'est
une espèce de pâture que l'imagination doit digérer et transformer'
(p. 627).

Colour emanates, then, from the temperament of the artist, especially in his free creations. But even in landscape painting, where his
aim is to reproduce the colours of nature, he cannot be purely imitative
and transfer what he sees on to the canvas, since the air and atmosphere are also important. If the painter painted only what he saw, the
result would be false, the distance between the spectator and
the canvas, the extent of air, being less than between the painter
and the natural scene. The artist has therefore to resort to ruse and
subterfuge, to the 'mathematics' of colour, in order to create the sense
of reality. In his initial description of the expanse of nature, Baudelaire
had insisted on the movement and vibration caused by the light and
atmosphere. But the even brush stroke of traditional painting is inadequate when it comes to rendering the effects of colour. The sense of
vibration is conveyed by the *touche* of the artist, which must be firm
and bold. Baudelaire states that an artist preoccupied by movement,
colour, and atmosphere will require 'un contour un peu indécis, des
lignes légères et flottantes, et *l'audace de la touche*' (p. 434).[42] Nor must
the touches merge with one another materially; the merging will take
place naturally for the eye if the spectator stands at some distance, and
the colour will thus also acquire more energy and freshness (p. 626).
Delacroix makes the same point in his *Journal* entry of 13 January
1857: 'A une certaine distance la touche se fond dans l'ensemble, mais
elle donne à la peinture un accent que le fondu des teintes ne peut
produire.'[43] Baudelaire further observes that Delacroix's painting abhors a vacuum. In painters who are not colourists there are always
empty areas, 'de grands trous produits par des tons qui ne sont pas de
niveau, pour ainsi dire; la peinture de Delacroix est comme la nature,
elle a horreur du vide' (p. 439). Clearly, Baudelaire has in mind such
works as Ingres's *Grande Odalisque* and Ary Scheffer's *Saint Augustin
et sainte Monique*, which contrast so unfavourably with the turbulent

---

[42] My emphasis.
[43] He also makes the point that neither contour nor touch exist in nature (612).

backgrounds of *La Barque de Dante*, *La Mort de Sardanapale*, *Les Adieux de Roméo et de Juliette*, and specifically the magnificent *Enlèvement de Rébecca*, with its 'parfaite ordonnance de tons, tons intenses, pressés, serrés et logiques', which makes of the whole picture a dramatic hymn to colour and movement. It will be recalled that in the definition of Romanticism intimacy, spirituality, and aspiration to the infinite are to be expressed 'par tous les moyens que contiennent les arts', with the result that composition, light and shade, modelling, brushwork, colour, outline, perspective, background, empty spaces, are in no way incidental but play an integral and vital role in the communication of the emotion and intimate drama of the subject matter.

Given Baudelaire's passionate promotion of the colourists, it is no surprise to see him subject bad colour to the most dismissive criticism. Thus Bigand is accused of making 'un tableau tout brun' (p. 370), a painting by Lécurieux has 'un aspect uniforme de café au lait' (p. 382), Hesse's colour is 'dure, malheureuse et amère' (p. 373), Saint-Jean's 'jaune et pisseuse' (p. 486). Planet (p. 371) and Glaize (p. 477) are reproached for their narrow range, and Lehmann for a pallor that depresses the poet 'comme un Véronèse ou un Rubens copiés par un habitant de la lune' (p. 461). On occasion Devéria (p. 365) and Chassériau (p. 367) produce little more than a *coloriage*, while Glaize's colour has the vulgarity of coffee- or opera-houses (p. 369). Troyon is capable of producing fine landscapes, spoiled however by the painful 'papillotage de ses touches' (p. 391); but nothing is worse than the excruciating discordance and *charivari* of Vernet.

Equally, his praise of great colourists is ample, especially Delacroix, whom he sees as belonging to the lineage of the Venetians, Rembrandt, and Rubens, and whose paintings he had in mind when expounding his views on colour. Of *Le Sultan du Maroc*, for example, he asks in 1845:

Véronèse fut-il jamais plus féerique? Fit-on jamais chanter sur une toile de plus capricieuses mélodies? un plus prodigieux accord de tons nouveaux, inconnus, délicats, charmants? Nous en appelons à la bonne foi de quiconque connaît son vieux Louvre;—qu'on cite un tableau de grand coloriste, où la couleur ait autant d'esprit que celui de M. Delacroix. (p. 357)

He is every bit as hyperbolic in 1855 about the *Chasse aux lions*, 'une véritable explosion de couleur' (p. 594): 'Jamais couleurs plus belles,

plus intenses, ne pénétrèrent jusqu'à l'âme par le canal des yeux.'[44]
Isabey, with his *Intérieur d'alchimiste*, 'est un vrai coloriste' (p.
382), but Baudelaire's predilection goes time after time to the exponents of
light, atmosphere, sky, clouds, sunsets, and marine landscapes. Although lacking firmness of touch, Héroult 'sait fort bien exprimer les
ciels clairs et souriants et les brumes flottantes, traversées par un rayon
de soleil. Il connaît toute cette poésie particulière des pays du Nord'
(p. 483); as a landscapist of the north reminiscent of Rubens and
Rembrandt, Rousseau 'aime les natures bleuâtres, les crépuscules, les
couchers de soleil singuliers et trempés d'eau, les gros ombrages où
circulent les brises, les grands jeux d'ombre et de lumière' (p. 484),
and Huet's marine and rustic canvases 'sont de véritables poèmes
pleins de légèreté, de richesse et de fraîcheur' (p. 664).[45] It is significant
here that Baudelaire admires those colourists who, like Bonington,
whom he ranks with Delacroix among the great painters of the century
(p. 611), have endowed their landscapes with a supernatural quality.
They were not *plein airistes*, preferring, like Huet,[46] to paint from
memory, though they did in some measure prepare the way for the
Impressionists who can be considered their descendants. It is also
significant that these scenes of land, sea and sky corresponded to a
major preoccupation in the poet's own mental universe.

Baudelaire's emphasis on the harmony of the natural scene in 'De
la couleur' has prompted Kelley, who has been followed by many
commentators since, to see the theory of colour as yet another aspect
of the law of contrasts governing the moral and physical order.[47] There
is no doubt that the theory fits the law, and the case is certainly
convincing. But it should be stressed that in 'De la couleur' Baudelaire
makes no claim that the harmony of colour is part of a wider philosophical view of nature. It should also be remembered that the idea
of the harmony of colour being inherent in nature was not new. In
particular, what Baudelaire says about light and atmosphere is already

---

[44] Cf. his note on *Chasse au tigre*: 'Delacroix alchimiste de la Couleur. Miraculeux,
profond, mystérieux, sensuel, terrible; couleur éclatante et obscure, harmonie pénétrante.
[. . .] Vert, lilas, vert sombre, lilas tendre, vermillon, rouge sombre, bouquet sinistre' (965).

[45] Among others praised for their colour, one should mention Fromentin (650), Jadin
(664), Noël (485) and, of course, Boudin (666).

[46] René-Paul Huet, *Paul Huet* (Paris: Laurens, 1911), 77.

[47] 'La théorie de la couleur, dont la base est l'harmonie, et qui repose toute entière sur
l'opposition de deux tons, d'un ton chaud et d'un ton froid, n'est qu'une application spéciale
de cette "loi des contrastes qui gouverne l'ordre moral et l'ordre physique" ' (*Salon de 1846*,
30).

present in Diderot. A crucial digression in the *Salon de 1763* takes the philosopher out of his study to contemplate an assemblage of diverse objects:

Assemblez confusément des objets de toute espèce et de toutes couleurs, du linge, des fruits, des liqueurs, du papier, des livres, des étoffes et des animaux, et vous verrez que l'air et la lumière, ces deux harmoniques universels, les accorderont tous, je ne sais comment, par des reflets imperceptibles; tout se liera, les disparates s'affaibliront, et votre œil ne reprochera rien à l'ensemble.[48]

The parallel with Baudelaire's natural scene is unmistakable; both men see the harmony in nature as the result of atmosphere, light, and reflection, and both show how the painter must 'cheat' in order to translate this harmony on to the canvas. But the point is that they understand this harmony, not within some overarching philosophical system positing nature as a unity in which contradictions are resolved, but as a question of perception, of empirical observation—just as it appears still to the detached twentieth-century observer without philosophical or metaphysical bias. It is significant also that in 'De la couleur' Baudelaire makes no mention of any such philosophy. It is of course true, as Kelley has convincingly shown,[49] that Fourierist artists and critics were attracted to colourism, not least because it squared with their *harmonien* view of nature and society. But one must be attentive to the relative position of carts and horses, and avoid a no doubt tempting illogicality which, if consistently applied, would transform Delacroix himself, greatly admired as he was by Fourierist critics, into a utopian dreamer. It is well known that Baudelaire moved in Fourierist circles and read *La Phalange* and *La Démocratie pacifique*;[50] but if he had been influenced in matters of colour or ideologically by critics like Laverdant then some more visible trace would surely have emerged in other parts of the *Salon*. In particular, one might have expected him to comment positively on works by well-known Fourierist artists; but if his attitude towards Papety's *Rêve de bonheur* (p. 387) is no more than lukewarm, his ridiculing of Gleyre's *Le Soir* (p. 372) is merciless; whereas Laverdant, who maintained that

[48] Denis Diderot, *Salons*, i. ed. Jean Seznec (Oxford: Clarendon Press, 1975), 217.

[49] *Salon de 1846*, 72–87, and 'L'Art: l'harmonie du beau et de l'utile', *Romantisme*, 5 (1973).

[50] For an account of Baudelaire's links with Fourierists see Peter Hambly, 'Idéologie et poésie: notes sur Baudelaire et ses contemporains', *Australian Journal of French Studies*, 16/2 (1979), 198–201.

every picture of Papety's was 'une page de la *Démocratie pacifique* mise en couleur', saw these two paintings as a diptych, 'Gleyre portraying the aspiration for happiness in *civilisation*, Papety showing its consummation in harmony.'[51] Such overt didacticism was alien to Baudelaire's way of thinking. Certainly, in 1845–6 he shared some of the Fourierists' enthusiasm for colourist landscapes, and Laverdant's view that the harmony in nature is paralleled by the inner harmony of the painter is not far from his own position. But the Fourierist attitude to painting was so capacious as to accommodate all but the most reactionary neoclassicists, so that similarities with their views on several fronts cannot be taken for an adherence to their ideology. It cannot be stressed too much that it was from his observation of Delacroix, 'le peintre le plus original des temps anciens et des temps modernes' (p. 353) that Baudelaire formed his ideas on colour.

That Baudelaire considers the harmony of colour in nature as a matter of empirical observation seems to be borne out by his positive references to nature, which are most frequent in the *Salons* of 1845 and 1846. The examples are so numerous that one can give only a few: Delacroix's drawing has 'un caractère insaisissable et tremblant comme la nature' (p. 356), *Le Sultan du Maroc* is 'gris comme la nature' (p. 357), Corot 'aime sincèrement la nature' (p. 389), colourists 'dessinent comme la nature' (p. 426) and imitate 'les palpitations éternelles de la nature' (p. 434), Decamps is praised for his 'goût minutieux de la nature' (p. 448), whereas Cabat makes the mistake of not trusting nature, and, finally, it was the Romantics' close study of nature that saved them and gave some allure to the modern school of landscape (p. 479). These statements stand in stark contrast to others which uncompromisingly reject nature: a statue by David is 'bête comme la nature' (p. 403) and indeed, sculpture as an art is 'brutale et positive comme la nature' (p. 487), the duty of the artist is to 'substituer l'homme à la nature et de protester contre elle' (p. 473), and Heine is praised for being, like Delacroix, a *surnaturaliste*, opposed to the outmoded idea of the '*imitation de la nature*' (p. 433). But the two views are not fundamentally irreconcilable; for if Baudelaire seems on the one hand to be putting forward a realist view of art, it is only in a very limited sense, in the representation of colour

---

[51] See Neil McWilliam, *Dreams of Happiness: Social Art and the French Left 1830–1850* (Princeton: Princeton University Press, 1993), 204.

and outline. What he is against, as much in 1846 as in 1859, is the slavish representation of external reality in place of that reality reflected in the mind and temperament of the artist. In both *Salons* nature is regarded as a dictionary to be used by the artist according to his vision, which replaces nature. Colour, as we have seen, is expressive and suggestive; as such, it need not follow the reality of the model or the outside world but must obey the laws of light, atmosphere, harmony, and contrast guaranteed by nature itself. Thus, *L'Enlèvement de Rébecca*, for example, or indeed any of Delacroix's works mentioned in 1846, can in no way be considered a direct imitation of nature, their colours being natural only to the extent that their interrelationship and harmony are in accordance with these laws, the recognition and exploitation of which have led to a revolution in modern art and a vast increase of vitality in painting.

Baudelaire's observations on colour serve to put his discussion of colourists and draughtsmen in much sharper focus, though a certain vagueness remains concerning the *contrastés* Spanish painters and the *harmoniste* Rembrandt, by which he perhaps means that while the Spanish favour the strong harmonies of contrast (red and green, orange and blue), Rembrandt prefers the softer ones of adjacent colours (red and orange, violet and blue). Clearly, Baudelaire does not consider them pure colourists like Delacroix or, for that matter, his great ancestor Rubens. To call the 'puissant idéaliste' Rembrandt a *harmoniste* was to accord great praise, since harmony is the basis of Baudelaire's view of colour and the quality he most admired in Delacroix in the *Salon de 1845*; but in 1846 it seems to indicate a position short of that of the colourist proper, a harmonious use of colour, which furthermore does not extend to outline and *touche*. The debate between colourists and draughtsmen was of course not a new one, having been much discussed in the eighteenth and nineteenth centuries, right up to the time of the 1846 *Salon*. The neoclassical view had been that draughtsmanship, with its emphasis on contour and outline, constituted the essence of painting; it was both the geometry and philosophy of art, colour being considered merely an additional ornament, which is why Baudelaire declares that pure draughtsmen are 'des philosophes et des abstracteurs de quintessence'. Draughtsmanship was rigorous and masculine, colour vague and feminine. To pronounce oneself a colourist was consequently to take up a modern, not to say revolutionary, position, in much the same way as the man of letters who espoused Shakespeare at the expense of Racine and classical drama;[52] and, like the men of letters, the colourist tended to defend his position by its fidelity to reality. Tragedy and comedy, artificially kept apart in classical drama, are not separate in real life; similarly, as Baudelaire indicates in his description of the natural scene, the harmony of colour and its vibrancy are inherent in nature. Draughtsmen, he claims, are exclusive, not having the time to see air and light, and being bent upon following outline in its most secret undulations. Their ability shows itself in the purity and finesse of outline, which of necessity excludes *touch*; whereas with the colourist, 'l'amour de l'air, le choix des sujets à mouvement, veulent l'usage des lignes flottantes et noyées'. In a word, particularly in the depiction of detail, 'la touche mangera toujours la ligne'.

It was common for traditionalists to consider Delacroix's draughtsmanship inferior to that of Ingres, the greatest contemporary *dessinateur* and head of his own school of *Ingristes*. An article by Desplaces redresses the balance, praising a charming oil, *Le Lever*, shown in the 1851 *Salon*, for the animation which the new method gives it and indicating the shortcomings of the Ingres school:

Cette figure est, en effet, d'un dessin et d'un modelé plein de vie et de relief. Un dessin vivant, une ligne qui joint le mouvement à la vérité, c'est là le grand problème, et que les Ingristes ont moins résolu qu'ils ne pensent. Ils ont la pureté de la ligne ou plutôt du contour, il leur manque l'animation du dessin.[53]

Baudelaire would, of course, have agreed with this view, as his outburst of 1855 shows;[54] but to the lack of animation in the works of

---

[52] In an often-quoted passage from 'Baudelaire en 1847' (*Etudes et témoignages* (Neuchâtel: La Baconnière, 1976), 99) Claude Pichois shows a link between social theories, aesthetic ideas, and political attitudes, claiming that to believe in flower symbolism and synesthesia, or to read Swedenborg could be construed as having socialist inclinations. He could have added being a colourist to his list.

[53] Quoted by Lee Johnson, *The Paintings of Eugène Delacroix: A Critical Catalogue*, vol. iii (Oxford: Clarendon Press, 1981–89), 7.

[54] 'Du dessin de Delacroix, si absurdement, si niaisement critiqué, que faut-il dire, si ce n'est qu'il est des vérités élémentaires complètement méconnues; qu'un bon dessin n'est pas une ligne dure, cruelle, despotique, immobile, enfermant une figure comme une camisole de force; que le dessin doit être comme la nature, vivant et agité; que la simplification dans le dessin est une monstruosité, comme la tragédie dans le monde dramatique; que la nature nous présente une série infinie de lignes courbes, fuyantes, brisées, suivant une loi de génération impeccable, où le parallélisme est toujours indécis et sinueux, où les concavités et les convexités se correspondent et se poursuivent; que M. Delacroix satisfait admirablement à toutes ces conditions [. . .]?' (595).

draughtsmen he would have added the lack of appeal to the imagination of the spectator. Their work tends to be too clear, much like a photograph, and too specific, too faithful to the detail of the model; whereas the colourist paints from memory, omitting accessory detail, as a consequence making the painting less specific and more general. The result, since 'l'imitation exacte gâte le souvenir', is that such painting, like Delacroix's, not only springs from the memory of the painter, but equally or more importantly it speaks to the memory of the spectator, who has less the sense of being confronted by something external to himself than of recognizing an experience already encountered at some level or other of awareness. No matter how astonishing the originality of the work, the spectator is drawn into it in a journey of discovery of another mentality, but above all a journey of self-discovery and exploration. This is no doubt what Baudelaire meant when, in *Prométhée délivré*, he wrote in February of the same year: 'la poésie d'un tableau doit être faite par le spectateur' (p. 9). The task, then, of the critic, or indeed of any spectator, is one of identification, re-creation and perhaps, above all, of recognition.

In addition to the clearly perceptible Neoplatonist overtones in this view of memory, a less obvious and more distant parallel with the poetic image springs to mind, in particular in connection with these 'comparaisons énormes', these extraordinary 'yankee' similes, which Laforgue admired and identified in Baudelaire, in which the inordinate gap between the two terms, between tenor and vehicle, has the power at once to astonish and invigorate.[55] Think of the clandestine pleasure which we squeeze, 'comme une vieille orange', the heart, 'meurtri comme une pêche', the anguish and terror which 'compriment le cœur comme un papier qu'on froisse', or the flesh of the lesbians clapping in the wind like 'un vieux drapeau'.[56] The physical, tactile, sensual quality of these images no doubt astonishes, since no poet had produced anything quite like them, but for all that, they appeal equally powerfully to the affective memory of the reader, who experiences the shock of a powerful originality together with an overwhelming sense of recognition.

In order, then, to maximize the appeal to the memory of the spectator, the painter must paint from memory, impose his own

---

[55] See my *Essai sur Laforgue et les 'Derniers Vers'* (French Forum Publications: Lexington, 1980), 97–8, 106–7.

[56] See 'Au lecteur', 'L'Amour du mensonge', 'Réversibilité' and 'Femmes damnées', *Oc.* i.

temperament, and universalize, omitting incidentals and subordinating detail to the ensemble of the painting. To ensure all this, the execution must be rapid, though its gestation may be drawn out. Much of the success of David's *Marat*, that 'triomphe du spiritualisme', is attributable to its most astonishing feature—that it has been painted with extreme rapidity (p. 410). Here, once again, Baudelaire's views find an echo in Delacroix, who records how the best head in *La Barque de Dante* was done 'avec une rapidité et un entrain extrêmes'[57] while a friend was reading him a canto of the *Inferno*, and it is said that the still life in the foreground of the *Lutte avec l'ange* in Saint-Sulpice was painted in an extraordinary twenty-two minutes.[58] Baudelaire himself records how Delacroix warned a young artist that if he was not capable of drawing a man in the time he takes to fall to the ground from a fourth-floor window, he would never be able to create 'de grandes machines'. The hyperbole reveals an enduring preoccupation which is to 'exécuter assez vite et avec assez de certitude pour ne rien laisser s'évaporer de l'intensité de l'action ou de l'idée' (p. 764). The result of these various requirements is that the painting will not have that finished appearance of academic, classical contructions; on the contrary, it will have something of the qualities of an *ébauche* rather than the finished work. This idea is so fundamental in Baudelaire's thinking that he returns to it in the discussion of the contemporary artists he most admires, Corot and Daumier, and makes of it an essential characteristic of the modernity of Constantin Guys. The idea was, however, far from new. In the *Salon de 1787* Diderot explains why a fine sketch pleases us more than a fine painting: 'L'esquisse ne nous attache peut-être si fort que parce qu'étant indéterminée, elle laisse plus de liberté à notre imagination, qui y voit tout ce qu'il lui plaît.'[59] The same idea is amply documented in Delacroix, who was convinced that 'L'exécution, dans la peinture, doit toujours tenir de l'improvisation.'[60] For him, as for Baudelaire, this unfinished quality was an essential part of the modern Romantic sensibility, impatient of the lack of vitality and imagination betrayed in the 'perfection' of

[57] *Journal*, 394, 24 Dec. 1853: 'Cette tête est celle de l'homme qui est en face, au fond, et qui cherche a grimper sur la barque, ayant passé son bras par-dessus le bord.'

[58] See Johnson, *Paintings*, v. 164.

[59] Diderot, *Salons*, iii, 242. He also associates speed of execution with the appeal to memory: 'Ce qu'il y a d'étonnant, c'est que l'artiste se rappelle ces effets à deux cents lieux de la nature, et qu'il n'a de modèle présent que dans son imagination; c'est qu'il peint avec une vitesse incroyable' (ibid. 160).

[60] *Journal*, 124, 27 Jan. 1847.

classical art. In another sphere Baudelaire's distaste for the limitations of the Comédie française finds a counterpart in Delacroix's dissatisfaction with the mediocre perfections of Racine (or Mozart) mentioned several times in the *Journal*: 'Je disais sur Racine ce que je pense et ce qu'on doit en dire, c'est-à-dire qu'il est trop parfait; que cette perfection et l'absence de lacunes et de disparates lui ôtent le piquant que l'on trouve à des ouvrages pleins de beautés et de défauts à la fois.'[61] Romantic art can be extravagant in conception and in subject matter; but it 'stravaigues'[62] in another way too, by going beyond prescribed boundaries of style and manner to exploit brilliantly, imaginatively, the lure of the irregular, eccentric, and bizarre. The 'irrégularités' and 'imperfections' of Shakespeare, 'les parties grossières et négligées' of Corneille, the 'défauts' of the 'hommes sublimes remplis d'excentricités', have a much greater appeal to the memory and imagination than the circumscribed perambulations of those meticulous but timorous spirits who have never ventured forth from the security of their own 'basse-cour'.[63]

A consideration of two of Baudelaire's *bêtes noires* will serve to set off the virtues of the modern school, and of Delacroix in particular: Horace Vernet inspires an extraordinary outburst of exasperation and venom, while Ary Scheffer attracts unalloyed contempt. Vernet unites in his person all the negative aspects of being French. His painting lacks depth of feeling, drama, or poetry; it is the work of a vaudevilliste, of one who is made dizzy by Michelangelo and whom Delacroix fills with a kind of animal-like stupor. Anything which has the qualities of the *abîme*, upwards towards the ideal, or downwards towards hell, causes him prudently to turn aside. More than anything, it is Vernet's unthinking, superficial nationalism and militarism that disgust and infuriate Baudelaire, who no doubt associates him with his stepfather General Aupick. At all events, he hates this art, which, like Béranger's poetry, is an obscene and grotesque flattery of national pride. His technical reasons for detesting Vernet are threefold. First, he substitutes *le chic* for draughtsmanship, *le chic* being the lack of reference to a model or to nature and their replacement by a

---

[61] *Journal*, 394, 24 Dec. 1853. See also p. 341, 9 May 1853. But see Baudelaire's comment (754) on the painter's praise of Racine.

[62] The expression (from Latin *extravagare*) is Scottish.

[63] The expression is Baudelaire's: 'Le Français est un animal de basse-cour, si bien domestiqué qu'il n'ose franchir aucune palissade. Voir ses goûts en art et en littérature' (*Oc.* i. 698).

pre-existing pattern, a stock figure with no counterpart in reality. It involves the abuse of memory, not the memory of the model recollected in order to be universalized and appeal to the memory of the spectator, but the memory of a cliché which the hand has learned to reproduce, hopelessly removed from real, lived experience. Instead of delving into his imagination and giving expression to his *naïve* temperament, the painter draws mechanically upon a stock of prefabricated images. The *chic* is consequently linked to the notion of *poncif*, which, however, applies more to postures and gestures, as for example when an actor places his hand on his heart to indicate undying love, or looks down at the stage, fists clenched, to signify desire for vengeance.

Vernet's second fault is to substitute discordance for harmony, and for colour a *charivari* of loud tones without the essential virtue of vibrancy. Lastly, he has no conception of the unity of a painting, which is lost in the proliferation of episodes. Here Baudelaire is probably thinking of the painting of the battle of Isly (1844) exhibited in the Salon, or those of Valmy and Jemappes (1792), so strangely lacking in drama, action, or movement.[64] No sense here of the courage and messianic fervour of the 'Morts de Quatre-Vingt-Douze' which Rimbaud was to celebrate. What we have are essentially static productions with lilliputian figures in bright military colours, dwarfed by the expanse of the canvas. Baudelaire frequently damns Meissonier for creating tiny pictures with tiny people, lacking that most essential quality of 'l'amour du grand' (p. 646). In spite of their larger scale, Vernet's canvases are no better; 'il fait des Meissonier grands comme le monde'. Here again, a comparison with Delacroix's extraordinary battle scenes drives home Baudelaire's point. The magnificent *Bataille de Taillebourg*, housed in Versailles, highlights the difference between Vernet's mediocrity and Delacroix's genius, in the handling of colour, in the unity of conception and execution, and the depiction of the heroic frenzy and violence of war. In Vernet, there is no passion, no *naïveté*, but an almanac-like memory and a photographic, documentary realism that records all the details of uni-

---

[64] National Gallery, London. In the *Salon de 1859* Baudelaire explains the difficulty of painting battles, which Vernet had 'overcome' 'par une série d'épisodes accumulés et juxtaposés' (642). See also his comment on *Judas et Thamar* (Wallace Collection, London): 'M. H. Vernet a résolu un problème incroyable: faire la peinture à la fois la plus criarde et la plus obscure, la plus embrouillée!' (413). Later he moderates his view in the light of Delacroix's admiration (765).

form, military accoutrements and decoration, as in the uniquely lack-lustre painting of Louis Philippe passing a review, ironically, at Versailles.[65]

The *éreintage* of Vernet, 'l'antithèse absolue de l'artiste', is so com-plete as to make one think one has reached the last circle of the damned. But with Ary Scheffer, the doubters and eclectics, one reaches new depths of mediocrity as one enters what Baudelaire calls the 'hospital of painting' (p. 472).[66] Great artists, whether colourists or draughtsmen, are strong, endowed with an immovable belief in their purpose and vision. Great painting, like great poetry, has faith: 'la grand poésie est essentiellement *bête*, elle *croit*' (p. 11).[67] Even Vernet did not suffer from the malady of doubt that afflicts the modern age, engendering the equally malignant malady of eclecticism. An eclectic is weak, like a ship trying to sail by all four winds; he has no faith, and neither star nor compass to guide him. Not having been created from an exclusive point of view,[68] his work can have no appeal to the memory. But worse than that, an eclectic not only copies other artists, he can be guilty of the supreme folly of bringing the means of another art form into his own, to cause one art to encroach upon another by the importation of the poetry of sentiment into that of painting. Such is the absurdity of Scheffer, a terminal case in this dismal hospital.

Saint Augustin et sainte Monique is a choice example of the aberra-tion which consists in confusing the means of poetry with those of painting; for the latter, says Baudelaire, is interesting only by nature of its colour and form, and resembles poetry only to the extent that poetry may similarly arouse in the reader ideas of painting—that is, presumably to the extent that it is concrete. The scarcely veiled refer-ence is to his own poetry and to that kind of Romantic poetry which,

[65] The full title of the work is *Louis Philippe accompagné de ses fils sort par la grande porte de Versailles pour passer une revue.*

[66] 'The hospital of painting' is even more insulting than 'le bagne de la peinture' (395) that Baudelaire had applied to the school of Lyon. It could be that the expression was prompted by Champfleury's *Salon*, published in *Le Corsaire-Satan* from 24 March to 23 May 1846: 'M. Scheffer [. . .] ne réussit qu'à nous montrer des gens souffreteux, aux yeux caves, bons à envoyer à l'hôpital' (Champfleury, *Son Regard et celui de Baudelaire* (Paris: Hermann, 1990), 100–1).

[67] A similar point is made about Haussoullier: 'Autre qualité énorme et qui fait les hommes, les vrais hommes, cette peinture a la foi—elle a la foi de sa beauté,—c'est de la peinture absolue, convaincue qui crie: je veux, je veux être belle, et belle comme je l'entends, et je sais que je ne manquerai pas de gens à qui plaire' (360).

[68] Cf. p. 473: 'Les éclectiques n'ont pas songé que l'attention humaine est d'autant plus intense qu'elle est bornée et qu'elle limite elle-même son champ d'observations. Qui trop embrasse mal étreint.'

based upon sensation rather than the abstractions of sentiment, can be thought to share, at least to some extent, the physicality of the visual arts. But to take the abstractions of loss or melancholy, or worse, as Scheffer has done, the vision of eternal life in some 'beyond' of time and space, 'what the ear has not heard and the eye has not seen' and to seek to give them concrete expression, is dispiritingly nonsensical. But that is what Scheffer has done in this 'peinture invisible' (p. 475), which shows Augustine and his unbelievably young mother looking for all the world like a conventional Virgin Mary in an equally conventional pose, with hands entwined and doelike eyes raised heavenward towards nothing at all. No movement, razor-sharp outlines, light and air without vibration, an abhorrent vacuum as background, the *poncifs* of expression and posture, all of which amounts to a biscuit-tin spirituality grounded not in physical beings of flesh and blood, but in two-dimensional cardboard cut-outs.[69]

Underlying Baudelaire's strictures on Scheffer is an idea that pervades his art criticism but is not fully stated until the *Salon de 1859*, that of the specificity of art forms. Although he himself did more than any other poet to develop the hybrid genre of the prose poem, his conservatism as an art critic renders him intolerant of any crossing of the genres or the confusing of the means of one art with another. Who, he asks, could without horror conceive of 'une peinture en relief, une sculpture agitée par la mécanique, une ode sans rimes, un roman versifié'? Such hybrids can only arise from an ignorance of the distinctive and defining qualities of an art form: 'Quand le but naturel d'un art est méconnu, il est naturel d'appeler à son secours tous les moyens étrangers à cet art' (p. 674).

The modern conception of pure art is of 'une magie suggestive contenant à la fois l'objet et le sujet, le monde extérieur à l'artiste et l'artiste lui-même' (p. 598). This conception, based on the power of physical things to suggest subjective states, stands in stark contrast to the outmoded stance of philosophic art, which sets out to imitate literature and convey a historical, moral, or philosophical message. The aim is outmoded since, claims Baudelaire, for several centuries there has been a separation of powers in the arts, so that certain subjects are the domain of painting, others of music, or of literature. The encroachment of one art on the other is yet another sign of decadence in the contemporary world. Readers of his literary criticism

---

[69] A later version of the painting can be seen in the National Gallery, London. Other works by Scheffer are housed in the Wallace Collection.

will feel themselves in familiar territory, and recognize a similarity with his well-known censure on didactic or moralizing literature in the essays on Gautier and Poe. The heresy of didacticism has contaminated also the German painters, the school of the 'ville philosophique' of Lyon, 'le bagne de la peinture', and Baudelaire's much esteemed friend, the erudite and brilliant conversationalist, Chenavard, whose *Palingénésie sociale*, a vast mosaic in *grisaille* relating the history of mankind, was intended for the Panthéon. But philosophic art, although peculiar to earlier stages of civilization (which Baudelaire never specifies), can have no place in the modern world. To be consistent, it would have to revert to the primitive hieroglyphs which characterized that art, to 'les innombrables et barbares conventions de l'art hiératique' (p. 605), to that 'language' of art which spelled out its message and which its consumers knew how to decipher.

Baudelaire's position seems clear, at least in its broad outlines, but on closer inspection it is not without ambiguity. The problem is that the argument is both diachronic and synchronic; diachronic because it distinguishes a modern from an early conception of art; synchronic because it sets forth a belief in the 'limites providentielles' and 'la constitution naturelle', which are given as fundamental to the essence of art and should not be violated. The propositions are irreconcilable, the earlier conception being at variance with the nature of art and its prescribed limits—unless one were to posit that art has found its true nature only in the modern era. Such a view would iron out the contradiction, but it would have the unfortunate effect of denying the earlier conception the status of art, and of making Baudelaire's views on modern art so categorical and overweening as to deprive them of credibility. The idea of an essential specificity of art is, of course, perfectly in keeping with his belief in an innate grammar and in the nature of rhetoric and prosody. Its incompatibility with a diachronic view is but another instance of a whole series of contradictions which are not so much imperfections in his thinking, as the signs of a questing, restless intellect, deeply aware of the dangers of imprisoning one's thought in a system 'pour y prêcher à [son] aise' (p. 577).

The ambiguity in the argument leads to an ambivalence in the poet's approach to 'philosophic' artists; and this again is hardly surprising in a poet several of whose own flowers of evil have a direct moral message,[70] and who sought in his 'petits poèmes en prose' to

---

[70] See F. W. Leakey, 'Baudelaire: the poet as moralist', in *Studies in Modern French Literature presented to P. Mansell Jones* (Manchester: Manchester University Press, 1961).

create a poetry of ideas, drawing from each object of his 'flânerie' 'une morale désagréable'.[71] That the moral lesson is often itself contradictory, ironic, or mystifying matters little, since a moral lesson of whatever kind might be thought incompatible even with this modern hybrid form, whose 'providential' limits have presumably not yet emerged. However that may be, Baudelaire's condemnation of the Lyon artists and Chenavard is unequivocal; but, crucially, his attitude towards the German school is much more nuanced. In particular, two works by Rethel are singled out for praise: *Première Invasion du choléra à Paris, au bal de l'Opéra* (*Der Tod als Erwürger*) and *Der Tod als Freund*, which, with their moral message conveyed by the allegorical figure of death, in the one as slayer, in the other as friend, were, interestingly, to have been the inspiration for two prose poems Baudelaire never completed.[72] In philosophic art, 'tout est allégorie, allusion, hiéroglyphes, rébus' (p. 600); there is, in short, a kind of coded language which has to be deciphered. But the appeal of Rethel is not in a one-for-one identification of hieroglyph with meaning, but in the way he has combined the hieroglyphs with more modern, 'suggestive' notations, such as the bird on the window-sill; 'vient-il écouter le violon de la Mort, ou est-ce une allégorie de l'âme prête à s'envoler?'[73] Rethel's virtue is, it seems, to have 'modernized' philosophic art by making it more suggestive, less explicit, endowing it with 'un caractère poétique, vague et confus', freeing the viewer from a straitjacketed response and allowing him to recreate the piece through his own memory and imagination. As with the greatest contemporary works, the viewer/critic has been involved in the creative act, and it is the 'traducteur qui invente *les intentions*'.

Allegory is, of course, a favourite and readily decoded hieroglyph of philosophic art, and Baudelaire's ambivalence towards it is not surprising. In the *Salon de 1845* he ranks it among the most beautiful of art forms (p. 368), regretting that Boissard has not been able to produce an allegorical picture representing Music, Painting, and Poetry;

---

[71] *Corr.* ii. 583, letter to Sainte-Beuve: 'j'ai l'espoir de pouvoir montrer, un de ces jours, un nouveau Joseph Delorme accrochant sa pensée rapsodique à chaque accident de sa flânerie et tirant de chaque objet une morale désagréable.' See also my *Baudelaire and 'Le Spleen de Paris'* (Oxford: Clarendon Press, 1987), Ch. 2.

[72] *Oc.* i. 374.

[73] Incidentally, it is in the other woodcut that death is playing on the 'violin' of a bone; in *Death as friend*, Death is tolling a bell. As so often (see in particular Ch. 4), Baudelaire is writing from memory.

and of course his own use of allegory is widely exemplified in the high art of *Les Fleurs du Mal*, and ironically in the more strident *Spleen de Paris*. It then seems odd that in the following year he should make no mention of Delacroix's use of allegory in his public decorations, but praise him for *not* painting Apollo and the Muses ('décoration invariable des bibliothèques'), and for yielding to his irresistible taste for Dante in painting the Luxembourg ceiling (p. 437). In the *Salon de 1859*, when his attitude towards sculpture has become much more positive, allegory is closely associated with what he seems to see as an essentially public art, in the splendid evocations of Harpocrates, Venus, and Hebe, the allegorized figures of Melancholy and Bereavement, and the sculptures of Ernest Christophe, which inspired 'Le Masque' and 'Danse macabre'. In discussing in the same *Salon* Penguilly's *Petite Danse macabre*, he regrets that modern artists neglect the magnificent medieval allegories 'où l'immortel grotesque s'enlaçait en folâtrant, comme il fait encore, à l'immortel horrible' (p. 652). On the other hand, he has no trouble in making fun of the abuse of allegorical titles and *rébus* in contemporary works that lack conviction and a proper sense of the modern. The work of the *pointus* appeals readily to the French mentality which is philosophic, lacking in imagination, incapable of responding to suggestive art, and most at home in deciphering the hieroglyphs of an art that aims to astonish, not by the means peculiar to it, but by 'des moyens étrangers à l'art' (p. 616). But behind the ironies about the bad taste of his contemporaries lies an uncertainty which is never completely dispersed: to what extent does he consider allegory the peculiar mode of sculpture; and, more importantly, to what extent can it be incorporated into a modern conception of a suggestive art without adulterating that art with hieroglyphs alien to its nature?

The great contemporary painter whom Baudelaire contrasts with Delacroix in the *Salons* of 1846 and 1859, and the *Exposition universelle (1855)*, is of course Ingres. His attitude towards this *dessinateur par excellence*, who was head of his own school and fêted as the greatest artist of his time, evolves considerably. In *Le Musée classique du Bazar Bonne-Nouvelle* of January 1846 Baudelaire lacks the space to praise, among others, *La Grande Odalisque* and Ingres's portraits which are not just snapshots of their subjects, but 'de vrais portraits, c'est-à-dire la reconstruction idéale des individus' (p. 412). He specifically mentions the portaits of M. Molé, Madame d'Haussonville, and arguably the most famous of all, that of M. Bertin, an entrepreneur of Balzacian proportions and founder of the important political *Journal des débats*. Baudelaire's attitude is flattering to the point of sycophancy; the eleven paintings shown at the exhibition enable one to appreciate 'toute la Genèse de son génie', in particular *La Petite Odalisque*, 'cette délicieuse et bizarre fantaisie', and the master's ability to paint beautiful women: 'Les muscles, les plis de la chair, les ombres des fossettes, les ondulations montueuses de la peau, rien n'y manque. Si l'île de Cythère commandait un tableau à M. Ingres, à coup sûr il ne serait pas folâtre et riant comme celui de Watteau, mais robuste et nourrissant comme l'amour antique.' He wishes to put right certain prejudices and misconceptions about Ingres, that his paintings are grey and lack colour, whereas if this 'nation nigaude' would only open its eyes it would realize that there never was painting which was 'plus éclatante, voyante, et même une plus grande recherche de tons'.

In the *Salon* of the same year, however, the tone is much more muted, no doubt because Baudelaire's ideas on colour and outline have been clarified and given a theoretical basis. He has also become more emphatic, convinced that the colourists now form the majority, colour being the most natural and the most visible of phenomena (p. 454). The chapters 'De l'idéal et du modèle' and 'De quelques dessinateurs' are particularly relevant here. In the first, where the argument is sometimes not without obscurity, he sets out to explain the principles guiding draughtsmen, often without their knowing it. The title of his chapter is, he says, a contradiction, or rather an agreement of contraries, by which he means that the *dessinateur* should synthesize ideal and model. Just as colour is composed of an infinite number of different tones, so in reality line is made up of a host of individual lines, each one being a feature of the model. The circumference of a circle, the ideal of the curved line, is comparable to an analogous figure made up of an infinite number of straight lines, and which should merge with it. But there is no such thing as a perfect circumference except in the ideal world of the geometer, and the foolish artist who does not realize this is led to the perpetual reproduction of the same unchanging ideal type: 'Les poètes, les artistes et toute la race humaine seraient bien malheureux, si l'idéal, cette absurdité, cette impossibilité, était trouvé. Qu'est-ce que chacun ferait désormais de son pauvre *moi*,—de sa ligne brisée?' Baudelaire repeats that exact imitation spoils memory; but so also does excessive generalization or idealization. The result is that the draughtsman should neither give a slavish imitation of the model, nor use it as a springboard out of reality to an ideal world of representation;

he must create his art, and his originality, in a middle way between these extremes if it is to have that essential appeal to the spectator. The essence man does not exist in nature, which offers nothing absolute or complete. Human beings are infinitely variable and no two are ever identical. But each individual is a harmony in itself,[74] and Baudelaire cites in support of his argument the work of the Swiss physiognomist Lavater, who drew up a taxonomy of noses and mouths which cannot go together. According to him, human beings are harmonious even in their ugliness, 'telle main veut tel pied; chaque épiderme engendre son poil' (p. 456), so that each individual has his own ideal. Baudelaire is not saying that there are as many original ideals as there are individuals, since the same mould can give many impressions; but that in the soul of the artist there are as many ideals as individuals and that a portrait (or figure) is a model complicated by an artist. The ideal, then, is not some kind of vague, academic abstraction; it is rather, in a justly famous definition, 'l'individu redressé par l'individu, reconstruit et rendu par le pinceau ou le ciseau à l'éclatante vérité de son harmonie primitive'. In order to do this, the artist must generalize somewhat, but at the same time exaggerate some feature to make the expression clearer. Drawing is a struggle between artist and nature, in which, with only a semblance of a paradox, the artist will succeed all the more readily if he understands the underlying intentions of nature. We have here, yet again, evidence of a belief, stressed by Kelley throughout his edition, in the underlying and inherent harmony of nature, as if the teleological intention of nature, which has been lost, were restored through the process of art and the imposition of the artistic temperament.

In the first chapter of the *Salon*, having just declared that criticism should be partial and passionate, Baudelaire had set out to appear impartial towards draughtsmen and colourists; for to exalt line to the detriment of colour or vice versa was to show, he declared, a great ignorance of individual destinies and the way that nature mingles in each artist the taste for line and the taste for colour. However, in the next chapter, in contrasting the 'naturalist' painters of the south and the imaginative painters of the north, a preference for the latter is suggested, while in the chapter on Delacroix a hierarchy is established between three kinds of drawing: the exact, the physiognomic, and the imaginative. The first is dismissed as stupid, 'incorrect à force de

---

[74] The same point is made by Diderot in the opening paragraphs of *Essai sur la peinture*.

réalité'. The second is 'un dessin naturaliste, mais idéalisé, dessin d'un génie qui sait choisir, arranger, corriger, deviner, gourmander la nature'; while the third and most noble can afford to neglect nature and represent another 'analogue à l'esprit et au tempérament de l'auteur' (p. 434).[75] The second type is associated with *passionnés* like Ingres, but the third is the privilege of geniuses and supreme artists such as Delacroix. There is no doubt about this hierarchy, though Ingres is still associated with the word 'genius'. In 'De quelques dessinateurs', however, where Michelangelo is said to be the only modern draughtsman with any inventive or imaginative genius, Baudelaire is much more trenchant. Generally draughtsmen are naturalists guided by reason, whereas colourists, whose method is analogous to that of nature, are guided by temperament. The differences had been set out before, but now the judgement is uncompromisingly negative: 'un dessinateur est un coloriste manqué', which is to say that he is hardly an artist at all. With this inauspicious aphorism Ingres is explicitly brought back into the discussion. His drawing is not called into question; indeed, he is said to draw admirably well, and rapidly, producing in his sketches the ideal naturally; in a sense he draws even better than Raphael, the great ancestor and king of draughtsmen. The fault lies with his colour, after which he vainly strives, loving it with the passion and lack of subtlety of a 'marchande de modes', and producing sometimes a discordant, but always a bitter and violent effect. His *Angélique* and the two *Odalisques* are deeply voluptuous, 'mais toutes ces choses ne nous apparaissent que dans un jour presque effrayant; car ce n'est ni l'atmosphère dorée qui baigne les champs de l'idéal, ni la lumière tranquille et mesurée des régions sublunaires' (p. 460). Baudelaire leaves the matter there, with the impression that there is somehow a mismatch between the sensuality of the figures and the quality of light in which they are placed.

It is clear that the *Salon de 1846* is built upon the opposition of colour and line, but to argue, as Kelley does in an effort to extend the theory of complementary contrasts, that Baudelaire manages to reconcile the opposed poles of this duality without destroying them and that the natural unity which is the French school in 1846 is 'la *résultante* des tendances opposées déterminées par Delacroix et Ingres'[76] seems to be

[75] Kelley talks of 'la création d'un univers autonome qui est néanmoins foncièrement naturel, puisqu'il obéit aux mêmes lois d'harmonie et d'unité que l'univers extérieur' (*Salon de 1846*, 31).

[76] Ibid. 46.

going beyond what the text itself will allow. True, Ingres's talent is recognized, but the praise seems faint alongside the eulogy of Delacroix, who at the end emerges as the supreme artist. Baudelaire's presentation of the issue appears to be tactical. If he is to persuade, he has to handle the immense reputation of Ingres with care, which is why he is impartial to begin with and then little by little tips the balance decisively in Delacroix's favour. Far from being presented with a coherent French school, the reader finds one that is split down the middle—with, in addition, figures like Vernet and Scheffer, whose presence in any harmony could only render it derisory.

In the *Exposition universelle*, however, Baudelaire casts aside all reserve; the indictment of Ingres's talent is unequivocal, and all the more wounding as he is still recognized as an artist of great renown. He begins by setting him against the great painters of the previous generation: David, 'cet astre froid', Guérin, and Girodet. Whatever their aims, whatever the solemnity of their subjects, whatever the inadequacy of their colour and use of light, they had the great merit of renewing in French art the taste for heroism and stoic virtue. But they were not as Greek and Roman as they might have intended, especially the latter two, in whose work there are signs of future Romanticism. Baudelaire sees something modern, something no doubt of 'la morale du siècle', in Guérin's Dido,[77] reminiscent as much of Chateaubriand and Balzac as of Virgil, and considers Girodet's *Atala* vastly superior to a host of insipid modern creations. With Ingres, however, whose origins were in the republican and imperial school, he experiences a strong sense of malaise, stemming from a first impression he has some difficulty in defining, something akin to the rarefied atmosphere of a chemistry laboratory with automatic figures too palpably alien from our experience, something negative, 'd'un ordre quasi maladif'. Devoid of *surnaturalisme*, Ingres's world appears as 'un milieu fantasmatique', or worse, as the imitation of such a milieu. The summing-up is without mercy: 'l'imagination qui soutenait les grands maîtres [. . .] l'imagination, cette reine des facultés, a disparu' (p. 585).[78] The judgement is all the more cruel as imagination is shown in the *Salon de 1859*, of which we have here a foretaste, to be the primary requisite for the artist, thus taking over from *naïveté* and temperament

---

[77] In *Didon et Enée* (1817), Louvre.

[78] Delacroix's opinion of Ingres was equally damning: 'Ingres a été pitoyable; c'est une cervelle toute de travers; il ne voit qu'un point. C'est comme dans sa peinture; pas la moindre logique et point d'imagination' (*Journal*, 405, 24 Mar. 1854).

celebrated in 1846. For Baudelaire imagination is by no means some
loose or unintellectual faculty; it has nothing to do with sentimentality,
effusions of the heart, or the detested 'style coulant' of the equally
detested Musset. On the contrary, it is essentially dynamic: 'elle sait
choisir, juger, comparer, fuir ceci, rechercher cela, rapidement,
spontanément' (p. 116). It is linked to good taste, enabling us to avoid
the bad and choose the good in art. Above all it is the faculty which
activates all the others: 'elle les excite, elle les envoie au combat'. It is
both analysis and synthesis (p. 620), and is essential for all creative
work in the arts or in science, in the world of action or of contemplation; one could no more imagine a mathematician or a general without
imagination than one could an artist. In painting it is imagination that
teaches the moral meaning of colour, outline, and scent. It presides
over the doctrine of correspondence and synesthesia: 'elle a créé, au
commencement du monde, l'analogie et la métaphore.' 'Elle crée un
monde nouveau.' 'Elle est positivement apparentée avec *l'infini*.'[79] Far
removed from the relaxed, facile, and dangerous faculty of fantasy, it
'bears a distant relation to that sublime power by which the Creator
projects, creates and upholds his universe' (p. 624).[80] Once again, as
with his definition of Romanticism, Baudelaire is positing a parallel
between art and religion through the functioning of imagination, the
highest, noblest queen of faculties.

Such a definition contrasts strongly with what might be called the
classical view which saw imagination, like memory, as the handmaid of
the intellect, providing images of past experience for it to work upon;
without it, the intellect could never make headway, but would always
be starting anew. Without the control and the legitimation of the
intellect, however, it gives rise to chimera and follies. For Pascal, it was
'cette partie décevante dans l'homme, cette maîtresse d'erreur et de
fausseté',[81] and for Samuel Johnson it was 'a licentious and vagrant
faculty, unsusceptible of limitations, and impatient of restraint'.[82] But
with Rousseau, Madame de Staël, and the German Romantics it is
higher than intellect itself and equates man with the Creator and his
creation; it bears witness to the divine in man. It is in this light that we
can understand the poet's forceful attack on photography and realism,
and his contempt for those who in painting, sculpture, or literature

---

[79] My emphasis.
[80] Baudelaire is quoting from Mrs Catherine Crowe, *The Night Side of Nature* (1848).
[81] Pascal, Pensée 82, Brunschvicg edition. Lafuma (44) gives 'cette partie dominante'.
[82] Samuel Johnson, *The Rambler*, no. 125.

strive to give an exact rendering of external reality. The imperfect world (as it had unequivocally become for Baudelaire by 1859) must needs be transformed by the artistic process, and be given order, unity, and force, art being an abstraction from reality and a sacrifice of detail to the ensemble. As for Delacroix, the world is a vast stock of images and signs which the imagination must digest and transform. It is clear Baudelaire's anti-realism springs from the *surnaturalisme* of 1846, and that the notions of *naïveté*, unity, and force of that year have become subsumed under the all-embracing notion of the imagination in the *Salon de 1859*.

It would be wrong, however, to think that the workings of the imagination are purely subjective, expressing only the temperament of the artist. Imagination, we are told, created analogy and metaphor at the beginning of the world. It takes the world apart and 'avec les matériaux amassés et disposés suivant des règles dont on ne peut trouver l'origine que dans *le plus profond de l'âme*,[83] elle crée un monde nouveau, elle produit la sensation du neuf' (p. 621). Baudelaire is reinforcing here the 1846 notion of an innate symbolism, a kind of innate language, which, because it is universal, is communicable directly to the mind of the consumer of the work. Analogy is inherent in the human psyche, part of its essential nature, in a way which seems distantly to prefigure Jung's universal archetypes dormant in the unconscious, or Chomsky's innate grammar. Nothing certainly could be further from a Lockian or Humean notion of the mind as a *tabula rasa* upon which the sensations of the outside world imprint themselves, and though Baudelaire's metaphysical anguish may bring him close to Pascal or the modern existentialists, his view of the configuration of the human mind indicates a strong essentialist conviction. Nor is this latter limited as it were to the thought structures of the mind; it extends to the forms in and through which it is expressed, so that rhetoric and prosody are by no means arbitrary tyrannies imposed upon the artist, but 'une collection de règles réclamées par l'organisation même de l'être spirituel' (p. 627).[84]

Ingres's works are devoid of imagination and, therefore inevitably, of movement. This, Baudelaire suggests, tongue-in-cheek, is possibly the result of a heroic sacrifice in favour of tradition and 'l'idéal du beau

---

[83] My emphasis.

[84] The same idea appears in note form in the poet's projected preface for *Les Fleurs du Mal*: 'comment la poésie touche à la musique par une prosodie dont les racines plongent plus avant dans l'âme humaine que ne l'indique aucune théorie classique' (*Oc.* i. 183).

raphaélesque' espoused by the *dessinateur*—a polite way of making a virtue of a fault. What aims does such an artist set himself? Not passion and sentiment, not great historical works, neither the sublimity of Christian inspiration, nor the ferocity of pagan subjects:

Je croirais volontiers que son idéal est une espèce d'idéal fait moitié de santé, moitié de calme, presque d'indifférence, quelque chose d'analogue à l'idéal antique, auquel il a ajouté les curiosités et les minuties de l'art moderne [. . .] Epris ainsi d'un idéal qui mêle dans un adultère agaçant la solidité calme de Raphaël avec les recherches de la petite-maîtresse. (p. 586)

So, coldness, calm, and no grandeur, nothing of the passion of Delacroix, or of Baudelaire's ideal for that matter, of Lady Macbeth, 'âme puissante au crime'.[85] Nothing of the extravagance of 'Hymne à la Beauté', the statuesque immobility perhaps of 'La Beauté', but with none of its mystery or antique grandeur, since with Ingres the antique has been adulterated and corrupted by the trivialities of contemporary fashion, the dispiriting 'afféteries' (p. 463) characteristic of *Ingrisme*.

Faults in the master's drawing are next in line for censure. Nature should, of course, be corrected, amended, represented as a whole, but Ingres is guilty of deceit and sleight of hand, so that his figures are often lacking in proportion and harmony in the sense intended by Lavater: 'Voici une armée de doigts trop uniformément allongés en fuseaux et dont les extrémités étroites oppriment les ongles, que Lavater, à l'inspection de cette poitrine large, de cet avant-bras musculeux, de cet ensemble un peu viril, aurait jugés devoir être carrés' (p. 587). No particular painting is specified, but there seems little doubt that he is thinking of *L'Angélique*, with her infinitely delicate fingers and robust limbs, which Baudelaire thinks owe a debt to Raphael. Elsewhere, he claims, we shall find 'un nombril qui s'égare vers les côtes, là un sein qui pointe trop vers l'aisselle'. Again, nothing is specified, but it takes little ingenuity to detect the once much praised *Grande Odalisque*, whose right breast appears to have been neatly pocketed like a billiard ball under the armpit, and whose navel appears too high, especially if one were to imagine her standing up. What was a virtue in 1846 has now in 1855 become a distortion, for a note in *Le Musée classique* admires in Ingres 'des recherches d'un goût particulier, des finesses extrêmes' (p. 413), which enable him in this painting, perhaps by using a negress as model, to accentuate 'certains développements et certaines sveltesses'. The parallel is too clear for

---

[85] See 'L'Idéal', *Oc.* i. 22.

one to doubt that he is talking of the same picture. Finally, in *Jupiter et Antiope* he declares himself disconcerted 'par une jambe sans nom, toute maigre, sans muscles, sans formes, sans plis au jarret'. In addition, he blames excessive emphasis on outline and insufficient modelling with the result that 'ses figures ont l'air de patrons d'une forme très correcte, gonflée d'une matière molle et non vivante, étrangère à l'organisme humain'. His women, in particular, seem to have lost whatever allure they once had, conveying none of the contained strength and vitality of, say, Delacroix's *Les Femmes d'Alger*.

Baudelaire's discussion of Ingres has little of the violence and rapidity of his drubbing of Vernet. On the contrary, it is reasoned, systematic, and comprehensive. Lacking the temperament which makes for the fatality of genius, Ingres is inevitably also of an eclectic disposition. His works draw upon multifarious sources: Titian, Renaissance enamellers, Poussin, Carraccio, Raphael, the German primitives, Persian and Chinese art. The chapter ends with the censure of two of his most famous works. *L'Apothéose de l'Empereur Napoléon Ier*, where his eclecticism includes features from Etruscan art, is made to appear absurd: the horses are not harnessed to the chariots and seem to be made out of the same wood as their Trojan ancestor; and Napoleon appears deprived of the epic beauty and aura of destiny recognized by contemporaries and historians alike. Here was a chance to depict a *modern* heroism, clothed in the Emperor's famous grey coat; but to crown everything, this strange stylized apotheosis lacks the essential ingredient of an apotheosis, 'le sentiment surnaturel, la puissance d'ascension vers les régions supérieures, un entraînement, un vol irrésistible vers le ciel, but de toutes les aspirations humaines et habitacle classique de tous les grands hommes' (p. 589). Having neither the 'aspiration vers l'infini' of Romantic modernism nor the heroism of modern life, it is the opposite of an apotheosis, and falls to earth under its own weight, like a balloon without gas. *Jeanne d'Arc* fares no better, though Baudelaire spares us an extended commentary, noting only the absence of any hint of what made her great, and any sense of *surnaturalisme*. The closing lines of the chapter seek to identify Ingres's virtues: his unremitting love of beauty and, for some eccentrics like Baudelaire himself, his *bizarrerie*. But the effect, no doubt intended, is to add condescension to affront, not least by turning Ingres's great energy and will-power into shortcomings, the abuse of will-power indicating not the creative energy of a Balzac or of a

Delacroix, but the pig-headed perseverance of a man caught in a rut from the outset of his career.

If Ingres's mistake was to sacrifice himself heroically to the tradition of Raphael, Courbet's was to sacrifice himself, in *his* war upon imagination, to 'la nature extérieure, positive, immédiate' (p. 586). Baudelaire's strictures on realism are prominent in 1855 and especially in the *Salon de 1859*, but, in spite of certain ambiguities in his attitude to nature, they were already well in evidence in 1846, when he declares that an eclectic is less than a man because he does not know that the first task of an artist is to 'substituer l'homme à la nature et de protester contre elle' (p. 473). He quotes with approval Heine (p. 432), who believed that the artist should avoid the direct imitation of nature since nature can never supply all the types required for his art, the most remarkable of which are revealed to him in his soul, 'comme la symbolique innée d'idées innées'. Nature is merely the pabulum which nourishes the artist's mind, or to use an image which he takes from Delacroix, nature is a vast dictionary 'dont il roule et consulte les feuillets avec un œil sûr et profond' (p. 433). As we have seen, the same idea is made even more explicit in 1859. The mistake of the realist, or rather of the positivist as he prefers to call him in 1859, is to copy the dictionary in the hope of producing a work of art, with the result that he produces a banality devoid of passion or imagination, the worthless photographic spectacle of 'la nature sans l'homme'. A painting can no more be an assemblage of diverse elements observed in the external world than a poem can be created by the arbitrary juxtaposition of words from a dictionary.

Baudelaire's silence about Courbet and failure to recognize his genius have caused much surprise, given their friendship from about 1847 and their shared political involvement from 1848 until the ideological break in 1852. Courbet's portrait of the poet, reused in *L'Atelier*, has been read as a homage of one artist to another, while the hashish-induced stupor of the *Somnambule*, the black frock coats in *Un enterrement à Ornans*, and the lesbian overtones of *Vénus et Psyché*[86] have been taken as proof of an affinity of temperament or preoccupation. Certainly, there is a case to be made for an influence of Baudelaire on the early Courbet, and recently Michael Fried has sought to 'baudelairize'[87] Courbet by interpreting his self-portraits as an exploration of his artistic quest. Though a list of the painter's works drawn

---

[86] Of 1864, later destroyed.
[87] In *Courbet's Realism* (Chicago and London: University of Chicago Press, 1990).

up by Baudelaire for the Salon of 1849 indicates a good knowledge of his production, Baudelaire's silence is perfectly understandable, since the Salons of 1845 and 1846 predate their friendship and in any case contained each only one minor work by Courbet.[88] By 1855 any flirtation with realism and the politics of the left had been left far behind, as the poet's views on imagination as the queen of faculties developed along with his rejection of 'nature', so that any praise of Courbet's work would have been out of line with Baudelaire's developing aesthetic. Though some have seen in his brief remarks in *Peintres et aquafortistes* (1862) a late recognition of Courbet's art ('Il faut rendre à Courbet cette justice, qu'il n'a pas peu contribué à rétablir le goût de la simplicité et de la franchise, et l'amour désintéressé, absolu, de la peinture'), it must be borne in mind that the eulogy is not without ambiguity, since the immense success of Courbet's paintings is explained by the contrast they form with the prettified superficialities of contemporary taste. No canvas of Courbet's is mentioned in *Peintres et aquafortistes*, and his virtues are moral rather than painterly. Baudelaire's definitive view is summed up in a jotting from the embittered *Pauvre Belgique!* where he deplores the disappearance of art from that country. The philosophy of Belgian artists, of these brutes as he calls them, is the same as Courbet's: 'Ne peindre que ce qu'on voit (Donc *vous* ne peindrez pas ce que *je* ne vois pas)' (p. 931). The result is that, instead of artists, there are only specialists, painters of the sun, moon, furniture, flowers, with infinite subdivisions, as in an industry, so that collaboration would become essential to make any one composition. Nowhere is Baudelaire's condemnation of photographic realism expressed with more wit or more venom.

But even before 1855 it is difficult to imagine the poet responding positively to the realism and lack of structure in Courbet's paintings, which make him most unlike Delacroix. *Les Lutteurs* (1853), for example, conveys little sense of struggle and compares negatively with Delacroix's magnificent *Lutte de Jacob* in Saint-Sulpice, which unites the muscular aggression of Jacob and the passive resilience of the angel.[89] Delacroix's own reaction to Courbet's canvas was far from flattering, condemning the way the figures are swallowed up by the background, and the lack of action and invention.[90] Similarly, he found *Les Baigneuses* offensive:

[88] *Le Guitarerro* and *Portrait de M****.
[89] See below pp. 69–25 for a discussion of this work.
[90] See *Journal*, 328, 15 Apr. 1853.

Une grosse bourgeoise, vue par le dos et toute nue sauf un lambeau de torchon négligemment peint qui couvre le bas des fesses, sort d'une petite nappe d'eau qui ne semble pas assez profonde seulement pour un bain de pieds. Elle fait un geste qui n'exprime rien, et une autre femme, que l'on suppose sa servante, est assise par terre occupée à se déchausser.[91]

The gestures of both nude and servant are indeed enigmatic, having a distant resemblance to certain religious paintings.[92] In particular, the figure of the nude has something of the lofty self-containment of Christ in Delacroix's *Le Christ au jardin des oliviers*, as he rejects the ministerings of the angels sent to comfort him. At the time, Courbet's painting attracted much criticism and incomprehension, notably for the 'dirtiness' and grossness of the bather (a Hottentot Venus, according to Gautier), its realism and apparent failure to integrate the figures and the landscape. The conservative Baudelaire is unlikely to have been more indulgent, and may well have found unacceptable or baffling the incongruity of gesture and situation, and the irreverent hint of irony which underpins it.

It is not known what Baudelaire thought of his own portrait, integrated into *L'Atelier* of 1855, though Bowness alleges disapproval.[93] His links with the painter must still have been close, since he persuaded him to remove the figure of Jeanne Duval, still visible in ghostly outline on the canvas. While this inveterate spinner of oxymorons may have appreciated Courbet's contradictory 'allégorie réelle', it is equally possible, or even likely, that he would have considered it a gratuitous mystification, a *rébus* incompatible with the demands of high art.[94]

The painting that has been thought most Baudelairean is, of course, the celebrated *Enterrement à Ornans* of 1850 which, in the view of many, represented more than any other contemporary work the modernity called for by the poet at the end of the *Salon* of 1845 and 1846. Though both texts, but especially the *Salon* of 1846, are dominated by the romantic modernity of Delacroix, there is an appeal for a different kind of modernity which would extend beyond sensibility to

---

[91] 328, 15 Apr. 1853.

[92] Abigail Solomon-Godeau writes of 'the histrionic gestures, the ghostly evocations of the *Noli me tangere*' of the painting, in Sarah Faunce and Linda Nochlin, *Courbet Reconsidered* (New Haven and London: Yale University Press, 1988), 114.

[93] 'Courbet and Baudelaire', *Gazette des Beaux-Arts*, 90 (Dec. 1977), 195: 'The portrait is a most arresting image, but it pleased neither the painter nor the poet, who refused it as a gift.'

[94] For Delacroix's positive reaction see his *Journal*, 529, 3 Aug. 1855.

include modern subject matter. The *Salon de 1845* ends with the famous assertion: 'Celui-là sera le *peintre*, le vrai peintre, qui saura arracher à la vie actuelle son côté épique, et nous faire voir et comprendre, avec de la couleur et du dessin, combien nous sommes grands et poétiques dans nos cravates et nos bottes vernies' (p. 407). The *Salon de 1846* declares: 'La vie parisienne est féconde en sujets poétiques et merveilleux. Le merveilleux nous enveloppe et nous abreuve comme l'atmosphère; mais nous ne le voyons pas' (p. 496), and expresses the wish for an epic art, not after the manner of the *Iliad* or the Greeks and Romans, but analogous to the great creations of Balzac—Rastignac, Birotteau, Vautrin. The specific character of the times is expressed also in contemporary dress, in 'le frac funèbre et convulsionné que nous endossons tous', the symbol of a perpetual mourning of modern man. The black coat, symbolizing equality, has its political beauty; it has also its poetic beauty, which is the expression of the public soul: 'une immense défilade de croque-morts, croque-morts politiques, croque-morts amoureux, croque-morts bourgeois. Nous célébrons tous quelque enterrement' (p. 494).

There seems little doubt that Courbet had Baudelaire's views in mind in painting the *Enterrement*. Champfleury had stated in 1851 that the painter from Ornans had completely understood the *Salon de 1846* and that great colourists can make colour with black coats, a white tie, and a grey background. Here indeed is an array of bourgeois, country bourgeois admittedly, in black coats, celebrating a burial. But that is as Baudelairean as the painting gets. No sense here of heroism, no sense of depth, emotion, spiritual energy, or Balzacian will-power, no sense of the anguish of bereavement and mourning. The colours are muted, 'dirty', and lacking vibrancy, the blacks *pace* Champfleury having little of the drama of *Boissy d'Anglas* or *L'Evèque de Liège*, the reds of the clergy having little suggestive power. In addition the horizontality of the composition (twice as long as it is high), the stasis of the figures, and their close-knit separation one from the other, play down any sense of a transcendence, which in any case seems mocked by the futile verticality of the crucifix set against a watery sky. The figures seem less to be celebrating a funeral, than going through the perfunctory mechanics of disposing of a corpse. In a word, there is nothing in the picture corresponding to the poet's aesthetic ideas and preferences of 1845 and 1846. By 1855, it was no doubt too late, but even then one might think Baudelaire's comments in the *Exposition universelle* of that year would have contained some recognition of his friend's talent, even if whatever enthusiasm there may have been had waned by that time. But there is no such thing. Courbet had been refused a place in the exhibition and had set up his own show in a *baraque* nearby. Friendship, one might think, would have dictated a bow in Courbet's direction, if at any time in the past Baudelaire had admired his work. There is praise for Courbet's fierce and tenacious will-power, and his vigorous temperament as a *protestant*[95] against the predominant orthodoxy; but his paintings, like those of Ingres, are damned for their *antisurnaturalisme*, indicating 'un esprit de sectaire, un massacreur de facultés' (p. 586). If this 'paragraphe mitigé', as it has been called (p. 1110), was intended as a protest against Courbet's exclusion from the the exhibition, it hardly carries conviction. On the contrary, two-edged, it damns, deftly, tellingly, with praise carefully directed to miss the mark.

The notes for *Puisque réalisme il y a* (p. 57) affirm against realism that 'La Poésie est ce qu'il y a de plus réel, c'est ce qui n'est complètement vrai que dans *un autre monde*', this world being considered as in 1846 a 'dictionnaire hiéroglyphique'. Had the piece been written up, it would have contained a denunciation of realism and an analysis '*de la nature, du talent de Courbet, et de la morale*', the content of which it is not difficult to imagine. A final cryptic note reads '*Courbet sauvant le monde*'. The allusion is to the painter's overweening pretensions, his arrogant transformation of a narrow, dogmatic, and misguided doctrine into a programme for the salvation of the world. Neither the brother nor the equal of his 'hypocrite lecteur', this artist has become a Messiah, his art, like that of Hugo, the exercise of a 'sacerdoce'.[96] Baudelaire's final word goes beyond a denunciation of Courbet's art to attack, for the first time, devastatingly, his character.

What is, however, surprising is that in the *Salon de 1859* Baudelaire should praise the works of two realist colleagues of Courbet's who sat under his presidency at the realists' meeting-place, the Brasserie Andler. Legros's *Angelus* and Armand Gautier's *Sœurs de charité* are cited as examples of the ability of modern artists to produce fine religious paintings, provided they have a sufficiently elevated imagination (pp. 629–31). The poet's admiration is no passing whim, since he praises other paintings by Legros in the *Exposition Martinet* of 1862.

[95] The compliment is two-edged, indicating praise for Courbet's revolt against conventional forms, and a rejection of the narrow, insensitive, unimaginative dogmatism Baudelaire associates with protestantism. See, for example, p. 621 and *Corr.* i. 522.

[96] See below p. 183.

The realism of the two works is striking: the one showing old peasant women in a simple church, with a Murillo-like urchin in the background tremblingly partaking of the 'confitures célestes' in a way that reminds the poet of the story of the philosopher's ass eating his macaroons; the other showing nuns in their simple attire, in little groups among some bare trees outside their church with its façade 'simple jusqu'à la pauvreté'. Before these suggestive paintings, the poet's imagination is set in motion, establishing associations with other works, Sterne, and the ass which appears in the prose poem 'Les Bons Chiens', with Lesueur and Philippe de Champaigne. It is significant that the poet's admiration is in no way impeded by the realist notations, on the contrary, it is stimulated by them; for what he objects to in realism, as curiously in the hopelessly unreal works of Ary Scheffer, is not the depiction of a recognizable physical reality, but the reduction of the human to that physical reality, amounting to a distortion of the conditions of life. The most pernicious art is that which 'dérange les conditions de la vie' (p. 41), a derangement which can operate in diametrically opposite directions, by a spurious idealization, or a reductive realism. In Legros and Armand Gautier, whose paintings are most unlike Delacroix's, the religious is expressed in and through the physical, as an essential ingredient of life. What Baudelaire rejected in realism, and this perhaps explains his silence about Courbet, was the unidimensional view of man, deprived of that 'aspiration vers l'infini', the duality which is an essential and permanent aspect of his humanity.

Delacroix

BAUDELAIRE WAS much obsessed by sunset. 'Harmonie du soir', the two 'Crépuscules', and his evocations of autumn, that twilight of the year, make clear what separates him from the banalities of the previous generation, and his own astounding originality. The sun that has drowned itself 'dans son sang qui se fige' shows how an original image can fascinate succeeding generations, inspiring Laforgue's 'soleil qui se crucifige', Mallarmé's 'Tison de gloire, sang par écume, or, tempête', and Apollinaire's 'Soleil cou coupé'.[1] But this obsession is expressed not just within a thematics of dissolution and recurrence, melancholy and optimism, in their relationship to the accidents of a sentimental experience or the travailing of a soul. It extends to his view of contemporary culture and, beyond that, to his religious pessimism: *'O splendeurs éclipsées, ô soleil descendu derrière l'horizon!'*[2] By his own declaration, the irresistible Night of 'Le Coucher du soleil romantique' refers to the state of contemporary literature, while the 'crapauds imprévus' and the 'froids limaçons' are the writers who are not of his persuasion. But his greatest scorn is for the painters of his time; none, except Delacroix, can be considered 'des Phares'.[3] David, Guérin, and Girodet have been replaced by 'la fausse école romantique' (p. 409). Doubt and eclecticism have replaced faith, temperament, and 'naïveté'; for great painting, like great poetry, 'est essentiellement *bête*, elle *croit*, et c'est ce qui fait sa gloire et sa force' (p. 11). In 1846 he declares that the great tradition has been lost and not

---

[1] Jules Laforgue, 'Complainte à Notre-Dame des Soirs'; Stéphane Mallarmé, 'Victorieusement fui le suicide beau'; Guillaume Apollinaire, 'Zone'.

[2] Baudelaire misquotes (110) from Hugo's 'Passé' in *Les Voix intérieures*. Gautier captures the importance of sunset in Baudelaire in his preface to the 1868 edition of *Les Fleurs du Mal* (16).

[3] G. Planche, *Etudes sur l'école française*, vol. i (Paris: Michel Lévy, 1855), 65: 'Gros, Géricault et Delacroix, voilà les trois grands noms que notre siècle va donner à l'histoire de la peinture! Voilà ce que l'écume de toutes les réputations qui bouillonnent autour de nous laissera surnager; voilà les phares imposants qui serviront à rallier nos souvenirs, et dont la lumière éclatante se réfléchira sur d'autres noms pour les sauver du naufrage.'

been replaced (p. 493), and in 1859 that 'la petitesse, la puérilité, l'incuriosité, le calme plat de la fatuité ont succédé à l'ardeur, à la noblesse et à la turbulente ambition, aussi bien dans les beaux-arts que dans la littérature' (p. 610). The rise of landscape painting is a sure sign of a general decline, and those who practise Catholic subjects lack the ability to infuse them with 'la morale du siècle', producing the kind of sentimental *poncif*-ridden shallowness of Delaroche and Ary Scheffer, those terminal cases in the hospital of painting. The idea of progress and the Voltairian optimism of the prevailing ideology have contributed to a spiritual decline, in which religious faith has also foundered. Baudelaire's Christianity was both vacillating and bleak, since he maintained a belief in original sin and the power of evil, without the accompanying redemption through the sacrifice of Christ. If there is salvation in this otherwise austere mental universe, it is to be found in suffering, in art, or in their combination. A famous passage of the *Journaux intimes* proclaims that the world is coming to an end, indicating that his own theology is distinctly negative; religion is 'la plus haute *fiction* de l'esprit humain' (p. 628). But even if God did not exist, 'la Religion serait encore Sainte et *Divine*'.[4] There is a sense in which the militant agnostic, if I may add a further oxymoron to the Baudelairean stockpile of philosophic and aesthetic *pétards*, is more religious than those who practise and confess, in the sense that his position has been reached through sustained meditation rather than passive acceptance of a ready-made ideology. A well-turned and challenging aphorism in the *Journaux intimes* approximates to this idea: 'Si la religion disparaissait du monde, c'est dans le cœur d'un athée qu'on la retrouverait.'[5]

Delacroix's professed attitude towards religion was that of a sceptic, or at most of a Voltairian deist, who might be thought to have thrown out, among other things, the baby with the bathwater. On this score, there is a parallel, both unexpected and obvious, with Baudelaire's own 'religion', in which this particular baby, Christ himself, is peculiarly absent or reticent. Baudelaire's Christianity without Christ was founded, as is well known, on the doctrine of the Fall, the 'idée catholique'[6] that presided over *Les Fleurs du Mal*, the prose poems, and his theory of the comic. By an extraordinary sleight of hand, he is able to extend this idea to Delacroix himself in the obituary essay of

---

[4] *Oc.* i. 665, 649.   [5] Ibid. 710.
[6] *Corr.* ii. 141: 'il [a certain priest who had condemned *Les Fleurs du Mal*] n'a même pas compris que le livre partait d'une idée catholique!'

1863, where the painter is credited with admitting sometimes that as a child he had been a monster, adding that it is only by pain, punishment, and the progressive use of reason that man can diminish his natural wickedness. Baudelaire's comment is typical: 'Ainsi, par le simple bon sens, il faisait un retour vers l'idée catholique. Car on peut dire que l'enfant, en général, est, relativement à l'homme, en général, beaucoup plus rapproché du péché originel' (p. 767). Less surprisingly, he extends to Delacroix his own 'crepuscular' obsession, noting that his colour produces an effect similar to that of tropical countries, 'où une immense diffusion de lumière crée pour un œil sensible, malgré l'intensité des tons locaux, un résultat général quasi crépusculaire' (p. 760). Furthermore, Delacroix's work, with its desolation and violence bearing witness to the eternal and incorrigible barbarity of man, is like 'un hymne terible composé en l'honneur de la fatalité et de l'irrémédiable douleur'. If to this are added Delacroix's Romanticism and modernity, we have the painterly counterpart of the poet himself, which goes a long way towards explaining why he thought that, of all contemporary artists, Delacroix alone excelled in the painting of religious subjects, and that he alone 'sait faire de la religion' (p. 436).

In these circumstances, it is odd that he should comment on so few of Delacroix's religious paintings, and that there should be no reference, for example, to any of the poignant crucifixion scenes, or to those of the sea of Galilee, with their dramatic treatment of the stormy waters, every bit as impressive as in the early *Barque de Dante*. In addition to the painting at Saint-Paul-Saint-Louis, and the murals at Saint-Denis-du-Saint-Sacrement and Saint-Sulpice, Baudelaire comments on only five canvases: *Saint Sébastien secouru par les saintes femmes*, *Annonciation*, *Mise au tombeau*, *Montée au calvaire*, and the very first painting to command his critical attention, the enigmatic and fascinating *Madeleine dans le désert*, first shown in 1845 (Pl. 1). Here is how he describes it in the *Salon* of the same year: 'C'est une tête de femme renversée dans un cadre très étroit. A droite dans le haut, un petit bout de ciel ou de rocher—quelque chose de bleu;—les yeux de la Madeleine sont fermés, la bouche est molle et languissante, les cheveux épars. Nul, à moins de la voir, ne peut imaginer ce que l'artiste a mis de poésie intime, mystérieuse et romantique dans cette simple tête' (p. 354).

It is not a mere laxity of writing that makes Baudelaire describe it first as a woman's head and only then identify her as Mary Magdalene.

His 'hesitation' is perfectly understandable and is justified by the work itself, and no doubt by the intention that presided over it, there being nothing in the painting to identify the figure as the repentant follower of Jesus. Without the title, the spectator would be bereft of any clue as to its meaning. Here, in an acute form, is a problem which arises from time to time in relation to Delacroix, the problem of how to interpret the work. This may at first seem strange, since so much of his production is of a literary and historical nature, whose principal characteristic, at least traditionally, might be thought to be its readability and transparency. Although his greatest and best-known paintings, such as *La Mort de Sardanapale* or *Scènes des massacres de Scio*, deal with a contemporary event or are inspired by contemporary literature, they have this in common with the great tradition of literary and historical works that their message and narrative function are intended to be clear. Nothing could be further from the self-referentiality of Manet's works and his modern descendants, and it is a mark of Baudelaire's artistic conservatism that he requires a strong narrative and literary content in the works that he admires; but it seems that from the beginning he found this narrative quality all the more alluring and effective if it was in some manner veiled, enigmatic, or bizarre.

This uncertainty about *La Madeleine dans le désert*, which has in addition a fragmentary quality, was registered even more acutely by some contemporary commentators, as Lee Johnson's admirable catalogue of Delacroix's works makes clear. Many 'felt that the image was ill suited to the subject and had difficulty in interpreting Delacroix's intentions'.[7] Houssaye, in a typical response, wondered 'si c'est la figure d'une femme qui rêve, d'une femme qui dort, ou d'une femme qui vient de mourir'.[8] In the passage from the *Salon de 1845*, Baudelaire captures much of the enigmatic quality of the work in words similar to those of the following year defining Romanticism as

[7] Johnson, *Paintings*, iii. 217.
[8] Quoted in Johnson, *Paintings*, iii. 218. *Salon de 1845*, 210.

An acquaintance with the story of the Saint's time in the desert as described by Jacques de Voragine might have guided critics towards a greater understanding of the picture: 'Cependant sainte Marie-Madeleine, désireuse de contempler les choses célestes, se retira dans une grotte de la montagne, que lui avait préparée la main des anges [. . .]. Il n'y avait ni cours d'eau, ni herbe, ni arbre; ce qui signifiait que Jésus voulait nourrir la sainte des seuls mets célestes, sans lui accorder aucun des plaisirs terrestres. Mais, tous les jours, les anges l'élevaient dans les airs, où, pendant une heure, elle entendait leur musique; après quoi, rassasiée de ce repas délicieux, elle redescendait dans sa grotte, sans avoir le moindre besoin d'aliments corporels' (*Le Légende dorée*, ed. Teodor de Wyzewa (Paris: Perrin et Cie, 1925), 343).

'intimité, spiritualité, couleur, aspiration vers l'infini' (p. 421), the latter being caught in the 'petit bout de ciel', the 'quelque chose de bleu' which gives this typically grotto-like enclosed space[9] the sense of an elevation and of an opening on to the infinite and the ideal. This notation is not just that of an enthusiastic colourist, seeming to announce the much greater liberties of the future Impressionists; it is to be understood above all within a typically Baudelairean thematics of sky and space, as in 'La Chevelure', 'Elévation', 'L'Aube spirituelle', and his commentary on Penguilly's *Petites Mouettes* in the *Salon de 1859*: 'l'azur intense du ciel et de l'eau, deux quartiers de roche qui font une porte ouverte sur l'infini (vous savez que l'infini paraît plus profond quand il est plus resserré)' (p. 653).[10]

But it is in the *Exposition universelle* of 1855 that Baudelaire more fully captures the mood of this painting of the Magdalene 'au sourire bizarre et mystérieux, et si surnaturellement belle qu'on ne sait si elle est auréolée par la mort, ou embellie par les pâmoisons de l'amour divin' (p. 593). The interpretation could hardly be more Baudelairean, pointing as it does to the ambiguities of life, death, and divine love, depicted not as abstractions but as an overwhelming physical sensation in which the erotic element is barely concealed. As such it can be equated to two passages in 'Fusées'. In the first, where love is likened to a torture or surgical operation, the patient's eyes are described as 'ces yeux de somnambule révulsés', and the human face is said to relax 'dans une espèce de mort'. The second contains his definition of the beautiful: 'une tête séduisante et belle, une tête de femme [. . .] qui fait rêver à la fois,—mais d'une manière confuse,—de volupté et de tristesse; qui comporte une idée de mélancolie, de lassitude, même de satiété'.[11] Baudelaire's interpretation, 'partiale et passionnée' (p. 418) though it may be, should not be seen as an intrusion or an imposition of the poet's temperament upon an innocent work. In this most discreet of Delacroix's paintings, which has something of the simplicity of a study, the suppression of context, situation, or locus, together with the interpretative burden which the artist gives to the title of this

---

[9] The grotto has a thematic force in Delacroix, as, for example, in *Médée* in the museum of Lille, and *Pietà*, Oslo, reproduced in Johnson, *Paintings*, iv, plates 79, 251.

[10] In an entry in his *Journal* on 17 Oct. 1853, Delacroix expresses a similar sentiment: 'Jean-Jacques dit avec raison qu'on peint mieux les charmes de la liberté quand on est sous les verrous, qu'on décrit mieux une campagne agréable quand on habite une ville pesante et qu'on ne voit le ciel que par une lucarne et à travers les cheminées' (*Journal*, 369).

[11] *Oc.* i. 651, 657.

otherwise anonymous head, seems to indicate that he also intended it
as a reverie, full of magical and suggestive power, on the way in which
the spiritual is rooted in the physical and in sensation—and of course
the penitent Mary Magdalene lends herself to such an interpretation
more perhaps than any other biblical figure.[12]

Baudelaire recognized himself in Delacroix, just as he was later to
recognize himself in Poe. It is a fundamental aspect of his poetic
universe that the opposites of heaven and hell, God and Satan, ideal
and spleen, 'extase de la vie' and 'horreur de la vie',[13] elevation and fall,
are not irremediably disjoined, but collapse and telescope into each
other. In this respect *La Madeleine dans le désert* presents a dramatic
parallel with his own poetry, which repeatedly illustrates how a spiritual elevation or aspiration towards the infinite can be diverted and
misdirected downwards into the physical and sensation. In 'Femmes
damnées' the lesbian lovers are said to be 'De la réalité grands esprits
contempteurs, / Chercheuses d'infini, dévotes et satyres', seeking a
transcendence in a love which goes counter to the order of nature. But
it is in *Le Poème du hachisch* that Baudelaire explicitly states that the
human thirst for the infinite is 'un goût qui se trompe souvent de
route'.[14] Crime, the intoxication of the artist, or the drunken stupor of
the down-and-out of the *faubourg* are all manifestations, not of a lack
of spirituality, but rather of one which, impatient and frustrated, seeks
to grasp eternal life within the here and now, within the temporal and
in sensation. It is in the light of this that we understand why
Baudelaire's ideal is not some 'beauté de vignette' got up in pseudo-
exotic or Spanish trumpery, but 'Lady Macbeth, âme puissante au

---

[12] In the 1845 *Salon* Baudelaire praises a *Vision de Sainte Thérèse brûlée d'une douleur
spirituelle* by Planet, a pupil of Delacroix's: 'La sainte Thérèse, telle que le peintre l'a
représentée, s'affaissant, tombant, palpitant, à l'attente du dard dont l'amour divin va la
percer, est une des plus heureuses trouvailles de la peinture moderne. [. . .] Ce tableau
respire une volupté excessive, et montre dans l'auteur un homme capable de très bien
comprendre un sujet—*car sainte Thérèse était brûlante d'un si grand amour de Dieu, que la
violence de ce feu lui faisait jeter des cris . . . Et cette douleur n'était pas corporelle, mais spirituelle,
quoique le corps ne laissât pas d'y avoir beaucoup de part*' (371). The quotation in italic is from
Vie de sainte Thérèse, translated by Arnaud d'Andilly (see 1273). Although the *idea* is similar
to Delacroix's and is made much more explicit, the treatment lacks drama and is not without
a degree of *mièvrerie*, as can clearly be seen from the reproduction in Mayne (ed.), *Art in
Paris*, plate 6.

In the *Salon de 1859* Baudelaire is critical of Baudry's *Madeleine pénitente*, which he finds
'un peu frivole et lestement peinte' (647).

[13] *Oc.* i. 703: 'Tout enfant, j'ai senti dans mon cœur deux sentiments contradictoires,
l'horreur de la vie et l'extase de la vie.'

[14] Ibid. 402.

crime, / Rêve d'Eschyle éclos au climat des autans'.[15] Precisely because of its impatience and frustration, such an inverted passion is
often associated with violence, as in 'Duellum', or 'A celle qui est trop
gaie', where love and hatred are inextricably intermingled. The
Journaux intimes compare love to a surgical operation;[16] in 'Les
Tentations' the Satan representing Eros has 'de brillants couteaux et
des instruments de chirurgie' affixed to a belt round his waist,
and Mademoiselle Bistouri is obsessed with surgeons who like to
'couper, tailler et rogner'. Though he was undoubtedly influenced by
Sade, one should not see in these 'sadistic' references simply a revolt
against eighteenth-century optimism and its facile acceptance of the
notions of perfectibility and the original goodness of mankind. One
should see also a frustrated desire to communicate, to penetrate and
get through to the other person, an exasperation at the insurmountable
otherness of people, a despair before the unacceptable truism that, as
for Constant, 'les autres ne sont jamais soi'.[17] Romanticism, and nowhere more acutely than in Baudelaire, is impatient of the distance
that separates human beings from the world, from other people, and
within themselves, a distance which the rationalist accepts as a fundamental and unalterable condition of conscious life. The Romantic, on
the contrary, sees it as tragic separation, and an incitement towards
the restoration of a unity lost. His inability to accept this condition
causes him to sell his soul, or lose it in impossible aspirations: 'tout
homme qui n'accepte pas les conditions de la vie, vend son âme'.[18]
Behind Baudelaire's sadism and violent love poems, one senses, as in
Constant's *Adolphe*, the veiled but unmistakable presence of the myth
of the androgyne and the transcendent unity it implies.

It was because of a similar confusion of love, death, and religion that
in his essay on *Madame Bovary* Baudelaire was able to recognize

---

[15] Jean Prévost sees a parallel here with Delacroix's painting *Lady Macbeth* (1849–50),
which belonged to Gautier: 'Baudelaire a vu souvent lady Macbeth dont le bras puissant tend
vers la nuit une main robuste et secrètement ensanglantée' (*Baudelaire* (Paris: Mercure de
France, 1953), 142). But the Lady Macbeth of Delacroix is the one, mad and defeated, whom
we find sleepwalking in Act V. Baudelaire's, on the contrary, is the one at the beginning of
the play, so 'puissante au crime' that she accuses her husband of infirmity of purpose and
commands him to give her the daggers to kill the king. Gautier wrote of the painting; 'il y a
quelque chose d'étrange, de hâve, de fou, d'automatique dans cette promeneuse nocturne'
(Johnson, *Paintings*, iii. 123).

[16] 'Il y a dans l'acte de l'amour une grande ressemblance avec la torture, ou avec une
opération chirurgicale' (*Oc.* i. 659).

[17] Maurice Blanchot, *La Part du feu* (Paris: Gallimard, 1949), 235.

[18] *Oc.* i. 438.

himself in Flaubert's 'bizarre Pasiphaé', pursuing the ideal 'à travers
les bastringues et les estaminets de la préfecture' (p. 84). In a brilliantly
provocative argument he elevates Emma to great heights and identifies
her with 'le poète hystérique' (p. 83). Her *bovarysme* lies not just in her
belief that the ideal can be made real in certain privileged times or
places, but also in her confusion of love, sensuality, and religion, no
more more tellingly illustrated than in the death scene, when 'collant
ses lèvres sur le corps de l'Homme-Dieu, elle y déposa de toute sa
force expirante le plus grand baiser d'amour qu'elle eût jamais
donné'.[19] The grotesqueness of the gesture should not be allowed to
conceal the intensity of her quest for some absolute value or experience, which has taken the wrong path and been misdirected into the
senses of which she remains prisoner to the end. Her confusion stems
from an inchoate and semi-conscious exasperation at the imperfections of a world in which action and dream are irrevocably disjoined,
and in which the 'aspiration vers l'infini' is constantly frustrated. The
novelist and the poet celebrate a yearning that can have no outlet
except in art; less lucid, but equally torn, Emma is duped by the
illusion of the immanence of the ideal in reality.

A related work to *La Madeleine dans le désert* is *La Madeleine avec un
ange*, which Baudelaire does not mention and probably did not know,
since, as Johnson says, it 'must have been little known to Delacroix's
contemporaries and was scarcely commented on in his lifetime'.[20] It
shows Mary Magdalene kneeling in some kind of grotto, her upper
body thrust back, her hands tightly clenched in prayer, her head lifted
upwards with an anguished expression, attended by an angel, with on
the right of the picture a much wider opening, allowing some light
from the upper air to pass into the scene. It is a powerful image of
repentance,[21] and indeed of carnality, but much more readable, and to
that extent more conventional, than its mysterious and fragmentary
counterpart.

Although entirely different in manner and subject matter, *La Mort
de Sardanapale* (1827–8) (Pl. 2) is thematically linked to *La Madeleine
dans le désert*, and it also finds a striking parallel in Baudelaire's own
mental universe. Again, it is surprising that he should say so little
about this extraordinary work, which represented what was most typi-

[19] *Madame Bovary* (Paris: Conard, 1930), 446.

[20] Johnson, *Paintings*, iii. 217.

[21] Alain Daguerre de Hureaux, following Johnson, calls it 'une poignante image de
l'humanité tourmentée par le remords' (*Delacroix* (Paris: Hazan, 1993), 223).

cal and Romantic in Delacroix's production. In 1846 Baudelaire had placed it among a series of paintings—*Dante et Virgile, Le Massacre de Scio, Le Christ aux Oliviers, Saint Sébastien, Médée, Les Naufragés, Hamlet*—which give the viewer the impression of witnessing 'la célébration de quelque mystère douloureux' (p. 440), and in his piece on the Exposition Martinet of 1862 his enthusiasm is unmitigated by the changes that had affected Delacroix's work over almost thirty years: 'Le *Sardanapale* revu, c'est la jeunesse retrouvée' (p. 734). It was probably Byron's tragedy *Sardanapalus* of 1821 that drew Delacroix's attention to the subject, though the two works are very dissimilar in conception. By his use of soliloquy at crucial points in the play, by his reporting of off-stage action, and above all in preserving a strict adherence to the unities of time, place, and action, Byron intended his play to be in the neoclassical mode of the French, of Alfieri and Grillparzer.[22] But on their own admission, the direct inspiration of both Byron and Delacroix was Diodorus of Sicily. Byron departs very considerably from the original, making of Sardanapalus a less extravagant figure and, above all, reducing the final scene to the suicide of Sardanapalus and his favourite Myrrha on a funeral pyre. As the notice in the *Salon* of 1827–8 indicates, Delacroix follows Diodorus more closely, adding either from his own imagination or possibly from some other source the slaying of the women and the animals, and the references to Aïscheh and Baleah:

Les révoltés l'assiegèrent dans son palais . . . Couché sur un lit superbe, au sommet d'un immense bûcher, Sardanapale donne l'ordre à ses eunuques et aux officiers du palais, d'égorger ses femmes, ses pages, jusqu'à ses chevaux et ses chiens favoris; aucun des objets qui auraient servi à ses plaisirs ne devait lui survivre . . . *Aïscheh*, femme bactrienne, ne voulut pas souffrir qu'un esclave lui donnât la mort, et se pendit elle-même aux colonnes qui supportaient la voûte . . . *Baleah*, échanson de Sardanapale, mit enfin le feu au bûcher et s'y précipita lui-même.

Somewhat more soberly, Diodorus records that 'he built an enormous pyre in his palace, heaped upon it all his gold and silver as well

---

[22] Byron, *The Complete Poetical Works*, ed. McGann and Weller, vol. vi (Oxford: Clarendon Press, 1991), 16: 'The Author has in one instance attempted to preserve, and in the other to approach the "unities"; conceiving that with any very distant departure from them, there may be poetry, but can be no drama. He is aware of the unpopularity of this notion in present English literature; but it is not a system of his own, being merely an opinion, which, not very long ago, was the law of literature throughout the world, and is still so in the more civilised parts of it.'

as every article of his royal wardrobe, and then, shutting his concubines and eunuchs in the room which had been built in the middle of
the pyre, he consigned both them and himself and his palace to the
flames'.[23] There may well have been other sources, and there has been
much speculation, notably by Beatrice Farwell and Lee Johnson,[24]
about what these may have been. It is possible that Delacroix found
inspiration in an Indian source for the enormous couch upon which
the Assyrian king is placed, with its elephant heads at each corner, and
there may be some Etruscan influence in the depiction of his treasures.
But the lack of attribution suggests that he concocted the passage in
the Salon catalogue for his own ends, to give a spurious historical
authenticity to the scene as he portrayed it. In any case, the search for
sources should not leave one blind to the use Delacroix invariably
makes of them, and to the extent that they serve as a point of departure
for his own prolific and uninhibited imagination. Think of the murder
of the bishop of Liège, which Baudelaire described as 'cette admirable
traduction de Walter Scott, pleine de foule, d'agitation et de lumière'
(p. 593), and the comparatively muted description of it in *Quentin
Durward*,[25] or the frenzied turbulence of *L'Enlèvement de Rébecca*, with
its swirling horses and the dramatic posture of Rebecca thrown on to
her back behind the saddle, against the flames and smoke of the
burning castle in the background. In *Ivanhoe* Scott devotes only two,
admittedly powerful, sentences to the conflagration, and Rebecca is
said merely to be 'placed on horseback before one of the Templar's
Saracen slaves, [. . .] in the midst of the little party'.[26] Similarly, there
is nothing of Delacroix's exuberance in any of his supposed sources for
Sardanapalus: the king, in spite of his beard, effeminate in posture as
in Byron and Diodorus, reclines in a manner not dissimilar to that of
the exiled poet in *Ovide chez les Scythes*, surveying impassively a scene
of carnage and eroticism. There are figures strewn in death, the con-
torted body of Aïscheh hanging from a silken cord, a horse being run
through by a black slave, the fearful gestures of those who are about
to die, the twisting torso of a concubine as she strives to avoid the
inevitable sword about to be drawn, while another naked woman,

[23] Diodorus of Sicily, ed. C. H. Oldfather vol. i (London: Heinemann, 1933), 441.

[24] Johnson, *Paintings*, i. 117. Beatrice Farwell, 'Sources for Delacroix's *Death of
Sardanapalus*', *The Art Bulletin*, xl (1958), 66–71. In particular Johnson points to possible
sources in Quintus Curtius, *History of Alexander* (see n. 37).

[25] In ch. xxii of *Quentin Durward*, entitled 'The Revellers', the Bishop of Liège is struck
down from behind at the end of a dignified and defiant denunciation of William de la Marck.

[26] *Ivanhoe*, (Edinburgh: T. C. & E. C. Jack, n.d.), 257.

reminiscent of Madeleine, swoons into a voluptuous death as if in love with the sword plunging into her body. The smoky-green background reveals a breach in the palace wall through which the rebels are about to pass, while the rest of the picture comprises the richest jewels, arms, silver, and gold which provide one of the most extraordinary still lifes to be seen in any picture. Black, brown, orange, yellow and above all blood red predominate in this immense canvas, which disorients the spectator not just because of its extravagant dimensions and the proliferation of incident, but by its impenetrability and its extraordinary use of perspective.

Critics have not failed to draw a parallel with Hugo's manifesto of Romanticism in the 'Préface' to *Cromwell* published in 1827, in which he justifies his conception of the 'drame romantique' with its rejection of the *bienséances* and the unities of time, place, and action to which Byron's play had remained faithful. Hugo's insistence on local colour and upon action on the stage as opposed to the classical *récit*, the complications of his plots as opposed to the Racinian 'action simple, chargée de peu de matière',[27] and his lyricism of passion, may all be said to have a counterpart in Delacroix's uneven masterpiece, which some saw as a challenge to Ingres's classical *Apothéose d'Homère*, causing as great a stir among traditionalists as Hugo's *Hernani* three years later. For many the painting appeared incomprehensible because of the strangeness of the treatment and, above all, the sheer proliferation of incidents. Even those familiar with the story of Sardanapalus[28] might have had difficulty in understanding what exactly was going on, unsure how to interpret, for example, the turmoil at the top right of the picture which, like the rest of the scene, only begins to be readable in the light of Delacroix's explanation published in the supplement to the *Salon*. Furthermore, many of the incidents seem allusive, fragmentary, or incomplete: the figures on the right, one with an outstretched arm, the other with his head between his hands, the horse being stabbed on the left and, further up on the same side, the head of the woman looking away, outside the painting, all these have been cut off by the frame in a manner unacceptable to the classical tradition of completeness and readability. The conservative critic Delécluze

---

[27] See Jean Racine, 'Préface' to *Britannicus*, *Théâtre complet* (Paris: Garnier, 1980), 256.
[28] For an account of various treatments of the story from the Renaissance to Romanticism, see J. Spector, *Delacroix: The Death of Sardanapalus* (London: Allen Lane, 1974), 50–8. A typically uncomprehending response to Delacroix's work is that of Louis Vitet in the *Globe* of 28 Mar. 1828 (81).

thought the painting an error on the painter's part: 'l'intelligence du spectateur n'a pu pénétrer dans un sujet dont tous les détails sont isolés, où l'œil ne peut débrouiller la confusion des lignes et des couleurs, où les premières règles de l'art semblent avoir été violées de partis pris'.[29] The sense of dolour and mystery is increased by the sheer magnitude of the painting (3.95 × 4.95 m.), and by the bizarrerie of the steeply rising perspective culminating in the impassive, and somewhat reduced, head of the king himself. Delacroix's treatment of space and his abuse of perspective had invited criticism right from the beginning. Lee Johnson's unequivocal view is that 'the spatial disunity between foreground and background reflects the artist's struggle with a primarily formal problem, that of fusing the neo-classical methods of his training with the Baroque style to which he was drawn by temperament', a problem which is fully resolved only in *Christ on the Sea of Galilee* of the 1850s.[30] If, as Spector has claimed, the spatial disjunction adds to the power of the work 'in displaying the opposed moods of pensive melancholy and animal energy, and of the detachment of the mental from the physical',[31] this can only be accidentally, according to the sceptical Johnson. Whatever the explanation of these defects, of which Delacroix himself was aware, there can be little doubt that for the viewer they increase the mystery and the attraction of the work, which at once overwhelms by its dimensions and draws one in by its mystery and its disturbing representation of spatial depth.

Baudelaire declared himself aware of Delacroix's faults, though he was unwilling to state what they were for fear of falling into critical platitudes:

Les défauts de M. Delacroix sont parfois si visibles qu'ils sautent à l'œil le moins exercé. On peut ouvrir au hasard la première feuille venue, où pendant longtemps l'on s'est obstiné, à l'inverse de mon système, à ne pas voir les

---

[29] Quoted by Maurice Tourneux, *Eugène Delacroix devant ses contemporains* (Paris: Jules Rouam, 1886), 49.

[30] Johnson, *Paintings*, i. 118. See also his discussion of *Christ on the Sea of Galilee*, ibid. iii. 233, for the resolution of the problem of spatial disunity: 'Delacroix retains the Baroque diagonal of the earlier picture, the helmsman in similar pose corresponding to Sardanapalus, but counteracts its recession by tilting the whole composition (not merely the foreground as in the earlier painting) into an almost vertical plane, and by placing limbs, oars and draperies parallel to the picture plane along the entire length of the diagonal. He thus preserves some of the spatial tensions of the *Sardanapalus* but resolves them by integrating them more fully into a dynamic unity.'

[31] Spector, *Delacroix*, 23.

qualités radieuses qui constituent son originalité. On sait que les grands génies ne se trompent jamais à demi, et qu'ils ont le privilège de l'énormité dans tous les sens. (p. 441)

The 'accident' of the technical defect in *Sardanapale* may well, however, have produced the kind of aesthetic bizarrerie which would have appealed to the poet for whom the beautiful is always bizarre (p. 578). Inevitably, he would have been drawn also by the colour, the movement, the violence, the 'draperies voltigeantes' (p. 434), the extravagant orientalism, the vastness of the work, and not least the eroticism of some of the postures. In a footnote to the *Salon de 1846* he mentions the 'foule d'études merveilleuses de femmes, dans les attitudes les plus voluptueuses' (p. 444) that Delacroix had made for the picture, and in 1855 he regrets the absence of the finished canvas from the Exposition universelle, since one would have seen 'de très belles femmes, claires, lumineuses, roses' (p. 593). The *Exposition Martinet* of 1862 ends with two questions whose urgency is a measure of his admiration for the sensuality of the work: 'Et tout ce harem de beautés si éclatantes, qui pourrait le peindre aujourd'hui avec ce feu, avec cette fraîcheur, avec cet enthousiasme poétique? Et tout ce luxe *sardanapalesque*[32] qui scintille dans l'ameublement, dans le vêtement, dans les harnais, dans la vaisselle et la bijouterie, qui? qui?' (p. 734). Eroticism is, of course, a central preoccupation in Delacroix, most visible in such early works as *Femme caressant un perroquet*, *La Femme aux bas blancs*, and *Odalisque allongée sur un divan*.[33] These nudes, as in the *Sardanapale*, are made all the more alluring as they have kept their jewels, emphasizing their nakedness and the play of light on their skin. There is here a clear link, noticed by several commentators, with Baudelaire's own poetry, in particular 'Les Bijoux', banned by the court in 1857, and almost certainly inspired by Delacroix:

> La très chère était nue, et, connaissant mon coeur,
> Elle n'avait gardé que ses bijoux sonores,
> Dont le riche attirail lui donnait l'air vainqueur
> Qu'ont dans leurs jours heureux les esclaves des Mores.

The potent mixture of eroticism and death, present also in the furtive approach of the Moor in Delacroix's *Othello et Desdémone*, was of

---

[32] Although Baudelaire italicizes the adjective, it had been in vogue during the Restoration. *Sardanapalique* is also found. In the sixteenth century, the usage had been *sardanapalin*. See Littré and Robert.

[33] Reproduced in Daguerre de Hureaux, *Delacroix*, 64–5.

course to find an echo in Baudelaire's own poetry, nowhere more macabrely than in 'Une martyre', that most calmly sadistic of flowers of evil which describes a woman's body on a sumptuous bed and her separated head resting upon a table 'comme une renoncule'. Did her vindictive lover, asks the poet, satisfy on her 'chair inerte et complaisante / L'immensité de son désir?' Prévost suggests a bold but convincing rapprochement between this poem and *Sardanapale*, for which Delacroix had made a sketch in which the voluptuous nude in the foreground was decapitated, and *Odalisque allongée sur un divan*, whose strangely turned head 'semble séparée du corps par son collier'.[34] Spector has attributed this kind of morbid preoccupation to Delacroix's own temperament, and there may be a degree of plausibility in his speculation; but more relevant than the accidents of an individual's evolution are the cultural determinisms and affinities which in this instance are much in evidence: Balzac's *La Fille aux yeux d'or* or *La Peau de chagrin*, for example, and the literature of orgies and suicides, characteristic of Romanticism and the texts discussed by Mario Praz in *The Romantic Agony*. Instead of being associated with life, health, exuberance, fulfilment, and procreation, love in Delacroix's painting as in many of Baudelaire's poems is linked to the unhealthy underside of things and to the anti-values of waste, despair, diminution, and death.

But it is with the figure of Sardanapalus himself that Baudelaire would have felt an inescapable affinity. Diodorus's description is of a complete *débauché*, spending his time with concubines, given to every excess and pleasure, and consorting sexually with both men and women. He sometimes dressed as a woman 'and so covered his face and indeed his entire body with whitening cosmetics and the other unguents used by courtesans, that he rendered it more delicate than that of any luxury-loving woman'.[35] Byron makes of him a much more complex personality, loving pleasure but also peace, and given to mercy rather than revenge and bloodlust. Though effeminate and dressing as a woman, he has a 'careless courage' and energy that have not been corrupted, and in the end he seeks bravely to save his palace and his nation, dying alone with his faithful favourite. Obsessed with death and the vanity of all things, he embodies a kind of Hamletian doubt and reluctance to act, combined with a poetic temperament

[34] Prévost, *Bandelaire*, 142.
[35] Diodorus of Sicily, 427.

which refuses to be dupe of his own emotions;[36] he appears, in short, as a Romantic hero, full of contradictions. Much of this has passed into Delacroix's interpretation, which of course centres on the death scene. The posture is languid and the dress tends towards the effeminate,[37] but what is most remarkable is his distraction and apparent indifference to the carnage around him. His gaze goes unseeingly beyond the stabbed concubine whose glazed and now sightless eye is lifted towards him, seeming to meet in indifference that of the distraught man with the outstretched arm on the right of the picture. What Delacroix has given us is a version of the Romantic aesthete, whose indifference, rooted in ennui, is not without a tinge of cruelty. As such, it is supremely Baudelairean, finding an echo in the last two stanzas of the opening poem, 'Au lecteur', of *Les Fleurs du Mal*:

> Dans la ménagerie infâme de nos vices,
>
> Il en est un plus laid, plus méchant, plus immonde!
> Quoiqu'il ne pousse ni grands gestes ni grands cris,
> Il ferait volontiers de la terre un débris
> Et dans un bâillement avalerait le monde;
>
> C'est l'Ennui!—l'œil chargé d'un pleur involontaire,
> Il rêve d'échafauds en fumant son houka.

Although Delacroix's exoticism does not extend to a hookah, he has supplied its thematic analogue in the wine vessel and goblet on the left of the king, signifying his need for inebriation and forgetfulness, 'pour ne pas sentir l'horrible fardeau du Temps'.[38] The figure of the indifferent or cruel prince is fundamental in Baudelaire, recurring in 'le roi d'un pays pluvieux' of 'Spleen' (LXXVII):

> Rien ne peut l'égayer, ni gibier, ni faucon,
> Ni son peuple mourant en face du balcon.

---

[36] Byron, *Poetical Works*, 19, 20, and especially p. 55 for the speech in which he declares his love of 'Chaldea's starry mysteries'.

[37] Baudelaire says that Sardanapalus is 'beau comme une femme' (593). The effeminacy of his attire finds a parallel in that of the Indian king, Sopithes, 'a man far surpassing all other barbarians in physical attractiveness', whom Johnson mentions as a possible source: 'His robe, which covered his legs as well as the rest of his body, was embroidered with gold and purple, he wore golden sandals studded with gems, his shoulders and arms were adorned with pearls and from his ears hung pearls conspicuous for whiteness and size, his golden sceptre was ornamented with beryl' (Quintus Curtius, *History of Alexander*, ix.i. 29–30, ed. J. C. Rolfe (London: Heinemann, 1946), ii. 373).

[38] See the prose poem 'Enivrez-vous', *Oc.* i. 337.

Du bouffon favori la grotesque ballade
Ne distrait plus le front de ce cruel malade [. . .]

This disturbing figure also appears in one of his most enigmatic and haunting prose poems, 'Une mort héroïque', which, together with Delacroix's painting, was to provide the intertext for Rimbaud's magnificent 'illumination' entitled 'Conte', which is at once an interpretation and an ironic subversion of its twofold intertext. Like these cruel princes, Sardanapalus is a victim of ennui, which in Baudelaire is not just *taedium vitae* or the lofty and elegant *vague à l'âme* of Chateaubriand's René, who enjoyed such a vogue among would-be aesthetes of the time that, in the words of Flaubert, he filled 'un demi-siècle du tapage de sa douleur'.[39] It stems rather from an intense awareness of original sin, which implies not just an innate propensity towards evil deeds and sins of commission, but more radically a fallen state which precedes any involvement in action. This state is one of imperfection, since from birth or from the expulsion from Eden man is projected into time and becoming, while having the 'memory' of a state of perfection, completeness, and being that remains for ever beyond his grasp. Baudelairean ennui, or spleen, as he more often calls it, is precisely a pathological apprehension of this imperfection, rooted not just in the intellect but in the physiology and in the nervous system. Escape is brief and illusory, being sought in perfect moments, in ecstasies and intoxications of the senses which momentarily re-create the conditions of oneness, only to be followed by a return to imperfection and an increased sense of ennui. Disenchantment is inevitable since eternity cannot be made permanent in the instant, the infinite within the finite, being within becoming. It may be that the aspirations of the soul are infinite, but the body and the senses are not, and he who seeks the one within the other condemns himself to an even greater sense of imperfection, an ever deeper immersion in spleen. Baudelaire's reveries of cruelty and sadism are not mere fantasies of violence for its own sake;[40] on the contrary, they betray an impatient and frustrated spirituality which seeks an outlet in the imagination of strong emotions. 'Au lecteur' shows a preoccupation with slaughter and instruments of death; Delacroix's *Sardanapalus* shows as

[39] Gustave Flaubert, *Par les champs et par les grèves* (Paris: Conard, 1927), 325.
[40] See, for example, in *Les Fleurs du Mal*, 'Duellum', 'A celle qui est trop gaie', and 'A une Madone', and in *Le Spleen de Paris*, 'Mademoiselle Bistouri' and 'Le Galant Tireur'.

it were the next stage, the impassive contemplation of death and the vanity of all things.

Sardanapalus's death is, of course, a suicide and to that extent it accords with an increasing obsession of Romanticism, which Baudelaire himself recognized. In classical works suicide often supplies the reasonable dénouement of the play, reasonable because the hero's position having become intolerable, he has no other way to act, in order to make amends, fulfil a patriotic duty, remain faithful to some lofty duty or principle, or avoid dishonour. The suicides of Brutus, Antony and Cleopatra, Othello, Mithridate, or Atalide in *Bajazet*, whether they stem from a philosophy of stoicism or from an impossible situation arising from a fault (pride, jealousy, or ambition) that brings an otherwise good person from 'high estate to low', provoke a powerful sense of catharsis or pathos in the audience; but they have nothing sinister about them and cannot be seen as a transgression of human or divine law or of some kind of taboo. Nor are they 'the coward's way out', as the unthinking cliché goes, but most often an honourable exit. But Romantic suicide concerns less a specific situation or aspect of a character than the totality of the character, and is linked much more closely and fundamentally to a view of the world affected by *mal du siècle* or nihilism. It is linked in the first place to the notion that, whatever the circumstances, life is not worth living, often because it fails to live up to the superior nature, intellect, insight or sensibility of the protagonist. That most extraordinary of all literary societies, the Suicide-Club, whose membership was, necessarily and perhaps mercifully restricted, gave places of honour to Goethe, Byron, and Chateaubriand, and proclaimed in article six of its constitution that 'seul peut autoriser le suicide, le dégoût de l'existence considérée comme mauvaise et indigne d'être vécue'.[41] The motive for Romantic suicide is often metaphysical despair, the perception of an irreparable rift between desire and reality, the conviction that, as in the famous poem of revolt, 'Le Reniement de Saint Pierre, 'l'action n'est pas la sœur du rêve'. Suicide rooted in such a despair is a manifestation of the kind of modern heroism Baudelaire celebrates in the final chapter of *Le Salon de 1846*, where he distinguishes the suicides of Hercules, Cato, and Cleopatra from the (alleged) suicide of Jean-Jacques Rousseau or of Raphaël de Valentin in *La Peau de chagrin*, who took their own lives 'pour changer de peau en vue de la métempsycose' (p.

---

[41] See Louis Maigron, *Le Romantisme et les mœurs* (Paris: Champion, 1919), 341.

494), out of a radical dissatisfaction with the conditions of life. It is linked also to a morbid preoccupation with the satanic and with the unnatural, and thus finds its place in the literature of the time alongside themes of madness, incest, homosexuality, criminality, or the taking of the side of Satan against God. Since St Augustine it had been accepted that, in Hamlet's words, the 'Everlasting had fixed / His canon 'gainst self slaughter', and Canto xiii of the *Inferno* reserves the most appalling fate for suicides, condemned to the seventh circle of hell, below heretics and murderers, in a dark wood where they grow for all eternity as warped, poisonous thorns, torn at by harpies, rehearsing the violence they had done themselves in life. In Christian theology suicide is the sin without remission, against hope and against the holy spirit, essentially an unnatural crime, the punishment for which is to be placed only two circles of hell from Judas, frozen in the icy coldness of his treachery.

The death of Sardanapalus reflects then the ambiguities of eroticism and death, the Romantic obsession with suicide, but also the disdainful silence of the superior individual faced with the inadequacies of the material world and the blind powers that ultimately overwhelm him. Here again the cultural resonances are very perceptible in the Byronic defiance, in the Vignian silence reminiscent of the end of 'Le Mont des Oliviers': 'Le juste opposera le dédain à l'absence / Et ne répondra plus que par un froid silence / Au silence éternel de la Divinité.' But its most obvious parallel is between the 'dandyism' of Sardanapalus and Baudelaire's 'Don Juan aux enfers', inspired by Molière and by Delacroix's *Naufrage de Don Juan*. The poem describes the Don, surrounded by the protest and admonitions of those he has wronged, impenitent and in a posture of calm indifference: 'Mais le calme héros, courbé sur sa rapière, / Regardait le sillage et ne daignait rien voir.' Dandyism and ennui have been elevated to a metaphysics of revolt. The dandy is, of course, a modern version of the Stoic, and as Baudelaire himself says, stoicism is a religion which has but one sacrament, which is suicide.[42]

Of the specifically religious works, Baudelaire mentions *Saint Sébastien* and *Le Christ aux Oliviers* only in passing for the gravity and profound sincerity that Delacroix brings to them (p. 436). The first is 'un délice de tristesse' (p. 634) because of the exquisite tenderness of the female figures attending the languid and wounded saint, and the

---

[42] 'Le stoïcisme, religion qui n'a qu'un sacrement,—le suicide!' (*Oc.* i. 664).

second, in the church of Saint-Paul-Saint-Louis, appeals more by
virtue of the subject matter than the execution. The rich colouring of
Christ's garments, the discreet but poignant representation of the
sleeping disciples, the spectral background, and the bizarre rock-like
surface upon which the angels are grouped, do not however compensate for the stiffness of Christ's posture or for the sense of academic
poncif in the gestures of the figures and the conventional halo, which
appear unrealistic, stylized, out of keeping with 'la morale du siècle'
captured in his other religious paintings. Escholier's lack of enthusiasm is understandable: 'Ce qui manque en effet à ce tableau religieux,
c'est la piété, c'est la foi et—fait exceptionnel chez Delacroix—c'est
l'inspiration.'[43] Daguerre de Hureaux observes that no contemporary
critic commented on the gesture of Christ 'qui repousse les anges
venus le secourir, comme s'il demandait à son Père d'éloigner de lui ce
calice',[44] whereas the traditional iconography emphasizes Jesus's acceptance of his passion: 'Not my will, but thine, be done.'[45] Baudelaire
appears to share Daguerre's reading when he quotes the gospel: 'Sei-
gneur, détournez de moi ce calice' (p. 632), but Christ's expression is,
in fact, much more one of resignation and acceptance than of anguished fear or an unwillingness to accept his fate. If Daguerre is right,
one would have to suppose that the frighted mien of the angels indicated some distress at not having accomplished their mission of
'strengthening him'[46] and that he was still intent on having the cup
pass; whereas the intensity and poignancy of the scene seem to lie in
his self-contained resolution which contrasts with their lack of fortitude, and their pity and fear at the inevitable outcome. However we
interpret Christ's gesture, what predominates is the powerful sense of
isolation of the central figure, accentuated by the averted posture and
closed eyes not just of Christ himself, but of the sleeping disciples and
of two of the three ministering angels who bury their faces in their
hands and in the shoulder of the grief-stricken third angel, who alone
is able to contemplate the scene. The drama of the Garden of Olives
has attracted the attention of many writers and poets. Pascal makes of
it a crucial moment in his apology of the Christian religion, while the
Romantic poets, Nerval and Vigny in particular, interpret it in terms
of humanistic revolt, seeing in Jesus a representation of abandoned

---

[43] Raymond Escholier, *Eugène Delacroix* (Paris: Cercle d'Art, 1963), 176.
[44] *Delacroix*, 214.
[45] Luke 22: 42.
[46] In Luke 22: 43 there is only one angel.

humanity. Something of this view passes into Baudelaire's own 'Le Reniement de saint Pierre', the third quatrain of which reads as follows:

—Ah! Jésus, souviens-toi du Jardin des Olives!
Dans ta simplicité tu priais à genoux
Celui qui dans son ciel riait au bruit des clous
Que d'ignobles bourreaux plantaient dans tes chairs vives [. . .]

Baudelaire seems in no way to have shared the misgivings of contemporary or subsequent critics about this early painting. On the contrary he felt that it overflowed with 'tendresse féminine et d'onction poétique' (p. 632), though it may well have been the depiction of the three angels and above all the appeal of the subject matter that enabled him to overlook any possible defects in the work.

A similar affinity no doubt drew Baudelaire to the murals Delacroix painted for la chapelle des Saints-Anges in Saint-Sulpice towards the end of his career. In his appreciation of *La Lutte de Jacob avec l'ange* (Pl. 3), Baudelaire restricts himself to quoting the story as it is told in Genesis 32: 23–32 and to a few brief comments on the scene, the still life in the foreground, and the contrasting attitudes of the wrestling figures. He points to 'les lueurs riantes et dorées du matin'[47] that suffuse the painting, the robust vegetation 'qu'on pourrait appeler patriarcale', the limpid stream of Jaboc on the left, on the right the tail-end of the caravan taking Jacob's presents to appease his brother Esau, and finally to Jacob and the angel:

L'homme naturel et l'homme surnaturel luttent chacun selon sa nature, Jacob incliné en avant comme un bélier et bandant toute sa musculature, l'ange se prêtant complaisamment au combat, calme, doux, comme un être qui peut vaincre sans effort des muscles et ne permettant pas à la colère d'altérer la forme divine de ses membres.

What is remarkable here is not so much what Baudelaire says as what he refrains from saying. He seems little inclined to convey to the reader 'la somme d'idées ou de rêveries' (p. 579) the work brings to his mind. On the contrary, one senses a reluctance to interpret 'cette bizarre légende, que beaucoup de gens interprètent allégoriquement, et que ceux de la Kabbale et de la Nouvelle Jérusalem traduisent sans doute dans des sens différents' (p. 730). He seems instead to be

---

[47] Vitet, erroneously, had blamed the full light of day in the work which he thought out of keeping with the dawn light of the account in Genesis. See Johnson, *Paintings*, v. 170.

following the painter's intention, attaching himself to the 'material' sense of the subject in order to draw 'tout le parti qu'un peintre de son tempérament en pouvait tirer'. The implication is that by dwelling on the material aspects of the scene, the painter, and the critic in his turn, have not imposed an arbitrary closure on the work, but have left its suggestiveness open to the viewer. If there is symbolism it is present only as a virtuality, operating in a manner similar to the elliptic symbols of later generations of artists, painter and critic being content to respect the simplicity and restraint of the biblical story. Baudelaire quotes Genesis at length, not as filler for his copy, but to show how Delacroix has produced a 'material' counterpart to the biblical account of Jacob's struggle with the angel. It is because for both men painting is the concrete art *par excellence* that it must be faithful to its means and seek to express the spiritual, not as an abstraction, but as something anchored in the physical. To seek to express the spiritual in an abstract manner is a contradiction, typical of eclectics like Ary Scheffer and the other 'singes du sentiment', who confuse the means of one art with those of another, the poetry of sentiment and feeling with the physicality of painting whose appeal is to sensation. Theirs is a kind of 'anti-painting' at the extreme opposite pole to Delacroix's impassioned creations which, like the works that inspired them, by Shakespeare, Dante, or Tasso, are full of colour and movement, and are essentially visual.

In *La Lutte de Jacob* one is struck immediately by the variety and richness of Delacroix's palette,[48] intensified by the pale orange light of dawn, which heralds, as in the biblical story, a new beginning, and which spreads from an unseen source on the right, where the chapel window is situated, on to one side of the trunk of the immense tree, the caravan at the bottom right and top left, and most dramatically on to the wrestling figures in the foreground. The effect is of light and darkness, clarity and mystery, befitting the turning-point in the fortunes of Jacob and the children of Israel. Another suggestive contrast is between the serpentine movement of the caravan of animals and people, and the supernatural struggle between the isolated figures of Jacob and the angel. For the caravan the dawn means the beginning of another day's labour; time is already on the march for them, but for Jacob the future will only begin to unfold itself again once his struggle is over and the outcome assured. The Jaboc, which in Genesis could be

[48] 'Jamais, [. . .] Delacroix n'a étalé un coloris plus splendidement et plus savamment surnaturel; jamais un dessin plus *volontairement* épique' (751).

interpreted symbolically,[49] occupies a tiny part of the bottom left of the painting and appears to have no other function than to emphasize the freshness of the scene, though Baudelaire specifically refers to it: 'A gauche, un ruisseau limpide s'échappe en cascades.' The dominant feature of the rich and robust vegetation is, of course, the immense tree whose twin trunks tower up into a black and almost impenetrable canopy of foliage. Readers of Delacroix's *Journal* have been quick to link it to the 'chêne d'Antin' described from his walks at Champrosay. Seen from a distance, it appears of an ordinary size; but from underneath its branches the impression is quite different: 'n'apercevant que le tronc auquel je touche presque et la naissance de ses grosses branches, qui s'étendent au-dessus de ma tête comme les immenses bras de ce géant de la forêt, je suis étonné de la grandeur de ses détails; en un mot, je le trouve grand et même effrayant de grandeur'.[50] Recalling the incident some years later, he records a sensation of the sublime, and it is clearly a similar distortion of perspective that ensures the grandeur and sublimity of the painting. Here is another of these intended disproportions, like the perspective in *La Mort de Sardanapale* or, as we shall see, the mare in *Ovide chez les Scythes*, which are characteristic of Delacroix's production. In a biblical context, the tree can be read as the Tree of Life in its various manifestations, from the Garden of Eden to the hill of Golgotha, but it can be read in a 'material' sense, as Baudelaire would no doubt have us do, as representing simultaneously the power of nature and of God. It embodies that sense of the numinous which caught the imagination of Lamartine and Hugo.[51] The caravan wends its way through time, but the struggle with the angel takes place beneath the timeless and awesome presence of the oak, whose massive strength is complemented by the pliant resilience of the wrestling angel. If Baudelaire invites us to read the work as an appeal to our material imagination, it is because he understood that Delacroix's impatient imagination had, here as elsewhere, broken free from the stultifying conformity of contemporary religious painting to the norms, means, and commonplaces of an outmoded tradition. It is also because, as with his own poetry, the

---

[49] As an obstacle to be passed. Cf. also Roland Barthes's analysis of the Genesis story in *L'Aventure sémiologique* (Paris: Seuil, 1985).

[50] See *Journal*, 9 May 1853. Recalling this impression on 25 Jan. 1857, he writes: 'Arrivé sous les branches mêmes, n'apercevant que des parties sans rapport avec l'ensemble, j'éprouve la sensation du sublime' (*Journal*, 341, 624).

[51] Lamartine, 'Le Chêne' in *Harmonies poétiques et religieuses*, and Hugo, 'A Albert Dürer' in *Les Voix intérieures*.

aspiration to the ideal, or the descent into spleen, is mediated through sensation and involvement in the world of objects.

As Lee Johnson's overview of the reception of the work shows, the painting was widely interpreted as depicting the struggles of the Romantic artist with his art, and Johnson himself believes that Delacroix was alluding to his 'personal trials as one of the elect'.[52] This interpretation has been shared by many critics since, notably by Dumur, who saw it as 'la *catharsis* de la tragédie antique, revécue à travers un mythe judéo-chrétien et la grande idée romantique de la mission de l'artiste et de son holocauste',[53] and Barrès read it as a 'page d'autobiographie suprême, résumé de l'expérience d'une grande vie, testament de mort inscrit par le vieil artiste sur les mur des Anges'.[54] Few would wish to object to such a view, and if Delacroix identified himself with the figure of Jacob, so no doubt also did Baudelaire. But this interpretation is perhaps too restrictive. In his invitations to the inauguration of the chapel Delacroix describes the painting, as is his wont, in the most factual manner:

Jacob accompagne les troupeaux et autres présents à l'aide desquels il espère fléchir la colère de son frère Esaü. Un étranger se présente qui arrête ses pas et engage avec lui une lutte opiniâtre, laquelle ne se termine qu'au moment où Jacob, touché au nerf de la cuisse par son adversaire, se trouve réduit à l'impuissance. Cette lutte est regardée, par les livres saints, comme un emblème des épreuves que Dieu envoie quelquefois à ses élus.[55]

The final sentence might appear to indicate a broadly traditional meaning of the story, were it not for the strong suspicion that it was intended as a *paratonnerre* to satisfy the church authorities, who might well have thought the powerful physicality of the work, its extravagance and bravura, so alien to the tradition of church decoration as to be out of place. However that may be, the whole conception and manner of execution of the mural situate it alongside Delacroix's other great works whose inspiration is religious in the broadest sense, on a level of universality. It is the struggle of the elect with the powers that surpass him, caught at the crucial moment when the angel lames him by touching the nerve in his thigh, a moment of defeat soon turned to

---

[52] Johnson, *Paintings*, v. 192.

[53] Guy Dumur, *Delacroix romantique* (Paris: Mercure de France, 1973), 204.

[54] Quoted by Daguerre de Hureaux, *Delacroix*, 239. Maurice Barrès, *Le Mystère en pleine lumière*, in *L'Œuvre de Maurice Barrès*, vol. xii (Paris: Club de l'Honnête Homme, 1967), 231.

[55] Quoted by Daguerre de Hureaux, *Delacroix*, 237. Delacroix, *Correspondance générale d'Eugène Delacroix*, ed. André Joubin (Paris: Plon, 1938), iv. 254.

victory as Jacob is blessed by the angel and given the new name of Israel. Smitten in his physical person, Jacob, like all those who answer the call of the divine, has, like the poet in 'Bénédiction', a curse upon his life, and a blessing upon his mission.

Baudelaire's comments on the other two paintings for the chapel are of lesser interest. Of *L'Archange saint Michel terrassant le démon* he suggests sources in Isaiah, Jude and Revelation, and mentions Milton's epic description of the event. Impressed by its dramatic magnificence, he finds, however, that the light from the upper part of the window makes it difficult for the spectator to enjoy the painting properly. As with *La Lutte de Jacob*, he cites the source for *Héliodore chassé du temple* in 2 Maccabees 3: 24–9, which relate how Heliodorus, sent by Seleucus to take the treasure from the Temple, is overcome by an angel who tramples him under the hooves of his horse, and is then whipped mercilessly by two other angels, 'pleins de force et de beauté, brillants de gloire et richement vêtus'. Baudelaire notes the splendour of the polychrome temple, the horse holding Heliodorus down with its hoof, the ferocity of the whipping, and the beauty and serenity of the angels, but makes no mention of the extraordinary posture of the angel swooping down vertically to punish his victim.[56]

There is no indication that Baudelaire gave any consideration to the three parts of the chapel as constituting a whole, and there would be little point in speculating on his possible reaction, were it not that Michele Hannoosh proposes an interpretation of the ensemble which is nothing if not Baudelairean, implying, if not directly stating, yet another parallel between painter and poet. Rejecting the safe interpretation of the cycle as representing the triumph of God over revolt, she argues that the murals express the interrelationship of 'material and spiritual, blasphemy and blessing, earthly and divine, damnation and election', reminiscent of the kind of collapsing of binary opposites familiar to students of Baudelaire. As a result, 'the message of the *Jacob* must be read back into the other two, and theirs

---

[56] Some commentators have suggested a link with 'Le Rebelle', published in the *Revue européenne* and *Le Boulevard* along with the piece on the Saint-Sulpice murals, and subsequently included in the posthumous edition of *Les Fleurs du Mal*. There is certainly a similarity between Delacroix's plunging angel and the first line of this irregular sonnet: 'Un Ange furieux fond du ciel comme un aigle'; but it is not developed. There is no mention of whipping, and the miscreant, who unlike Heliodorus persists in his revolt, is seized by the hair and belaboured with punches. There is also the possibility, based on Prarond's recollection, that the poem dates from the 1840s (see Pichois's comment in *Oc.* i. 1106.).

into it',[57] so that all three paintings reflect the same ambiguity of divine
and demonic, election and damnation, and the artist becomes a kind
of Lucifer or Heliodorus pillaging the temple. The sensuality of
Delacroix's art and its materiality were thought by some contemporaries to be almost blasphemous, and it was precisely because of
these qualities that Baudelaire thought Delacroix alone capable of
producing religious paintings in keeping with a modern, Romantic
sensibility. But if Delacroix painted the treasure and jewels of the
temple with the same brio and sensuality as in *Sardanapalus*, it was not
out of some kind of Luciferan desire to pillage the temple, but because
jewels *are* alluring, otherwise they would not have attracted the covetousness of Seleucus and his messenger Heliodorus. Delacroix understands, like Baudelaire, that since vice is seductive, 'il faut le peindre
séduisant' (p. 41). If this were not so, both vice and virtue would be
gratuitous, without justification or merit. Also, there is little indication
in the painting of 'nobility', as Hannoosh has argued, in the youthful
figure of Heliodorus, struck down by the angels and divine horsemen
like the demon in the cupola. On the contrary, his posture in defeat
seems ignoble, and it is difficult to make out whether he is handsome
like the divine horseman or not, since his countenance is mostly hidden. But even if one were to admit that he is handsome, this would not
be a ground for thinking the painting ambiguous. It would merely
show that Delacroix, like Baudelaire, did not indulge in an oversimpli-
fied depiction of the vicious as ugly and the virtuous as beautiful. What
can be generally accepted is that the tripartite work shows three kinds
of revolt and their outcome. *Saint Michel* stands on high on a cosmic
level, while the *Heliodorus* and *Jacob* on the walls are rooted in human
time and the real world. But the contrast between them does not
impair the unity of the total work, as Hannoosh argues it does. They
can be viewed rather as complementary, the one showing the punishment for covetousness and sacrilege, the other the revolt that can be
used by God's grace and transformed into blessing in the unfolding of
his plan for Israel, and for humankind. Jacob's struggle with the angel,
like the protestations of Job, or the weakness that Paul acknowledges to
be the source of his strength, belong to a paradoxical theology of
suffering clearly reflected in Baudelaire's own world-view. Baudelaire
sensed an element of *décadence* (p. 751) in these works, which display

---

[57] *Painting and the* Journal *of Eugène Delacroix* (Princeton: Princeton University Press,
1995), 190, 186.

more artistic self-assertion than conventional piety or restraint, and no doubt by contemporary standards Delacroix's Romanticism was excessive and incompatible with the conventions of church decoration, as it was in the equally excessive *Pietà*. But Romantic excess does not necessarily imply Luciferan or Heliodoran revolt. On the contrary, by a curious paradox, Delacroix's church decorations may be judged as giving a more powerful expression to the mystery and depth of these biblical events than in any other artist of his time. Their orthodoxy shines through the bravura, for what Delacroix has produced for the chapel of the holy angels is three instances of the intervention of divine messengers and a synthetic view of revolt, culminating in that of Jacob as a sign of grace and election. As Baudelaire himself puts it, 'les phénomènes engendrés par la chute deviendront les moyens du rachat' (p. 528).

It is, however, in his commentary on the *Pietà* (Pl. 4) in the church of Saint-Denis-du-Saint-Sacrement that we see most clearly why Baudelaire considered that Delacroix alone knew how to paint religious subjects. As a preliminary to his comments on the painting, he praises the grandeur and universality of Delacroix who has freed himself from 'la symbolique et les traditions primitives' which third-rate artists adopt 'pour remuer et faire chanter la corde religieuse' (p. 435). The uninhibited artist is able to impose his own temperament and naïvety without having recourse to the superannuated bric-à-brac of past ages and traditions, and that is why his paintings are not academic or pedantic exercises, but modern and original expressions, if not of religious belief, then of a deeply felt religious anguish or tension.[58] Nothing, indeed, could be further from Ary Scheffer or the *saint-sulpiceries* of his contemporaries[59] than this magnificent mural in the church of Saint-Denis-du-Saint-Sacrement, 'où la majestueuse reine des douleurs tient sur ses genoux le corps de son enfant mort, les deux bras étendus horizontalement dans un accès de désespoir, une attaque de nerfs maternelle' (p. 435).[60] Baudelaire is not interested in the identity of the various figures, which has animated much of the

---

[58] Delacroix writes of his enthusiasm while painting the mural to the music of the church services: 'Je me rappelle mon enthousiasme, lorsque je peignais à Saint-Denis du Saint-Sacrement et que j'entendais la musique des offices; le dimanche était doublement un jour de fête' (*Journal*, 24 Dec. 1853, 394).

[59] Cf. Papety, *Consolatrix afflictorum*, reproduced in Kelley, *Salon de 1846*, plate 58.

[60] In the *Salon de 1845* Baudelaire had, however, praised *L'Evanouissement de la Vierge* by Auguste Hesse: 'Il a d'abord un mérite singulier—c'est de ne rappeler, en aucune manière, les motifs convenus de la peinture actuelle, et les poncifs qui traînent dans tous les jeunes

discussion about the work, and makes no speculation about the three male figures who support the Virgin, nor about the two 'saintes femmes' who help support the dead Christ, the one on the left being certainly Mary Magdalene. What interests him is the suggestive power of the dress and above all of the actions and postures of the contrasting figures, the one, dark-haired, on the left, holding Christ's feet and looking anxiously and intently towards the distraught Virgin Mary, the other, fair-haired, supporting his arm and shoulder, eyes red with grief, looking out of the picture towards the spectator: 'la première rampe convulsivement à terre, encore revêtue des bijoux et des insignes du luxe; l'autre, blonde et dorée, s'affaisse plus mollement sous le poids énorme de son désespoir'. The three men at the back direct their gaze towards the elongated body of the fainting Virgin, her eyes shut and arms inordinately and bizarrely spread out as if she in turn were being crucified, while at a distance, on the right of the picture, completing the 'round' of gazes, two men, one of whom is young and elegantly dressed, look on, the one in awe, the other in sorrow, bringing our eyes back to the central scene and so heightening the sense of drama. Of the background Baudelaire writes:

Le groupe est échelonné et disposé tout entier sur un fond d'un vert sombre et uniforme, qui ressemble autant à des amas de rochers qu'à une mer bouleversée par l'orage. Ce fond est d'une simplicité fantastique, et E. Delacroix a sans doute, comme Michel-Ange, supprimé l'accessoire pour ne pas nuire à la clarté de son idée. Ce chef d'œuvre laisse dans l'esprit un sillon profond de mélancolie.

The background has indeed that greeny-brown turbulence, inter-spersed with vague streaks of light, that is a feature of many of Delacroix's works and gives them a spectral depth setting off the central scene, all the more so as in this picture the garments of the three men are rich and of a deep blood red. The absence of minor detail contributes to the universal quality of the painting, as does the absence of any of the conventional Christian symbolism that Baudelaire thought marred contemporary religious painting.

His commentary contains a puzzling reference to *Hamlet*: 'L'un des deux personnages qui soutient et modère sa douleur est éploré comme les figures les plus lamentables de l'*Hamlet*, avec laquelle œuvre celle-

ateliers' (373). From the description in the *livret* of the *Salon*—'La Vierge à la vue de son fils qui va disparaître dans le sépulcre, vaincue par la douleur, tombe évanouie dans les bras de Marie-Madeleine et de l'autre Marie' (1274)—it would appear to have at least a superficial resemblance to Delacroix's *Pietà*.

ci a du reste plus d'un rapport.' Claude Pichois (p. 1299) thinks that the reference is to the paintings and lithographs Delacroix made on the subject, and it may be that Baudelaire, who in 'La Béatrice' saw himself as an 'ombre d'Hamlet', was fascinated by Shakespeare's fatherless prince not just as a cultural figure, but because of a personal affinity.[61] While it is extremely doubtful that there is any parallel with *Hamlet et Horatio au cimetière* of 1835, there is an unmistakable resemblance between the headgear, beard, face, and attitude of the head of the figure on the right of the *Pietà* (identified as Joseph of Arimathea) and those of Horatio in the 1839 painting of the same name, housed in the Louvre. What further specific links there may be with Hamlet might indeed, as Pichois suggests, be fruitfully sought in the lithographs, most convincingly, I would suggest, in the one depicting Hamlet and his mother, in which her features and the tension of her body have much in common with those of the Virgin.[62] But one wonders whether the two detached figures[63] standing at some distance on the right of the *Pietà* do not also have a Hamletian quality. Bullemont identifies the elegant young man as St John, which seems implausible given his modern apparel. Whatever Delacroix's intentions, the effect of the separation of the two figures and their sorrowful countenance is, clearly, to increase the drama of the central scene and the isolation of the mourners. What would be more daring and more plausible in this most profound of paintings would be to suggest a connection between the figures and the Danish prince, in particular in the graveyard scene, where he meditates on death in the most general manner, before his shocked recognition that it is Ophelia who is to be buried. In all three of Delacroix's gravedigger scenes Hamlet's meditative expression bears a resemblance to that of the principal onlooker in the *Pietà*, whose serene sorrow at human mortality contrasts poignantly with the grief-stricken agony of those who have just lived the reality of the death of their God.

The suggestion of other possible links with the play continues, however, to puzzle the critical will. The contemporary critic Prosper

---

[61] Baudelaire acquired the Hamlet lithographs to decorate the Hôtel Pimodan.

[62] See *Hamlet et la reine*, in Loys Delteil, *Le Peintre-graveur illustré*, vol. iii (New York: Da Capo Press, 1969), plate 112. Baudelaire draws a parallel between *Une Sibylle qui montre le rameau d'or* and the lithographs: 'La tête rappelle un peu l'indécision charmante des dessins sur Hamlet' (356).

[63] Similarly, in *La Mise au tombeau* (Boston Museum of Fine Arts), Delacroix has two sets of detached figures in the background to increase the drama and isolation of the mourners.

Haussard thought the *Pietà* a new kind of painting, 'sans analogue ni précédents chez les maîtres de la peinture, mais qui s'inspire à de grandes sources de poésie, et renvoie des reflets de Dante et de Shakespeare, de Goethe et de Byron',[64] and it is here that we can begin to understand what Baudelaire thought the other links might be. He was not perhaps thinking of anything specific, but rather of a similarity of intellectual climate. Though far removed in time, Dante and Shakespeare were judged by Baudelaire, Delacroix, and many of their contemporaries to be eminently modern in sensibility and in manner. Delacroix's superb tribute to Dante in the Luxembourg ceiling placed him in the lineage of the great epic poets of the ancient world— Homer, Ovid, Statius, and, of course, Virgil. For modern artists the *Divine Comedy* bore witness to the exalted mission of the artist as visionary, as the Orphic explorer of the mysteries of death and the underworld, captured with such passion and drama in *La Barque de Dante*, which Baudelaire greatly admired. In the *Pietà*, the anguish and terror of death are made all the more pressing by the sense of the grave, with its suspicion of a dim light, opening up before the desolate group.[65] As in Hugo's *Préface de Cromwell* and Stendhal's *Racine et Shakespeare*, Shakespeare in particular represented an art which had freed itself from the conventions and stylization of the past, and so Delacroix's *Pietà* may be considered Shakespearean to the extent that the attitudes and gestures of the figures do not conform to a preconceived idea of what is beautiful.[66] Because they were natural, and above all passionate, they escaped from any notion of *bienséance* and appeared to some contemporary viewers to border upon the grotesque, at variance with the inherent sublimity of the subject matter. Nothing, it is true, could be further removed from the Raphaelesque ideal of beauty aimed at by Ingres and his followers, and it was no doubt this perception that provoked the outrageous and anonymous attack upon the work and upon Delacroix in the *Journal des artistes*, which railed at 'ces figures repoussantes', Mary Magdalene 'aux yeux avinés', the Virgin 'crucifiée, inanimée, plâtrée et défigurée', and the 'corps hideux,

---

[64] Johnson, *Paintings*, v. 84. P. Haussard, 'Le Christ au sépulcre', *Le National* (10 Nov. 1844).

[65] Timothy Raser, *A Poetics of Art Criticism: The Case of Baudelaire* (Chapel Hill: University of North Carolina Press, 1989), 104, makes the excellent point that the light 'must come from within the tomb'.

[66] Ary Scheffer's *Le Christ consolateur*, shown in the Salon of 1837, is an example of religious art thought to be acceptable to contemporary taste. See McWilliam, *Dreams of Happiness*, 131.

putréfié, affreux, qu'on ose nous présenter comme l'image du Fils de Dieu'.[67] Similarly, for the cultural conservatives, Shakespeare was still the barbarous histrion he had been for Voltaire, producing in *Othello*, for example, not so much a study of jealousy, as the depiction of the savage butcher of Desdemona.[68] Baudelaire was clearly aware of such criticism, since he mentions a fashionable young artist who referred to the work as 'peinture de cannibale'; but he underlines its uniqueness, declaring that one could not find in the most elaborate palette or in a dictionary of rules anything remotely like this 'sanglante et farouche désolation, à peine compensée par le vert sombre de l'espérance'.

In addition to any specific similarities with the Hamlet works, what for Baudelaire particularizes this religious painting is freedom of execution and naturalness and passion of gesture. Delacroix's most powerful paintings, he says, are those where he chooses his own subjects and can use his imagination unfettered;[69] but if he excels also in religious paintings, where the subjects are set in advance through a long tradition, it is because 'la tristesse sérieuse de son talent convient parfaitement à notre religion, religion profondément triste, religion de la douleur universelle, et qui, à cause de sa catholicité même, laisse une pleine liberté à l'individu et ne demande pas mieux que d'être célébrée dans le langage de chacun,—s'il connaît la douleur et s'il est peintre' (p. 436). Like the actor and the poet, the painter does not have to believe in religion to produce great religious paintings. What he needs above all is imagination and a belief in the reality of what he is depicting during the execution of the work (p. 629). It is clear that the appeal of such works lies above all in the depiction of a sorrow that resonates beyond the specifically Christian context to give expression to mankind's eternal and fundamental sense of abandonment and despair. In this *Pietà* whatever religious sentiment there is appears negative, contradicted by the apparent dirtiness of Christ's body, which appears almost in a state of decomposition, and strangely out of proportion. If the painting contains any consolation, it is not in an implicit or conventional message of hope in a victory following defeat, or in the known outcome of the Christian story, which is celebrated, for example, in Titian's *Pietà*, with the Virgin Mary pointing serenely

[67] Johnson, *Paintings*, v. 83.
[68] Prévert catches this attitude well in the reaction of Count Edouard de Montray to Frédéric Lemaître's interpretation of Othello in the film *Les Enfants du paradis*.
[69] Baudelaire calls these works 'de fantaisie' in 1846. By 1859 his attitude towards 'fantaisie' has changed fundamentally (644).

upwards. In spite of Delacroix's impatience with the term, Baudelaire was right to see him as a religious painter in the broadest sense, since so many of his works are not just literary or historical, but seem in addition to give expression to that 'douleur universelle', which Laforgue was later to call 'l'universel *lamasabaktani*',[70] just as in the *Pietà* the despair of Christ's followers overflows any sectarian limits to merge with that of all humankind. In this context, the apparently minor detail of the two bystanders in the *Pietà* is confirmed as a stroke of genius essential to the meaning of the work;[71] for we as spectators cannot view the scene with their equanimity. We see them seeing, and detach ourselves from them to return to the 'sanglante et farouche désolation', not as a moment in history but as evidence of the recurrent and inevitable defeat of the will to transcendence. The spectator is not given the impression of being installed in some safe, neutral position outside the painting. This is not just the death of Christ; it is ours.

In Baudelaire's commentary on the *Mise au tombeau*[72] in the *Salon de 1859* a similar universalizing tendency is evident. He begins by asking the reader if he has ever seen a better expression of the solemnity required by the subject, and if Titian could have invented such a thing, without apparently being aware that Delacroix had copied Titian's *Entombment* at the beginning of his career.[73] Delacroix's conception of the scene is indeed very different from Titian's, much less academic, and owing much, according to Gautier,[74] to the influence of Rembrandt. Gautier's commentary is not only very perceptive; it has in addition a distinctly Baudelairean ring: 'Les figures ont des mouvements si vrais, si dramatiques, si passionnés, dans leur savante négligence; elles font si bien ce qu'elles font, que l'imagination les achève, quoique souvent elles soient à moitié perdues dans l'ombre et à peine indiquées en cinq ou six touches grossières: le geste fait supposer le bras et le regard remplace l'œil.' Again Baudelaire dwells on the figure of Christ's mother, who, as in the *Pietà*, is not some 'femmelette d'album', and has none of the cloying sentimentality of some renderings to be found in 'ce capharnaüm de faux *ex-voto*, dans

[70] Laforgue, 'Préludes autobiographiques' in *Les Complaintes*.

[71] The bystanders, interestingly, do not appear in the two sketches for the *Pietà*, reproduced in Johnson, *Paintings*, vi, plate 39.

[72] Now in the National Museum of Western Art, Tokyo.

[73] See Johnson, *Paintings*, ii, plate 9 for a black-and-white reproduction.

[74] Ibid. iii. 248: 'On [le] prendrait pour un Rembrandt inconnu.' Théophile Gautier, *Salon* (Paris, 1859).

cette immense voie lactée de plâtreuses sottises' (p. 631), that is the 1859 Salon. On the contrary she has 'un geste et une ampleur tragiques qui conviennent parfaitement à cette reine des mères' (p. 634). Even she is universalized, being referred to not by name or as the Virgin but as the *Mother*, as if in some way she were the mother of all: 'La *Mère* va s'évanouir, elle se soutient à peine!' Baudelaire is sensitive also to the image of the cave itself, whose suggestive quality Delacroix was able to exploit in the fearsome *Médée furieuse* and in *La Résurrection de Lazare*. It corresponds to his own obsession with tombs, 'escaliers sans rampe', dungeons, and underground chambers.[75] In this *Mise au tombeau* the spiralling steps and the mingling of daylight in the upper part and torchlight in the lower depths transform the burial place into what Bachelard would have called an archetype of the unconscious, what Baudelaire calls an 'emblème de la vie souterraine que doit mener longtemps la religion nouvelle'. The *sfumato* of the principal figures is an invitation to reverie, creating in the viewer an impression which is not so much historical as poetic, religious, universal, as he contemplates 'ces quelques hommes qui descendent soigneusement le cadavre de leur Dieu au fond d'une crypte, dans ce sépulcre que le monde adorera, "le seul, dit superbement René, qui n'aura rien à rendre à la fin des siècles!"'.

The titles of the paintings discussed so far indicate an explicit religious intention. Other paintings are interpreted by Baudelaire as being implicitly religious. Of those inspired by his Moroccan visit in 1832, *Les Femmes d'Alger* (Pl. 5) is assuredly one of the finest. Baudelaire is aware of the impression made by this journey on the mind of the painter: 'là il put à loisir étudier l'homme et la femme dans l'indépendance et l'originalité native de leurs mouvements, et comprendre la beauté antique par l'aspect d'une race pure de toute mésalliance et ornée de la santé et du libre développement de ses muscles' (p. 430). This comment is so close to Delacroix's own alleged exclamation on entering the house of the Algerian women ('C'est beau! C'est comme au temps d'Homère!'[76]) and to others in his correspondence that one is tempted to think that Baudelaire must have had some second-hand knowledge of them.[77] What he and Delacroix are

---

[75] See, for example, 'Confession', 'Spleen' nos. 76, 78, 'L'Irrémédiable', 'Brumes et pluies'.

[76] Quoted by Johnson, *Paintings*, iii. 166.

[77] To Pierret Delacroix writes: 'Imagine, mon ami, ce que c'est de voir couchés au soleil, se promenant dans les rues [. . .] des personnages consulaires, des Catons, des Brutus,

referring to here is the 'classical' dignity of a proud and unmixed race, a kind of modern paganism, far removed from the degenerate world of contemporary Paris. Other critics have pointed out how the Moroccan journey brought to his work a documentary realism and at the same time a new balance and classicism. But given Baudelaire's failure to mention at any point the development of Delacroix's manner of painting, it seems most unlikely that he is referring to anything other than the figures in the paintings.[78] Here, at all events, is the Orient, not as he had imagined it in the extravagant turmoil of *La Mort de Sardanapale*, but with a real interior, showing the richly attired and bejewelled women seated on their carpets and attended by a black servant among the draperies, mirrors, recesses, doors, hookahs, *babouches*, and other local trinkets. Unlike the paintings of Arabs on horseback or of hunting scenes, unlike *Les Convulsionnaires de Tanger*, whose frenetic swirling movement is captured also in one of Guys's *Pompes et solennités* (p. 704), *Les Femmes d'Alger* is an essentially inward and above all static creation whose very stillness is accentuated by the graceful, gentle movement of the negress with her raised arm, her head and upper body turned slightly to the left and her right foot arched in its forward movement above the elegant slipper. Pierre Daix has caught this aspect of the work extremely well: '*Les Femmes d'Alger* si on les compare aux grandes toiles de la période précédente sont immobiles, saisies dans un instant qui est aussi l'éternité [. . .] A la peinture d'élan succède la peinture de description, d'analyse. La couleur qui était rythme, mouvement, devient piège à durée.'[79] Having given us this invitation to reverie, he goes on however to call it 'la toile

auxquels il ne manque même pas l'air dédaigneux que devaient avoir les maîtres du monde.' And to Jal: 'Les Romains et les Grecs sont à ma porte: j'ai bien ri des Grecs de David, à part bien entendu, sa sublime brosse. Je les connais à présent: les marbres sont la vérité même, mais il faut y avoir lire, et nos pauvres modernes n'y ont vu que des hiéroglyphes' (*Correspondance générale*, vol. i, 319, 330). Baudelaire's enthusiasm for the nobility of Catlin's North American Indians is evident in the *Salon de 1846* (446).

[78] It is a remarkable feature of his criticism that Baudelaire never points to any development in Delacroix's painting. At most he is aware of different styles dictated by subject-matter rather than by evolution, as the following passage from the *Exposition universelle* indicates: 'On croit découvrir par-ci par-là des échantillons de progrès; mais si de certains tableaux plus récents témoignent que certaines importantes qualités ont été poussées à outrance, l'esprit impartial perçoit avec confusion que dès ses premières productions, dès sa jeunesse (*Dante et Virgile aux enfers* est de 1822), M. Delacroix fut grand. Quelquefois il a été plus délicat, quelquefois plus singulier, quelquefois plus peintre, mais toujours il a été grand' (590).

[79] Pierre Daix, *Delacroix le libérateur* (Paris: Club des Amis du Livre progressiste, 1963), 178.

1. Delacroix, *Madeleine dans le désert*

2. Delacroix, *La Mort de Sardanapale*

3. Delacroix, *La Lutte de Jacob avec l'ange*

4. Delacroix, *Pietà*

5. Delacroix, *Les Femmes d'Alger*

6. Delacroix, *Ovide chez les Scythes*

7. Guys, *Turks conveying the sick to Balaclava*

8. Guys, *Turks conveying the sick to Balaclava* (as published in *The Illustrated London News*)

9. Guys, *Lord Raglan's Head-quarters at Balaclava*

10. Guys, *Captain Ponsonby riding in Alexandria*

11. Guys, *Consecration of a Burial Ground at Scutari*

12. Guys, *La Loge de l'Empereur*

13. Manet, *Lola de Valence*

14. Manet, *La Musique aux Tuileries*

15. Manet, *Le Balcon*

16. Manet, *Olympia*

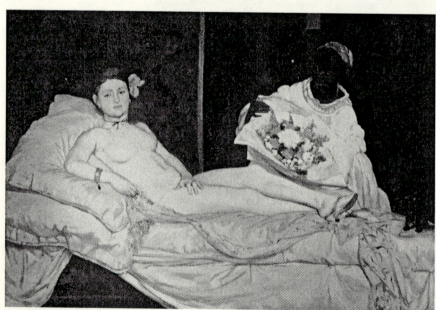

réaliste par excellence' and to castigate Baudelaire, blinded by his disapproval of Courbet and Champfleury, for not being sensitive to Delacroix's realism.[80] Gustave Planche, on the other hand, had seen the painting, which he considered Delacroix's most resounding triumph, as an example of art for art's sake, in which the subject matter was of little or no importance: 'Intéresser par la peinture réduite à ses seules ressources, sans le secours d'un sujet qui s'interprète de mille façons et trop souvent distrait l'œil des spectateurs superficiels, pour n'occuper que leur pensée qui estime le tableau selon ses rêves ou ses conjectures, c'est une tâche difficile, et M. Delacroix l'a remplie [. . .] c'est de la peinture et rien de plus, de la peinture franche, vigoureuse, vivement accusée.'[81]

Lee Johnson rejects this Art-for-Art's-sake interpretation and nuances the realist one by adding to the documentary intention of familiarizing the viewer with an Algerian interior and costumes the 'higher ideals of fine art'.[82] Although aware that the details of the picture are so accurate that an ethnographic museum had recently used the picture to illustrate the costumes of the time,[83] he is sensitive above all to the use of light and the gradation of the costumes from the plainest on the right to the most elaborate on the left, though he remains more than sceptical about Baudelaire's suggestion of a 'parfum de mauvais lieu' in what the poet considers to be Delacroix's 'tableau le plus coquet et le plus fleuri'.[84] According to Jules Buisson, Delacroix himself was irritated and bored by his admiring poet-critic who praised his painting for its atmosphere of illness and relentless melancholy.[85] The reference seems to be directly to *Les Femmes d'Alger*, and one is indeed aware here of a discrepancy between the painting and Baudelaire's mention of illness and perhaps especially of 'la tension des nerfs'.

Ce petit poème d'intérieur, plein de repos et de silence, encombré de riches étoffes et de brimborions de toilette, exhale je ne sais quel haut parfum de

---

[80] Ibid. 230.

[81] G. Planche, *Etudes sur l'école française*, vol. ii, 248. Quoted in Johnson, *Paintings*, iii. 169.

[82] Johnson, *Paintings*, iii. 169.

[83] *Delacroix, Le Voyage au Maroc*, catalogue of the exhibition at the Institut du monde arabe (Paris: Flammarion, 1994), 116.

[84] Gautier probably had Baudelaire's phrase in mind when he called *Les Femmes d'Alger* 'ce bouquet de fleurs vivantes' (*Ecrivains et artistes romantiques* (Paris: Tallandier, 1929), 239).

[85] See *Lettres à Baudelaire*, ed. Claude Pichois (Neuchâtel: La Baconnière, 1973), 112.

mauvais lieu qui nous guide assez vite vers les limbes insondées de la tristesse.
En général, il ne peint pas de jolies femmes, au point de vue des gens
du monde toutefois. Presque toutes sont malades, et resplendissent d'une
certaine beauté intérieure. Il n'exprime point la force par la grosseur des
muscles, mais par la tension des nerfs. C'est non seulement la douleur qu'il
sait le mieux exprimer, mais surtout,—prodigieux mystère de sa peinture,—
la douleur morale! Cette haute et sérieuse mélancolie brille d'un éclat morne,
même dans sa couleur, large, simple, abondante en masses harmoniques,
comme celle de tous les grands coloristes, mais plaintive et profonde comme
une mélodie de Weber. (p. 440)

However much one might wish to nuance Baudelaire's hyperbole, it
is true that nothing could be further from a realist or art-for-art's-sake
interpretation. His criticism is creative, responding to the poetry, the
mystery, the suggestiveness and sensuality of this *mundus muliebris*,[86]
and producing a kind of poetic prose, a literary analogue of the visual
art. Whereas in the 'riches étoffes' the realist would see only a documentary fact of the harem, the poet recognizes a moral quality; for they
are rich not just in their colour and fineness but in the associations
and emotive depth they connote. Even the apparently dismissive
'brimborions de toilette' have their suggestive function, guiding the
poet's imagination from these instruments of the women's toilette
towards their sensuality and the heavy sexuality of the harem, where
the silence and repose of the women are inherent in their function
which is to still the desire of their master. Typically, this sensuality,
this 'luxe, calme et volupté', are not devoid of spirituality and a quasi-
religious 'aspiration vers l'infini' that opens on to a limbo of melancholy, suggested by the black make-up round the women's eyes, and
accentuated in the case of the one on the left by a shadow falling from
the brow across the cheekbone. As Baudelaire says in 'L'Eloge du
maquillage', 'ce cadre noir rend le regard plus profond et plus
singulier, donne à l'œil une apparence plus décidée de fenêtre ouverte
sur l'infini' (p. 717). Where the realist might attribute the suggestion
of sadness to the social and cultural position of the women who cannot

---

[86] The expression occurs in ch. 10, 'La Femme', of *Le Peintre de la vie moderne*, where it
is followed by an equally poetic passage, which is relevant to Delacroix's painting: 'La femme
est sans doute une lumière, un regard, une invitation au bonheur, une parole quelquefois;
mais elle est surtout une harmonie générale, non seulement dans son allure et le mouvement
de ses membres, mais aussi dans les mousselines, les gazes, les vastes et chatoyantes nuées
d'étoffes dont elle s'enveloppe, et qui sont comme les attributs et le piédestal de sa divinité;
dans le métal et le minéral qui serpentent autour de ses bras et de son cou, qui ajoutent leurs
étincelles au feu de ses regards, ou qui jasent doucement à ses oreilles' (714). See also *Oc*. i.
499, where he uses the Latin expression as meaning 'world' rather than 'attire'.

escape their sumptuous prison, the poet gives it a metaphysical quality. Clearly, these 'limbes'[87] are not those of Dante's virtuous pagans,
but of Romantic ennui, which Sainte-Beuve describes as 'une inertie
mêlée d'angoisse, d'une angoisse dont on n'a plus présents les motifs,
mais qui subsiste comme une fièvre lente dont on compte les
battements'.[88] It is this feverish langour that Baudelaire sees in the
Algerian women, which explains their illness, their deep inner beauty,
and their 'douleur morale'.

In a typical flourish this purple passage ends with a splendid sense
of 'l'expansion des choses infinies', as it opens out to other colourists
to establish an analogy, a kind of critical synesthesia with the music
of Weber, with which Baudelaire also associates the prose poem
'L'Invitation au voyage' and the verse poem 'Les Phares' where 'des
fanfares étranges / Passent, comme un soupir étouffé de Weber.' Here
is a criticism which fulfils the prescriptions of *Le Salon de 1846*; that it
must be partial and passionate and produced from an exclusive point
of view 'qui ouvre le plus d'horizons' (p. 418), making of the painting
an invitation to a journey of memory and analogy.

Encouraged by the poet, the viewer finds further spatial depths
that are not just topographical, but the physical analogues of
the spiritual intensity of the painting, in the 'miroir profond' with
its suspicion of a reflection, the gleaming silver vessels which
are linked thematically to 'les meubles luisants/Polis par les ans'
of 'L'Invitation au voyage', in the recesses behind the curtain about
to be closed, in the stroke of genius of the enticingly half-open
red door, in the absent window which is the source of light, in
the beautiful bare feet of the women and the discarded slippers
which contrast with the delicate, stealthy, and fleet-footed ease of
the black servant whose Matisse-like two-dimensionality serves to
increase the sense of depth of the room, and finally in the *narguilé*
and the opium dream it suggests; an interior that gives on to no
outside, and is indeed the counterpart of the inwardness of the women
themselves, whose eyes neither meet nor see in their self-contained
dreaminess. Even the Koranic text on the curtain indicates less
a realist notation than the lure of the mysteries of an alien
culture. For a realist, the background no doubt 'diminishes in
substance', and the figures similarly betray their origins as separate

---

[87] Baudelaire had thought of *Les Limbes* as a possible title for *Les Fleurs du Mal.*
[88] Sainte-Beuve, *Volupté* (Paris: Gallimard, 1986), 264.

studies;[89] but for the viewer who responds to the appeal to the memory and imagination which Delacroix's great paintings make, every detail of 'splendeur orientale' in this magnificent canvas is 'morally' eloquent of the intimate drama and yearning it contains.

The same could not be said of the much smaller version[90] of the subject, painted in 1849 and now in the Musée Fabre in Montpellier. Here there is no outside source of light but a warm suffused glow that seems to emerge from behind the woman on the right of the picture; there is no door, and the depths are screened by various draperies, the mirror on the wall is devoid of reflection, there are very few objects and details to stimulate the imagination, and the black servant is much more static, seeming to merge with the featureless curtain she is lifting in order to depart. Of the three seated women, only the one on the right maintains her inwardness, the other two appearing more aware of their surroundings. Some commentators have thought that a passage in Delacroix's *Journal* dated 17 October 1853 refers to the two versions of the painting, and indicates a preference for the later work:

Je n'ai commencé à faire quelque chose de passable, dans mon voyage d'Afrique, qu'au moment où j'avais assez oublié les petits détails pour ne me rappeler dans mes tableaux que le côté frappant et poétique; jusque-là, j'étais poursuivi par l'amour de l'exactitude, que le plus grand nombre prend pour la vérité.[91]

Lee Johnson notices 'un effet de rêverie léthargique des plus poétiques', as if Delacroix had remembered the scene 'à travers un voile de mémoire teinté',[92] while a contemporary critic reviewing the Salon of 1849 had praised its superior colour and the replacement of the bizarre and discordant background in the earlier version by 'un demi-jour d'intérieur calme et vrai'.[93] More recently, Mras has noticed the disappearance of the tiles on the floor, the playing-down of the Moorish patterns in the women's dresses, and generally the suppression of detail and local colour. He goes on to conclude that 'under the erosive effect of time, it achieves, by way of compensation, a more striking and poetic power in which the langour and lassitude inherent

---

[89] F. A. Trapp, *The Attainment of Delacroix* (Baltimore and London: Johns Hopkins University Press, 1971), 128.

[90] The dimensions are as follows: 1834, 1.80 × 2.29 m.; 1849, 0.84 × 1.11 m.

[91] *Journal*, 369.

[92] See *Delacroix, le voyage au Maroc*, 118.

[93] Cailleux in *Le Temps*, 28 June 1849. Quoted by Daguerre de Hureaux, *Delacroix*, p. 181.

in the theme gain an aura of pathos which adds [a] further poetic dimension to this evocation of harem life'.[94] It is of course true that the later version conforms much more closely to Baudelaire's requirement that art must proceed from memory in order to speak to the memory of the beholder, and that as a consequence the artist must sacrifice the incidental details in favour of the ensemble. However, although theoretically the appeal to the imagination should be greater in this perhaps more intimate work, which has furthermore a stronger resemblance to a watercolour or to an *ébauche* than to a completed picture, the 1834 version in fact possesses greater depth; and this is precisely because the various details and objects have, in addition to any documentary function, the ability to draw in the imagination of the viewer and to 'faire rêver'. Nothing could be further from the 'mémoire d'almanach' (p. 470) which Baudelaire had condemned in Vernet. On the contrary, each object is an invitation to an inner journey.

Delacroix's women were not universally admired by his contemporaries. Victor Hugo is reported to have called them 'grenouilles' (p. 593), claiming to have looked in vain for 'une seule femme vraiment belle' in his paintings with the exception of the somewhat mannered angels in *Christ aux Oliviers* and the nude in *Scènes des massacres de Scio*. In his view *Les Femmes d'Alger*, 'cette orientale étincelante de lumière et de couleur', represented 'le type de cette laideur exquise propre aux créations féminines de Delacroix',[95] which might seem extraordinary to us nowadays. Baudelaire shows himself aware of such misgivings by admitting that, generally speaking, Delacroix does not paint pretty women, not at any rate from the point of view of fashionable society, since they almost all appear ill, and that theirs is an inner beauty. The idea is developed in 1855 in a page of the *Exposition universelle* which is important for *Les Femmes d'Alger*. He divides Delacroix's women into two groups, the first transparent and decorative, like the nymph seen from the back in the left-hand corner of the Galerie d'Apollon in the Louvre, to which he might have added the angelic figures that pleased Hugo. The others (Cleopatras, Desdemonas, Ophelias, Virgins, or Mary Magdalenes) are what he

---

[94] George P. Mras, *Eugène Delacroix's Theory of Art* (Princeton: Princeton University Press, 1966), 58. Champfleury (*Son Regard et celui de Baudelaire* (Paris: Hermann, 1990), 122) also prefers the later work, and T. J. Clark (*The Absolute Bourgeois*, London: Thames and Hudson, 1973, 132) finds it 'more shadowy and spacious, owing more to Rembrandt than the first'.

[95] See Charles Hugo, *Victor Hugo en Zélande* (Paris: Lévy, 1868), 210.

calls 'femmes d'intimité', representing modern woman in her 'manifestation héroïque, dans le sens infernal ou divin', and the ideal of Romanticism and spirituality set out in the *Salon de 1846*. Whether they owe their distinction to the allure of crime, as with the savage jealousy of Medea about to kill her children, or to the odour of sanctity, as with *La Madeleine dans le désert*, whether their gestures are languid or violent, 'ces femmes malades du cœur ou de l'esprit ont dans les yeux le plombé de la fièvre ou la nitiscence anormale et bizarre de leur mal, dans le regard, l'intensité du surnaturalisme' (p. 594). The echo from 'Hymne à la Beauté' is unmistakable:

> Que tu viennes du ciel ou de l'enfer, qu'importe,
> O Beauté! monstre énorme, effrayant, ingénu!
> Si ton œil, ton souris, ton pied, m'ouvrent la porte
> D'un Infini que j'aime et n'ai jamais connu?

This feminine heroism, which lies in a certain spiritual intensity and has its counterpart in Sardanapalus and in Baudelaire himself, is expressed through a physical type which adds to the air of reverie 'la gorge abondante, avec une poitrine un peu étroite, le bassin ample, et des bras et des jambes charmantes'. We are here as far from the bland inhuman figures of Ingres as we are from the massive creations of Rubens or Courbet, whose 'poitrines' are too broad to set off sufficiently the opulence of the bosom. Médée and 'les femmes d'Alger' are the most perfect illustrations of this kind of physical and moral beauty, the one in its frenzied postulation towards evil, the other in its enigmatic and understated spirituality tinged with a brooding and curiously suspect sensuality.

The theme of exile and abandonment, common to both painter and poet, most often appears to go beyond its immediate or specific cause to take on a metaphysical dimension. Baudelaire had recognized in *Les Femmes d'Alger* a melancholy similar to that which in other paintings by Delacroix is summed up by 'une figure plus désolée, plus affaissée que les autres, en qui se résument toutes les douleurs environnantes; ainsi la femme agenouillée, à la chevelure pendante, sur le premier plan des *Croisés à Constantinople*; la vieille, si morne et si ridée, dans *Le Massacre de Scio*' (p. 440). In these works, as for Malraux, 'Why hast thou forsaken me?' has become the cry of all mankind.[96] For this reason there is little triumph on the part of the Crusaders in their entry into Constantinople. The posture of the woman bent over the body in

---

[96] André Malraux, *Les Voix du silence* (Paris: NRF, 1951), 628.

the foreground is matched by the fearful gestures of the old men on the left of the picture, by the glimpses of continuing violence in the background on the right, and above all by the melancholy and world-weariness of the central figure of the victorious Boudoin, before yet another scene of dolorous mystery.

Here is a great historical and literary scene, originally described by Villehardouin in the *Conqueste de Constantinople*. Typically Baudelaire's own description is not so much an interpretation as a kind of 'transposition d'art', a piece of poetic prose, a lyrical prose poem, quite different from the kind he was later to practise in *Le Spleen de Paris*:

Mais le tableau des *Croisés* est si profondément pénétrant, abstraction faite du sujet, par son harmonie orageuse et lugubre! Quel ciel et quelle mer! Tout y est tumultueux et tranquille, comme la suite d'un grand événement. La ville, échelonnée derrière les *Croisés* qui viennent de la traverser, s'allonge avec une prestigieuse vérité. Et toujours ces drapeaux miroitants, ondoyants, faisant se dérouler et claquer leurs plis lumineux dans l'atmosphère transparente! Toujours la foule agissante, inquiète, le tumulte des armes, la pompe des vêtements, la vérité emphatique du geste dans les grandes circonstances de la vie! Ces deux tableaux sont d'une beauté essentiellement shakespearienne. Car nul, après Shakespeare, n'excelle comme Delacroix à fondre dans une unité mystérieuse le drame et la rêverie. (p. 592)

What is remarkable here, as in so many of Baudelaire's commentaries on literary or historical paintings, is the way the subject matter is set aside. Clearly, he is sensitive to the drama of a great historical moment, but it is the incidentals that form the substance of the transposition— the sky, the sea, the banners, the town, the crowd, the costumes, and the gestures, in a word, all that makes up the 'magie suggestive' of the painting. The action and the event itself which would have occupied the attention of the historian are subordinated to these visual elements; and yet typically, paradoxically, and perhaps inevitably in this most literary of art critics, Shakespeare is brought in at the end, not just in order that Delacroix should be seen to take his place among the greatest creative minds, but because there is a definite and identifiable similarity between them. The final sentence of the paragraph is an original insight into the art of Delacroix, and also of Shakespeare, whose ability to combine drama and reverie can be seen, for example, in the scene with Duncan before Macbeth's castle or Ophelia in her madness distributing flowers.

Gesture and posture are fundamental preoccupations of Baudelaire's criticism, as is revealed in his comments on the *Pietà*, *La Lutte de Jacob avec l'ange,* or the remarkable *Roméo et Juliette* in which Juliet throws back her head in a movement of animal pleasure: 'ce mouvement vigoureux de la nuque est particulier aux chiens et aux chats heureux d'être caressés' (p. 439). One could add the servant in *Les Femmes d'Alger,* Virgil's arm raised in fear in *La Barque de Dante,* or the furtive twist of Medea's body away from her children to see if she is being observed. The gestures he picks out are never frozen or stylized, but are integral to the intensity and movement of the scene, like the fluttering draperies and the vibration of colour. Stasis is inimical to imagination, which may be a reason why Baudelaire is indifferent to still life. Gesture is essentially dramatic, indeed theatrical, having a continuation in the mind of the spectator; and so it is not by chance that he draws a parallel with the theatre, considering Delacroix unrivalled except by the great actors of the time, Frédéric Lemaître and Macready (p. 441). As we have seen, in the *Salon de 1846,* colour and outline were fundamental to great painting; in the obituary essay he adds gesture, which makes Delacroix especially attractive to literary men and poets: 'ce mérite très particulier et tout nouveau de M. Delacroix, qui lui a permis d'exprimer, simplement avec le contour, le geste de l'homme, si violent qu'il soit, et avec la couleur ce qu'on pourrait appeler l'atmosphère du drame humain' (p. 745). Gesture has its part in the suggestive art of the painter and its appeal to the memory, making of his painting 'une espèce de mnémotechnie de la grandeur et de la passion native de l'homme universel'.

Another great literary painting is the magnificent *Ovide chez les Scythes* of 1859 (Pl. 6) which Baudelaire comments on at some length in the *Salon* of that year. Here again Delacroix has departed considerably from his sources, the *Tristia* and the *Epistulae ex Ponto* in which the banished Roman poet laments his lot among a barbarous people in an inclement land:[97]

Harsh voices, grim faces, surest indication of their minds, neither hair nor beard trimmed by practised hand, right hands not slow to stab and wound with the knife which every barbarian wears fastened to his side. Among such men, alas! your bard is living, forgetful of the loves with which he played: such

---

[97] The following passage from the Supplement to Delacroix's *Journal* is clearly related to *Ovide chez les Scythes*: 'Cadre pour l'histoire du sentiment d'un cœur et d'une imagination malade, celle d'un homme qui après avoir vécu de la vie du monde se trouve devenu esclave chez les barbares, ou jeté dans une île déserte comme Robinson, forcé d'user des forces de son corps et de son industrie,—ce qui le fait revenir aux sentiments naturels et calme son imagination' (839).

men he sees, such men he hears, my friend. Would he might live and not die among them, so that his shade might yet be free of this hated place![98]

He himself appears a barbarian since he is not understood by them: 'barbarus hic ego sum, qui non intelligor ulli'.[99] Delacroix brings out well the contrast between the languid, 'feminine' poet[100] in his civilized garb with his detached melancholy and ennui, and the barbarous, primitive people clad in animal hides among whom he must spend his exile. Their crude dwellings, instruments, and arms, their beards, basic activities, and closeness to nature and animals, indicated by the mother with naked child, the wolflike dog and above all the disproportionate mare which is being milked to provide sustenance, serve no doubt to emphasize the exile of the poet of the *ars amatoria*; but the effect is much more pastoral than in Ovid, and the barbarians, far from presenting a threat, seem compassionate as well as curious, with offerings of wild fruits in addition to the mare's milk.[101] Delacroix's notice for the *Salon* which Baudelaire commends for its brevity reads simply: 'Les uns l'examinent avec curiosité, les autres lui font accueil à leur manière, et lui offrent des fruits sauvages et du lait de jument' (p. 636).[102]

Baudelaire's critical strategy is somewhat different here from in the previous painting, and there is no attempt to produce a *transposition d'art*. His comments are relatively few and general, evoking the posture of the exiled poet: 'le voilà couché sur des verdures sauvages, avec une mollesse et une tristesse féminines, le poète illustre qui enseigna l'*art d'aimer*' (p. 635), resigned to exile and death among a savage people. He then quotes a page from Chateaubriand's *Les Martyrs* in which the Christian exile Eudore, prisoner of Pharamond, describes

[98] Ovid, *Tristia: Epistulae ex ponto* (London: Heinemann, 1988), p. 237.

[99] Ibid. 248. Baudelaire quotes the same line in his account of *La Double Vie* by Asselineau (91).

[100] Cf. ibid. 107: 'I, who once shunned affairs, who was born for a carefree life of ease, who was soft and incapable of toil, am now suffering extremes'; and 109, 111: 'Aweary I lie among these far-away peoples in this far-away place, and thoughts come to me in my weakness of everything that is not here.'

[101] Similarly, in the fifth cupola of the Palais Bourbon showing 'Ovide chez les barbares' the poet is being offered sustenance by the barbarians.

[102] *Herminie chez les bergers*, inspired by Tasso, is also a painting of 1859, closely linked to *Ovide chez les Scythes* in the depiction of the primitive life of the shepherds, and of the sky, lake, mountains and distant perspectives. Zacharie Astruc writes of it: 'Le sentiment général est une rudesse aimable, une farouche grâce, une naïveté, une grandeur simple et bonne, une paix austère et bienveillante à l'âme agitée de passions, qui sont le pur écho de l'âme du Tasse.' (Quoted by Johnson, *Paintings*, iii. 148.)

his unexpected discovery of Ovid's grave, covered in vegetation in the midst of the wilderness, with a laurel tree growing on it. There follows a meditation on exile, the inability of talent to ensure happiness, and the ingratitude of Rome towards its illustrious poet, whose memory is still kept by the barbarous people who welcomed him as an Orpheus amid its forests. The passage is rendered all the more significant and moving as it marks the moment of Eudore's liberation, the culmination of his physical and spiritual wanderings from his childhood Christianity through a period of profligacy and loss of faith, and from the security of his family in Rome through a long exile and travail in majestic and savage landscapes. The theme of transience and death is constantly accentuated as Eudore's account of his wanderings pauses at the Simois and the tomb of Achilles, in the 'ville désolée' of Corinth, at the tomb of Scipio Africanus with its inscription, 'Ingrate patrie tu n'auras pas mes os', at Posilipo and Avernus with their Virgilian associations, in the Catacombs, and at the tomb of Cecilia Metella.[103] Baudelaire cites the passage not just because it is relevant to Ovid's death in exile, but because

le ton mélancolique du poète des *Martyrs* s'adapte à ce tableau, et la tristesse languissante du prisonnier chrétien s'y réfléchit heureusement. Il y a là l'ampleur de touche et de sentiments qui caractérisait la plume qui a écrit *Les Natchez*; et je reconnais, dans la sauvage idylle d'Eugène Delacroix, une *histoire parfaitement belle* parce qu'il y a mis la *fleur du désert, la grâce de la cabane et une simplicité à conter la douleur que je ne me flatte pas d'avoir conservées.*

The phrases in italic are taken from the epilogue to *Atala*,[104] so that in this brief passage we have an allusion to three works by Chateaubriand. What Baudelaire has done is to find a literary counterpart to the painting, which he calls a 'verdoyant *exil*', a kind of *correspondance* or analogue between painting and literature, giving a sense of expansiveness and depth. The exile in the painting *corresponds* to the sense of exile, everywhere present in Chateaubriand's work and indeed his life, whether it is that of René in the North American wilderness, of the émigré author in London, or of the Christian Eudore, all of which are muted variations on the exile of the Christian

---

[103] Cecilia Metella had a huge tomb built for herself on the via Appia.

[104] The only painting by Delacroix inspired by Chateaubriand is *Les Natchez*, which interestingly represents a scene from the epilogue to *Atala*: 'Une jeune Canadienne traversant le désert avec son époux est prise par les douleurs de l'enfantement et accouche; le père prend dans ses bras le nouveau-né' (*Journal*, 5 Oct. 1822, 28).

soul in time and space. There is a long tradition, going back to Dante, which sees Virgil as a link between the pagan and the Christian worlds. In *Les Martyrs*, in the symbolic liberation of Eudore at the tomb, there is a similar suggestion that for Chateaubriand, Ovid, who is described as an Orpheus figure, has replaced the writer of Book VI of the *Aeneid*. This perhaps explains why Baudelaire should strive to introduce into this remarkable commentary allusions (delicate and unobtrusive no doubt) to Christianity and its inevitable sense of disproportion between the temporal and the eternal. By multiplying the allusions to Chateaubriand and above all by placing his commentary at the end of the section on religious paintings, he has drawn this essentially pagan work into a context far removed from the intentions of its author, by what must be seen as a calculated rhetorical strategy to Christianize it.

Baudelaire, who must have identified himself with this exiled and unrecognized Orpheus, develops the sense of a correspondence by interpreting the painting not just as a moment in the unhappy life of the poet, but as the visual and pictorial counterpart to the poetic world of Ovid: 'Tout ce qu'il y a dans Ovide de délicatesse et de fertilité a passé dans la peinture de Delacroix; et, comme l'exil a donné au brillant poète la tristesse qui lui manquait, la mélancolie a revêtu de son vernis enchanteur le plantureux paysage du peintre.' The sense of a suggestive depth which Baudelaire admires in all great art is amply present in this splendid landscape: 'l'esprit s'y enfonce avec une lente et gourmande rêverie, comme dans le ciel, dans l'horizon de la mer, dans des yeux pleins de pensée, dans une tendance féconde et grosse de rêverie'. If the foreground depicts the poet's surroundings, the middle and background are the physical and objective correlative of his state of mind, being not some kind of realist backdrop, but an invitation to dream. The unruffled surface of the lake, the blue heights of the mountains and the sky, the magnificent clouds reminiscent of the works of Boudin which Baudelaire discovered in the same year, and the perspective retreating into the farthest distance, all indicate a depth corresponding to the Latin poet's sense of longing and exile. Appropriately, it was Chateaubriand himself who removed from literature the fauns, satyrs, and nymphs of neoclassicism 'pour rendre aux grottes leur silence, et aux bois leur rêverie',[105] and who, in

---

[105] Chateaubriand, *Essai sur les révolutions: Génie du christianisme* (Paris: Gallimard, 1978), 719.

opening up the depths of landscape, unlocked also those of the self and the imagination, without which a painting like *Ovide chez les Scythes* might perhaps have been inconceivable in France.

At no point is it clearer why Baudelaire considers Delacroix 'le plus *suggestif* de tous les peintres, celui dont les œuvres [. . .] font le plus penser, et rappellent à la mémoire le plus de sentiments et de pensées poétiques déjà connus, mais qu'on croyait enfouis pour toujours dans la nuit du passé', and why he regards his work as 'une espèce de mnémotechnie de la grandeur et de la passion native de l'homme universel' (p. 745). But the associations aroused by the painting do not stop there, but lead us into the heart of Baudelaire's own mental universe, as the coy allusion to the charm it must have 'aux tempéraments nerveux et poétiques' indicates. The specific allusion is to Fromentin, about whom he promises to speak shortly, but there can be little doubt that he includes himself among such spirits, so that the thematic resonances of the painting reach back to his own poetry, to 'les grands ciels qui font rêver d'éternité', the seas, mountains, valleys, and lakes of 'Elévation', to 'le petit lac immobile' set amid the mountains and the depth of sky and sea in the prose poems 'Le Gâteau' and 'Le *Confiteor* de l'artiste', to the green eyes of 'Le Poison' which are 'Lacs où mon âme tremble et se voit à l'envers', and to the fertility of Cybele in 'J'aime le souvenir . . .' and 'Bohémiens en voyage'. The suggestion of fertility emanates of course from the mare, with its proud and powerful head caught in a dramatic movement towards the viewer. Harshly criticized at the time for being so out of proportion as to be unreal, it was judged by one wit to be the partner of the Trojan Horse.[106] Delacroix, however, was not interested in realism, but in objects in their relationship to the characters in a painting and in what he called their 'exactitude pour l'imagination'.[107] The disproportionate size of the mare, which literally foregrounds the sense of the vital, the primitive, and the barbarous, may be read as another of these characteristic and intentional *bizarreries* of Delacroix's art which have the power to astonish and add drama to his paintings. But whatever one may think, the mare finds a thematic analogue in the 'louve au coeur gonflé de tendresses communes' of 'J'aime le souvenir . . .', and negatively with the she-wolf in 'Le Cygne', that other great poem of exile,

---

[106] See P. de Saint-Victor in 1859, of the 'bête gigantesque qui encombre le premier plan': 'On dirait la jument du Cheval de Troie.' (Quoted by Johnson, *Paintings*, iii. 151.)

[107] *Journal*, 10 Oct. 1855, 552.

which nurtures those 'qui s'abreuvent de pleurs / Et tettent la
Douleur comme une bonne louve'.

This question of thematic analogues has to be handled with care.
Claude Pichois, following Crépet/Blin and Adam, suggests that
Baudelaire was thinking of Boudin and *Ovide chez les Scythes* when in
1861 he composed the octosyllabic sonnet 'Horreur sympathique',
which carries an allusion to the author of the *Tristia* in the second
quatrain: 'Je ne geindrai pas comme Ovide / Chassé du paradis
latin.'[108] But the 'ciel bizarre et livide / Tourmenté comme ton destin'
of the sonnet and the clouds which are 'les corbillards' of the poet's
dreams are the exact opposite of the luminous, ideal skyscapes of
Boudin and Delacroix's masterpiece. Similarly, one should be wary of
making of 'Le Cygne' too close a thematic analogue of Delacroix's
painting, in spite of a direct reference to Ovid and the shared theme of
exile. The allusion is to the *Metamorphoses*, where the creator orders
man to fix his gaze on the skies and stars,[109] but the intention is clearly
ironic, since the swan seems to be reproaching God instead of finding a justification for its suffering. The links in 'Le Cygne' are not
with Delacroix, but intratextually, with 'Les Aveugles' of the same
'Tableaux parisiens' section with their eyes lifted upwards, and
intertextually with Vigny's 'La Maison du Berger' in which mankind
'cherche en vain au ciel ses muets Spectateurs'.[110]

It is a critical commonplace that the 'spleen' poems and 'Tableaux
parisiens' accentuate the sense of discordance, while many of the
earlier poems in the collection such as 'Elévation' and 'La Chevelure'
give the sense of a rising of the mind and of expansiveness amid the
proliferation of analogies and memories. In 'La Chevelure' especially,
past, present, and future merge into one dimension, in which the poet
is installed without feeling the anguish of the passage of time. The
point of departure is the extraordinary image in the first stanza: 'Pour
peupler ce soir l'alcôve obscure / Des souvenirs dormant dans cette

[108] *Oc.* i. 983.
[109] Ovid, *Metamorphoses*, 1.84–6:

> pronaque cum spectent animalia cetera terram,
> os homini sublime dedit caelumque videre
> iussit et erectos ad sidera tollere vultus.

[110] Clearly in 'Les Aveugles', as is borne out by his use of the rhyme 'beugle / aveugle',
Baudelaire is thinking of Vigny's poem:

> Sur ce taureau de fer qui fume, souffle et beugle
> L'homme a monté trop tôt. Nul ne connaît encor
> Quels orages en lui porte ce rude aveugle.

chevelure, / Je la veux agiter dans l'air comme un mouchoir!' In order
to understand this image, we should need not so much the power to see
it with the inner eye—indeed to give it too precise an outline would be
absurd—but rather the faith and the creative power to live it, or rather
relive it, as a journey of discovery, a deliverance from the restrictions
of the present, the unfolding of a past with all its memories, and above
all as an opening on to the future. By spreading out over the three
dimensions of past, present, and future, memory brings about a transfiguration of time, which loses its threat, its uncertainties, and its
irreversibility. Through the echantment of memory, the poet finds
himself in a time which is, so to speak, circular; the past is projected
into a future that is both open to joy and closed to anxiety, and the
future is endowed with the reassuring certainty of the past while still
keeping its appeal to adventure and novelty. Similarly, the intimate
space of the alcove, following the expansive dynamism of the
poem from 'la langoureuse Asie' to 'la brûlante Afrique', takes on the
dimensions of the infinite, without, however, losing anything of its
finite and intimate quality; and this infinite space, obeying the same
development and impulsion of memory and time, undergoes a parallel
transformation, and is changed into an habitable milieu without
vertigo or claustration. The effect of the hair and of the memories it
contains is to make the azure blue of the sky 'immense et rond'; and
this roundness of time and space is the essential characteristic of the
dreamed-of perfection, in which past and future, alcove and
abyss, claustrophobia and vertigo, time and eternity cease, as in
Breton, 'd'être perçus contradictoirement'.[111] These privileged moments, when space and time are transfigured, are truly lyrical
moments, what Baudelaire identifies in Banville as 'les belles heures de
la vie' (p. 163), in which the inner man 's'élance en l'air par trop de
légèreté et de dilatation, comme pour atteindre une région plus haute'
(p. 164).[112] Delacroix's paintings similarly seem to him to be 'la
traduction des beaux jours de l'esprit' (p. 596) and '*l'âme dans ses
belles heures*' (p. 637), nowhere more successfully or movingly than in
the great canvas of *Ovide chez les Scythes*. It is a dream that is so
recorded, and by that he means not the disordered 'capharnaüms de la
nuit', but a vision which is the fruit of an intense meditation, analo-

---

[111] André Breton, *Œuvres complètes* (Paris: Gallimard, 1988), i. 781.
[112] Cf the following statement in the first essay on Gautier: 'La poésie lyrique s'élance,
mais toujours d'un mouvement élastique et ondulé. Tout ce qui est brusque et cassé lui
déplaît, et elle le renvoie au drame et au roman de mœurs' (126).

gous to the high moments of his own lyricism, and which he defines as 'l'infini dans le fini'.[113]

But even at this high point of convergence the links with the painting are not exhausted; for just as Delacroix has produced a visual analogue to the poetic world of Ovid, so Baudelaire in 'Les Phares' sums up in one famous quatrain the painterly world of his ideal artist. Criticism, he claims in 1855, must seek 'plutôt à pénétrer intimement le tempérament de chaque artiste et les mobiles qui le font agir qu'à analyser, à raconter chaque œuvre minutieusement' (p. 583). It is in 1855 too that he cites and explains the quatrain in order to bring the reader to a deeper understanding of Delacroix's mental universe and what makes him *sui generis*.

> Delacroix, lac de sang, hanté des mauvais anges,
> Ombragé par un bois de sapins toujours vert,
> Où, sous un ciel chagrin, des fanfares étranges
> Passent comme un soupir étouffé de Weber.

He then explains these verses 'dont la sincérité peut faire passer la bizarrerie': '*Lac de sang*: le rouge;—*hanté des mauvais anges*: surnaturalisme;—*un bois toujours vert*: le vert, complémentaire du rouge;—*un ciel chagrin*: les fonds tumultueux et orageux de ses tableaux;—*les fanfares de Weber*: idées de musique romantique que réveillent les harmonies de sa couleur.' Here in miniature is the kind of criticism which was to be central to the critical preoccupations of Proust and, later, Georges Poulet and his Genevan followers.

Poulet is one of the few critics who have sought to define Baudelaire's critical method, claiming him in *La Conscience critique* as the illustrious precursor of the school of 'la critique d'identification', of which Poulet himself was the leading exponent. Seeing a parallel between Baudelaire's method as poet and as a critic, Poulet argues that just as the 'poète-flâneur' experiences 'cette sainte prostitution de l'âme qui se donne tout entière, poésie et charité, à l'imprévu qui se montre, à l'inconnu qui passe', so also the poet as critic will experience a similar pleasure by entering into the skin of his writer and assimilating his work, in much the same way as he espouses the crowd; so that, like Poulet's, Baudelaire's criticism has as its starting point a

---

[113] For an excellent account of the possible sources of this phrase see Pichois's note (1397). See also Delacroix's *Journal*, 8 Oct. 1822, 29: 'chez [le peintre], comme dans la nature extérieure, la part est faite franchement à ce qui est fini et à ce qui est infini, c'est-à-dire à ce que l'âme trouve qui la remue intérieurement dans les objets qui ne frappent que les sens'.

movement of participation in and identification with the experience of
the author, reminiscent, one might say, of the posture of the young
Marcel in front of the hawthorn bushes at Tansonville, as in an effort
to define the charm they hold for him, he strives to 'm'unir au rythme
qui jetait leurs fleurs, ici et là, avec une allégresse juvenile'.[114]
Baudelaire does not, it is claimed, hold the work at a distance in order
to understand it. On the contrary, he is more like the actor, Rouvière
for example, who endeavours to step inside his role, so that his task is
in a sense mimetic, involving not a relation of subject to object, but
rather of subject to subject. In this posture of *disponibilité* the poet,
whose poetry is eminently suggestive, becomes as critic, according to
Poulet, 'une âme suggestible' responding to the suggestions and
promptings inherent in the work.

But clearly, argues Poulet, what is received by the critic is not the
same as what is transmitted, the 'cause' in the work and in the mind of
the artist is not identical to the 'effect' in the reader or spectator. What
is received is something analogous to the experience of the artist,
something which, arising from the memory of the critic, is 'equivalent', but not identical. Poulet gives as an example of this process
Baudelaire's piece on Marceline Desbordes-Valmore in which her
poetry appears to him as a 'simple jardin anglais, romantique et
romanesque' (p. 149). In this essay the poet states that he had always
taken delight in seeking in external nature 'des exemples et des
métaphores qui me servissent à caractériser les jouissances et les impressions d'un ordre spirituel' (p. 148), and from this statement and
from the image of the garden Poulet concludes that in the final analysis
Baudelaire's criticism is primarily concerned with finding the metaphoric equivalent of the work in question. It is essentially metaphorical, since the act of identification consists in finding 'un ensemble
d'images, où se reflèteront les images appartenant à l'univers poétique
que cet acte s'est donné pour fin de définir'.[115]

What Poulet says of Baudelaire's critical approach is convincing,
but he seems over-hasty to generalize, since other examples of the
approach are hard to find in the literary criticism. It is principally in
his *art* criticism that Baudelaire exploits the idea of a metaphorical
reaction to a painting or drawing. In the *Salon de 1846* he suggests that
since a fine picture is nature reflected by an artist, the best criticism
would be this picture reflected by an intelligent and sensitive mind:

[114] *A la recherche du temps perdu*, vol. i (Paris: Gallimard, 1987), 136.
[115] Georges Poulet, *La Conscience critique* (Paris: José Corti, 1971), 46.

'Ainsi le meilleur compte rendu d'un tableau pourra être un sonnet ou une élégie' (p. 418), and there is of course no lack of such transpositions in *Les Fleurs du Mal*. But the finest example of this metaphorical criticism is beyond doubt the essay on Wagner, itself a kind of transposition, in which his stated aim is to demonstrate that 'la véritable musique suggère des idées analogues dans des cerveaux différents' (p. 784). Even here however, as with the writings on art, the idea of a metaphorical criticism has to be approached with some circumspection, since what is involved is not so much a critical method as a prescriptive aesthetic which seeks to distinguish between good and bad contemporary art. Baudelaire's denunciation of draughtsmen and praise of Delacroix are motivated by his belief that great art, proceeding as it does from the memory of the artist, speaks directly to the memory of the spectator. Poulet's argument appears in the end tautological or circular, since, if the specific quality and intention of art is to address itself to the memory, then the critic whose memory is not so aroused is merely insensitive and incapable of responding to the suggestive magic of the work. The so-called critical method is in fact merely the inevitable counterpart to the prescriptive aesthetic.

At other times Baudelaire seeks to isolate the 'speciality'[116] of a writer or artist, what makes him *sui generis*, or more generally to 'm'informer du pourquoi, et [. . .] transformer ma volupté en connaissance' (p. 786). As a critic/journalist he adopts many strategies, depending on whether he is moved by admiration, friendship, anger, financial necessity, or the pressure of colleagues. He can strive to present his subject as faithfully as possible to a wider public, or use him to define his own attitudes and ideas, and to promulgate them. Clearly, his contempt of eclecticism does not extend to the less exalted *métier* of criticism. Though it is by no means his only posture, Baudelaire does practise a criticism of identification, nowhere more successfully than when he is writing about a form of art other than literary, in the essay on Wagner, or in his pages on Delacroix, which involve a discourse that is the critical counterpart of the high moments of lyricism in *Les Fleurs du Mal*, similarly dominated by echoes and analogies. Unlike the academic critic whose fingers have been paralysed by his pen, those of the poet–critic run with agility 'sur l'immense clavier des *correspondances*' (p. 577). But above all, his art criticism is metaphorical to the extent that it conjures up the work of

---

[116] Delacroix himself is given to comparisons and contrasts to define the 'speciality' of a painter.

another artist, working most often in a different medium; a criticism that sees *Hamlet* in the *Pietà*, Weber in *Les Femmes d'Alger*, and Chateaubriand in *Ovide chez les Scythes*. In his brief account of the 'spirit' of the Luxembourg ceiling which follows a lengthy quotation from the passage in Dante which inspired it, he praises Delacroix's use of light and the way he has combined historical and landscape painting, but the most suggestive notations are those that establish links with other works: 'Cela fait penser aux pages les plus verdoyantes du *Télémaque*, et rend tous les souvenirs que l'esprit a emportés des récits elyséens' (p. 438). Even the uncharacteristic blue and white sky gains in resonance as it is linked to the ideal transparency of Bonington's watercolours. As a creative artist Baudelaire excelled in the least expansive genres—sonnets, fixed forms, 'petits poèmes en prose'—and this predilection for brevity and compactness also characterizes his moments of critical enthusiasm. It is significant that he is at his most expansive in his *éreintages*, of Vernet or Scheffer, and in the communication of his anger and contempt. In his early art criticism, especially the *Salon* of 1846, even his exposition of theory can be allusive, presenting not so much an elaborate exposition as a series of terse, suggestive, and memorable pronouncements. It is in his praise of an artist that he is at his most dense and explosive, and that he shows his *spécialité* as a critic, what makes him *sui generis*. Gita May has perfectly understood his method: 'Baudelaire, au lieu de *conter* un tableau ou une statue, ne s'attarde volontiers que devant ce qui fait exquisément vibrer sa sensibilité.' Whereas Diderot's descriptions are '*impressionnistes* et *analytiques*', the poet's are '*mnémoniques* et *synthétiques*'.[117]

---

[117] Gita May, *Diderot et Baudelaire: critiques d'art* (Paris and Geneva: Minard/Droz, 1957), 109, 120.

3

De l'essence du rire

THERE EXISTS a splendid photograph of Baudelaire,[1] taken by Neyt in Brussels in 1864, and dedicated by the poet to his friend Auguste Malassis, 'le seul être dont le rire ait allégé ma tristesse en Belgique', with a caption adapted from a famous poem by Horace, 'Ridentem ferient ruinae'.[2] In front of this portrait one feels an unease, born of the discrepancy between the poet's expression and the Latin inscription. Baudelaire appears, already considerably aged, in an aristocratic posture, his abundant though greying hair swept back from the forehead to show its breadth and nobility, his lips set in a stoical expression befitting the Horatian moral of a man whom the ruins of the world would strike unafraid. Dignified, haughty even, sad, above all impassive, there is nothing in the portrait to suggest laughter, and certainly not the ironic and revolted laughter promised by the inscription. That admirable head, which is not without bitterness, is of a sage who neither laughs nor trembles, and if Malassis's laughter had lightened his sadness, one would not have guessed it from the evidence of the photograph.

This is not the only place where the reader is left puzzled and uncertain by Baudelaire's attitude to laughter; for in *De l'essence du rire*, which unlike the *Salons* has aroused comparatively little critical attention, one finds alongside the familar notions of man's first disobedience and the Fall passages describing a state analogous to what is commonly referred to as 'le fou rire'. Furthermore, in pages where he writes of a 'hilarité folle, excessive, et qui se traduit en des déchirements et des pâmoisons interminables' (p. 535), and where he declares that the laughter aroused by the grotesque contains something profound, axiomatic, and primitive which is nearer to innocence and absolute joy than the laughter caused by the comedy of manners,

---

[1] *Baudelaire: documents iconographiques*, ed. Claude Pichois and François Ruchon (Geneva: Pierre Cailler 1960), plate 57.

[2] Horace, *Odes*, III. 3: 'Si fractus inlabatur orbis / impavidum ferient ruinae.' Baudelaire also refers to the ode in the *Salon de 1859* (624).

we feel momentarily disoriented, uncertain of recognizing the creator of the sombre and sinister world of *Les Fleurs du Mal* and *Le Spleen de Paris*. But what is even more puzzling is that there are moments when our appreciation of the power and clarity of this remarkable essay is replaced by a feeling of unease before a certain slippage in the terms used, by ambiguities in tone and obscurities in the development of the principal ideas.

The first moment of unease comes early in the essay, at the beginning of the second section, after the brief two-page introduction. The opening paragraph is so odd as to be worth quoting in its entirety:

Le Sage ne rit qu'en tremblant. De quelles lèvres pleines d'autorité, de quelle plume parfaitement orthodoxe est tombée cette étrange et saisissante maxime? Nous vient-elle du roi philosophe de la Judée? Faut-il l'attribuer à Joseph de Maistre, ce soldat animé de l'Esprit-Saint? J'ai un vague souvenir de l'avoir lue dans un de ses livres, mais donnée comme citation sans doute. Cette sévérité de pensée et de style va bien à la sainteté majestueuse de Bossuet; mais la tournure elliptique de la pensée et la finesse quintessenciée me porteraient plutôt à en attribuer l'honneur à Bourdaloue, l'impitoyable psychologue chrétien. Cette singulière maxime me revient sans cesse à l'esprit depuis que j'ai conçu le projet de cet article, et j'ai voulu m'en débarrasser tout d'abord. (pp. 526-7)

Much scholarly time has been spent in tracking down the compelling maxim that opens the argument. James Patty's subtle and learned article,[3] in which its origin is traced to Bossuet's *Maximes et réflexions sur la comédie* of 1694, has, however, won universal assent. The essence of his argument is that the maxim is a conflation of two passages. In the first Bossuet refers to a verse in Ecclesiasticus: 'le fou éclate en riant, mais le sage rit à peine à petit bruit', adding in explanation, 'et d'une bouche timide'. In the second he claims of another maxim in Ecclesiasticus,[4] 'Qui méprise les petites choses, tombe peu à peu', that the believer 'doit toujours trembler à cette sentence du sage'. Patty's argument could hardly be more convincing, and one has the impression of being in the presence of a definite source.[5]

---

[3] James Patty, 'Baudelaire and Bossuet on Laughter', *Publications of the Modern Language Association of America*, 80 (Sept. 1965), 459–61.

[4] Ecclesiasticus 21: 23, and 19: 1.

[5] Poinsinet de Sivry, *Traité des causes physiques et morales du rire* ([1768] Exeter: Exeter University Publications, 1986), 29, quotes the following passage from a Comte Oxenstiern which is clearly modelled on Ecclesiasticus 21: 23: 'Le rire immodéré d'un sot est le partage [. . .] / Que tout homme d'esprit, & le sage sur-tout, / Ne rit jamais sans un peu de scrupule.'

What is less convincing, however, and causes unease, is the suggestion that the conflation is the result of Baudelaire's bad memory, excusable by the lapse of time between the first version of his essay, which may have been as early as 1845, and its publication in 1855.[6] Patty is surely right in thinking that Baudelaire would not have hesitated to modify the maxim 'if his artistic instincts had dictated such an alteration'. And indeed it seems most unlikely that his unconscious mind, aided by a faulty memory, would have come up with such a perfect formulation uniting the rhythm of a well-crafted octosyllable and the classical 'ne . . . que' form with the depth and suggestiveness of what has been called Baudelaire's 'aphorismes-abîmes'.[7] In addition the maxim is both mysterious and endowed with the explosive power of a squib, its suggestive magic being all the greater for its lack of an immediate explicit meaning. It contrasts sharply with, for example, such maxims from La Rochefoucauld as 'Tout le monde se plaint de sa mémoire, et personne ne se plaint de son jugement', which is almost self-sufficient, or 'L'hypocrisie est un hommage que le vice rend à la vertu',[8] which, though immediately comprehensible, requires considerable development and explication. But here with Baudelaire the maxim appears at first as a puzzle, requiring several pages to spell out and make explicit the idea which its perfect form both contains and partly conceals. Furthermore, the puzzling aspect is increased by the double meaning of 'en tremblant', which indicates, as the essay goes on to demonstrate, that the Sage's status as Sage is threatened by laughter, and at the same time turns the maxim into a truism, since all laughter involves some degree of trembling or 'convulsion'. The maxim which set out to distinguish the Sage from other human beings seems curiously to reduce him to their level, casting doubt on its own validity in the process. All of this inclines one to the conclusion that the poet's obsession with the maxim and his uncertainty about its origin are feigned,[9] a kind of tactical 'spoof', whose rhetorical *raison d'être* is at least twofold.

First, anyone acquainted with Baudelaire's use of maxims has

---

[6] See Pichois, 'La Date de l'essai de Baudelaire sur le rire et les caricaturistes', in *Etudes et témoignages*, 80–94.

[7] See my *Baudelaire and 'Le Spleen de Paris'* (Oxford: Clarendon Press, 1987), p. 51–4.

[8] La Rochefoucauld, *Maximes*, nos. 89, 218.

[9] Here I agree with the broad lines of Michele Hannoosh's analysis of the 'sources' of the maxim in *Baudelaire and Caricature: From the Comic to an Art of Modernity* (Pennsylvania State University Press, 1992), 15 ff., though she tends to see ironies where I would prefer to be more guarded.

learned to be on guard, fearful of falling victim to his ambiguities and unstable ironies, and of not being sure, as with Flaubert, whether 'on se fout de lui, oui ou non'.[10] The opening sentence of *Choix de maximes consolantes sur l'amour* of 1846 contains a maxim which seems to destroy itself in the utterance: 'Quiconque écrit des maximes aime charger son caractère;—les jeunes se griment,—les vieux s'adonis- ent.'[11] The validity and wisdom normally considered essential to max- ims are here undermined by the intentions of the creators of maxims. The young affect the wisdom of their elders, while those same elders give themselves the allure and elegance of the young. Since the idea is couched in the form of a maxim, its reliability is immediately put in question, and it takes on something of the Cretan liar paradox, because in order to 'make sense' it has to be seen as true and false at the same time, which is unsettling. This is not the only place in Baudelaire where the use of maxims produces a sense of unreliability, at variance with the genre's function and its, at least, traditional inscription in a world of fixed truths and essences. The artist in 'La Corde',[12] for example, is made to appear an insensitive and superficial charlatan because of his self-satisfied sententiousness, and his constant recourse to maxims arouses the suspicions of the reader, who is eventually guided towards a more complex interpretation of the poem than the one proposed by the narrator.

But it may be asked what good purpose can be served by such an irony at a crucial point in a philosophical essay on laughter, in which the poet is bent upon convincing his reader of the validity of his argument? Though many may have been taken in by the apparent candour of the passage (it was one of the misfortunes of Baudelaire's life that his ironies were sometimes believed), it seems clear from the number of possible sources that he is throwing his reader a line, and a fairly clear indication of the true origins of the maxim. Could it be part of the legendary wisdom of Solomon? If so, it would be easy enough to check. Joseph de Maistre? But no, since it was probably a quotation from another source. It seems to have something of the intellectual rigour of Bossuet, but then the elliptic style suggests Bourdaloue. The implication is surely that the maxim is to be found in none of these authorities, all of which are plausible but none wholly satisfactory. Baudelaire's display of his reading and literary awareness does not

[10] Gustave Flaubert, *Correspondance* (Paris: Gallimard, 1973), i. 679.
[11] *Oc.* i. 546.
[12] See below, pp. 246–9.

appear genuine, nor is it meant to. With more than a suspicion of arrogance, and only a semblance of modesty, what Baudelaire is doing here, tongue in cheek, is to give his maxim the prestige and the authority of the spiritual giants among whom he is implicitly ranking himself.[13] Here is a thought, he seems to be saying, so rich and so deep that it might have come from the pen of the greatest religious thinkers; but I would not make so bold as to claim in public such genius for myself. His sleight of hand is strategic: to give authority to a new and startling theory from an intelligent, but still relatively unknown and unrecognized writer. But the disproportion is clear, and the irony bends back on the author, who appears to be claiming a wisdom beyond his age, on a par with that of these great canonical figures.

His choice of names from the Bible and the great figures of Christian *spiritualité* is also strategic. There is no mention of the philosophers of the ancient world—Plato, Aristotle, Cicero, Quintilian; no mention of Hobbes, Kant, Voltaire, or Descartes. By referring solely to the Christian tradition, he has subtly disposed his reader to think along such lines and to accept his theory more readily. His rhetorical trick is to suggest that the maxim came first, and that his obsession with its tormenting obscurities gave birth to the theory, whereas the truth is that he has fabricated the maxim in order to persuade the reader of the excellence of his theory, which is grounded, not in some moral speculation, but in metaphysics and theology, in the certainties of the Christian view of the human condition.[14]

The analysis of the proposition is conducted in three rapid paragraphs which pass from a consideration of the Sage to that of his opposite, the fool, and then to a conclusion, thus following, however tentatively, something not far removed from the traditional pattern of thesis, antithesis, synthesis. If the Sage fears laughter as he fears temptation, it is because there is a hidden contradiction between his nature as Sage and the primordial nature of laughter. Baudelaire hastens to corroborate immediately 'le caractère officiellement chrétien'

---

[13] There is nothing exaggerated or comic (*pace* Michele Hannoosh, *Baudelaire and Caricature*, 17) in Baudelaire's references to Maistre as 'ce soldat animé de l'Esprit-Saint', to 'la sainteté majestueuse' of Bossuet, or 'la finesse quintessenciée' of Bourdaloue. His admiration for them would be difficult to exaggerate. The joke is that he is indirectly applying these qualities to himself.

[14] M. A. Ruff, *L'Esprit du mal et l'esthétique baudelairienne* (Paris: Armand Colin, 1955), 257: 'c'est une question proprement esthétique, que Baudelaire essaie de résoudre par la métaphysique et la théologie'.

of the maxim, by supporting the view that the Sage *par excellence*, the Word made flesh, never laughed, though the gospels relate that he knew both anger and tears.[15] Driving his argument home, he emphasizes that for the writer of the maxim,'un chrétien, sans doute', the Sage will be wary of allowing himself to laugh, and that the comic vanishes from the point of view of absolute knowledge and power. If the Sage does not laugh readily, it stands to reason, if one inverts the proposition and considers its antithesis, that laughter is the mark of madmen and fools, implying always some degree of ignorance and weakness. The synthesis follows without delay in words that are powerfully axiomatic: 'le rire humain est intimement lié à l'accident d'une chute ancienne, d'une dégradation physique et morale'. What is interesting about the conduct of the argument is that at each stage Baudelaire is moved, a sceptic might say forced, to lay down benchmarks from Christianity, particularly at the weak or doubtful points: by citing Jesus as the Sage *par excellence*, by insisting that the author of the maxim is probably a Christian, and by preceding his 'synthesis' by the crucial condition, 'si l'on veut se mettre au point de vue de l'esprit orthodoxe'. It is clear that without this Christian display the argument would lack the force and momentum to take it through its various stages to the desired conclusion. One would be left with the Sage's distrust of laughter, which would not take us much further than Ecclesiasticus and Bossuet's addendum, or Lavater's dictum, which George Clapton suggested as a possible source, 'Le Sage sourit souvent et rit rarement.'[16]

In support of his point that laughter is linked to the doctrine of the Fall, Baudelaire borrows and adapts a page from his contemporary, Chennevières, claiming that in the garden of Eden,

---

[15] For the Christian prejudice against comedy and spectacles, see Tertullian, *De spectaculis*, and Jacques-Bénigne Bossuet, *Maximes et réflexions sur la comédie* (1694). Not all Christian writers, however, disapprove of laughter. Pascal, in the eleventh *Lettre provinciale*, claims that the first words of God to Adam after the fall show 'un discours de moquerie, et *une ironie piquante*, selon les Pères' [. . .] 'il se moqua de luy en cét estat par ces paroles de risée: *Voilà l'homme qui est devenu comme l'un de nous: Ecce Adam quasi unus ex nobis. Ce qui est une ironie sanglante et sensible* dont Dieu le *piquoit vivement*, selon S. Chrysostôme et les interpretes.'

In Jacob Bidermann's Jesuit play *Philemon Martyr* the actor–buffoon is converted and martyred in one day, whereupon there is rejoicing and laughter in heaven.

For the idea that God or Christ cannot laugh, see, among Baudelaire's contemporaries, Félicité de Lamennais, *Esquisse d'une philosophie* (Paris, 1840), iii. 371; Paul Scudo, *Philosophie du rire* (Paris: Poirée, 1840), 134, 139, 147.

[16] 'Lavater, Gall et Baudelaire', *Revue de littérature comparée* xiii (1933), 444.

c'est-à-dire dans le milieu où il semblait à l'homme que toutes les choses créées étaient bonnes, la joie n'était pas dans le rire. Aucune peine ne l'affligeant, son visage était simple et uni, et le rire qui agite maintenant les nations ne déformait point les traits de sa face. [. . .] Au point de vue de mon philosophe chrétien, le rire de ses lèvres est signe d'une aussi grande misère que les larmes de ses yeux. (p. 528)

Once again, he is at pains in this borrowed page to underline the Christian origins of the thought and suggest a continuity from the creator of the original maxim, his Christian philosopher, to the decription of the earthly paradise, the loss of which is evoked in the Pascalian overtones of the expression *misère*.

Fearing that his argument may appear too general and tinged with mystical apriorism, he typically hastens to provide a concrete illustration, inviting the reader to imagine the impossibly innocent Virginie from Bernardin de Saint-Pierre's sentimental novel *Paul et Virginie*, freshly disembarked from her tropical island paradise, and confronted in Paris by some gross caricature depicting the supposed outrages of Marie-Antoinette or some 'bonne farce de boxeurs, quelque énormité britannique, pleine de sang caillé et assaisonnée de quelques monstrueux *goddam*' (p. 529). Virginie's reaction is one of incomprehension, since all she had known on her island had been the love of family and the sexless companionship of Paul; and yet with a 'reploiement d'ailes subit' and a 'frémissement d'une âme qui se voile et veut se retirer', this 'angel' feels, instinctively, 'que le scandale était là'. The intertextual reference is unmistakably to Vigny's *mystère*, 'Eloa', where the angel of pity, tempted by her very nature to descend into the depths of hell from the luminous heights of heaven, averts her eyes heavenwards from the spectacle of the convulsive sorrow of the half-repentant Satan.[17] Had Baudelaire wished to find a similar reaction he could have found it in Bernardin's novel itself, in the scene where Virginie pleads to the evil owner for mercy for his fugitive slave. Eyeing her knowingly, he swears that he will forgive the slave not for

[17] *Œuvres complètes* (Paris: Gallimard, 1986), i. 29:

Mais sitôt qu'elle vit sur sa tête pensive
De l'enfer décelé la douleur convulsive,
Etonnée et tremblante, elle éleva ses yeux;
Plus forte, elle parut se souvenir des cieux,
Et souleva deux fois ses ailes argentées,
Entrouvrant pour gémir ses lèvres enchantées,
Ainsi qu'un jeune enfant, s'attachant aux roseaux,
Tente de faibles cris étouffés sous les eaux.

love of God, but for love of Virginie herself, whereupon our angelic heroine takes flight in distress and fear.[18] In all these instances the situation and reaction smack of the cliché and the *poncif*, which no doubt explains why Baudelaire adopts ironically and almost blasphemously a biblical expression to lead into his conclusion: 'Et, en vérité, je vous le dis, qu'elle ait compris ou qu'elle n'ait pas compris, il lui restera de cette impression je ne sais quel malaise, quelque chose qui ressemble à la peur.'

In the third section he argues that a proof that laughter is one of the pips in the paradisal apple is the agreement among commentators that it stems from a sense of one's superiority. Though he mentions no names, it is possible that he was thinking of Hobbes's definition: '*Sudden glory*, is the passion which maketh those *Grimaces* called LAUGHTER; and is caused either by somme sudden act of their own, that pleaseth them; or by the apprehension of some deformed thing in another, by comparison whereof they suddenly applaud themselves.'[19] A more likely source, however, is Stendhal, according to whom laughter springs from our pride, from '*la vue soudaine de notre propre supériorité*'.[20] Baudelaire is quick to comment that this idea is not very profound; but with a minimal addition of two exclamations—'Idée satanique s'il en fut jamais! Orgueil et aberration!'—he lends it depth and shunts it into line with his own, orthodox, thinking. It was of course Lucifer's pride and sense of superiority over the other angels that brought about his downfall and with it the change of his name to Satan. For confirmation of the theory, argues Baudelaire, one has only to think of the laughter of madmen, whose madness lies most often in the idea of their own superiority, or to imagine Virginie contaminated by the capital, gaining in knowledge of the world, and developing with the idea of her superiority the capacity for laughter. Why, he asks, do we laugh at someone falling in the street?

Qu'y a-t-il de si réjouissant dans le spectacle d'un homme qui tombe sur la glace ou sur le pavé, qui trébuche au bout d'un trottoir, pour que la face de son frère en Jésus-Christ se contracte d'une façon désordonnée, pour que les

---

[18] *Paul et Virginie* (Paris: Garnier-Flammarion, 1966), 105.

[19] *Leviathan*, ed. R. Tuck (Cambridge: Cambridge University Press, 1991), I. VI.

[20] 'Qu'est-ce que le rire?', in *Molière, Shakespeare: la comédie et le rire* (Paris: Le Divan, 1930), 321.

muscles de son visage se mettent à jouer subitement comme une horloge à midi ou un joujou à ressorts?' (p. 530)[21]

It is unconscious pride that triggers the sudden and irresistible outbreak of the laugher; I am not so stupid, absent-minded, unaware, not to notice the obstacle or pitfall. The effect of falling is to precipitate our walker from the time of projects and efficacious action into that of imperfection and absurdity. Here he was, hastening towards some action or project belonging to a whole system of values, decisions, judgements, and choices that form the very stuff of his life, giving it both meaning and direction. But the sudden intervention of his fall changes all that, and the person going about his business with so much haste and élan falls less on the pavement, one might say, than into irony, which denies and nullifies his enthusiasm and his involvement in the world of action. And the more he is serious, eager, absorbed, the more sudden and violent will be the convulsions of the laugher.

That suddenness plays an important role in the production of laughter has been noticed by many commentators, Stendhal and Hobbes among them, as we have seen. In *De institutione oratoria* Quintilian[22] states that the cause of laughter is often uncertain and that it 'often breaks out against our will'; and Kant thinks that it is '*an affection arising from a strained expectation being suddenly reduced to nothing*'.[23] Though it is important in many instances, suddenness is not, however, essential. To realize this, one need only compare the unforeseen and hysterical convulsions of unrestrained laughter with the sardonic grimace which is but a pretence, without gaiety or convulsion, or indeed with the laugh of the villain of melodramas with which Baudelaire clinches his theory: 'Tous les mécréants de mélodrame, maudits, damnés, fatalement marqués d'un rictus qui court jusqu'aux oreilles, sont dans l'orthodoxie pure du rire.' Why do villains cackle, if not out of their superiority over ignorant, stupid, or tearful innocence? Charles Maturin's Melmoth is the archetype from whom all other such villains derive their existence. In this magnificent story, which Baudelaire had planned to translate, Melmoth, condemned to

---

[21] Cf. Denis-Prudent Roy, *Traité médico-phylosophique sur le rire* (Paris: Crochard, 1814), 234: 'L'on voit une personne tomber, et l'on rit; qui peut rendre si irrésistible et si pressant le besoin d'éclater alors en dépit de la raison et des convenances?'

[22] Quintilian, VI. iii. 9.

[23] *Critique of Judgement* (Oxford: Clarendon Press, 1986), 199 (my emphasis).

perpetual wandering in time and space, has sold his soul to the devil for immortality upon earth; but tired of his burden, he seeks in vain to pass it on. At this point Baudelaire brings out the full significance of the convulsion in laughter, which had been noticed by other thinkers but not understood. Quintilian notes that it 'extorts confession of its power not merely from our face and voice, but convulses the whole body as well'; and Kant maintains that something absurd 'must be present in whatever is to raise a hearty convulsive laugh'. Melmoth's laugh, which punctuates the novel, indicates his vast superiority, physical and intellectual, over the rest of mankind; but it also denotes his weakness, 'un côté faible, abject, antidivin et antilumineux'. What could be more indicative of a physical weakness than the 'convulsion nerveuse' of laughter? But it also indicates an inherent moral weakness. His laugh is the result of his double and contradictory nature, infinitely greater than other men, and infinitely vile in relation to absolute Truth and Goodness. He is a living contradiction, a magnified and exaggerated exemplification of that *grandeur* and *misère* which Pascal saw as fundamental to humankind. Profounder by far than 'le rire en pleurs', such laughter is not sudden and has nothing comic about it, its function being to punctuate the time of imperfection and irony, and to emphasize the irremediable nature of his condition: 'And he laughed with that horrible convulsion that mingles the expression of levity with that of despair, and leaves the listener no doubt whether there is more despair in laughter, or more laughter in despair.'[24]

Baudelaire's originality in this remarkable theory was to put the comic in the laugher instead of the object of laughter, since one laughs at someone not just out of superiority, but also in a sense out of identification, the convulsions indicating that the laugher is as threatened as the object. In extreme cases, one could have died laughing,[25] as the popular phrase goes, with one's breathing and indeed time itself being interrupted by breaches and convulsions which are the negation of the continuity of life. That laughter should indicate the superiority of the laugher and his physical and moral weakness can, of course, be

---

[24] *Melmoth the Wanderer* (Harmondsworth: Penguin, 1977), 457–8. Balzac wrote a variation, *Melmoth réconcilié*, in 1835.

[25] Many commentators, among them Baudelaire (533), mention the story of Philemon, who dies laughing on seeing an ass eating his figs, and inviting his servant to pour it some wine. For the origin of the story see the note by Pichois (1348), who thinks Baudelaire may have found it in Rabelais, *Gargantua*, ch. 20.

seen as an orthodox view, totally in keeping with the doctrine of the Fall. For fallen humanity there can be no safe position ethically, since it can always be corrupted by pride, or by a modesty that can never clear itself of some trace of falseness. Take the problem of motive, which provides an interesting parallel with laughter.[26] Can a motive ever be pure of any trace of self-love and pride? Good deeds engender conceit and self-satisfaction, but my awareness of that can never free me totally from pride, since my admission that my motive is tinged with imperfection becomes in turn a cause of pride and superiority over those who are not similarly aware. I am modest in the admission that my motive can never be perfect, but pride of such know-ledge immediately ensues, and the process can repeat itself in an endless descending spiral of superiority and imperfection.[27] That is why Christian theologians (of the kind that Baudelaire approved of: Augustinians, Jansenists, Pascal) have maintained that salvation cannot be through good works, but through grace. This is the logical consequence of the Fall, the 'idée catholique' which presides over Baudelaire's thinking and was the starting point of Les Fleurs du Mal. It is equally logical and orthodox that, as Baudelaire himself puts it, tongue in cheek no doubt, 'les phénomènes engendrés par la chute deviendront les moyens du rachat' (p. 528). That is precisely why in 'L'Irrémédiable' the one guiding light for the introspective fallen creature is the infernal 'phare ironique' of 'La conscience dans le Mal'; and that, as he says in 'La Fausse Monnaie', 'le plus irréparable des vices est de faire le mal par bêtise'. And so it is with laughter. I may laugh at the impossible innocence of Virginie or of Immalee in Melmoth, and that laughter proves my intelligence and superiority, but inevitably it bends back on my imperfection, which of course is why Baudelaire jokingly states that as analyst and critic he would not dare affirm that his intelligence is greater than Virginie's. His quip shows that the laugher cannot escape, any more than the person who would wish to convince one of the purity of his motives. By laughing at the person who trips and falls, we bring him back to his 'fallen' reality, and this 'hypocrite promeneur' becomes 'mon semblable, mon frère', a

---

[26] In Le Poème du hachisch Baudelaire pokes fun, mercilessly, at Jean-Jacques Rousseau's inability to believe in his own fallen nature and moral weakness: 'L'enthousiasme avec lequel il admirait la vertu, l'attendrissement nerveux qui remplissait ses yeux de larmes, à la vue d'une belle action ou à la pensée de toutes les belles actions qu'il aurait voulu accomplir, suffisaient pour lui donner une idée superlative de sa valeur morale. Jean-Jacques s'était enivré sans hachisch' (Oc. i. 436).

[27] As is well known, this dilemma is brilliantly exploited by Camus in La Chute.

companion in the web of imperfection, brought down to his true level of reality which he shares with me and the rest of humanity. It has been said that the function of the poet in *Les Fleurs du Mal* is to record a spiritual journey, the travailing of a soul in the modern world, and to live out for his hypocritical fellow human beings the realities of their condition. Equally, laughter, comedy, and caricature could be said to have a similar function of bearing witness to the one central truth of the Christian religion, about which Baudelaire's belief rarely seems to have faltered.

His criticism of tragedy in *Le Salon de 1846* and *Le Peintre de la vie moderne* is not unrelated to his idea of laughter. It is not just for the stilted *poncif*-ridden acting encouraged by the Comédie française that he shows his contempt. It is for the genre of tragedy itself which he says 'consiste à découper certains patrons éternels, qui sont l'amour, la haine, l'amour filial, l'ambition, etc., et, suspendus à des fils, à les faire marcher, saluer, s'asseoir et parler d'après une étiquette mystérieuse et sacrée' (p. 480). In his belief that a tragic poet could never comprehend the infinite variety of human beings and the 'différentes morales' that govern them, there is an echo from Hugo who had maintained that, while there can be only one sublime, there are a thousand types of the ugly: 'le beau n'a qu'un type; le laid en a mille'.[28] It emerges that, like his appreciation of laughter and caricature, Baudelaire's preference for the superior genre of comedy is justified by its realism and ability to give expression to the diversity and stridency of the modern world.

Although Baudelaire makes no reference to the Ancients or to the many treatises of the seventeenth and eighteenth centuries, he was aware of the main issues raised and the possible approaches to them. In spite of some similarities of idea and expression, it is unlikely, however, that he knew Poinsinet de Sivry's *Traité des causes physiques et morales du rire* of 1768, but I mention it because it provides a useful overview of theories with which Baudelaire was almost certainly familiar. The treatise is in three parts, in which three *philosophes*, Destouches, Fontenelle, and Montesquieu, seek to justify their theory against views they consider untenable. At the end Montesquieu's idea that laughter stems from pride prevails over Destouches's preference for joy and Fontenelle's for madness.[29] For us, Montesquieu's argu-

---

[28] *Théâtre complet* (Paris: Gallimard, 1963), i. 420.
[29] Rosemary Lloyd, *Baudelaire et Hoffmann: affinités et influences* (Cambridge: Cambridge University Press, 1979), 170, quotes from an article by a certain Brazier in *L'Artiste* of 1840

ment is the most interesting, not, curiously, for what it affirms, but for what it denies. In its early stages there is a passage which rejects an idea that contains *en puissance* Baudelaire's later synthesis:

Quelques personnes ont encore prétendu que le rire devoit sa naissance *à l'indécision de l'âme entre deux mouvemens.* Il est bon de savoir comment les défenseurs de cette opinion s'y prennent pour la soutenir. Ils conviennent que lorsque la joye est simple & surtout excessive, le rire n'en résulte point; non plus que de la douleur, lorsqu'elle est sans mélange d'aucune autre sensation. Mais s'il arrive, disent-ils, que l'ame soit en suspens entre le plaisir & la peine, à la rencontre de quelque objet d'une essence ambigue & douteuse; alors, dans le combat qu'exige d'elle la concurrence de ces deux impressions, l'ame fait un effort pour prendre un parti; & cette secousse communiquée aux organes produit le mouvement du rire. Voilà, me semble, bien du rafinement en pure perte; car en supposant qu'il fût possible d'appliquer ce principe à deux ou trois occasions particulieres, il est mille qui ne quadrent point avec cette explication, & deux mille qui la détruisent formellement.[30]

The reference is almost certainly to Laurent Joubert's *Traité du ris*[31] of 1579 which puts forward a similar idea of indecision between two conflicting states, an idea which in turn bears some similarity to Descartes's in article 126 of *Des passions de l'âme*[32] in which, having established that joy and laughter are incompatible, he detects in the latter a mixed reaction: 'il y a toujours quelque petit sujet de haine, ou du moins d'admiration'. From the point of view of Baudelaire's theory, these references to an ambiguity in laughter appear as a missed opportunity, not just in Poinsinet de Sivry, but in many of the other authors as well, who are for the most part obsessed by the notions of joy and pride. Denis-Prudent Roy's *Traité médico-phylosophique sur le rire* of 1814, which Baudelaire could well have come across, also contains some parallel passages; but the study which comes closest to his own thinking is *Philosophie du rire* of 1840, by Paul Scudo, who incidentally must have read Roy since he includes in his bibliography all the titles listed by him. That Baudelaire may have known the work is borne out by an anonymous reference to Scudo, who was a music critic, in the essay on Wagner where the pretentious critic S appears,

[30] Poinsinet, *Traité*, 36.
[31] Paris, 1579.
[32] Descartes, *Œuvres et lettres* (Paris: Gallimard, 1953), 753.

appropriately, as an idiot laughing, 'comme un maniaque', at the extraordinary originality of Berlioz's music (p. 781). It is borne out also by the similarity of certain ideas and formulations, but most of all by the central thesis. After an introductory quotation modelled on Descartes 'Je pense, donc je ris', chapter IV, entitled 'Le rire décèle notre imperfection', proceeds to the following resounding statement: 'Le rire est à la fois le signe de la superiorité de l'homme, et de son imperfection. Il rit parce qu'il pense, mais il rit aussi parce qu'il est méchant.'[33] It is true that Scudo does not develop the idea of imperfection or link it specifically to the doctrine of the Fall, nor does he see the importance of the accompanying convulsions; but the quasi-identity of the theories prevents one from excluding it as a possible source. The only other text which comes anywhere near to Baudelaire's is one which he almost certainly did not know, Bonaventura's *Nachtwachen* of 1804, mentioned by Bakhtin in *Rabelais and his World*. It claims that laughter was sent to earth by the devil, but appeared under the mask of joy to facilitate its acceptance.[34]

The grotesque was of course a major preoccupation of the previous generation of Romantic writers, especially Hugo, towards whom Baudelaire had ambivalent feelings, but whose comic genius he admired.[35] The best-known example is possibly Quasimodo, the terrifyingly misshapen hunchback of *Notre-Dame de Paris*,[36] whose grotesque body hides the sublimity of his soul, revealed in his selfless love for the divinely beautiful Esmeralda, with whom he is united in death. A similar antithetical schema is evident in the figure of Tribulat, the buffoon of *Le Roi s'amuse*, behind whose cynical wit lies total devotion to his daughter, and in Hugo's most fascinating creation on the theme of laughter, *L'Homme qui rit* of 1869. It is the story of Gwynplaine, a victim in childhood of the *comprachicos*, who maim and distort human bodies and faces in order to show them as grotesques at fairs. It is revealed in the course of the novel that his true identity is not that of a *forain*, but Lord Clancharlie, cheated out of his birthright in

---

[33] Scudo, *Philosophie du rire*, 133.

[34] Mikhail Bakhtin, *Rabelais and his World* (Bloomington: Indiana University Press, 1984), 38. See *Die Nachtwachen des Bonaventura*: 'um sich an dem Weltmeister zu rächen, schickte er das Gelächter ab, und es wusste sich geschickt und unbemerkt in der Maske der Freude einzuschleichen, die Menschen nahmen's willig auf, bis es zuletzt die Larve abzog und als Satire sie boshaft anschaute' (Edinburgh: Edinburgh University Press, 1972), 290.

[35] In the first essay on Gautier, Baudelaire writes of 'le nombre et l'ampleur' of Hugo's faculties; 'je veux parler du rire et du sentiment du grotesque' (110).

[36] *Notre-Dame de Paris*, bk. one, v.

infancy. His hideously deformed countenance is made to contain a continual grimace: '*Bucca fissa usque ad aures, genzivis denudatis, nasoque murdridato, masca eris, et ridebis semper.*'[37] Like Quasimodo, Gwynplaine is outwardly grotesque, but inwardly tragic and sublime. He is beloved of the beautiful Dea, who, mercifully blind through having been born in an appropriately pure snowstorm on Chesil beach, sees only his soul. For all the extravagance of its plot and characters, this extraordinary novel is marked by the simplistic antitheses of Hugo's Romantic dramas in which he sought to mingle comedy and tragedy, the sublime and the grotesque, not just to make the sublime more exalted, but to be nearer the *truth* about humanity, and because Christianity, the religion of our times, teaches that man is body and soul, earthly and heavenly, temporal and eternal, good and evil, sublime and grotesque: 'La poésie née du christianisme, la poésie de notre temps est donc le drame; le caractère du drame est le réel; le réel resulte de la combinaison toute naturelle de deux types, le sublime et le grotesque, qui se croisent dans le drame, comme ils se croisent dans la vie et dans la création.'[38]

But for all its daring, Hugo's view of the sublime and grotesque was disappointing, not so much in theory as in practice. It led to an abuse of antithesis and a lack of psychological subtlety, as indeed Baudelaire himself was to observe.[39] The breakthrough and originality were to lie not in the mechanical juxtaposition of opposites, but in their fusion, in the creation of figures, situations, images, so fused and intermingled as to form a synthesis of opposing elements. It was the special merit of writers like Flaubert and Baudelaire himself to view comedy and tragedy dialectically. The clash of the antithesis comedy upon the thesis tragedy results not in Romantic drama or the hybrid genre of tragicomedy, but in irony; not the irony made of the discrepancy between expectation and achievement, dream and reality, but the irony that is a vision of the world in which it is uncertain where the

---

[37] *L'Homme qui rit* (Paris: Flammarion, 1982), i. 240: 'La bouche fendue jusqu'aux oreilles, les gencives mises à nu, le nez écrasé, tu seras un masque, et tu riras toujours.'

[38] *Théâtre complet*, i. 425.

[39] 'M. Victor Hugo laisse voir dans tous ses tableaux, lyriques et dramatiques, un système d'alignement et de contrastes uniformes. L'excentricité elle-même prend chez lui des formes symétriques. Il possède à fond et emploie froidement tous les tons de la rime, toutes les ressources de l'antithèse, toutes les tricheries de l'apposition' (431).

Hugo himself had seen the genius of Shakespeare as lying in the use of antithesis. See *William Shakespeare*, 'Totus in antithesi. Shakespeare est tout dans l'antithèse' (*Œuvres dramatiques et critiques complètes* (Paris: Pauvert, 1963), 1391).

comedy ends and the tragedy begins, which makes of Emma Bovary both a foolish and misguided blasphemer and the seeker after an impossible ideal of perfection, a vision in which a whole range of binary opposites, of which spleen and ideal are the archetype, is inextricably interfused.

Hugo's view of laughter is similarly disappointing since it serves either as a mask, or to express the superiority and confidence of the laugher. It does not represent a complex psychology, but the revolt and subversive power of the individual or social group. There is a strong sense in which the laughter of the buffoon, servant, or underdog is an affirmation of their dignity in the face of oppression. It is a negation of their status as underlings and an affirmation of their future and place in the world. In the smile there is consent, says Hugo, while 'le rire est souvent un refus'.[40] There is then the superior laughter of the king, and there is the laughter from below which denies and affirms at one and the same time.[41] The whole of the carnivalesque side of *Notre-Dame de Paris*, with its 'Mardi Gras' excesses, is clearly linked to the underground laughter of the people. Indeed, the laughter and the carnivalesque in Hugo have much the same function as defined by Bakhtin, who sees the latter as revolution itself: it 'discloses the potentiality of an entirely different world, of another order, another way of life'.[42] Like the carnivalesque of Rabelais, the laughter and the grotesque in *Notre-Dame de Paris* is positive and affirmative. In this connection Victor Brombert is right to disagree with Bakhtin's view that the grotesque in Hugo, as in Romanticism in general, is subjective and destructive.[43] Bakhtin declares that in Romanticism the grotesque 'became the expression of subjective, individualistic world outlook very different from the carnival folk concepts of previous ages'. The destructive humour of Jean-Paul Richter is directed against all reality. Deprived of the positive and regenerating power of the carnivalesque, it is not directed against 'isolated negative aspects of reality but against all reality, against the finite world as a whole'. It is conceived as 'an escape from all that is finite', as a 'transfer to the spiritual sphere', and is consequently linked to the sense of an '*interior infinite*' of the indi-

---

[40] *L'Homme qui rit*, i. 68.

[41] 'Vulcain pour le rire d'en haut, Thersite pour le rire d'en bas', *William Shakespeare*, 1358.

[42] Bakhtin, *Rabelais*, 48.

[43] Victor Brombert, *Victor Hugo and the Visionary Novel* (Cambridge, Mass.: Harvard University Press, 1984, 73.

vidual 'unknown to the medieval and the Renaissance grotesque'.[44] Clearly, Richter's view, for whom the greatest humorist of all would be the devil, is closer to Baudelaire's, and it is precisely to the extent that laughter in Hugo is not subjective, is not linked to some sense of the inner infinite, and does not bend back upon the laugher, that it appears less subtle, both in theory and in practice, and that in spite of its diversity and its seminal role in Romanticism it appears curiously out of date when set against the shifting and self-destructive ambiguities of his contemporaries.

In the light of the theories of previous and contemporary thinkers, one's instinctive admiration for *De l'essence du rire* is readily justified. Baudelaire's *tour de force* is to have explained laughter by one simple, powerful and synthesizing idea, that of the Fall of man: the idea that it is intimately linked 'à l'accident d'une chute ancienne, d'une dégradation physique et morale'. Laughter is contradictory, a Pascalian manifestation at one and the same time of man's *grandeur* and of his *misère*. Such a synthesis, like Bergson's, which defines the comic as 'du mécanique plaqué sur du vivant',[45] has the power and simplicity of a stroke of genius, all the more striking as Baudelaire claims he is not writing a treatise, but simply conveying to the reader 'quelques réflexions qui me sont venues souvent au sujet de ce genre singulier' (p. 525). Although the ideas of Bonaventura and Scudo may have been in the air, and although the passage from Chennevières may be said to contain the theory in embryonic form, Baudelaire's genius was to transform an intuition about the idea of superiority and the satanic origin of laughter into a general theory embracing diverse aspects of comedy in literature and the plastic arts.[46]

But here again one cannot help feeling a certain malaise, which is not at first easy to locate or define, but springs from the conduct of the argument and the elaboration of the detail. Felix Leakey[47] states that

---

[44] Bakhtin, *Rabelais*, 36, 42, 44.

[45] H. Bergson, *Le Rire* ([1924] Paris: Presses Universitaires de France, 1956).

[46] Michele Hannoosh, *Baudelaire and Caricature*, 12, sees the full title of the essay, *De l'essence du rire et généralement du comique dans les arts plastiques*, as a joke, 'deflating with one stroke the swollen seriousness of its excessive length and the enormous project which it announces'. But the title is perfectly true to the subject matter and evinces nothing in the way of self-conscious irony. His project not to write a treatise, but merely to give the reader some reflections on the subject is a literary commonplace of authorial modesty. Furthermore, a treatise is traditionally a short work, see to name but a few Joubert, Poinsinet de Sivry, Roy, Scudo, and Voltaire.

[47] F. W. Leakey, *Baudelaire and Nature* (Manchester: Manchester University Press, 1969), 44.

the argument is increasingly subtle, which may be an intentional understatement, while Rosemary Lloyd[48] more trenchantly asserts that it
has a tendency to 's'embrouiller', though she does not say how or why.
The first problem arises from the distinction between laughter and
joy. Baudelaire admits that one could object to his theory that laughter
is diverse, that we do not always laugh out of superiority, and that
many things amuse us which are innocent and have nothing to do with
sinfulness. But this, he argues, is only the case if we fail to distinguish
joy from laughter. Joy is one, whereas laughter is double, hence the
convulsions. To make the point more forcefully he contrasts the
diabolical laugh of Melmoth with the joy of children,[49] which opens
like a flower: 'c'est la joie de recevoir, la joie de respirer, la joie de
s'ouvrir, la joie de contempler, de vivre, de grandir'. But no sooner has
he established this vital distinction than he undermines it by a typically ironic *soubresaut*, which, reminiscent of the prose poems, passes
abruptly from the myth of the child to its fallen reality: 'Et pourtant,
remarquez bien que si le rire des enfants diffère encore des expressions
du contentement animal [by which he means the wagging of dogs'
tails[50] or the purring of cats], c'est que ce rire n'est pas tout à fait
exempt d'ambition, ainsi qu'il convient à des bouts d'hommes, c'est-à-
dire à des Satans en herbe' (p. 535). It seems a fundamental weakness
in the argument that joy which is one should at the same time be held
to be double. If the joy of children, so near to undivided nature, is thus
contaminated, what hope can there be for the so-called innocent
amusements and joys of adults, *a fortiori* of poets and artists? But,
having weakened a vital distinction, Baudelaire leaves the matter
hanging unresolved, and to the consternation of the reader goes on to
raise 'un cas où la question est plus compliquée', the crucial case of the
'comique absolu' itself.

    This kind of laughter, which he also calls the grotesque, springs
from the contemplation of fabulous creations, beings 'dont la raison, la

[48] Lloyd, *Baudelaire*, 182.
    [49] Cf Roy, *Traité*, 210: 'Un enfant qui rit de tout son cœur, ne s'abandonne pas à ce plaisir
parce qu'il se met au-dessus de ceux qui le font rire; s'il rit quand on le chatouille, ce n'est
pas assurément parce qu'il est sujet au péché mortel de l'orgueil.' Also Félicité de
Lamennais, *De l'art et du beau* (Paris: Garnier, 1872), 244, where he defines the laughter of
the child as 'la joie d'être et d'être à soi'. Scudo, more subtly, suggests that the child 'ne
commence à sourire que lorsqu'il commence à comprendre' (*Philosophie*, 134).
    [50] Scudo also (*Philosophie*, 125–6) refers to the wagging of a dog's tail in distinguishing
human laughter from the happiness of animals. In his chapter on comedy his position is near
to Baudelaire's: 'Rire, c'est l'acte d'une créature imparfaite, mais perfectible; au-dessus et
au-dessous de l'homme, on ne rit plus' (156).

légitimation ne peut pas être tirée du code du sens commun'. It involves not so much an imitation of nature as a new creation, and this new creation can give rise to the helpless hilarity which some have difficulty in associating with the poet. With the grotesque the notion of superiority is still present, but it is a superiority not of man over man, as with 'le comique significatif', but of man over nature. This kind of laughter is a veritable 'épuration de la comédie', presenting itself 'sous une espèce une' and creating a sensation close to joy. It is characterized by the 'vertige de l'hyperbole' and 'de gros éclats de rire, pleins d'un vaste contentement'. It is the comic with all its convulsions, taken to an extreme. But the contradiction is flagrant. How can there be oneness in convulsion, joy within an awareness of the Fall? How can one feel superior to nature while being at the same time a prey to irony and derision? How can one be convulsed without trembling, since 'Le Sage ne rit qu'en tremblant'? As if sensing an objection, Baudelaire warns us that we must not find this idea too subtle. If it seems far-fetched, he says, that is because it is nearer to innocence and absolute joy than 'le comique de mœurs'. While the latter is double, being divided into art on the one hand and moral idea on the other, the grotesque, like the joy previously mentioned, 'se présente sous une espèce une', being seized by intuition rather than by the intellect.[51] With 'le rire significatif' whose appeal is to our powers of analysis and judgement, we may have to wait for the penny to drop, whereas with the grotesque laughter is sudden, violent, and immediate. But here again, as with the joy of children, Baudelaire feels obliged to qualify in a paragraph which Professors Leakey[52] and Pichois (p. 1349) think is a later addition from a time when the poet was more concerned with the idea of original sin and after Poe and Maistre had replaced Hoffmann in his thinking: 'J'ai dit: comique absolu; il faut toutefois prendre garde. Au point de vue de l'absolu définitif, il n'a plus que la joie. Le comique ne peut être absolu que relativement à l'humanité déchue, et c'est ainsi que je l'entends' (p. 536). This qualification has all the signs of an afterthought, reinforcing a vital point that had got lost in the course of the argument and without which it would have appeared that the grotesque was breaking away from the synthesizing notion of the Fall of man. But if, as the

---

[51] Charles Mauron states that with the 'comique absolu', which he defines as a 'création absurde, étrangère à toute signification morale', Baudelaire 'retrouve la liberté et l'innocence de l'artiste pur' ('Le Rire baudelairien', *Europe* (Apr.–May 1967), 59). He fails, however, to see the contradiction in the argument.

[52] Leakey, *Baudelaire*, 150, n. 2.

addition claims, the comic can be absolute only relatively to fallen humanity, we would of necessity have to accommodate within it the idea of the duality of man, which in any case, one supposes, is exemplified by his convulsive laughter. In other words, Baudelaire has shown us man's superiority over nature, but has forgotten or omitted its necessary corollary, his *misère* springing from his remoteness from the earthly paradise, lost through revolt and disobedience. And this omission is all the more striking as we have just read the splendid passage evoking Virginie in her tropical, earthly paradise, a passage which, incidentally, resembles the description of Immalee in *Melmoth*.[53] When, at the end of the essay, the dominant idea of superiority is said to be essential to both forms of laughter, and where Baudelaire writes of the spectator's and the reader's 'joie de sa propre supériorité et la joie de la supériorité de l'homme sur la nature', we are tempted to echo an earlier part of the essay and add 'idée satanique s'il en fut jamais!', and wonder how this joy (or laughter) can remain one and not contradictory.

It seems that Baudelaire had difficulty in fitting the grotesque and the laughter it engenders into his overall theory. Leakey surely sensed this when he suggested that the specific references to the doctrine of original sin were interpolated at a later date than the original drafting of the essay. But this would involve a very drastic solution to the problem; for if all references to the doctrine were to be removed, we would be left with no theory of laughter at all, apart possibly from the distinction between the two types of comic, and a handful of anecdotes and allusions. The conclusion must be that the idea of original sin (which after all he did not have to look for in Poe or Maistre) was already there in the first version, and that he had reinforced the idea (which, besides, was latent in the Chennevières passage and the description of Virginie) in an unsuccessful effort to accommodate the grotesque. The doctrine of the Fall, an essential and inevitable part of his Catholic education, also suited his temperament, and it is likely that at the time of writing it coexisted in his mind with other less sombre notions. In the description of Virginie there had been a glancing, possibly ironic, reference to the socialist belief in a future earthly

---

[53] *Melmoth*, ch. XV, opening sentence, 374: 'The sole and beautiful inmate of the isle, though disturbed at the appearance of her worshippers, soon recovered her tranquillity. She could not be conscious of fear, for nothing of that world in which she lived had ever borne a hostile appearance to her.'

paradise, and later in the essay he speculates on a future state of purity and intelligence in which laughter will have disappeared:

nous voyons que les nations primitives, ainsi que Virginie, ne conçoivent pas la caricature [. . .] et que, s'avançant peu à peu vers les pics nébuleux de l'intelligence, ou se penchant sur les fournaises ténébreuses de la métaphysique, les nations se mettent à rire diaboliquement du rire de Melmoth; et, enfin, que si dans ces mêmes nations ultra-civilisées, une intelligence, poussée par une ambition supérieure, veut franchir les limites de l'orgueil mondain et s'élancer hardiment vers la poésie pure, dans cette poésie, limpide et profonde comme la nature, le rire fera défaut comme dans l'âme du Sage. (pp. 532–3)

The passage is disturbing because of the contradiction it contains. With the increase of intelligence in civilised nations comes a corresponding increase in caricature and laughter, and yet an ultracivilized intelligence will rise beyond laughter. Clearly, Baudelaire is referring to himself and to the heights of lyricism in *Les Fleurs du Mal*. The ideal and 'les beaux jours de l'esprit' are not compatible with irony and laughter. However, the contradiction remains, and this curious coexistence of a belief in the Fall and its ultimate demise, which finds a parallel in the ideas of laughter as convulsion and laughter as joy, does little to alleviate the unease aroused by the essay.

It is remarkable that the same contradiction should be repeated in the essay on Banville of 1861:

le poète sait descendre dans la vie; mais croyez que s'il y consent, ce n'est pas sans but, et qu'il saura tirer profit de son voyage. De la laideur et de la sottise il fera naître un nouveau genre d'enchantements. Mais ici encore sa bouffonnerie conservera quelque chose d'hyperbolique; l'excès en détruira l'amertume, et la satire, par un miracle résultant de la nature même du poète, se déchargera de toute sa haine dans une explosion de gaieté, innocente à force d'être carnavalesque. (p. 167)

Following a long definition of lyricism and 'les beaux jours de l'esprit', the contradiction is all the more surprising as it precedes a passage in which Baudelaire identifies the essentially demonic nature of modern art. Banville's lyricism has none of the characteristics of Byron, Maturin, or Poe: 'Aussi, dans ses œuvres, vous n'entendrez pas les dissonances, les discordances des musiques du sabbat, non plus que les glapissements de l'ironie, cette vengeance du vaincu.' As in the essay on laughter Baudelaire has managed, in two vertiginous pages, to remove the demonic from laughter, and to place it at its heart.

There are other moments of hesitation and uncertainty in the argument, which may well be explained by the discrepancy between first composition (around 1845) and publication in July 1855 and September 1857. It could be that the essay, which was to have as its title *Histoire de la caricature*, then *Une physiologie du rire*, was written both hurriedly and over a long time, creating startling transitions or hiccoughs in the flow of ideas. Take, for example, the two passages where Baudelaire sums up the argument, the first occurring at the beginning of the fourth section, only one-third of the way through the essay. Here he rehearses for a second time the idea of the satanic origin of laughter revealing the contradictory nature of man, an idea which he has just abundantly explained in the previous paragraph dealing with laughter in melodrama and in *Melmoth*. One has the impression of the argument marking time as the writer takes his bearings to see how far he has got, as if picking up the thread of his thought after some time and starting a new chapter with a summary of the argument so far: 'Maintenant, résumons un peu, et établissons plus visiblement les propositions principales, qui sont comme une espèce de théorie du rire.'

The second summing-up is placed, legitimately one might say, at the very end of the essay. But two things stand out: first, Baudelaire's undisguised impatience to round off the article and be finished with it: 'Ainsi, pour en finir avec toutes ces subtilités et toutes ces définitions, et pour conclure, je ferais remarquer une dernière fois qu'on retrouve l'idée dominante de supériorité dans le comique absolu comme dans le comique significatif, ainsi que je l'ai, trop longuement peut-être, expliqué.' Second, not only do we sense Baudelaire's impatience, but looking back over the article we are aware that not all the subtleties have been explained, and that not all the difficulties have been resolved. What is more, in the conclusion there is no longer any reference to original sin, nor indeed is there in the long final section dealing mainly with Hoffmann, and it seems strange, given the importance of the doctrine in the earlier part of the essay, that the notion of superiority alone, without its gloomy and satanic overtones, is said to be the dominant idea in both forms of the comic, in the 'comique significatif' and in the 'comique absolu'.

As we have seen, theoretically the grotesque is one, and so is not divided into art on one side and moral lesson on the other; and this is indeed borne out by the hilarious example of the English pantomime which he describes with gusto in the sixth and final section of the essay. It involves a scene in which the thieving Pierrot is brought to justice with much moaning like a bull to the slaughter, and guillotined. After the descent of the fearful knife, his head rolls across the stage, 'montrant le disque saignant du cou, la vertèbre scindée, et tous les détails d'une viande de boucherie récemment taillée'. But then his truncated body, still impelled by the irresistible urge to steal, rises up after the execution and walks off triumphantly with his own head in his pocket. There can be no question here of a moral lesson, and indeed, it would take a grotesque effort of serious-mindedness to make of it a protest against capital punishment. The effect on the audience could not be more dramatic; for pantomime is 'l'épuration de la comédie; c'en est la quintessence', 'une ivresse de rire, quelque chose de terrible et d'irrésistible' (pp. 539–40). The scene, and its vertiginous prologue in which all the characters make the most frantic and extravagant gestures, are characterized by violence, which Baudelaire sees as a fundamental and distinctive ingredient in this kind of laughter. He writes of its suddenness and explosive effect, of the 'émanation, explosion, dégagement de comique' (p. 543), the explosion indicating in Baudelaire an outburst of creative energy. The hyperbolic gestures and convulsions of the laughers are the visible signs of an ecstatic intoxication, of joy at having triumphed over nature and death, as if one had made a leap into a surreal sphere, free from the laws of the physical world: 'tout cela s'opère avec de gros éclats de rire, pleins d'un vaste contentement'. But the convulsions are so violent and extreme no doubt because at the height of the ecstasy one remains, paradoxically, aware that the liberation is illusory, that the breakthrough belongs to the world of imagination and fantasy. One goes beyond the real world through the trickery of the pantomime, but at the same time one is held back by common sense—and it is precisely this discrepancy and imbalance that are expressed in the hyperbolic convulsions.

This is the highest expression of the grotesque in Baudelaire, but it is hardly exemplified in his own creative work. For him the comic, especially the grotesque, is eminently a mute art that is compromised to the extent it is involved with words, since laughter depends on an explosion within the instant, whereas words entail an unfolding in time. Analysis is hostile to the comic, which is why Baudelaire takes his examples of the grotesque from outside literature, with the exception of Hoffmann. Of course, the essay is on the essence of laughter and generally on the comic in the plastic arts, as the full title indicates; but it is noteworthy that he should cite Molière, Voltaire, and Rabelais as examples of the 'significatif', but look to an English pantomime for the best illustration of the 'absolu', the pantomime being the quintessence of the comic, purified of any extraneous element. For Baudelaire the grotesque is above all a visual phenomenon, on stage or in a drawing. Like the best caricatures, pantomime is successful because it is mute—he criticizes Grandville for giving his characters speaking-bubbles, and praises Daumier for his brief captions which he thinks superior to Gavarni's long commentaries. At its highest the comic is visual, sudden, and unmediated through language.[54] There may be many reasons why, in 'Une mort héroïque', almost twenty years after the composition of the essay on laughter, this 'parfait magicien ès lettres françaises' should appear to take leave of his own genius and present himself in the paradoxical and usurping mask of a mute clown. This 'aphasic' reverie is perhaps linked to his childhood dream of being an actor; it is certainly linked to his evolving pessimism about the nature and function of art; but it should also be stressed that it springs first and foremost from his meditation on the nature of the comic.

'Une mort héroïque', one of the most profound and enigmatic of Baudelaire's prose poems, contains a pantomime. It concerns a brilliant buffoon, by name of Fancioulle, who has entered a foolhardy plot against the tyrannical prince, whose favourite he is. The prince, 'amoureux passionné des beaux-arts', a minor Nero, afflicted by *Ennui*, decides to set up a spectacle, at which the plotters would be present, and in which the actor would play one of his best roles. Using the occasion 'pour faire une expérience physiologique d'un intérêt *capital*', he wishes to see how the actor will perform under the sentence of death. Fancioulle gives a magnificent performance which wins thunderous applause from the admiring audience. Enchanted and humiliated, the prince orders a page-boy to give 'un coup de sifflet' in the middle of the act, whereupon the stricken Fancioulle falls stone dead on the stage.[55]

---

[54] The titles of Baudelaire's prose poems have something of the immediacy and pithiness of the captions of caricatures: 'Chacun sa chimère', 'Un plaisant', 'Laquelle est la vraie?', 'Le Galant Tireur'. The 'caricatural' visual quality of the poems is caught in the descriptive *vignette*s of some of his characters. See my 'Les Poèmes en prose de Baudelaire et la caricature', *Romantisme*, 74 (1991), 57–64.

[55] The intertext is Stendhal's comparison of politics in a work of literature to 'un coup de pistolet au milieu d'un concert' (*Le Rouge et le Noir*, and *La Chartreuse de Parme* (Paris: Garnier, 1973), 360 and 435 respectively).

The poem contains a series of fascinating contradictions and paradoxes which are almost impossible to fathom: Fancioulle, who is merely a buffoon, excels in 'ces drames féeriques dont l'objet est de représenter symboliquement le mystère de la vie'; comedy, we are told, can reach the heights of an ecstatic joy re-creating, through artistic genius and even on the brink of death, 'un paradis excluant toute idée de tombe et de destruction'; and most importantly in the present context, joy and convulsion appear compatible as in the English pantomime: 'Ce bouffon allait, venait, riait, pleurait, se convulsait . . .'. His tears, laughter, and convulsions indicate his wretchedness, and yet he keeps 'une indestructible auréole autour de la tête [. . .] où se mêlaient, dans un étrange amalgame, les rayons de l'Art et la gloire du Martyre', so that even in his buffoonery and fallen state he represents a perfect idealization.

'Une mort héroïque' suggests, if not a coincidence of opposites, then at least a kind of equilibrium, whereas the other prose poems show the sudden and ironic passage from one to the other. The most common pattern is the passage from ideal to spleen, from exaltation to triviality, from dream to reality, and it is clear that in *Le Spleen de Paris* the emphasis falls almost exclusively on discord, disproportion, contradiction and the impossibility of uniting dream and reality, or poetry and prose. In spite of the final whistle-blow which marks the passage from art and illusion to reality, 'Une mort héroïque' seems to be an exception, since the contradictions of joy and convulsion, subtlety and grossness, the mystery of life and buffoonery remain unresolved. The contradictions in Fancioulle, whose name, from the Italian for boy or child, indicates that poetic genius is nothing other than 'l'*enfance retrouvée* à volonté' (p. 690), are easy to identify, but the problem is how to arrive at a satisfactory interpretation of this exceptional poem, that would synthesize and resolve what appears to be incompatible.

Most interpretations agree, very broadly, with that of Charles Mauron,[56] who sees in Fancioulle and the cruel prince an incarnation of aspects of the poet, the one representing the artist as martyr and idealist, the other the cynic, the negator, the agnostic aware of what separates art from reality. For Mauron the poem shows the triumph of the social self over the artist. This interpretation is satisfactory, but only up to a point, since it resolves the antagonism between the prince and the buffoon, but fails to take account of the contradictions within

---

[56] Charles Mauron, *Le Dernier Baudelaire* (Paris: José Corti, 1966).

Fancioulle himself. Another critical possibility would be to interpret the poem in the light of the analysis of the artist as clown, presented by Jean Starobinski in *Portrait de l'artiste en saltimbanque*.[57] According to this view, Fancioulle, like Emma Bovary and Don Quixote as seen by Daumier and Unamuno, is at one and the same time a buffoon and serious, comic and tragic, grotesque and sublime, since he adheres to an ideal which by definition cannot take root in the real world. In a world where 'l'action n'est pas la sœur du rêve',[58] only a fool could live out such a tension, with the result that Fancioulle appears, like Emma Bovary herself, in whom Baudelaire recognized a sister soul, as an alter ego of the 'poète hystérique'.

But in its turn this interpretation gets nowhere near exhausting the complexities of this highly suggestive and elusive text; and the reason lies not just in the poet's ability to create elliptic allegories with the power to puzzle and stimulate the imagination of the reader, but in the absence of any information about the pantomime played by Fancioulle. With his laughter and exaggerated tears, he represents 'le mystère de la vie', but what is the plot, and what actually happens on the stage? The pantomime with the guillotined Pierrot is intelligible at least in its broad lines, whereas 'Une mort héroïque' appears as a pure virtuality, less as a representation taking place on a real stage, than the possibility of an action, indeed as a sort of experiment on the part of the author, an empty space for the reader to fill. It is up to the reader to conceive of a plot, or the outline of a plot, which would show in a mute piece of buffoonery the deepest mysteries of life, and which would reconcile what, in Baudelaire's theory of the comic, was irreconcilable from the first composition of the essay, not so much laughter and tears, as joy and convulsion.

The final section is dominated by the description of the English pantomime as an example of the 'comique absolu'. The rest is given to the subdivisions of the comique, and somewhat cursorily to Hoffmann. In addition to the fundamental philosophic division of the comic into 'significatif' and 'absolu', Baudelaire explains that there can be further categories depending on the specific qualities the artist or his national origins. The 'comique féroce', for example, is an exaggeration of the 'significatif', while the 'comique innocent', found in Italy or in the drawings of Jacques Callot, is a mitigated form of the grotesque. Although in passages of Rabelais and certain plays by

---

[57] Published by Skira (Geneva) in 1970.
[58] *Oc.* i. 122.

Molière such as *Le Bourgeois Gentilhomme* and *Le Malade imaginaire* there are elements of the grotesque, the French genius lies predominantly in the 'significatif', Voltaire being the best and most coherent example. 'La rêveuse Germanie' is said to excel in the 'comique absolu', while the Spanish genius for the comic is often cruel 'et leurs fantaisies les plus grotesques contiennent souvent quelque chose de sombre'. The subdivisions are developed and exemplified in the two companion essays, *Quelques caricaturistes français*, and *Quelques caricaturistes étrangers*, and will form the subject of the next chapter.

It is, however, what Baudelaire says about Hoffmann in the last three pages of the essay that concerns us at this point. The short story Baudelaire praises most, describing it as 'un catéchisme de haute esthétique' (p. 542), is *La Princesse Brambilla*. He also mentions *La Fiancée du roi*, *Maître Puce* (which he calls *Peregrinus Tyss*), and *Le Pot d'or*; but there is little indication that he meditated on them at any length. Of the latter two he says nothing, and is content to draw attention as an example of the grotesque to the scene in *La Fiancée du roi* (*Daucus Carota*) where the peasant girl, enamoured of the fine regiment of carrots in their red uniforms and green hats, sees them for their true worth in their barracks: 'cette masse de soldats rouges et verts dans leur épouvantable déshabillé, nageant et dormant dans la fange terreuse d'où elle est sortie. Toute cette splendeur militaire en bonnet de nuit n'est plus qu'un marécage infect.' The transformation of the splendid carrots into loutish soldiers is clearly a fine example of the grotesque; but it is important to notice that Baudelaire qualifies the distinction between the two kinds of comic which he had made in the previous section: 'Le comique significatif est un langage plus clair, plus facile à comprendre pour le vulgaire, et surtout plus facile à analyser, son élément étant visiblement double: l'art et l'idée morale; mais le comique absolu, se rapprochant beaucoup plus de la nature, se présente sous une espèce *une*, et qui veut être saisie par l'intuition' (pp. 535–6).

In the fifth section he had left no doubt that the two kinds of laughter are quite separate, establishing between them the same distinction as between didactic literature (what he calls 'l'école littéraire intéressée') and Art for Art's sake. 'Le comique significatif' pursues a moral aim, the correction of manners, while the grotesque is comedy for its own sake. But now in the final section, it appears that these distinctions are not hard and fast, and the categories which had previously appeared separate begin to overlap, in Hoffmann precisely, who is said to unite French satire, Italian gaiety, and 'le profond comique germanique'. Baudelaire claims indeed that Hoffmann, the finest creator of the grotesque, has mingled both involuntarily and quite voluntarily the grotesque with a certain dose of 'comique significatif': 'ses conceptions comiques les plus supra-naturelles, les plus fugitives, et qui ressemblent souvent à des visions de l'ivresse, ont un sens moral très visible'. In *Daucus Carota* the moral lesson lies in the discrepancy between illusion and reality; but Baudelaire's contention is that the grotesque and surreal predominate to such an extent that the world of rational parallels and resemblances has been left far behind. To make the point clearer one might contrast the carrots with Voltaire's description of the two armies in chapter three of *Candide*. The moral message in both stories is similar, the discrepancy between military illusion and reality; but the means are totally different. In Voltaire, the contrast is between the pomp and splendour of the armies before the battle and the 'boucherie héroïque' of their engagement, the soldiers remaining themselves throughout. But in Hoffmann the world is turned upside down. The soldiers are not *like* carrots. The carrots exist in this surreal world in their own right, as independent creations. The soldiers are not compared to carrots; on the contrary in a splendidly surreal inversion, it is the carrots that are compared eventually to soldiers. The comic power of the grotesque derives from the absence of a comparison or simile, and from a vision which at first is surreal and only later reveals itself to be metaphoric. In the beginning we have only the carrots 'sous une espèce *une*' as it were, which then turn out to be soldiers; whereas the 'comique significatif' maintains a duality throughout, and is irremediably split like a simile. The appeal of the simile is to the rational mind, even in the most extravagant instances, since the two elements are kept apart. With the 'new creation' of the grotesque, however, the appeal is to another, more imaginative, 'synthetic' faculty, which Baudelaire calls intuition. The parallel with the poetic image could not be clearer, since the comic charge of the grotesque could be compared to the greater poetic charge of the metaphor, and more particularly of the elliptic metaphor over that of the simile or comparison. It is clear then that there is no inconsistency in the grotesque having a moral meaning, just as a great work of literature, such as *Les Fleurs du Mal*, can perfectly well have a moral result without being overtly didactic and without having an explicit moral aim.[59] The grotesque is compatible with a moral lesson provided it is implicit in the new creation of the artist and does not constitute his primary aim.

The other example of the grotesque with a moral import is the figure of Giglio Fava in *La Princesse Brambilla*, 'le comédien atteint de dualisme chronique': 'ce personnage *un* change de temps en temps de personnalité, et, sous le nom de Giglio Fava, il se déclare l'ennemi du prince assyrien Cornelio Chiapperi; et quand il est prince assyrien, il déverse le plus profond et le plus royal mépris sur son rival auprès de la princesse, sur un misérable histrion qui s'appelle, à ce qu'on dit, Giglio Fava'. Here again, the moral lesson, that is to say the insight into the duality of human nature, a Baudelairean obsession if ever there was one, is seen to be perfectly compatible with the grotesque creation of a character whose memory is incapable of bridging the two parts of his personality.

It should be stressed that that is all Baudelaire says specifically about Hoffmann, since the final point of the essay involves him only in the most general way. The last three paragraphs are given to his observation that one of the peculiar signs of the 'comique absolu' is to appear to be unaware of itself, just as the funniest animals, such as monkeys, are those that have the most gravity. The point leads him to sum up the argument, in the curious manner we have seen, stressing the permanent duality of the artist who, comic or serious, has the power to be both himself and someone else at the same time. When Hoffmann creates the 'comique absolu' he is perfectly aware of what he is doing, though the essence of this kind of comic is to appear to be unaware of itself, just as an artist is an artist only on the condition of being double 'et de n'ignorer aucun phénomène de sa double nature'.

Baudelaire does not go much beyond seeing in Hoffmann a fine example of the humour of 'la rêveuse Germanie'. From the evidence of the essay it is not certain that he read Hoffmann closely or that he explored in detail the intricate complexities of his works. If *La Princesse Brambilla* is 'un catéchisme de haute esthétique', it is because it exemplifies better than any other work the nature of 'le comique absolu'. Ingeborg Köhler, Rosemary Lloyd, and Michele Hannoosh

---

[59] Cf. Benjamin Constant's view, which is similar to Baudelaire's, that 'un ouvrage d'imagination ne doit pas avoir un but moral, mais un résultat moral' (Benjamin Constant, *Œuvres* (Paris: Gallimard, 1957), 868). See also the poet's strictures on *Les Misérables* in which he says that 'la morale entre directement *à titre de but*' (218).

have analysed the essay and this story very closely in an attempt to establish parallels between the two authors. There is, however, a danger of highlighting the similarities at the expense of the differences, and blurring the focus. Agreeing that for Baudelaire Hoffmann is the best theoretician of the 'comique absolu',[60] Köhler spoils a sound analysis by identifying the grotesque in several poems of *Les Fleurs du Mal*, claiming that 'cette ironie "absolue" se rencontre un peu partout dans le recueil'; but it is extremely doubtful that one could find any such example in his poetry, and certainly not in 'Danse macabre' or 'Une martyre' as she alleges, because in these poems, as elsewhere, Baudelaire's irony lacks that sense of innocence and joy which is essential to the grotesque and which characterizes so much of Hoffmann, not least *La Princesse Brambilla*.

Similarly, one wonders if Rosemary Lloyd, in her otherwise excellent study, does not overstate the similarity between the lessons of the fountain of Urdar and Baudelaire's idea of the grotesque. The fountain figures in the story of King Ophioch and Queen Liris. An intelligent young man, endowed with some poetic sensibility, Ophioch is given to an incurable melancholy born of the discrepancy between the prelapsarian world of harmony he yearns after, and the desolate chaos of the real world in which he lives. The beautiful but empty-headed Liris, on the other hand, is given to perpetual and equally incurable giggling for no reason that anyone has been able to discover. The unhappiness of this couple, who otherwise seem made for each other, is beyond remedy, until the good Magus Hermod causes them to look into the limpid waters of the Urdar fountain, whereupon their lives are transformed and their eternal happiness assured:

As they beheld the shining blue sky, the bushes, the trees, the whole of nature, and their own selves, mirrored upside-down in its infinite depths, they felt as though dark veils were being rolled back to disclose a magnificent new world full of life and joy, and as they perceived this world they felt a delight such as they had never known or suspected. After gazing into the pool for a long time, they rose, looked at each other—and laughed: for the physical expression not only of intense well-being but also of joy at the victory of inner spiritual forces must be called laughter.[61]

---

[60] Ingeborg Köhler, *Baudelaire et Hoffmann* (Uppsala: Studia Romanica Uppsaliensia, 1979), 84: 'Hoffmann ist für Baudelaire der bislang beste Theoretiker des absolut Komischen, vorzüglich im Märchen.'

[61] E. T. A. Hoffmann, *The Golden Pot and other Tales*, trans. Ritchie Robertson (Oxford: Oxford University Press, 1992), 166.

By seeing the world upside down in the waters of the spring, they come to a true knowledge of the world and above all of themselves, as if they had awakened from a bad dream. The king's melancholy and the Queen's vacuous giggling are replaced by a joyous and contented laughter, and the pernicious effects of thought are replaced by the beneficent insight of intuition; for 'thought destroys intuition, and man [. . .] reels around without a home, prey to mad illusions, blind and insensate, until the veritable mirror of thought supplies thought itself with the knowledge that he *is*'.[62] The similarity between Baudelaire's thought and Hoffmann's is immediately perceptible. The grotesque is linked in both to intuition rather than to intellection, and it engenders in both laughter and a deep sense of joy, stemming in the one from a triumph over the limits of the natural world, in the other from a vision of the world upside down. It is surely an unconscious memory of this Hoffmannian vision that explains why Baudelaire erroneously refers to Grandville's book of drawings *Un autre monde* as *Le Monde à l'envers*, a work in which the caricaturist had striven to 'refaire la création' and had effectively put 'le monde sens dessus dessous' (p. 558). But in emphasizing the parallels between the two authors, Lloyd has overlooked the extent to which Baudelaire, fascinated by Hoffmann, has strayed from his original linking of laughter with the doctrine of the Fall. When, in the fifth section of the essay, he had first analysed the grotesque, describing the laughter it gives rise to as 'une hilarité folle, excessive, et qui se traduit en des déchirements et des pâmoisons interminables' (p. 535), there was no doubt a sense of innocence and joy, but there was also something deeply distressing and disturbing in the hyperbolic convulsions. In the final section, however, as has been pointed out, the baleful aspects of laughter give way to a prevailing sense of joy, as if his sombre thought had been dispelled by Hoffmann and the balanced and serene world of *La Princesse Brambilla*.

Lloyd gives an excellent account of humour in Hoffmann:

Le comique et le tragique sont, aux yeux d'Hoffmann, 'rayons d'un seul foyer', le point où les deux éléments convergent étant l'humour. C'est grâce à lui que l'homme se rend compte à la fois de sa propre grandeur et de sa propre misère: c'est grâce à lui aussi que cette connaissance mène à cette diminution de la tension qu'est le rire. Le vrai comique, ce qu'Hoffmann appelle le 'wahrhaftig Komische', provoque 'un rire de joie merveilleuse, création, en

---

[62] Ibid. 167.

effet, de chagrin et de désespoir'. Loin de la frénésie du carnaval et du rire agaçant de Liris, l'humour est l'expression du 'triomphe de la force intime et spirituelle'.[63]

Whatever the stresses in his other works, we can see here how humour in *La Princesse Brambilla* brings about, or at least seems to, a state of inner balance and harmony. It appears as a spiritual triumph, a higher wisdom, a *sagesse* which permits laughter without trembling, and in which the sense of superiority gives way to one of serenity. It is as if, at their point of convergence, tragedy and comedy had been disarmed of their most wounding weapons or had had their stings removed, so that whatever despair there is is shot through with joy and wonder. It is to this kind of recuperation in Hoffmann that Jean Starobinski is referring in an article of 1967: 'Nothing prevents the ironist from conferring an expansive value to the freedom he has conquered for himself: he is then led to dream of a reconciliation of the spirit and the world, all things being reunited in the realm of the spirit.'[64] Starobinski's reading of Hoffmann is similar to Baudelaire's in the last pages of the essay; but, as we have seen, such a balance and harmony are not compatible with Baudelaire's convulsive laughter, nor is it compatible with the ironic vision that informs much of his production, a vision born of the dialectical clash of the antithesis comedy upon the thesis tragedy. Far from producing balance, the resulting synthesis remains full of ambiguities, stridencies, and tensions, in which no unequivocal statement can be proffered without simultaneously calling up its opposite. In such a view, there can be no privileged position, no transcendence, and the sage remains as powerless as any other man.

Paul de Man is surely right to criticize Starobinski on this count, basing his argument on Friedrich Schlegel's theory of irony which fits Baudelaire's practice perfectly: 'Irony divides the flow of temporal existence into a past that is pure mystification and a future that remains harassed for ever by a relapse within the inauthentic. It can know this inauthenticity but it can never overcome it.'[65] Hannoosh sees that 'irony does not lead to synthesis or a stable recovered unity'; but seeks, if not a way out, then some kind of consolation in *dédoublement* and in the realization of dualism an opening of the boundaries of the self, 'the means by which others reach the same level

---

[63] *Baudelaire*, 175.
[64] Quoted by Paul de Man in 'The Rhetoric of Temporality', *Blindness and Insight*, 2nd edn. (London: Methuen, 1983), 217.
[65] Ibid. 222.

of understanding'.[66] But it is one thing to extend Baudelaire's concern for his 'hypocrite lecteur' in *Les Fleurs du Mal* to his theory of laughter and his other more strident works; it is quite another to talk of some kind of transcending of dualism which, she maintains, 'consists in maintaining it'. This sounds suspiciously like philosophically having one's cake and eating it, and the resulting realization of the 'self's—every self's—dependence on others' seeks to strike an optimistic humanist note which accords not at all with the disharmonies of the texts themselves, providing an illusory foundation amid the shifting sands of his irony.

De Man's article takes us back to Schlegel and Romantic irony, appropriately, since the debate sprang from Hoffmann. But for Baudelaire laughter and irony are grounded in the much older Judeo-Christian doctrine of the Fall, so that just as for fallen humanity there can be no safe position ethically, there can be no such position aesthetically or philosophically. Irony of irony implies the same downward spiral as pride and modesty, in an endless repetition which permits of no transcendence. Romantic irony is of course a phenomenon inextricably linked to a moment in European consciousness and to the emergence of a self-conscious, dialogical literature which has become the principal characteristic of what is now loosely called 'modernity'. The previous literature was of a different kind, or at least seemed so, and although Christian moralists kept people aware of their spiritual and moral wretchedness, literature itself seemed to have been spared the same anguished or despairing questioning of its action and status; but when the lessons of the Fall are extended to literature, their effects bear a close similarity to those of Romantic irony and the modernity which sprang from it.

[66] Hannoosh, *Baudelaire and Caricature*, 73.

4

Caricature

Quelques Caricaturistes Français

'Un homme étonnant fut ce Carle Vernet. Son œuvre est un monde, une petite *Comédie humaine*; car les images triviales, les croquis de la foule et de la rue, les caricatures, sont souvent le miroir le plus fidèle de la vie' (p. 544). An expression of enthusiasm, a hyperbolic and scarcely veiled comparison to the greatest novelist of the century, and a startling paradox, provide the arresting opening to the essay on French caricaturists. The idea that Vernet's drawings constitute a human comedy is readily justified by a rapid overview of his work, with its street scenes and various types, sellers of cherries, cocoa, brandy, sausages, rabbit skins, its blind people, 'ennuyeux chez eux', tailors, its *Brodeuse, Vielleuse*, and bagpipe players. The paradox is that this apparently throwaway and caricatural drawing can produce in miniature an image of reality as faithful as Balzac's depiction of contemporary French society which belongs to the domain of great art. The implication is that just as Balzac's 'realism' is rooted in his creative imagination and his status as *visionnaire* (p. 120), so also the truth of Vernet's time is caught in the deforming mirror of his sketches and caricatures. The parallel between exaggeration and realism, caricature and modernity is thus established at the outset and is implied throughout the essay until it is again made explicit at the beginning of *Le Peintre de la vie moderne*. Baudelaire goes on to say that often the caricatures, like the engravings of fashion, appear more caricatural as they become outmoded and the difference between past and present is emphasized. The distancing power of the passage of time can produce a comic effect that was not in the original drawings and was not perceptible to contemporaries, or not to the same extent—so that what was stiff and upright in the figures was not so much a caricatural comment on the manners of the time as a reflection of

The essays on caricature were first published in Oct. 1857, but, like *De l'essence du rire*, existed in a different form probably as early as 1845–6.

historical truth: 'chaque citoyen avait l'air d'une *académie* qui aurait passé chez le fripier'. Vernet emerges as a painter of manners, and it is history that is the caricaturist, the comic being less in the artist than in the detached perception of the observer looking back with the questionable benefit of hindsight. The accuracy of this observation, Baudelaire claims, can be supported by personal experience, by our childhood memories of those who frequented our parents' drawing-rooms.

In Baudelaire's opinion one of his most successful works represents a gaming house. It is not in fact by Vernet, but is an engraving by Darcis from a drawing by Guérain entitled *Le Trente-un, ou la maison de prêt sur nantissement*:[1] 'il y a là des joies et des désespoirs violents; de jeunes joueurs fougueux et brûlant la chance; des joueurs froids, sérieux et tenaces; des vieillards qui ont perdu leurs rares cheveux au vent furieux des anciens équinoxes' (p. 545). Although aware of its stiffness and aridity, Baudelaire considerably exaggerates its impact, making much of two female figures, one with her back to the viewer, the other blandly looking on while furtively putting money into her handbag. It has been suggested that this drawing is the inspiration for 'Le Jeu' in 'Tableaux parisiens',[2] and it could certainly have provided the initial spark for this poignant evocation of the corruption of the capital city. But the differences between poem and drawing are more conspicuous than any similarity. The relative smallness of the figures, the rigidity and stylization of their postures, and their distance from the viewer do little to convey the potential drama and torment of the subject matter. In the poem, on the other hand, there is something grotesque and hallucinating in the description of the gamblers with their colourless lips and toothless jaws, and the old courtesans, 'Pâles, le sourcil peint, l'œil câlin et fatal, / Minaudant, et faisant de leurs maigres oreilles / Tomber un cliquetis de pierre et de métal', reminiscent of Goya's hags clinging in vain to a youth long past. Furthermore, the second half of the poem shifts the emphasis from the corruption of the gambling den to the poet's reaction to the scene and his awareness of his own fallen condition. In a nightmarish vision he sees himself seeing, and in a triple remove envying these hideous figures who are able to desire and feel at ease in the world of phenomena and time. The tender heart which in 'Harmonie du soir' had hated 'le néant vaste et noir' and revolted against the death of time and memory in the cosmic

---

[1] Reproduced by Hannoosh, *Baudelaire and Caricature*, 90.
[2] *Oc.* i. 1028.

expungement of sunset, has identified itself with the despairing voice of 'Obsession' in its quest for 'le vide, le noir et le nu'. In the end the poem has little to do with gambling, and gives little insight into the mind of the gambler.[3] Unlike the drawing, its impact is not social but metaphysical, showing as poignantly as any of the *Fleurs du Mal* the duality of a modern soul imprisoned in a world without transcendence.

Baudelaire's attitude towards Pigal is distinctly lukewarm, the only reason for his brief mention being that he is a transitional figure between Vernet's essentially outmoded manner and the modern style of Charlet. If there is an innocence about Pigal's creations, it is measured, with none of the brio of the Italians, and his 'vérités vulgaires' have none of the harshness of the British. Lacking imagination, originality and even humour, his work shows sureness of touch, verisimilitude, and sound observation, and his popular scenes are said to be good; 'presque toujours des hommes du peuple, des dictons populaires, des ivrognes, des scènes de ménage, et particulièrement une prédilection involontaire pour les types vieux' (p. 545). Clearly, Baudelaire is thinking of such of the *Scènes parisiennes* as *Qui s'y frotte s'y pique*, *Parlons peu et parlons bien*, or *J't'aime tant!*, with its red-faced drunk embracing a terrified and extremely ugly woman. Had he known Pigal's more sinister drawings of suicides, he would almost certainly have mentioned them. He might even have appreciated them more, for example, the one showing a man who has failed to win the lottery hanging himself,[4] while another throws himself from a bridge, or *Vanité des vanités!*,[5] with a man on the heights of the Père-Lachaise cemetery contemplating 'tour à tour la ville qui remue et la ville qui dort'.

But clearly the introductory paragraphs on Vernet and Pigal are intended as a lead-in to a figure who exemplifies in Baudelaire's eyes all that is misconceived and mediocre in art, his *bête noire*, Charlet. It might seem bizarre to devote more than three pages to an artist he despises and whom, like Pinelli, he would have omitted had it not been for the demands of public opinion. But his strategy becomes clear in the subsequent pages on the greatest French caricaturist, Daumier,

---

[3] Unlike Malraux's depiction of Clappique's 'frénésie de perdre' at the gaming table in *La Condition humaine* (pt. 5), or Dostoevsky's *The Gambler*. See also Walter Benjamin, *Charles Baudelaire: A Lyric Poet in the Era of High Capitalism* (London: NLB, 1973), 135–8.

[4] The caption reads: 'Quand on a tout perdu, quand on n'a plus d'espoir . . .'.

[5] Mentioned by Champfleury, *Histoire de la caricature moderne* (Paris: Dentu, 1872), 284.

whose works are the exact opposite of Charlet's, and whose genius is given greater relief and impact by the brutal contrast with the third rate. The criticism of Charlet matches almost point for point that of Horace Vernet in the *Salon de 1846*: as an exclusive patriot he lacks the universal, cosmopolitan spirit essential to artistic genius and would not be understood beyond the Rhine or Pyrenees; he flatters his public, confirming them in the security of their prejudices instead of alerting them to a different reality through the subversive power of the comic; even his representations of monks are feeble, designed merely to please and flatter the anti-clericalism of the *soldat laboureur*, with none of the vigorous beauty in ugliness of Goya's monstrous creations; he idealizes the soldier and the child, and is blind to their reality. Baudelaire alludes to no particular drawing, but a good example of what so irritates him would be *L'Allocution*,[6] which shows mature soldiers and boys in noble, valiant postures preparing for battle. Like Horace Vernet's work it is nothing but *poncif*, aggravated by the *chic* of the abuse of memory deprived of a model, with the result that the figures appear as prefabricated *patrons* producing the kind of art that Baudelaire thinks above all pernicious since it deforms reality and 'dérange les conditions de la vie' (p. 41).

One drawing about which Baudelaire is grudgingly positive is the macabre *Voilà peut-être comme nous serons dimanche!* It depicts robbers in a forest looking at a hanged man: 'un pendu, déjà long et maigre, prend le frais de haut et respire la rosée, le nez incliné vers la terre et les pointes des pieds correctement alignées comme celles d'un danseur' (p. 548). But the praise is soon dissipated by an unfavourable comparison with the lines in which Villon is said to have evoked his comrades eating beneath the gibbet on a dark plain.[7] Another half-hearted effort is made to find merit in the early *Uniformes de la garde impériale* of 1819–20 before Charlet became convinced of his own greatness: 'les personnages ont un caractère réel. Ils doivent être très ressemblants. L'allure, le geste, les airs de tête sont excellents.' But the final summing-up is an unequivocal *éreintage*, in which Charlet is committed with Horace Vernet and Bérenger, 'ses cousins germains en ignorance et en sottise', to sleep 'dans le panier de l'indifférence'.

---

[6] British Museum, London.

[7] Again, Baudelaire's memory fails him, that is, if he is thinking of 'L'Epitaphe de Villon en forme de ballade', in which the bodies of the poet and his friends on the gallows have been eaten by crows.

1. Charlet, *L'Allocution*

The astonishing thing is that Baudelaire's god, Delacroix, took a diametrically opposite view of Charlet, whom he had known since his youth and admired as much as Bonington and Géricault. Hannoosh has analysed Delacroix's article in *La Revue des deux mondes* and has suggested various passages as possible retorts to the poet's strictures for which the master had reproached him.[8] That their attitudes should have been so fundamentally different is hard to explain. The article does contain some minor reservations, and it is possible that Delacroix was reacting out of fidelity to an old friend and to the spirit of the times in which much of his work was produced. Whether or not he was trying to redress what he saw as an injustice in Baudelaire's intemperate criticism must remain a matter of speculation; but one tends to side with the poet as far as the question of idealization is concerned, and to the extent that as caricatures Charlet's lithographs are singularly lacking in humour.

[8] *Baudelaire and Caricature*, 109–13. See also Baudelaire's account of his meeting with Delacroix: 'il m'a fait venir une fois chez lui, exprès pour me *tancer*, d'une façon véhémente, à propos d'un article irrespectueux que j'avais commis à l'endroit de cet enfant gâté du chauvinisme' (764).

It is, however, Daumier who dominates the article. Baudelaire considers him one of the most important figures not only in caricature but in modern art in general, a man whose works are familiar to the public, but who remains anonymous since people do not take the trouble to read the initials on the drawings. What is odd about Baudelaire's discussion is that, after a few introductory facts about Daumier's beginnings, he embarks on a digression on the caricatural fever following the revolution of 1830: 'C'est un tohu-bohu, un capharnaüm, une prodigieuse comédie satanique, tantôt bouffonne, tantôt sanglante, où defilent, affublées de costumes variés et grotesques, toutes les honorabilités politiques' (p. 549). The vocabulary of chaos and violence, reminiscent of the English pantomime in *De l'essence du rire*, suggests a buffoonery akin to the 'comique absolu', all the more powerfully as this fantastic epic is punningly crowned by Philipon's famous representation of Louis-Philippe as a pear, 'par la pyramidale et olympienne *Poire* de processive mémoire'.[9] In exaggerating a harmless and obliging comparison into a metaphor, like Hoffmann with his carrots, Philipon has created a surreal comedy, and at the same time a kind of shorthand, an 'argot plastique' (p. 550) immediately comprehensible to the opponents of the regime who used it as a negative standard round which to rally.

In this gory buffoonery, full of massacres, imprisonments, arrests, trials, searches, and beatings-up, the King plays the role of ogre or assassin, or of a Gargantua with an insatiable appetite. A striking feature is that the works referred to remain anonymous, unidentified by Baudelaire, who describes them from a faulty memory, which reinforces the point that he is writing not as a historian or philosopher, but as a journalist, bent less on accuracy than on getting his message over to his public as economically as possible. The essays are full of inaccuracies and misattributions. A letter to his mother shows he was aware of the shortcomings of what he hoped would become a 'gros travail': 'Tu verras quelques pages étonnantes sans doute; le reste n'est qu'un ramas de contradictions et de divagations. Quant à l'érudition, il n'y en a que l'apparence.'[10] The first caricature, bearing the Shakespearean caption 'Have you pray'd tonight, Madam?', shows a pear-headed Othello-Philippe with the burly shoulders of a worker in the

---

[9] The pun is clearly on 'couronnée' and 'pyramidale', from Latin *pirum*, a pear. Baudelaire tells the often repeated story of how Philipon, in order to prove to the court the innocence of his caricature, made four successive drawings, beginning with a perfect likeness of the King and ending with the fatal pear.

[10] *Corr.* i. 178.

halles about to strangle innocent Liberty. The message, and its gro-tesqueness, would have been all the more direct and powerful as the play had been brought to the attention of the public in Vigny's trans-lation *Le More de Venise*, Rossini's opera, and Delacroix's paintings. Another caricature shows Liberty, in Phrygian hat and bearing the innocent coquetry of a democratic *grisette*, surrounded by the King and his ministers making indecent propositions; another, convincingly identified by Hannoosh as *Une exécution sous Louis XI* by Traviès, shows her before some gothic court of the King with his leering ministers, while yet another pictures her in the torture chamber with recognizable figures as her executioners, 'les bêtes noires de l'opinion'. The only reference to Daumier in all this is oblique, to the scatological lithograph of December 1831 for which he served a six-month prison sentence. It represents the Pear as Gargantua, enthroned on a *chaise percée*, swallowing the tribute of his toiling subjects and excreting divers medals and honours to his grateful deputies. Baudelaire declares that since the February revolution, he had seen only one caricature equal in ferocity to those that followed July 1830. It shows a body on a stretcher, riddled with bullets, during the massacres of Rouen in April 1848: 'A genoux devant la civière, enveloppé dans sa robe de juge, la bouche ouverte et montrant comme un requin la double rangée de ses dents taillées en scie, F. C.[11] promène lentement sa griffe sur la chair du cadavre qu'il égratigne avec délices. —Ah! le Normand! dit-il, il fait le mort pour ne pas répondre à la Justice!' (p. 552). As with the other works, its impact stems from the overt vio-lence, the grotesque or incongruous expressions of the principal and background figures, and the contrast with the central drama. But this unidentified caricature, which Timothy Clark thinks was probably never published,[12] can be thought so to outstrip the others in its macabre and surreally perverted logic as to belong to a separate cat-egory, akin to the black humour defined and popularized by André Breton.

What is striking about the pages on the 1830 revolution is the discrepancy between some of the scenes and Baudelaire's inflated vocabulary. On the one hand he stresses the violence, chaos, and exaggeration; on the other we have the relative stasis, for example, of the Traviès cartoon, in which the characters appear almost too di-minutive to have much effect on the viewer. A possible explanation is

[11] Frank-Carré, president of the court of Rouen.
[12] Clark, *Absolute Bourgeois*, 143.

that Baudelaire sees the grotesqueness not so much in the individual drawings as in their sheer volume, in the cumulative effect of so much savagery and madness. As elsewhere in his criticism, there is a sense of accumulation, of a momentum which, once set in motion, threatens to engulf reason, order and balance, a proliferation conveyed by the repeated 'tohu-bohu', and the adjective 'tous/toutes' added to every noun. What is evoked is not the world of one artist, but of a generation, a decade of history given over to the sound and fury of insanity. Here is the Fall, not as it affects individuals, but a society.

The role of Daumier in the battle against the government is nowhere more tellingly exemplified than in the lithograph of the massacre of la rue Transnonain during the uprising of the Lyons weavers in February 1834. This famous work is among the most powerful of his output, one in which Baudelaire believes he proves himself a great artist. It shows a simple room, its basic furniture scattered about, and the dead body of a worker, half propped against an unmade bed, half stretched-out on the bloodstained floor, in his nightcap, his shirt indecently revealing his bare legs. A woman's feet emerge from the gloom on the left, and on the right is seen the head of an old man, cut off by the edge of the drawing, while under his body the father crushes the corpse of his child: 'Dans cette mansarde froide il n'y a rien que le silence et la mort' (p. 552). This, writes Baudelaire, is not exactly caricature; for though the undignified postures and the arbitrary obscenity of violent death are chillingly grotesque, there is not the same macabre or sick humour as in the previous works. No trace here of the 'comique absolu';[13] 'c'est de l'histoire, de la triviale et terrible réalité', conveying with all the emotive power and mastery of a great artist the scandal of a brutal historical event of legalized murder. The work stands on its own as a totally engaged and effective protest, which elevates it above the minor art of caricature to put it on the same level as great art. We are no longer in the domain of satire or the comic of whatever sort; Daumier's peers are not Goya, Hogarth, or any of the French caricaturists. Baudelaire's description recalls David's *Marat assassiné*, with the hand hanging from the bath, still holding his pen, the wound in the chest, the mouth agape with his last breath, the blood in the water and on the paper, the kitchen knife on the floor, and the 'misérable support de planches' which serves as a working table with its simple and poignant inscription 'A Marat, David'. 'Tous ces détails

---

[13] *Pace* Hannoosh, *Baudelaire and Caricature*, 137.

sont historiques et réels, comme un roman de Balzac; le drame est là, vivant dans toute sa lamentable horreur, et par un tour de force étrange qui fait de cette peinture le chef-d'œuvre de David et une des grandes curiosités de l'art moderne, elle n'a rien de trivial ni d'ignoble' (pp. 409–10). The historical reality, the drama, the cruelty, the lamentable horror, the coldness of the scene, are all shared by Daumier's piece, the difference being the triviality of the one, and the nobility of the other. In Daumier, nothing but silence and the insignificance of an anonymous death; in David the added triumph of spirituality and 'le parfum de l'idéal' conferred by the sublime demise of 'le *divin* Marat', transformed from his real ugliness into an Apollo-like beauty, 'tel qu'en lui-même enfin l'éternité le change'. Here are two forms of modernity, one poignant in its trivial reality devoid of transcendence, the other in which the reality of history has been transformed into the sublimity of epic, 'un don à la patrie éplorée'.

At this point Baudelaire alludes to two series of satirical portraits of politicians, the one full-length, the other in bust, which appeared in *La Caricature* and *Le Charivari* in 1833–4. What interests him, however, is not the political dimension, which he does not even mention, but Daumier's excellence as a portraitist, his ability to combine comic verve with the precision of a Lavater. His *charges* remain within bounds, those ordained by nature and observed by the Swiss physionomist. His fidelity to nature keeps him within the constraints of reality, protecting him from the excesses of *fantaisie*, while the discipline of Lavater ('telle main veut tel pied') endows his figures with a natural unity and harmony. Baudelaire sees in these portraits less a political document related to a specific time than a study of manners and the fundamental corruption of human beings. Here, as elsewhere, his attention is not to the specific or circumstantial, but to the general and enduring. No particular politician or incident is mentioned. What these animal-like faces show is 'toutes les pauvretés de l'esprit, tous les ridicules, toutes les manies de l'intelligence, tous les vices du cœur', thus participating in the category of 'le comique significatif', though, as previously, there is a hint of the 'absolu' in the way the accumulated works appear to exhaust the categories of corruption. Though ostensibly still about the political satire of the 1830s, this passage already contains the basic elements of Baudelaire's conclusion, in which two and a half pages later the series devoted to the infamous Robert Macaire is defined as the decisive inauguration of 'la caricature de mœurs'. Just as in the seventeenth century the *Satire Ménippée* gave way to Molière, so caricature moves from the political and the particular to concern itself with the actions and manners of all the citizens, thus passing into a domain which most closely resembles that of the novel.

Among the works from Daumier's earlier period, which Baudelaire believes generally lack the lightness of touch and sense of improvisation of his later manner, he singles out *La Liberté de la presse* as particularly successful, being 'très fini, très consciencieux et très sévère', in spite of a suspicion of heaviness. As so often, he is content to describe the caricature without analysis, and allow it to speak for itself. It shows, he says,[14] amid the instruments of his trade 'un ouvrier typographe, coiffé sur l'oreille du sacramentel bonnet de papier, les manches de chemise retroussées, carrément campé, établi solidement sur ses grands pieds' (p. 553) with his fists clenched and frowning

2. Daumier, *Rue Transnonain*

[14] From his reference to the instruments of the typographer's trade, absent in the caricature, it would appear that once again Baudelaire was writing from memory, confusing in his mind *La Liberté de la presse. Ne vous y frottez pas!* (1834; see ibid. 147) with *Ah! tu veux te frotter à la presse!!* (*La Caricature*, 3 Oct. 1833).

eyebrows, while in the background the eternal Philippe and his minions skulk, but dare not intervene. What humour there is lies in the contrast between the noble defiance of the muscular worker, and the craven impotence of the miniscule figures of the King and his police. Here the atmosphere is quite different from the drawings in which Liberty is endangered by her grotesque attackers. In the latter, the satire is foregrounded, while in the former it is proud defiance. With this work, in which the humour is minimal, there is a strong case for considering Daumier the artist who most successfully gave expression, albeit in a minor genre, not just to the scandals and inequities of modern life as in *Rue Transnonain*, but to its heroism.[15]

3. Daumier, *Le Dernier Bain*

[15] A letter of July 1861 to Martinet mentions a study on Daumier (*Corr.* ii. 176). Whether it was a recycling of what Baudelaire had already written or a new study is not known, since it was never published and has been lost.

Baudelaire goes on to describe four caricatures from different genres to illustrate the seriousness and diversity of Daumier's work, which he compares to a labyrinth or forest: *Le Dernier Bain, A la santé des pratiques*, a scene from *Némésis médicale*, and a plate from *Les Philanthropes du jour*. The diversity of these drawings and their varying degrees of humour do not conceal their common preoccupation with violence and death, to which Baudelaire seems instinctively attracted. *Le Dernier Bain* of 1840 is the most caricatural because the most exaggerated in gesture, posture, and contrast:

Sur le parapet d'un quai, debout et déjà penché, faisant un angle aigu avec la base d'où il se détache comme une statue qui perd son équilibre, un homme se laisse tomber roide dans la rivière. Il faut qu'il soit bien décidé; ses bras sont tranquillement croisés; un fort gros pavé est attaché à son cou avec une corde. (p. 553)

On the other side of the river, a bourgeois gives his insouciant attention to the delights of angling. Baudelaire captures the stiffness and the statue-like rigidity of the suicide and his posture. Clearly, the resemblance to a statue was intended by Daumier, who underscores it with a kind of visual pun, since the stone round the man's neck is not some rough boulder but has the size and the shape of a plinth. The implication is that the man has lost whatever prestige he had, and that whatever raised him in the eyes of others has now been taken from him and is the macabre instrument of his watery demise; which is no doubt why Baudelaire talks of him as fleeing the spectacle of civilization. He also notices 'la redingote chétive et grimaçante' with the man's bones showing through, a caricatural equivalent of 'la pelure du héros moderne' (p. 494); but, though he does not mention that the man has tied his feet with the meticulous preparation of the suicide, he embroiders on the spectacle, adding a serpent-like cravat and a pointed Adam's apple, which are not in the picture. The grim humour is in the exaggerated stiffness of the man's body, and in the impossible angles between him and the parapet, and between his neck and the perpendicular rope with the stone tied to it. It arises also from the contrast between his resolute and anguished expression accentuated by the frenzy of his windswept hair, and the carefree pleasure of the angler, intent on what may come out of the river, but unconcerned about what may go into it. The angler in turn conjures up, in a grating piece of ironic intertextuality, Brueghel's famous painting of the fall of Icarus, unnoticed by the ploughman who pursues his humble and useful task, oblivious of Promethean enterprises. It would be idle to speculate on what self-reflexive irony may lie behind Baudelaire's assertion that it is not the suicide of a poet who wishes to be fished out and talked about; but there can be little doubt that the poet who had contemplated suicide in 1845,[16] who had pondered that of Nerval (pp. 156, 236, 306), who in 1846 had exalted the heroism of 'suicides *modernes*', who had written of Stoicism that it is a religion whose only sacrament was suicide,[17] was peculiarly drawn to this 'caricature sérieuse et lamentable' of a temptation born of despair.

The second plate, whose title Baudelaire does not remember, and some details of which are inaccurate, is equally macabre, but in a quite different way, having much more social import. *A la santé des pratiques*[18] shows what appears to be a doctor drinking to the health of his clients at the 'Rendez-vous des bons vivants', in the company of a gleefully smiling and top-hatted skeleton, complete with his inevitable scythe, reading a pamphlet promoting some infallible panacea, the certain and profitable results of which can be seen in the background in the form of a hearse, followed by mourners with appropriately bowed heads. The theme of death figures also in *Choléra-Morbus* from *Némésis médicale*, but without the element of social satire. In both drawings Baudelaire emphasizes the fierce sunlight; the 'soleil de plomb' in the one, in the other the splendid, white sky of Paris, 'incandescent d'ardeur' (p. 554), that ironically accompanies great scourges and political upheavals alike. The reference is to the epidemic that struck Paris on 26 March 1832, and to the torrid days of revolution in 1789, July 1830, and June 1848. This, as Alison Fairlie has pointed out,[19] is the same ironic sun of 'Une charogne' and 'Le Cygne'; it is also the sky of the even more gratingly ironic prose poems, 'la coupole spleenétique du ciel' of 'Chacun sa chimère', or the indifferent exuberance of the 'œil brûlant' of the sun in 'Le Fou et la Vénus', matched only by 'le soleil ivre [qui] se vautrait tout de son long sur un tapis de fleurs magnifiques engraissées par la destruction' in 'Le Tir et le cimetière'; so that the drawing can be said to reflect some of Baudelaire's own obsessions. In the foreground a dead man lies sprawled across the pavement, while a woman enters a house with her

---

[16] See his letter of 30 June 1845 to Ancelle (*Corr.* i. 124).

[17] *Oc.* i. 664.

[18] Published in *Le Charivari*, 26 May 1840, its full title adds *association en commandite pour l'exploitation de l'humanité*.

[19] *Imagination and Language* (Cambridge: Cambridge University Press, 1981), 196.

4. Daumier, *A la santé des pratiques*

hand over her nose and mouth, and in the backgound there are two hearses similar in size and shape to the one in *A la santé des pratiques*. The posture of one of the horses mirrors exactly that of a famished dog skulking across the square, its tail between its legs. Here again the humour is minimal, confined to the postures of the animals and people, and it is the thought that is foregrounded, showing humanity as a victim of disease and sudden death under a blistering and cruel sun that hastens the progress of the plague. The drawing makes no social comment, but Baudelaire is quick to exploit its potential and supply one of his own. The reference to 'les grands remue-ménage politiques' and the square 'plus désolée qu'une place populaire dont l'émeute a fait une solitude' invite the inescapable comparison of political uprising to a scourge as inhuman and destructive as a plague.

The final example of Daumier's serious thinking is a plate from *Les Philanthropes du jour*,[20] representing a prison scene with a well-dressed philanthropist seated between two vicious-looking convicts, 'stupides comme des crétins, féroces comme des bouledogues, usés comme des loques' (p. 554), one of whom admits to frightful crimes. The caption reads: 'Ainsi donc, mon ami, à vingt deux ans vous aviez déjà tué trois hommes . . . quelle puissante organisation, et combien la société est coupable de ne l'avoir mieux dirigée! . . .—Ah! voui, monsieur! . . . la gendarmerie a eu bien des torts à mon égard . . . sans elle je ne serais pas ici!' It is easy to see how the joke would have appealed to Baudelaire, whose belief in human imperfection was fortified by his Catholic upbringing and his reading of Joseph de Maistre on the redemptive effect of capital punishment. What he most often picks out in Daumier is the blackly humorous preoccupation with death, in the form of suicide, murder, plague, or poisoning, and even when talking about his work in general terms, with its depiction of the manias and monstrosities of the bourgeois in the capital city, he notes the incidence of dead bodies, 'le cadavre vivant et affamé, le cadavre gras et repu', as if always aware of the skeleton beneath the flesh.

Having listed the principal series of Daumier's caricatures, Baudelaire gives a paragraph to l'*Histoire ancienne*, which seems to him important as the best paraphrase of Joseph Berchoux's famous line 'Qui [nous] délivrera des Grecs et des Romains?' (p. 46). Just as in 1852 the poet had levelled his excoriating wit against the puerilities of 'l'école païenne' with its absurdly anachronistic cult of the ancient world and its deities, so Daumier ridicules 'la fausse antiquité'; 'et le bouillant Achille, et le prudent Ulysse, et la sage Pénélope, et Télémaque, ce grand dadais, et la belle Hélène qui perdit Troie, et tous enfin nous apparaissent dans une laideur bouffonne qui rappelle ces vieilles carcasses d'acteurs tragiques prenant une prise de tabac dans les coulisses' (p. 556). These fixed types with their inevitable and unchanging epithets, devoid of psychological verity or nuance, conforming to fixed patterns of utterance and action, may have dignified the epics and tragedies to which they belonged in their time; but in the real world of the nineteenth century with its stridency and

---

[20] See Hannoosh, *Baudelaire and Caricature*, 143.

5. Daumier, *Les Nuits de Pénélope*

uncertainties they are hopeless anachronisms, impeding the expression of a modern outlook and sensibility. Irony is more than just a dominant feature in this sensibility; it has become a vision in its own right, finding its natural expression in comedy and caricature. Those, says Baudelaire, who have little respect for Olympus and tragedy, will have reason to be delighted, no doubt because they share his predilection for comedy over tragedy which he thinks incapable of giving expression to the complexities of modern life and the modern psyche. He gives no example from this hilarious series of fifty drawings; but *Les Nuits de Pénélope* must be among the most outrageous; it shows a haggard and completely drained Penelope, collapsed in her chair, her night's work of embroidery undone, casting a desperately faithful eye upon the idiotically grinning, self-satisfied effigy of Ulysses on the wall. Here is the lofty world of epic, demythologized and endowed with the caricatural realism of everyday existence, just as in Baudelaire's own work the lyrical is brought down to earth and made absurdly literal[21] in the shrill realities of *Le Spleen de Paris*.

To conclude the section, Baudelaire has three brief paragraphs defining Daumier's art and the moral that emerges from it. Placing him among the greatest draughtsmen, as he had in the *Salon de 1845*, he praises his sureness of touch, and the ease and abundance of his draughtsmanship, which appears as a sustained improvisation. Daumier draws from memory, but unlike Charlet, Vernet, and Scheffer, he never falls into the trap of the *chic*. His observation and fidelity to nature keep him within the limits prescribed by Lavater, but they also prevent his art from reaching the heights of 'le comique absolu'. His comedy is reasonable, 'significatif', avoiding anything that is not immediately understandable by a French public. Like Molière's, it goes straight to the point, there being no barrier between the visual and one's understanding of it. The great merit of his drawings is in the immediacy of the idea, the moral message or simply the humour, '[qui] se dégage d'emblée', as if the humour were involuntary, springing not from an idea but from a vision which imposes itself independently of the artist. The caption, if it exists at all, is brief, and the drawing is most often sufficiently eloquent to do without it. One need think only of *Les Nuits de Pénélope*, or *L'Odorat* or *La Vue* (showing the sense of smell or sight) to appreciate the accuracy of Baudelaire's observation.

---

[21] Baudelaire's prose poems are often marked by a 'caricatural' literality, as, for example, in 'Le Mauvais Vitrier', where he wishes to see 'la vie en beau' through coloured windows, or in 'Le Galant Tireur' to '*tuer* le Temps'.

His final judgement is that all Daumier's work is marked by a fund of decency and good nature, without rancour or gall, and that he avoided certain subjects because they went beyond the limits of the comic and might upset people. Here again, we notice Baudelaire seeming to play down the political side of Daumier, some aspects of which might be thought to participate in the 'comique féroce', in favour of the benign humour that characterizes his later work.[22]

An arresting paradox marks the final brief paragraph which claims that Daumier's drawing is naturally coloured, and that his lithographs and wood engravings 'éveillent des idées de couleur' (p. 557). Typically, the claim is allusive, but makes sense in the context of the rest of Baudelaire's aesthetic. The function of Daumier's pencilwork is not just to define contours; by implication, it is to indicate the structures and masses that form the harmony of the drawing. And if indeed one holds a Daumier at a distance, one notices these constitutive masses, which are the lithographic counterpart of the colour masses in a Delacroix painting, and have the same function. It was already a flattery to compare him to the greatest draughtsmen, but the supreme accolade was surely to put this essentially black and white art on the same level as that of the greatest colourist of the time, and to have recognized in it the vitality of his palette. Baudelaire is not just indulging in hyperbole and paradox for their own sake; he is identifying something in Daumier's art that distinguishes it from that of any of the other caricaturists he mentions. A brief comparison of one of his drawings, a court or street scene, with a Gavarni or a Grandville will distinguish the comparative rigidity of their gestures and postures, and the stasis of their scenes which seem posed for the camera, from the verve and movement of Daumier's fleeting creations, caught in mid-flight by the action camera of the *flâneur* on the lookout for the idiosyncratic, monstrous, or droll. The next step would have been to recognize in Daumier a great colourist, in fact, and a great creator of oil paintings; but here, as with Courbet and Manet, Baudelaire is curiously silent, possibly because Daumier came so late to oil on canvas that Baudelaire never got to know his work in that medium.

The transition to Monnier[23] is not arbitrary, but part of a strategy to highlight Daumier's genius by placing him between two mediocre talents. The tone is devastating. If Monnier has been successful in

---

[22] The final quatrain of Baudelaire's 'Vers pour le portrait de M. Honoré Daumier' states that his laughter 'rayonne, franc et large, / Comme un signe de sa bonté!' (*Oc.* i. 167).

[23] Henri Monnier (1799–1877) is best known for his *Scènes populaires*, published in 1830.

bourgeois circles and in artists' studios it is because, like Julius Caesar, he filled three functions: actor, writer, and caricaturist. His art is essentially bourgeois, since his ability in each domain is the exact opposite of what ideally it should be: as an actor he is cold, unlike Rouvière; as a writer finicky, unlike, say, Balzac; and as an artist he has contrived the surreally impossible feat of creating *chic* from nature. Like all realists he is obsessed with detail, and is thus incapable of seeing things 'en grand'. His archetypal bourgeois, Monsieur Prudhomme, is 'monstrueusement vrai', to the point of being a traced-out copy, or *sténographie*[24] of Monnier's endless observations in cafés and other such places. One cannot deny they are appealing, for to do so would be to deny the charm of the camera; 'mais Monnier ne sait rien créer, rien idéaliser, rien arranger' (p. 558). His works lack *naïveté*, having the cold limpidity of a mirror reflecting the passer-by. To understand the inadequacy of Monnier's art, one need only compare his passivity with the vitality and passion of the true *flâneur*, of the man of the crowd who gives himself 'poésie et charité, à l'imprévu qui se montre, à l'inconnu qui passe'.[25] If these drawings are inadequate aesthetically, they can be considered inadequate morally as well, as the reference to the reflection of the passer-by indicates. What Monnier produces does not belong to the domain of art, irony, or caricature; it appears rather as a flattery of the unthinking and self-satisfied bourgeois who, like the Paris crowd, 'se complaît dans les miroirs où elle se voit' (p. 119). Before Monnier's reflection, the bourgeois is reassured and confirmed in his status and condition, like the hideously ugly man in the prose poem 'Le Miroir' who affirms his immortal and inalienable right, given by 1789, to admire himself in his mirror.[26]

If Baudelaire's damning of Monnier is unequivocal, his page on Grandville is elliptic and ambiguous. The burden of his two paragraphs is that Grandville is 'un esprit maladivement littéraire' (p. 558) who has strayed into the visual arts. Like the unspeakable Ary Scheffer, guilty of trying to give expression to literary abstractions in the supremely concrete medium of oil painting, he has confused one medium with another, being constantly on the lookout for hybrid means of projecting his thought into the domain of the visual arts. So

[24] Champfleury tells how in the 1840s 'un poète taquin' [Baudelaire] explained that 'les *Scènes populaires* n'étaient pas de l'art. Il manquait à la plupart de ces sténographies un reflet de la personnalité du créateur; tout était traité sans idéalisation, par menus détails, jamais par masse, et par là les types restaient à l'état de croquis d'après nature' (*Histoire*, 244).

[25] See 'Les Foules', *Oc.* i. 291.

[26] See my *Baudelaire and 'Le Spleen de Paris'*, 78–80 for a discussion of this poem.

convinced is Baudelaire of this failing that he accuses him of attaching speech-balloons to the mouths of his characters, though one would be hard put to find evidence of this in his published drawings.[27] Though he touched upon various questions, being neither a philosopher nor an artist, he fell inevitably between two stools. This imbalance and lack of creative cohesion or focus would be of interest to a philosopher or doctor who could produce a fine psychological and physiological study of Grandville, and it is for this reason no doubt that Baudelaire is interested more in the man than in his drawings. It is possible that he felt some affinity with this *homo duplex*, since duality is rooted in the human psyche nowhere more firmly than in that of modern man. But the specificity of art forms, their distinctive virtues and competence, constitute a fundamental tenet in his aesthetic, and such a duality cannot be other than a fatal weakness if installed within the artist, torn between incompatible genres.

And yet Baudelaire's admiration is unmistakable for this man who, with superhuman courage, has passed his life in redoing creation: 'il la prenait dans ses mains, la tordait, la rarrangeait, l'expliquait, la commentait [. . .] Il a mis le monde sens dessus dessous.' The extraordinary world of *Un autre monde* (which Baudelaire mistakenly calls *Le Monde à l'envers*) may be amusing for some, but he finds it frightening, with its systematic disorder, its cornices propped up by the floor, furniture with its feet in the air, drawers opening inwards, its defiance of the laws of nature. The extravagance and absurdity of this other world must surely bring it close to the 'comique absolu'. Furthermore, the moral message seems drowned in the flights of imagination, as in *Les Poissons d'avril*, which shows fish angling for human beings in a topsy-turvy world. The distorted perspectives, the duel of the sugar cane and beetroot, 'dispute qui ne s'est terminée que par l'intervention (tardive, hélas!) de la carotte', his procession of bizarre animals representing some unthinkable menu—'lièvre faisandé, oie en matelotte, homard saumoné, perdreau à queue d'écrevisse, escargot-tortue, cochon-dinde rôti'[28]—show the artist's domination of nature which he recasts in accordance with his fantasy, creating an art that is primarily joyous. Baudelaire makes no mention, however, of the 'comique absolu' or of any other kind, and reverts to negative criticism,

---

[27] See J. J. Grandville, *L'Œuvre graphique complète de Grandville* (Paris: Arthur Hubschmid, 1975).

[28] J. J. Grandville, *Un autre monde* (Paris: 1844), 64, 36. A 'poisson d'avril' is an April fool's joke.

6. Grandville, *Crime et expiation*

declaring that, though capable of some good things, Grandville lacks flexibility and is incapable of drawing a woman. It is the mad side of his talent that is important, as in his late drawings just before his death in 1847, which Hannoosh has identified as *Crime et expiation* and *Une promenade dans le ciel* from *Deux Rêves*.[29] Here, says Baudelaire, Grandville 'appliquait sa volonté, toujours opiniâtre, à noter sous une forme plastique la succession des rêves et des cauchemars, avec la précision d'un sténographe qui écrit le discours d'un orateur. L'artiste-Grandville voulait, oui, il voulait que le crayon expliquât la loi d'association des idées' (p. 559). Baudelaire's view is that his courage, stubbornness and will-power have been misdirected in an impossible task and the result is failure.

From his beginnings in *Métamorphoses du jour* (1828) Grandville had been obsessed with the general idea of analogy. Following a tradition going back to Le Brun that exploits analogies between human and animal traits, he had shown on a sliding scale the metamorphosis of a human face into that of a fish, and of a dog into a human being; but Baudelaire again underlines the failure of the drawings, since Grandville did not know how to capitalize on the process: 'il cahotait comme une locomotive déraillée'. The technique is akin to Philipon's with his Pear—with this crucial difference that Philipon succeeded in creating a new metaphor, a visual neologism in the slang language of caricature, whereas Grandville's doggedness and perseverance appear repetitive and inconsequential. For all its variety, his work is monotonous, marked above all by a lack of insight into the moral or social truths of contemporary life or of the permanent truths of human nature and the conditions in which it evolves. The analogies, in other words, stop short, without expansion, as indeed in *Deux Rêves*, the first of which is an elaborate narration based on association of ideas, mainly pertaining to shape. A murderer clubs to death a man whose head takes the form of the roots of a tree, signifying that his life has been uprooted. A cross marking the place of death, becomes a fountain, then a sword, then the scales of justice, a pan of which becomes an eye which grows bigger, pursuing the criminal, knocking him off a column (symbol of his pride and self-respect), until it is finally transformed into a giant fish about to devour him, as he stretches out towards a luminous cross of redemption. Narrative here is quite different from that of a Greuze genre painting, for example, such as *Le Fils prodigue*,

[29] Hannoosh, *Baudelaire and Caricature*, 169.

where it is constructed from the attitudes and gestures of the participants in the drama, each element of which is caught simultaneously, within the instant. In Grandville's caricature the narration evolves from one figure to the next in a dramatic and temporal succession, in a way that might be thought incompatible with the essential simultaneity of a visual art. Baudelaire seems to have sensed this, and seen it as proof of a morbidly literary talent. In the reference to the stenographer, there is an implied criticism of a dogged and unthinking fidelity to the dreams and nightmares, rather than a control or a direction of them, as if, to adapt a phrase from Nerval, Grandville were undergoing his dream instead of guiding it.[30] Baudelaire's conclusion could not be more negative: Grandville is very funny, but often without knowing it.

One might, of course, have expected the poet of 'Correspondances' to approve of this transcription of the dream world and exploitation of the resources of analogy; but the defect in Grandville lies less in the use of analogy than in the type of analogies and what triggers them. Whereas Baudelaire's are dynamic and mind-expanding, having 'l'expansion des choses infinies', or outrageous, strident, and ironic as in some of the 'Tableaux parisiens' or prose poems, Grandville's, in *Deux Rêves* at least, for all the dreamlike quality of the ensemble, are triggered purely by resemblance, the arbitrary similarity of shapes—a cross, a fountain, the scales of justice, and so on. To that extent, they lack autonomy as well as expansion, springing not so much from the depths of the imagination as from a fantastic but superficial wit. They are most unlike Goya's hallucinating creations that impose themselves on the viewer before their message has been grasped intellectually; most of all, perhaps, they lack that essential quality of all art, high or low, the ability not just to make us laugh or weep, as Flaubert said, but to 'faire rêver'.[31]

Baudelaire seems to have known only the works he mentions or to which he alludes; for had he been aware of the 'fiel et ténacité'[32] of Grandville's more directly political caricatures such as *La Guillotine*, *La France livrée aux corbeaux*, *L'Enterrement de la Liberté*, or the

[30] 'Je ne demande pas à Dieu de rien changer aux événements, mais [. . .] de me laisser le pouvoir de créer autour de moi un univers qui m'appartienne, de diriger mon rêve éternel au lieu de le subir' (Gérard de Nerval, *Œuvres*, vol. i (Paris: Gallimard, 1974), 435).

[31] 'Ce qui me semble, à moi, le plus haut dans l'Art (et le plus difficile), ce n'est ni de faire rire, ni de faire pleurer, ni de vous mettre en rut ou en fureur, mais d'agir à la façon de la nature, c'est-à-dire de *faire rêver*' (Flaubert, *Correspondance*, ii. 417).

[32] Arsène Alexandre, *L'Art du rire et de la caricature* (Paris, 1892), 171.

macabrely humorous *Voyage pour l'éternité* with its ubiquitous skeletons, he might have nuanced his opinion. In what he states directly and what he implies he seems to have been guided by Gautier's article of 1847,[33] influencing in his turn Champfleury's opinion in his history of caricature.[34] Other contemporaries were more generous, but it was later generations who responded most positively. Rimbaud, in a famous letter to Izambard, asks admiringly if there has ever been anything 'de plus idiot que les dessins de Grandville',[35] thus preparing the way for the Surrealists' craze for what they took to be his exploration of the unconscious mind, and Benjamin, basing his interpretation on *Un autre monde*, has seen in his work an indication of the commodification of the universe and a covert denunciation and exemplification of advertising.[36] The common belief is that he is important because of 'le côté fou de son talent'; but, unlike those who came after, Baudelaire was ambiguous in saying so, expressing praise and reservation at the same time. He knew, as did subsequently Benjamin, that Grandville fell into madness and died in a *maison de santé*. Whatever his extravagant works tell us incidentally about the state of society and culture, it was the madness in the man that was of primary interest to Baudelaire; the madness in the work was more doubtful, and his art remained flawed and unable to release its 'mad' potential since it never overcame the disparity between the visual and the literary.

Anyone acquainted with Baudelaire's dismissive lines on Gavarni in 'L'Idéal'—'Je laisse à Gavarni, poète des chloroses, / Son troupeau gazouillant de beautés d'hôpital'—might be astonished to find him referred to as 'bien autrement important' (p. 559), much more important than Grandville. One has at first the impression that the transition is justified by his greater talent, but Baudelaire's reservations soon become apparent, alerting us retrospectively to the overtones of the adjective 'important', implying that he is important because he is known to a wider public and has published more. It is significant that no mention is made of the excellence of Gavarni's art or of his genius. He is not entirely a caricaturist, or even only an artist; 'il est aussi un littérateur'. The logic of the transition is clear; Gavarni is no doubt

---

[33] Published in *La Presse*, 24 Mar. 1847, and in *Portraits contemporains* (Paris: Charpentier, 1874), 231–3.

[34] Champfleury, *Histoire*, 287–98.

[35] Arthur Rimbaud, *Œuvres complètes* (Paris: Gallimard, 1972), 238.

[36] Walter Benjamin, *Paris capitale du XIXe siècle: le livre des passages* (Paris: Editions du Cerf, 1993), 173, 175, 850.

more important, but, like Grandville, he is a kind of hybrid, half artist, half man of letters. His drawings depend wholly upon their captions for their intelligibility, so his art is fundamentally dual, being divided into drawing on the one hand, and message on the other. Far removed from Daumier, whose message is seized immediately in an explosive illumination, it has all the weaknesses of 'le comique significatif', and none of its strengths.

So strong is his prejudice against the literary quality of Gavarni's art that he is blind to its positive qualities, its modernity and power to catch the dress and fashion of contemporary society, its gestures, postures, and what we now call body language. The Goncourt brothers are particularly sensitive to this aspect of his art: 'Voilà nos bras, nos jambes, nos torses, nos renversements, nos horizontalités, nos accoudements, notre marche et notre pas; toutes ces postures lâches où nous nous complaisons ainsi que dans des pantoufles faites; un portrait en pied pour lequel le dix-neuvième siècle a posé comme il était dans la rue, dans sa chambre, sans prendre une pose.'[37] In addition there is the naturalness of the drawings, their intimacy, and the sense they give the viewer of intruding incognito into a private world of domestic interiors, bourgeois, demi-monde or student, which he is privileged to observe almost in the posture of a voyeur. And like the voyeur, he is vouchsafed the sense of a discovery of the truth, not as things are with their public façade, but as they are in their reality and spontaneity, when precisely we as witnesses are not there. Here Gavarni excels as a *peintre de mœurs*, as painter of modern life, not in its public aspects, as we shall see with Guys, but in its private and secret recesses. His works, which Baudelaire lists—*Les Étudiants, Les Lorettes, Les Actrices, Les Enfants terribles*—are so many 'scènes de la vie privée', wittily and cynically portrayed, but with none of the drama or overstatement of a Balzac.

It is strange also that having underlined the importance of the captions, Baudelaire should say nothing about their wit, their variety, their lexical and stylistic richness, which would merit a study in their own right. The only example he gives is among the least typical, a drawing from *Les Balivernes parisiennes* showing a foppish young man pleading for a kiss from a pretty woman who disdainfully replies: 'Repassez ce soir, on a déjà donné à votre père ce matin' (p. 560). There is no indication of the diabolical candour of the *enfant terrible*,

---

[37] *Gavarni: l'homme et l'œuvre* (Paris: Fasquelle, 1925), 144.

the bitchiness of the *lorette* or the actress, the argot of the student, artist, concierge, or maid, which bear witness to Gavarni's powers of linguistic observation to complement the visual. The naturalness and lack of restraint of the figures are supported by the jauntiness of the caption which seems to impose itself independently of the will of the artist: 'Quand je fais mon dessin en vue d'une légende faite, j'ai beaucoup de mal, je me fatigue, et cela vient toujours moins bien: *les légendes poussent dans mon crayon, sans que je les prévoie ou que j'y aie pensé avant.*'[38]

As Sainte-Beuve was to point out,[39] Gavarni was too much of a thinker to be political, just as he was too elegant to be a caricaturist. He produced only one political caricature, against Charles X in 1830, and regretted it for the rest of his life. Baudelaire makes no mention of it, but has understood that Gavarni's talent lies elsewhere, and that he found his ideal political climate in the *apaisement* of the last years of the July monarchy rather than in the turmoil of 1830 or 1848: 'La république a un peu effacé Gavarni [. . .] Il était né avec l'apaisement, il s'éclipse avec la tempête' (p. 560).[40] Nor does he mention *Les Lorettes vieillies*, and could not have known his later work after his visit to England, depicting the hideous Thomas Vireloque,[41] in which, according to Sainte-Beuve, 'Le Gavarni-Fragonard passait insensiblement au La Bruyère.'[42] It is the Gavarni-Fragonard that Baudelaire is acquainted with, and for whom he has a mitigated admiration. He sees in him something of the elegance, understatement, and tenuousness of Marivaux. For all the modernity of his fashionable figures, his invention of the *lorette* and the *débardeuse*, and his reinvention of the spirit of carnival, Gavarni's cast of mind seems to belong more to the eighteenth century. He prefers to flatter than to bite, to encourage than to blame; like all men of letters he is slightly tainted with corruption; his hypocrisy is charming; his cynicism wears 'un vêtement gracieux', and so his thought 'caresse les préjugés et fait du monde son complice'.

---

[38] Quoted in ibid. 151.

[39] *Nouveaux Lundis* (Paris: Michel Lévy, 1866), vi. 151–2.

[40] There is no reason to think that Baudelaire is making an adverse comment here, or implying that Gavarni would have been better if his work had reflected the political turmoil of 1830 or 1848. Daumier's art had had to change during the *apaisement* (p. 555). Baudelaire's aim is to define the specific quality of Gavarni's art.

[41] *Les Propos de Thomas Vireloque.*

[42] Sainte-Beuve, *Nouveaux Lundis*, 193. Baudelaire did, however, know a drawing from *Paris le soir*, which shows considerable satirical bite (ibid. 164, and my *Baudelaire and 'Le Spleen de Paris'*, 104).

There is in his work a tolerant and cynical urbanity typical of the eighteenth century, whose echo is prolonged in Stendhal in the figures of the Marquis de la Mole and Count Mosca. Incapable of caricature, 'il n'a jamais fait une figure grimaçante exagérée',[43] and his characters are so handsome that they served as models, for the *lorette* or the art student, rather than representations of moral faults to be corrected by the power of laughter. There was something of this in Baudelaire himself, the admirer of the licence of Fragonard and Boucher; but it was accompanied by the moral rigour of the doubting Catholic who kept the discipline of the 'examen de conscience'. His own humour was intolerant to the point of savagery, notably in the prose poems and *Pauvre Belgique!* In spite of the subtlety of Gavarni's captions, some of which are 'très entortillées', his work is easy to understand, which explains why many prefer him to Daumier. Here Baudelaire is showing his powers of understatement and reticence, making a virtue out of a shortcoming. To sum up, he sees in Gavarni a *littérateur* and implies he is superficial, or at best an anachronism within the strident vices of nineteenth-century France.

The last two and a half pages of the essay deal cursorily with Trimolet, Traviès, and Jacque, with little attempt to define their art. Baudelaire's remarks on Trimolet, whose melancholy destiny was to die in 1842 at the age of thirty, are brief. His early death, at a moment when his artistic powers were in full development, is a telling example of *le guignon*. No one could possibly suspect, says Baudelaire, from the graceful and childlike buffoonery of his works, that his poor life had been assailed by so many afflictions and sorrows. His work has a unique savour, characterized by 'la plus folle et la plus innocente gaieté' (p. 561), reminiscent of Callot or the Italians. Also, since he works directly on to the plate, his drawings have the spontaneity and imprecision of a *croquis*. Baudelaire detects also the clear influence of Cruikshank. These qualities are apparent in *Le Comic—Almanach pour 1842*, in, for example, *Mai—Parties de campagne,* which shows a fat man and woman on an old nag whose tail is being pulled by a little boy, causing both man and horse to fall. As in *Novembre* , which shows a horse being startled by a torch in the fog, the parallel with Cruikshank is evident in the chaotic movement of the tiny topsy-turvy figures and the joviality of 'le comique innocent'.

---

[43] Sainte-Beuve, *Nouveaux Lundis*, 151.

The one picture of Trimolet's that Baudelaire describes is *Le Vieux Mendiant*, correctly identified by Hannoosh:[44]

dans une nuit sombre et mouillée, un de ces vieux hommes qui ont l'air d'une ruine ambulante et d'un paquet de guenilles vivantes s'est étendu au pied d'un mur décrépi. Il lève ses yeux reconnaissants vers le ciel sans étoiles, et s'écrie: 'Je vous bénis, mon Dieu, qui m'avez donné ce mur pour m'abriter et cette natte pour me couvrir!' Comme tous les déshérités harcelés par la douleur, ce brave homme n'est pas difficile, et il fait volontiers crédit du reste au Tout-Puissant. (p. 561).

In spite of what unthinking optimists might think, there are, says Baudelaire, men of genius who have passed such nights. It is easy to see why he was drawn to this further example of *le guignon*. The expression of contentment and resignation on the face of the beggar with his folded hands and outstretched feet is reflected in his prayer and his 'quietist' acceptance of God's bounty; and the serenity of the work is matched by the transparency of its message. But nothing could be further from the despair and the discordant ambiguities of Baudelaire's prose poem, 'Le Vieux Saltimbanque', of 1861, and any attempt to bring the two together runs the serious risk of distorting both works.[45] His swipe at the optimists is an aside, independent of the picture, and the meaning and the 'comedy' of the piece remain unaffected, whereas in the prose poem, the inadequacies of the narrator and his inability to contemplate the parallel with himself are integral elements in the enigma of the work.

The fate of Traviès, an eminent artist not sufficiently recognized in his time and now almost forgotten, was similarly unfortunate. Baudelaire implies that he is at once the victim of *le guignon* and its celebrant, particularly among *le peuple*. His muse is a nymph of the faubourg, 'pâlotte et mélancolique' (p. 562), and he shows a deep feeling for the joys and griefs of the people and *la canaille*. Baudelaire thinks his *Scènes bachiques* a remarkable work, and is much impressed by his rag-pickers: 'ses chiffonniers d'ailleurs sont généralement très ressemblants, et toutes ces guenilles ont l'ampleur et la noblesse presque insaisissable du style tout fait, tel que l'offre la nature dans ses caprices'. Whether or not he was influenced by Traviès in 'Le Vin des

[44] *Baudelaire and Caricature*, 184. Jonathan Mayne, following Jacques Crépet, had suggested it was *La Prière*, which figured in the Salon of 1841 (*The Painter of Modern Life and Other Essays* (London: Phaidon, 1964), 184).

[45] *Pace* Hannoosh, *Baudelaire and Caricature*, 185.

chiffonniers', there is an obvious thematic link with *Les Fleurs du Mal*, which may explain Baudelaire's admiration in spite of his 'défaillances' and lack of the sureness of touch that marks great artists. Baudelaire makes little of Traviès's most famous creation, the sleazy and deformed trickster and profiteer, Mayeux, who is to Traviès what Robert Macaire and M. Prudhomme were to Daumier and Monnier, and who was inspired by the grimaces of a 'physiognomanic' clown, called Leclercq, who performed in taverns, drinking dens, and little theatres. His great success was to represent a hunchback; 'il imitait à s'y méprendre la bosse, le front plissé d'un bossu, ses grandes pattes simiesques et son parler criard et baveux'. From this was born the idea of Mayeux at the time of the July revolution.

A final very brief paragraph on Jacque brings the essay to an abrupt and arbitrary end. This excellent artist also is praised in fulsome but vague terms for his caricatures, the best known of which are *Militairiana* and *Malades et Médecins*: 'sa caricature a, comme tout ce qu'il fait, le mordant et la soudaineté du poète observateur'. One is left with the impression that, having exercised his analytical powers on the major French caricaturists—Daumier, Grandville, and Gavarni—Baudelaire, this self-confessed 'paresseux nerveux' whose creative difficulties are well documented,[46] has run out either of inspiration, or of time to meet the deadline for publication.

Quelques Caricaturistes étrangers

About half the length of the essay on the French, the essay on foreign caricaturists is divided into four brief sections, given in turn to the English, Spanish, Italian, and Flemish. It thus exemplifies the argument of *De l'essence du rire* that caricature, like laughter, can be defined by national characteristics. In practice, however, each artist is defined, in what is little more than a vignette, by his own artistic personality, and a deeper structure seems to emerge of alternating contrasts, between Hogarth and Cruikshank (and Seymour), and between Goya and Pinelli, with Brueghel placed at the end in a unique and extreme category which serves to define the limits of communicability of the comic.

In the first sentence Baudelaire declares his enthusiasm for

[46] See Pichois, 'Baudelaire ou la difficulté créatrice', in *Baudelaire: études et témoignages*, 242–61.

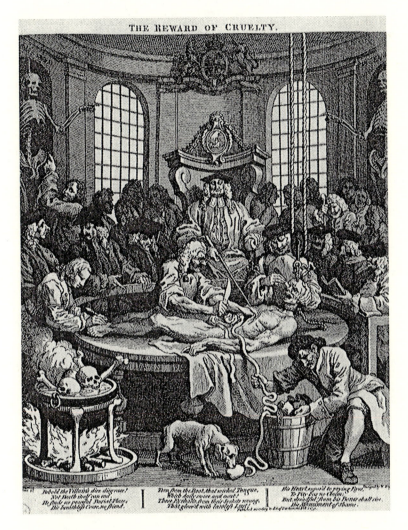

7. Hogarth, *The Reward of Cruelty*

Hogarth, 'un artiste des plus éminents en matière de comique, et qui remplit la mémoire comme un proverbe' (p. 564). Having often heard it said of him: 'C'est l'enterrement du comique', he finds in the remark a firm basis of truth, since his talent comprises something cold, astringent, and funereal. Like much of British humour, it is brutal and violent. With, however, more than a hint of reservation he sees Hogarth as always preoccupied with the moral sense of his compositions, to such an extent that, like Grandville, 'il les charge' (a clear play on words) 'de détails allégoriques et allusionnels' in order to convey his thought. Like Grandville, he is too explicit and too literary, so that the viewer is sometimes more impeded than aided in his understanding, as with *Mariage à la mode*. But his manner is varied, and in *The Rake's Progress*, *Gin Lane*, *The Enrag'd Musician*, and *The Distress'd Poet* he shows greater freedom and spontaneity. As an example of his most typical work, Baudelaire describes without naming it, from memory and with some minor inaccuracies, one of his most disturbing plates, *The Reward of Cruelty*, the last of the series of *The Four Stages of Cruelty*. Typically, he takes the caricature as a self-sufficient work, making no mention of its place in the series or of the three-stanza caption detailing the misdemeanors for which the defunct miscreant is being punished.[47]

'Sur une poulie ou toute autre mécanique scellée au plafond se dévident les intestins du mort débauché. Ce mort est horrible, et rien ne peut faire un contraste plus singulier avec ce cadavre, cadavérique entre tous, que les hautes, longues, maigres ou rotondes figures, grotesquement graves, de tous ces docteurs britanniques, chargées de monstrueuses perruques à rouleaux. Dans un coin, un chien plonge goulûment son museau dans un seau et y pille quelques débris humains.'[48]

[47] Behold the Villain's dire disgrace!
Not death itself can end.
He finds no peaceful Burial Place;
His breathless Corse, no friend.

Torn from the Root, that wicked Tongue,
Which daily swore and cursd!
Those Eyeballs from their Sockets wrung,
That glow'd with lawless Lust!

His Heart expos'd to prying Eyes,
To Pity has no Claim;
But, dreadful from his Bones shall rise,
His Monument of Shame.

[48] In fact the pulley is attached to the victim's head, and the dog appears to be eating the man's heart, which has fallen to the floor.

Among the details not mentioned by Baudelaire, one notices the principal 'surgeon', knife resolutely gripped in one hand, thrusting his other hand with grim, scientific determination into the gaping chest from which the intestines tumble to the floor; a studious young man making a more delicate incision into the foot; the gleeful abandon of a middle-aged dissector stirring a knife in the eye-socket while firmly supporting the head of the deceased, whose neck retains the rope with which he was hanged; the 'soup' of skulls and bones bubbling over a fire on the left, and the bucketful of offal on the right into which a coarse individual plunges a hand. The master surgeon presides like a judge giving instructions, with a long pointer to the place where his colleague should next operate, while on either side of the semi-circle two skeletons suspended in niches bearing their names extend arm and finger as if literally pointing out the moral of the macabre scene, above which are set the arms of the monarch with crown, lion, and unicorn. Sinister, violent, and resolute, Hogarth's work almost always involves instances of violent death, as in *The Gin Palace*. Beyond the detail of his drawings, his dominant characteristic, what makes him *sui generis*, is not so much the death of the comic as 'le comique dans l'enterrement' (p. 565).

But in spite of the trenchancy and the aphoristic character of the definition, there remains some uncertainty, since, though he has indicated the extent to which Hogarth is British, Baudelaire has not situated him in relationship to the fundamental categories of the 'comique significatif' and the grotesque. At the outset, he had stressed the moral sense of his compositions, but had then detected in works like *The Reward of Cruelty* an easing of this moral sense. By detaching the work from its place in the series of four, he himself has further lessened the moral preoccupation, and by the same stroke brought it nearer to the category of the grotesque. Indeed, if we look only at the caricature, what springs to mind is not some sense of punishment for past misdeeds, but the nightmare, half comic, half terrifying, of a world given over to violence and an absurd and unfeeling logic, a world turned upside down and inside out. The surgeons with their monstrous wigs and caricatural expressions are comic above all in their impassive concentration and serene acceptance of the macabre torture imposed on the dead man. Here is the emanation, the explosion of a comic so inhumanly and hyperbolically surreal as to have left the familiar world of human actions and emotions far behind. To read a moral into the scene seems both an absurdity and an irrelevance, an insane and doomed attempt to restore some semblance of measure to a world governed by the logic of madness. One senses a contained outburst or a restrained paroxysm. As such, it finds to some extent a parallel with 'Assommons les pauvres!', 'Le Galant Tireur', 'Portraits de maîtresses', and 'Mademoiselle Bistouri', and above all with the uncontrolled violence of that most disturbing of Baudelaire's prose poems, 'Le Mauvais Vitrier', in which the poet shatters the glazier's panes for not having ones that will allow him to see 'la vie en beau'. It is significant that Breton includes this poem in his *Anthologie de l'humour noir* and cites Hogarth as a similar spirit and practitioner of black humour. This kind of humour causes convulsions as severe as those in the pantomime with the guillotined Pierrot, but instead of giving on to joy at man's superiority over nature and his triumphant, though illusory, liberation from its restrictions, it involves a macabre and intensified awareness of a fallen humanity given over to unreason and violence. Like the grotesque, it implies a transcendence, but downwards. Breton's notion of black humour has its source in Hegel's objective humour and the independence of the self, but it owes also much to Freud. To the extent that it implies the invasion of the super-ego by the libido, it points to a victory of the pleasure principle over the law of the father. Humour, writes Freud, 'implique non seulement le triomphe du moi, mais encore du principe du plaisir qui trouve ainsi moyen de s'affirmer en dépit de réalités extérieures défavorables'.[49] As a result, it has much in common with Baudelaire's idea of the grotesque, though in the last analysis the emphasis in the latter's black humour is less on a joyous liberation than on defiance and derision of the forces that oppress humankind.

Although, like his compatriots, Seymour is presented as an *ultra* of caricature, favouring the excessive and brutal, *The deep, deep Sea* exemplifies a much more light-hearted comic than Hogarth's. It shows a rowing boat called *The Water Nymph* with two sailors, heads twisted backwards as they gawp at the scene, while at the stern sits a portly Londoner in top hat, cigar poised in his left hand, in beatific contemplation of the watery element only a few yards off the city of London. A picnic hamper and three champagne bottles are the obligatory accompaniment of the outing. What no one has noticed is that this imbecile's wife has taken accidentally to the water, from which emerge like two stumps from the knee 'upwards' the sturdy legs of this invol-

---

[49] See Breton, *Œuvres complètes*, ii. 1758 for the quotation and the influence of Hegel and Freud.

untary sea nymph. 'Tout à l'heure ce puissant amant de la nature cherchera flegmatiquement sa femme et ne la trouvera plus' (p. 566). The humour is accentuated by the caption, which Baudelaire does not mention: 'Mr Dobbs singing "—Hearts as warm as those above lie under the waters cold"'(p. 1361). Though he does not assign it to a category, the caricature with its death by drowning seems to nudge 'le comique significatif' towards the 'féroce'.

The paragraph on Seymour leads to the more relaxed humour of George Cruikshank, the special merit of whose art lies in 'une abondance inépuisable dans le grotesque' (p. 566). More than in any other artist Baudelaire finds in Cruikshank the essential ingredients of this highest form of the comic: 'la violence extravagante du geste et du mouvement, et l'explosion dans l'expression'. It is unclear how well he knew Cruikshank's work; he speaks of his abundant production but of no caricature in particular. It seems likely, however, that he was thinking neither of the caricatures of Napoleon, nor of *The Gin Shop* with its allegorical figure of death, reproduced one knows not why in the catalogue of the 1968 exhibition, but of scenes with no sense of the 'comique féroce' or of the macabre. The explosive expression could not be better exemplified than in *The Colic* which, for all its energetic little devils pulling at the lady's digestive system, is light-hearted, showing the comic of a person acutely aware of her dependence on her physical state. Similarly, *A Skaiting Party*, *A Party of Pleasure*[50] with its sinking boatful of seasick holidaymakers, and *The Comforts of a Cabriolet*, with its human content scattered chaotically on the road and in the air in extravagant disarray, make no searing statement about the accidents that flesh is heir to, but express the sense of hilarity and joyous innocence essential to the 'comique absolu'. In these drawings, with their hyperbolic gestures and movement, the laws of nature, of gravity in particular, appear either exaggerated or suspended, creating an upside-down world after the manner of Grandville: 'Tous ses petits personnages miment avec fureur et turbulence comme des acteurs de pantomime [. . .] Tout ce monde minuscule se culbute, s'agite et se mêle avec une pétulence indicible, sans trop s'inquiéter si tous ses membres sont bien à leur place naturelle.' It is an innocent buffoonery, reminiscent of Callot or Hoffmann, devoid of any disquieting or macabre element, and of any moralizing or social dimension.

[50] *A Skaiting Party* is reproduced in Mayne (ed.), *The Painter of Modern Life*, plate 46, and *A Party of Pleasure* in my 'Les Poèmes en prose de Baudelaire et la caricature', 61.

8. Cruikshank, *The Comforts of a Cabriolet!*

In spite of some deficiencies—Baudelaire thinks him insufficiently attentive to the natural posture and position of his figures' limbs—Cruikshank is the artist who represents the grotesque in its purest form. His captions are always brief, adding little if anything to our understanding of the caricature. They merely define in words what is immediately clear to the eye. In order that in these delightful extravagances there should be 'émanation, explosion, dégagement de comique' (p. 543), the verbal element is reduced to a minimum, to the point of tautology; for, as we have seen, the art of the grotesque or the comic is eminently a mute art, which is compromised to the extent that it encumbers itself with words. It is in no way surprising that he should compare the actions of Cruikshank's characters to those of actors in a pantomime, this innocent mute art *par excellence*. Nor indeed is it surprising that this innocent grotesque, the highest form of the comic, is nowhere in evidence in his own creative writings.

Baudelaire's knowlege of Goya seems to have been slight. Claude Pichois lists the oil paintings he may have seen (1363), and a letter to Nadar in 1859 shows that he was much interested in the erotic *Maja desnuda* of which he tried to acquire a copy.[51] Unaware of *Los Desastres*

---

[51] *Corr.* i. 574.

de la guerra and *Los Disparates*, which were not published until 1863–4, he probably got to know *Los Caprichos* through Gautier, whose famous study in the *Voyage en Espagne* of 1845[52] shows through his own pages on the Spanish artist. He is particularly struck by the caricatures of monks—'moines bâillants, moines goinfrants, têtes carrées d'assassins se préparant à matines, têtes rusées, hypocrites, fines et méchantes comme des profils d'oiseaux de proie' (p. 568).[53] He finds it paradoxical that such a mind, coming after the Enlightenment, should have been so obsessed by witches, sabbaths, devilish cruelty, 'toutes les débauches du rêve, toutes les hyperboles de l'hallucination'. But typically the paradox goes straight to the centre of Goya's mental universe, showing that he understood well that the rationalist's conviction that the sleep of reason produces monsters does not prevent him from being obsessed and even tempted by them. The nightmares of the rationalist indicate less a confidence in the power of reason than an agonized awareness of the dangers to which it is exposed—just as it is the mathematician Pascal who is most open to the fear of infinite space, and the philosopher Sartre to the terrors of the absurd. The other aspect of Goya that fascinated Baudelaire is the world of prostitution, with go-between hags preparing slender Spanish girls for 'la prostitution du soir, sabbat de la civilisation', in *Bellos consejos*, *Bien tirada está*, and *Ruega por ella*.[54]

Without naming them, Baudelaire describes two engravings exemplifying Goya's hallucinatory world. The first is easily identified as *Los Caprichos* 62, *Quién lo creyera!*, which shows two witches involved in what appears to be a struggle to the death in an indeterminate place:

Est-ce un coin de Sierra inconnue et infréquentée? un échantillon du chaos? Là, au sein de ce théâtre abominable, a lieu une bataille acharnée entre deux sorcières au milieu des airs. L'une est à cheval sur l'autre; elle la rosse, elle la dompte. Ces deux monstres roulent à travers l'air ténébreux. Toute la hideur, toutes les saletés morales, tous les vices que l'esprit humain peut concevoir sont écrits sur ces deux faces, qui, suivant une habitude fréquente et un

[52] It is probable that he had also read Gautier's article in *La Presse* of July 1838 (1362).
[53] As, for example, in *Caprichos* 13, 78, 79, 80.
[54] See *Caprichos* 15, 17, 31. Baudelaire may have been thinking of the following passage in Gautier: 'Le type de la *mère utile* est merveilleusement bien rendu par Goya, qui a, comme tous les peintres espagnols, un vif et profond sentiment de l'ignoble; on ne saurait imaginer rien de plus grotesquement horrible, de plus vicieusement difforme; chacune de ces mégères réunit à elle seule la laideur des sept péchés capitaux; le diable est joli à côté de cela'(Théophile Gautier *Voyage en Espagne* (Paris: Charpentier, 1879), 120).

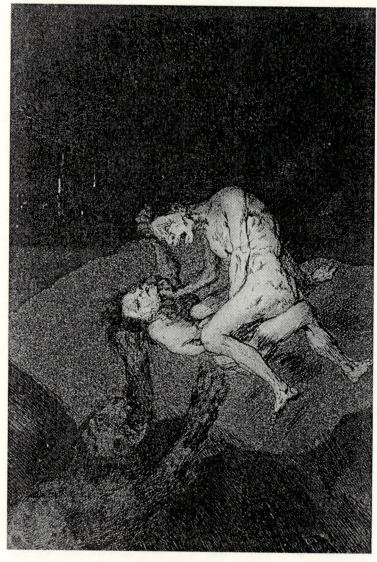

9. Goya, *Quién lo creyera!* (Capricho 62)

procédé inexplicable de l'artiste, tiennent le milieu entre l'homme et la bête. (p. 569)

As is often his wont, he makes little effort to interpret the work, being content to convey the sense of a surreal and frantic violence.

Jean Prévost[55] was among the first to see a parallel between this engraving and 'Duellum' from *Les Fleurs du Mal*, which can be read as a kind of transposition in which the duel is of the sexes, 'D'une jeunesse en proie à l'amour vagissant'. By a typical 'soubresaut de la conscience' Baudelaire upsets our expectations as readers, taking us in a vertiginous progression from the ferocious onset of the duel to the wailings of young lovers, locked in the ardour of an eternal hatred. He has also hijacked the original by making the witches male and female, whereas in Goya they were of indeterminate sexuality, probably female. Furthermore, he has imposed on the struggle an explicit and definitive closure which permits us to interpret it in only one way. What is interesting, however, is that, although he departs considerably from the original, in some respects he is more faithful, by including the wild beasts of the deserted region that had been omitted in the essay. The ravine 'hanté des chats-pards et des onces', is obviously inspired by the leopard-like monsters of the engraving reaching out with fearsome gestures from below and above the witches, who in their fury remain unaware of the danger threatening them.

Goya's title gives little indication of the meaning of the engraving, and the spectator finds himself in much the same position as Baudelaire's hypothetical amateur who, though ignorant of the political or social background, would none the less experience 'une commotion vive' at the artist's technical skill and imagination. Here again, the appeal is to the memory of the viewer who is able to recognize something of his own experience, beyond the historical, social, or political particularities of the satire, 'quelque chose qui ressemble à ces rêves périodiques ou chroniques qui assiègent régulièrement notre sommeil' (p. 568). In other words, he is able to identify what is eternal and permanent in these fleeting caricatures, almost all of which are, however, 'suspendues aux événements'.

In *Quién lo creyera!* the eternal significance is in no way obscured by the transitory or sociopolitical, there being no reference to any event in contemporary Spain. The inscription on the preparatory drawing reads: 'The proudest witches are hurled down from the highest point

---

[55] *Baudelaire*, 148.

of their flight', and the Prado commentary suggests that the struggle is about which of the two is more of a witch, adding that villains can be accomplices but never friends.[56] What the drawing suggests is a hell, in which the witches, like deformed Lucifers, fall eternally in a rocky and monstrous chaos. Baudelaire was clearly sensitive to this suggestion, for in the poem the Sierra becomes typically a 'gouffre', a hell 'de nos amis peuplé'. Both artists understand that in hell there can be no pact, no accommodation, no hint of a positive value, no respite from violence and imperfection. Such are the moral implications of both drawing and poem. With the drawing, however, one senses that the vision came first, before the idea, and imposed itself upon the artist, which is why the fantastic has the power at once to perturb and appeal to the memory of the spectator, who has the feeling of being confronted by a spontaneous emanation from his own unconscious. The sense of the autonomy of the drawing is reinforced by the curious caption chosen by Goya as if in astonishment and incomprehension at his own creation. Whereas Baudelaire's title designates the battle of the sexes which the poem illustrates and makes explicit, Goya's is an exclamation in the guise of a question, indicating not so much the artist's desire to guide the viewer to a proper understanding of the drawing as an invitation to share in his astonishment at the unbelievable and hallucinating spectacle that has surged into being. Who indeed would believe it? With Goya's captions generally, it is as if the artist were as helpless as the viewer before the grotesque emanations of the fantastic, reduced to a baffled questioning or to an uncomprehending and 'behaviouristic' description of what is going on, that leaves out the essential element that would make sense of the figure. Instead of closing the gap of meaning, the caption often seems to increase it. Nothing could be further from the defining clarity of Cruikshank's *The Colic*, Hogarth's *The Reward of Cruelty*, or Daumier's *Le Dernier Bain* than *Buen Viage*, *Volaverunt*, *Las rinde el Sueño*;[57] which perhaps explains why Goya's commentaries on the drawings are intended to act as explanations, but may be seen at the same time as rationalizations of the monsters produced by the sleep of reason.

In this connection *Y aún no se van!*[58] is significant. Baudelaire describes it thus:

[56] *Goya: The Complete Etchings and Lithographs* (New York: Prestel, 1995), 70.
[57] *Los Caprichos* 64, 61, 34.
[58] *Los Caprichos* 59.

10. Goya, *Y aún no se van* (Capricho 59)

L'autre planche représente un être, un malheureux, une monade solitaire et désespérée, qui veut à toute force sortir de son tombeau. Des démons malfaisants, une myriade de vilains gnomes lilliputiens pèsent de tous leurs efforts réunis sur le couvercle de la tombe entre-bâillée. Ces gardiens vigilants de la mort se sont coalisés contre l'âme récalcitrante qui se consume dans une lutte impossible. Ce cauchemar s'agite dans l'horreur du vague et de l'indéfini.

Perhaps because he was describing the drawing from memory, the detail is not accurate, since there are no demons weighing down on the tombstone and the other figures are placed behind or beneath the struggling 'monad'. It may be that Baudelaire had confused this drawing with the description he had read in Gautier of *Los Desastres de la guerra* 69, showing a decomposed body in a grave holding a piece of paper with the inscription *Nada*. Around his head 'tourbillonnent, à peine visibles dans l'épaisseur de la nuit, de monstrueux cauchemars illuminés ça et là de livides éclairs',[59] and it is possible that it is these monsters that Baudelaire has transposed into the plate with the grave-stone. Whatever the reason for his confusion, he has interpreted *Y aún no se van!* subjectively, drawing it into his own mental world, and apparently deaf to the promptings of the title. The theme of death is everywhere present in *Les Fleurs du Mal*, often with the attendant imagery of gravestones and their thematic analogues such as lids or ceilings, as in the first two lines of 'Le Guignon' ('Pour soulever un poids si lourd, / Sisyphe, il faudrait ton courage!'), 'le mourant qu'écrasent les blessés' of 'L'Irréparable', and 'le ciel bas et lourd' of 'Spleen' weighing down on the spirit 'comme un couvercle'. There is also an obvious parallel between Goya's *Nada* and 'Le Rêve d'un curieux', where the poet dreams he is dead but is denied any revelation: 'La toile était levée et j'attendais encore.' Here is a clear case of the poet imposing his own preoccupations, and depriving the work of its ambiguity and suggestive power. This he has been able to do because he is describing it from memory and because the nightmarish atmosphere of the drawing which 's'agite dans l'horreur du vague et de l'indéfini' invites such a reaction. The vagueness of the print, together with the characteristic interaction of light and shade, is an invitation to such an appropriation, just as in 'Les Fenêtres' the dark recesses of a room seen through a window provide a spur to the imagination. But Baudelaire's response, though imaginative, does not do justice to the

[59] Gautier, *Portraits contemporains*, 123. A few trial proofs of *Los Desastres* were known to a very small number of people before they were published as a volume in 1863.

ambiguity of the work suggested by the title, *And still they don't go away!*, which seems to convey the permanent threat of superstition and unenlightenment, or the oppressive presence of the dead among the living.

The final print mentioned is a lithograph, *Dibersión de España*, from near the end of Goya's career when his eyesight was deteriorating. It shows a bullfight in which a bull furiously attacks one of the fighters, lifting trouser and shirt with its horn to reveal to public view the posterior of the wounded unfortunate. What attracts Baudelaire more than the obvious grossness is the sense of chaotic activity in these late lithographs 'où règnent un tumulte et un tohu-bohu admirables' (p. 569), and the way the bullfights, with their teeming, antlike crowds are made to appear as 'vastes tableaux en miniature'. They share something of the topsy-turvy world of Cruikshank with his myriad figures in frantic activity, with this difference that in Goya the violence does not have his innocent exuberance, but appears darkly threatening and sinister. There is also the sense that their smallness is in inverse proportion to their explosive effect on the viewer, just as in the prose poem or in the short story the appeal to the imagination can be greater than in the novel. These lithographs conform therefore to a fundamental requirement in Baudelaire's 'oxymoronic' aesthetic whereby large and small, concentration and expansion, *centralisation* and *vaporisation* are not perceived as contradictory, but as complementary. Oddly, but without fundamental paradox, the sublime world of Delacroix showing 'l'infini dans le fini' finds its counterpart in the grotesque scenes of Goya's vast pictures in miniature.

Other Goya prints not directly mentioned by Baudelaire have had an influence on his poetry, none more than *Tu que no puedes*, which is transposed in 'Chacun sa chimère'. The *capricho* shows two Spaniards bent under the weight of asses with faintly human expressions mounted on their backs. The moral is clear, that Spain is groaning under the oppression of fools. Typically, Baudelaire universalizes the drawing, setting aside its social and political message and implying that men are in the grip of a huge chimera of which they know nothing and which impels them independently of their will. Whereas Vigny's 'Les Destinées', to which the prose poem can be compared, sees men in the grip of fate or predestination, Baudelaire makes of the chimera something resembling the dictates of the unconscious mind. In his desolate landscape there is nowhere to go, and the aspirations that give unfailing hope to those 'qui sont condamnés à espérer toujours' can never be made real. This view of mankind is made even more bleak in the final paragraph, where the poet seeks in vain to understand the nightmarish vision, but stops short, overwhelmed by indifference weighing on him even more heavily than the 'chimères' on their victims.

Another echo of Goya can be detected in the second tercet of 'La Lune offensée', evoking the poet's mother, 'Qui vers son miroir penche un lourd amas d'années, / Et plâtre artistement le sein qui t'a nourri!' There is a clear parallel with works like *Capricho* 55, *Hasta la muerte*, or *El Tiempo*,[60] which depict the hideous coquetry of grotesque old women in front of their mirror seeking to repair the irreparable ravages of the years.[61] There are also muted resonances from Goya in the frightful crones of 'Le Jeu', in the 'terrains cendreux, calcinés, sans verdure' and 'démons vicieux' of 'La Béatrice', in the 'sorcières faméliques' and 'vieillards lubriques' of 'Sépulture', and in some of the more extravagantly grotesque elements in such prose poems as 'Le Gâteau', 'Les Tentations', 'Le Crépuscule du soir', or 'Le Miroir'. There is, particularly in *Le Spleen de Paris*, a fantastic element that aligns Baudelaire with Goya, though one should be aware that whereas the latter's imagination is resolutely concrete, his human beings and demons often taking the form of animals, Baudelaire has a tendency towards abstractions and allegorical figures, which often anchors his work firmly in a world of ideas rather than things. A case in point would be 'La Chambre double', with its 'cortège de Souvenirs, de Regrets, de Spasmes, de Peurs, d'Angoisses, de Cauchemars, de Colères et de Névroses'. These 'figures' remain abstract, with nothing of that haunting and terrifying presence and physicality of Goya's monsters, and it would be misleading to see any specific presence of the Goyesque in this kind of intellectualized fantasy.

It is in the fantastic that Baudelaire places Goya's originality, whose genius is neither in the *comique absolu* nor in the *significatif* of the French, though on occasion he can rise to the former or plunge below the latter into the *comique féroce*. Here, Baudelaire does not mean by fantastic the dangerous and gratuitous licence he denounces in the *Salon de 1859* (p. 644). On the contrary, he sees Goya's fantastic as disciplined, so that what is monstrous does not depart into another

---

[60] *Le Temps* (otherwise called *La Vieille*) shows an ancient hag looking into a mirror with 'Qué tal?' written on its reverse side (Musée de Lille).

[61] Cf. the 'vieilles au miroir' in 'Les Phares'.

realm, but remains plausible. He may create monsters, but by what is yet again only an apparent contradiction they are harmonious, viable, marked above all by verisimilitude; he has no doubt a deep sense of the absurd, but of an absurd that is possible. The diabolical and animal grimaces are imbued with *humanity*, and as in Lavater the harmony of the parts to the whole is preserved even in the most outrageous creations, so that it is impossible to determine at what point the real or the natural merges with the fantastic that trancends it. The result is that though we recognize immediately the elements of our world in these extraordinary prints, what is alienating and what makes the fantastic art of this 'jovial' Spaniard so profoundly disturbing is that it is not always possible to make sense of the actions and gestures depicted.

In the final two sections of the essay a strong impression once again emerges that Baudelaire has gone to print before he has researched and fully thought out his argument. He seems at a loss to exemplify what is specifically Italian in the work of any one caricaturist. Leonardo's drawings represent Italian pedantry rather than joyous exuberance, being scientific, objective studies executed with great accuracy by a natural historian rather than by a caricaturist; they appear to be copies rather than an expression of reality. Bassano is said to express the Italian genius in his pictures of the carnival of Venice, in which frivolous southerners indulge in an innocent gaiety full of sausages, legs of ham, and macaroni. The mention of the carnival immediately evokes *La Princesse Brambilla* with its German artists at the Café Greco, appreciating the innocent humour of the Midi, which, however, has none of the depth associated with 'la rêveuse Germanie'. Finally, by a paradox which is not without its own humour, it is a French artist, Callot, who with his 'figures carnavalesques' best represents this kind of humour which is found in the temperament of the Italians rather than in their art.

The rest of the Italian section is given to Pinelli, a *croqueur* of picturesque scenes rather than a caricaturist. Baudelaire mentions him only because in his youth he had heard him endlessly praised for belonging to what can only appear as the hopelessly contradictory type of '*caricaturiste noble*'. But the caricature is infinitesimal, and the nobility appears to lie in an Ingresque obsession with outline and outmoded subject matter, and an equally Ingresque aspiration to 'style'. He claims he would not have introduced Pinelli, just as he would not have introduced Charlet, but feared being accused of serious omissions (p.

549). As we saw, the reason for bringing in Charlet was strategic, to set off the genius of Daumier. In the essay on foreign caricaturists, Pinelli serves as a pretext for a page on the relationship between an artist's work and his life. Baudelaire's studies of the artists he admires contain few biographical details; in the case of Gautier there were none, 'rien qu'une immensité spirituelle!' (p. 104). Pinelli's originality was in his disordered and bohemian life, not in his art, but in his charlatanism and posturing. His domestic life was full of strife between his wife and daughter, whose disputes he copied on to paper, showing thereby the intellectual laziness of the artist who cannot escape the tyranny of the real. Whether Pinelli has been unfairly represented in his legend, he is used to confirm the truism that nothing resembles the perfect bourgeois so much as the 'concentrated' artist of genius. The adjective and the approval it implies send us to Baudelaire's quotations from Emerson's *The Conduct of Life*: 'the hero is he who is immovably centred'; 'the one prudence in life is concentration; the one evil is dissipation'.[62] The reader will no doubt remember that for Baudelaire, Delacroix, the most creatively original genius of his time, was the perfect incarnation of these virtues.

The final section also bears the marks of Baudelaire's haste. Ostensibly about the Flemish and Dutch whose works are 'd'un caractère vraiment spécial et indigène' (p. 572), though no indication is given of what this might be, it comprises a page and a half on Brueghel the Elder whose drawings, like those of the later Grandville, show all the power of hallucination: 'visions d'un cerveau malade, hallucinations de la fièvre, changements à vue du rêve, associations bizarres d'idées, combinaisons de formes fortuites et hétéroclites'. Baudelaire divides his work into two classes. The first comprises political allegories and allusions, scenes where nature is constantly transformed into a puzzle, which he thinks almost totally indecipherable in the nineteenth century. So impenetrable are these allegories that one can never be sure that they do not belong to the more interesting second category, which his unthinking contemporaries would qualify as fantasies, but which he believes contain 'une espèce de *mystère*'. Neither the latest medical research nor the common-sense reductionism of Voltairians has been able, he claims, to unravel the secrets of the mind. It is typical of Baudelaire to dwell upon its deep mysteries at the expense of the social and historical considerations, on the eternal at the expense of the

[62] *Oc.* i. 674.

transitory. How, he wonders, can a human intelligence contain 'tant de diableries et de merveilles, engendrer et décrire tant d'effrayantes absurdités?' Though Brueghel's works engender vertigo, an essential ingredient of 'le comique absolu', the result is far from joyful in this 'capharnaüm diabolique et drolatique' which can be explained only by a special, satanic grace. This contradictory notion scarcely casts light on the mystery, which he says remains as dark if we replace it by madness or hallucination. Readers of *Les Fleurs du Mal* will remember its appearance in the plural in the sombre 'L'Irrémédiable': 'Un phare ironique, infernal, /Flambeau des grâces sataniques, / Soulagement et gloire uniques, /—La conscience dans le Mal!', where it celebrated the only consolation for the irremediably damned. A satanic grace can never be perfect, can never deliver, but only bring the light of awareness to their eternal slavery. Pichois (p. 1366) links it to *Le Poème du hachisch*, where drugs are seen as a means whereby the Spirit of Darkness enslaves human beings. Flaubert had criticized Baudelaire for blaming hashish and insisting on the power of Evil; but in his reply the poet had been firm in his conviction that certain human actions can be explained only by the intervention of an evil power external to man.[63] Without going so far as to claim that Brueghel had seen the devil, Baudelaire cannot help noticing that the prodigious flowering of monstrosities in his work coincides with what he refers to as the famous and historic '*épidémie des sorciers*', by which he means, in modern as in more remote times, a contagion, a poisoning of the moral atmosphere, an invasion of the human mind by the powers of evil. The collective counterpart to the imp of the perverse he recognized in Poe and some of his own uncontrolled outbursts of satanic energy, it would appear to represent that part of the unconscious mind that harbours the destructive anti-values of madness and cruelty. The implication is that through such a satanic grace Brueghel had access to that inhuman world and expressed it in his art. But there is also the implication that in the exploration of these uncharted depths his art has reached, if not gone beyond, the limits of communicability.

[63] Claude Pichois, *Lettres à Baudelaire*, 155. *Corr.* ii. 53.

5

From Landscape to the Painting
of Modern Life

BAUDELAIRE DEVOTES an increasing number of pages in his *Salons* to landscape painting, but his enthusiasm is in inverse proportion to the space covered. Much of what he writes after 1845 expresses his misgivings, and as his aesthetic ideas evolve he becomes increasingly intolerant of the genre which was to predominate in the second half of the century, at the expense of religious and historical painting, which had for long maintained their position at the top of the hierarchy. Although in the *Salon de 1859* he admits that the modern school of landscape painters is singularly strong and skilful, he repeatedly expresses his disenchantment at the cult of nature for its own sake, and twice refers to landscape as an 'inferior' genre, attracting only second-rate talents. In a damning conclusion, which must be taken as his definitive position, he complains that among landscape painters he has found only 'des talents sages ou petits, avec une très grande paresse d'imagination' (p. 668).

In 1845, however, his tone had been much more positive. Huet, Haffner, Flers, and Kiörböe all meet with approval, and like Corot, Rousseau, and Daumier, Français is said to exemplify '*l'amour de la nature*'. The absent Théodore Rousseau is praised for the *naïveté* and originality he shares with Corot, and for an even greater charm and sureness of execution; but it is the latter who, as the head of the modern school of landscape painters, is given the greatest attention. Baudelaire alludes to his *Paysage avec figures*, exhibited the year before, which depicts a woman playing a violin, in a pastoral scene likely to appeal to the poet who, in 'Mœsta et errabunda', was to evoke the nostalgic charm of violons 'vibrant derrière les collines'.[1] There is

---

[1] In fact the woman is playing a cello (1280–1). See also Jean Prévost's comment in *Baudelaire*, 190.

praise for his use of colour[2] and for his *touche* which is 'spirituelle, importante et bien placée', giving the lie to those 'demi-savants' who, accustomed to the 'morceaux luisants, propres et industrieusement *astiqués*' of conventional academic painting, have maintained he was gauche and did not know how to paint. Such critics do not understand that there is a great difference 'entre un morceau *fait* et un morceau *fini*—qu'en général ce qui est *fait* n'est pas *fini*, et qu'une chose très *finie* peut n'être pas *faite* du tout'. Baudelaire is impressed by the powerful structure of Corot's works, by what he calls in *Le Peintre de la vie moderne* the 'barbarie' of his eye which, 'synthétique' and 'abréviateur', is able to set out from the beginning the principal outlines of a landscape, giving it 'son ossature et sa physionomie' (p. 698).[3]

In the same *Salon Daphnis et Chloé* is noted for its charm; but it is *Homère et les bergers* that attracts the longer comment. Baudelaire finds its composition faultless, there being nothing superfluous, not even the two little figures 'qui s'en vont causant dans le sentier' in the background. Critics have pointed to Poussin's *Orphée et Eurydice* as having inspired the painting (p. 1281), but Baudelaire thinks that Homer resembles too much David's *Bélisaire*, and indeed the shape and posture of the head are similar, as is the position of the legs. He admires the three little shepherds and their dog, which he feels might be found on the bas-reliefs of ancient statues. Though the original story of Homer and the shepherds goes back to Herodotus, the immediate literary inspiration was Chénier's twenty-sixth 'Bucolique', as the title in the Salon clearly indicates: *Homère et les bergers, paysage, André Chénier: L'Aveugle*. The literary subject matter, rare in Corot, must have attracted Baudelaire, and the setting, which is not some idealized classical or Italian landscape but is based on a modest sketch of the village of Royat, may also have pleased him in a picture whose charm lies in the balance between the classical dignity of the founder of western literature, and the simplicity of the scene, with the shepherds and their dog, and the shadowy group in the background.

---

[2] 'Il sait être coloriste avec une gamme de tons peu variée—et [. . .] il est toujours harmoniste même avec des tons assez crus et assez vifs' (390).

[3] Prévost, *Baudelaire*, 83 sums up Baudelaire's view of Corot: 'Au paysage observé, il préfère le paysage construit; il louera toujours Corot de ses qualités de composition, plutôt que de son sens exquis des valeurs; s'il préfère Corot à Théodore Rousseau, dont la couleur lui plaît bien davantage, c'est pour l'harmonie de ses paysages.'

In the *Salon de 1846* Corot receives only a passing mention for *Vue prise dans la forêt de Fontainebleau*,[4] which depicts a rural scene with cows beside a pond, with no historical or narrative element. Fittingly, the unity of the composition is linked to the *naïveté* of the artist, and to the fact that it was painted from memory. Several other painters are favourably mentioned, but again, it is the absent Rousseau who receives the greatest praise, as 'un paysagiste du nord'. But considerable space is given to the negative aspects of the genre, Baudelaire's greatest scorn being for the *extravagants* and *fanatiques* who have *ingrisé* landscape. The expression is first used of Flandrin in 1845, but applies equally well to Desgoffe, Chevandier, Aligny, and the other landscape painters of the Ingres school. It may be permissible, concedes Baudelaire, to dampen down reflected lights in a portrait, as Ingres does, but in landscape painting, whose essence and poetry lie in the interplay of light and shade, such a procedure is a folly and a contradiction.

At the beginning of 'Du paysage' Baudelaire expresses affection for 'le paysage de fantaisie', which reflects man's natural need of 'le merveilleux', but he sees it mainly as a northern genre, not much practised or appreciated in France, and in any case in need of revitalization. Given his praise of Corot's *Homère et les bergers* in the previous year, his attack on historical landscape is not surprising, since it has degenerated into *poncifs* perpetrated by those who have such a fear of the natural that they would imagine hell 'sous l'aspect d'un vrai paysage, d'un ciel pur et d'une nature libre et riche'. Like historical and religious painting, landscape has its Horace Vernets and Ary Scheffers—but Baudelaire spares his readers, and the perpetrators, their names.

In the *Salon de 1859* his disenchantment is even more marked. Few are praised, most are blamed for the mindless cult of nature at the expense of structure and imagination: Daubigny's paintings lack solidity, having 'la mollesse et l'inconsistance d'une improvisation', Troyon exemplifies 'habileté sans âme', while Rousseau and Corot fall sadly from the favour they had previously enjoyed. Rousseau mistakes a simple study for a composition: 'Un marécage miroitant, fourmillant d'herbes humides et marqueté de plaques lumineuses, un tronc d'arbre rugueux, une chaumière à la toiture fleurie, un petit bout de nature enfin, deviennent à ses yeux amoureux un tableau suffisant et

---

[4] Corot had sent four works, three of which were refused.

parfait' (p. 662). And in the praise of Corot's rigorous composition and 'abbreviated' and rapid drawing, there is embedded criticism that his contrasts are not forceful enough, his light is too soft and 'crepuscular', his work lacks energy and the ability to dazzle and astonish. In a word, Corot 'n'a pas assez souvent le diable au corps' (p. 663).

Baudelaire's criticism of Millet is particularly severe. Some of the ridicule directed against Ingres's pupils in the chapter on portrait painting is made to stick also to him, but it is not because Millet has *ingrisé* landscape painting or is unaware of the importance of light surrounding an object, or keeps only a semblance of colour in his pictures. On the contrary, he strikes one emphatically as a colourist rather than a draughtsman, as Baudelaire himself seems to recognize when he mentions the fine qualities 'qui attirent tout d'abord le regard vers lui'. Millet's great mistake is rather to have sought out 'style', by which is meant the neglect of the natural poetry of a subject and the imposition of one that is foreign to it. Like Ingres and his pupils, he has a preconceived idea of style, borrowed from the past or some extraneous source. Baudelaire is intolerant of the self-consciousness and serious-mindedness of Millet's peasants who have too high an opinion of themselves: 'Qu'ils moissonnent, qu'ils sèment, qu'ils fassent paître des vaches, qu'ils tondent des animaux, ils ont toujours l'air de dire: "Pauvres déshérités de ce monde, c'est pourtant nous qui le fécondons! Nous accomplissons une mission, nous exerçons un sacerdoce!" [. . .] Dans leur monotone laideur, tous ces petits parias ont une prétention philosophique, mélancolique et raphaélesque' (p. 661).[5] His reference to their various activities shows he knew *Le Repas des moissonneurs* (1853), *Le Semeur* (1850), *La Tondeuse de moutons* (1853) and, Millet's only work to be shown in the Salon of 1859, *Femme faisant paître sa vache*. Whether or not he was taking exception to the religious dimension Millet increasingly bestowed on his painting, as in *Le Repas des moissonneurs*, which adds to the 'Homeric' postures of the harvesters the Old Testament monumentality of Ruth and Boaz, his impatience with the sculptural solemnity of the figures and their timeless, stylized postures is unmistakable.

An oblique note on the Crabbe collection in 1864 is his only other reference to Millet: 'Millet. La bête de somme de La Bruyère, sa tête

---

[5] Here Baudelaire is not referring to Raphael's draughtsmanship, as in ch. III of the *Salon de 1846* (421), but to what he calls 'la solidité calme' of his compositions (586). For further irony on *sacerdoce*, see *Oc.* i. 665.

courbée vers la terre' (p. 964).[6] Claude Pichois (p. 1524) thinks the reference is to *Une famille de paysans*, while T. J. Clark suggests perhaps more plausibly *L'Homme à la houe*.[7] Whether he had any particular painting in mind or not, the note has been said to show that Baudelaire was beginning to see merit in his depiction of peasants. There may be little more than wishful thinking in this view; but to be fair to the Baudelaire of 1859 the criticism is not without foundation, since the female figures in *Femme faisant paître sa vache* and *L'Angelus* (which he may also have known since it belongs to the same period), resemble nothing so much as wooden effigies of saints, radiating an inauthentic Raphaelesque and philosophical pretension inconsistent with the rigours of their lives as peasants. And if there is any substance in the opinion Gambetta was to express much later on *L'Angelus*—'[la peinture] s'élève et prend un rôle moralisateur, éducateur; le citoyen passe dans l'artiste et avec un grand et noble tableau nous avons une leçon de morale sociale et politique'[8]—then Baudelaire's understanding of Millet's work, if not his judgement on it, would appear to be vindicated.

Boudin

There is, however, one landscape painter whom Baudelaire does single out for praise: Eugène Boudin, whose reputation had not yet been established and whom he had met at Honfleur in the same year (1859) in the company of Alexandre Schanne and Courbet. The page devoted to him is extraordinarily dense, poetic, and paradoxical. The opening sentences, however, are not surprising. In line with the main thesis of the *Salon*, they proclaim that 'l'imagination fait le paysage' and denounce those who copy nature directly. When a painter is taking notes on the spot, he has clearly no time to abandon himself to the 'prodigieuses rêveries contenues dans les spectacles de la nature présente'. It is only in the tranquillity of the studio that the deeper work of transformation, elaboration, and construction can be brought about. If these misguided artists had seen, as Baudelaire had, the

---

[6] The reference is to La Bruyère, *Les Caractères*, ed. R. Garapon (Paris: Garnier, 1962), 339: 'animaux farouches, des mâles et des femelles, répandus par la campagne, noirs, livides et tout brûlés du soleil, attachés à la terre qu'ils fouillent et qu'ils remuent avec une opiniâtreté invincible'.

[7] Clark, *The Absolute Bourgeois*, 97.

[8] Quoted in *Jean-François Millet* (London: Hayward Gallery, 1976), 88.

several hundred pastels improvised by Boudin in front of sky and sea, they would understand the distance separating a study from a picture. Boudin knows that the rapid open-air study will have to be transformed into a picture by a process of recollection, and would not be so foolish as to pass off his notes and studies as finished works. Here, Baudelaire is once again taking a conservative stance; for although open-air painting was established in France in the first two decades of the nineteenth century, there was a marked distinction between such sketches and the structured and idealized picture produced in the studio. The traditional view was put forward in the *Salon de 1824* by Delécluze, who denounced 'Shakespearean' painters for their subservience to effects in nature, commending those who impose upon observation a strong conceptual framework. What is remarkable is not just that Baudelaire mentions no completed picture by Boudin with admiration,[9] but that, as the passage progresses, he becomes increasingly lyrical about these fleeting pastels which capture the most unstable and evanescent of perceptions, until the remarkable outburst of poetic prose describing Boudin's skyscapes which so impressed Gaston Bachelard that he gave it a conspicuous place in his discussion of 'l'imagination dynamique du nuage':[10]

Ces études si rapidement et si fidèlement croquées d'après ce qu'il y a de plus inconstant, de plus insaisissable dans sa forme et dans sa couleur, d'après des vagues et des nuages, portent toujours, écrits en marge, la date, l'heure et le vent; ainsi par example: *8 octobre, midi, vent de nord-ouest.* Si vous avez eu quelquefois le loisir de faire connaissance avec ces beautés météorologiques, vous pourriez vérifier par mémoire l'exactitude des observations de M. Boudin. La légende cachée avec la main, vous devineriez la saison, l'heure et le vent. Je n'exagère rien. J'ai vu. A la fin tous ces nuages aux formes fantastiques et lumineuses, ces ténèbres chaotiques, ces immensités vertes et roses, suspendues et ajoutées les unes aux autres, ces fournaises béantes, ces firmaments de satin noir ou violet, fripé, roulé, ou déchiré, ces horizons en deuil ou ruisselants de métal fondu, toutes ces profondeurs, toutes ces splendeurs, me montèrent au cerveau comme une boisson capiteuse ou comme l'éloquence de l'opium. Chose assez curieuse, il ne m'arriva pas une

---

[9] Baudelaire seems to share Boudin's lack of enthusiasm for *Le Pardon de Sainte-Anne-Palud au fond de la baie de Douarnenez.* Though he had submitted it to the Salon, Boudin thought it mediocre: 'Plein de défauts [. . .] trop de choses et rien qui caractérise la Bretagne: d'ailleurs le coloris, la lumière laissent à désirer, il faut arriver à plus de pureté, plus de rayonnement [. . .] pas de centre. Un intérêt éparpillé' (quoted by Pascale Lemoine in *Eugène Boudin, roi des ciels* (Lausanne: Bibliothèque des Arts, 1981), 26).

[10] *L'Air et les songes* (Paris: José Corti, 1950), 222.

seule fois, devant ces magies liquides ou aériennes, de me plaindre de l'absence de l'homme. (pp. 665–6)

What we are left with at the end of the passage is the prestige of this ephemeral and intoxicating art which combines the most alert and delicate observation with an evident sense of the supernatural, to such an extent that, in a wry reference to the sociable Robespierre, 'qui avait soigneusement fait ses *humanités*', the poet whose preference is avowedly for paintings endowed with human drama claims not to have felt the absence of people. Clearly, the point of departure of the paragraph has been lost in the heady enthusiasm for the fleeting and the incomplete, and one is left with the strong impression that these rapid sketches, which were done merely to stimulate the memory of the artist in the tranquillity of his studio, have become for Baudelaire works of art in their own right.

We have already noted Baudelaire's admiration for Delacroix's rapidity of execution as a necessary adjunct to the dominance of the artist over the subject-matter and for the consequent appeal to the memory of the spectator. For Boudin to capture the constantly changing formation and colours of the clouds according to the direction of the wind and the hour of the day, this rapidity of execution is a condition *sine qua non*, to such an extent that he was often moved to apply the pastel directly without passing through the intermediary stage of the pencilled line.[11] Apart from cloud and sea the subject is almost nothing at all: a line of coast or estuary, a sandbank, a suspicion of vertical sails, the black spectre of a mast amid the uniform volume of sky and water. For the most part, except for masts or a headland, the effect is strongly horizontal, with streaks and bands of colour stretching from one side of the picture to the other. Roger-Marx's observation that 'Boudin cherche les champs illimités' and has little interest in things vertical is as valid for these pastels as for the later fashionable beach scenes.[12] But one magnificent piece[13] shows a setting sun about to be engulfed by sea or sky, low in the middle of the picture, with

[11] Gilbert de Knyff, *Eugène Boudin raconté par lui-même* (Paris: Meyer, 1976), 352: 'Pour ses études de ciels qu'il aimait turbulents, il employait presque toujours le pastel appliqué directement sur le papier sans passer par le dessin au trait.'

[12] Claude Roger-Marx, *Eugène Boudin* (Paris: Crès, 1927), 28. Contrasting the vanishing perspectives of Jongkind, Hamilton makes a similar point, stating that 'Boudin preferred pictures made of superimposed layers, a technique learned from Corot' (*Boudin at Trouville* (London: John Murray, 1992), 150).

[13] Reproduced in Laurent Manœuvre, *Eugène Boudin: dessins* (Arcueil: Editions Anthèse, 1991), 27.

above it a towering mass of crimson, green, dark blue, black, gold, and orange, whose turbulent verticality is accentuated by a pale blue break at the top of the composition opening on to a sense of the infinite, made all the greater for being 'plus resserré', as in Penguilly's *Les Petites Mouettes* mentioned in the same *Salon*. In the lyrical vision[14] of these tiny studies which seem to capture 'l'infini dans le fini' (p. 636), there is a strong sense that through weightlessness and constant metamorphosis the material world has been set free, desubstantialized into pure spirit. Other sunsets and studies of the rising moon are so devoid of recognizable features and boundaries between the elements as to be totally abstract; they are nothing but colour and movement, the work of a colourist *à l'état pur*, the *touch* having almost completely devoured the outline. To find its parallel in contemporary painting, you would have to look to some of Bonington's watercolours,[15] or to part of a Delacroix canvas, as if that part had been excised from the work and made to stand on its own. One might think of the astonishing background to his extravagantly original *Nature morte aux homards* of 1827, which Baudelaire probably did not know, and which unites in one canvas a still life, a hunting scene, a landscape and skyscape; or *Le Christ sur le lac de Génézareth, Hamlet et Horatio au cimetière* (1859), or indeed any of his great canvases, historical, religious, or literary, which have for their background some natural scene.

The comparison with Delacroix is not gratuitous. Cahen[16] reports that Burty thought the pastels reminiscent of the cloud studies Delacroix's admirers fought over at the posthumous sale of his cartoons, and Baudelaire himself complains at the end of the chapter on landscape that in the modern landscape painters he has found nothing of 'le charme naturel, si simplement exprimé, des savanes et des prairies de Catlin', of the magnificent imagination that flows in Victor Hugo's drawings, or of 'la beauté surnaturelle des paysages de Delacroix' (p. 668). It is unlikely that he is referring here to Delacroix's landscape paintings as such, about which he knew apparently little. Indeed, in commenting in the *Salon de 1846* on the Lux-

---

[14] See Roger-Marx, *Eugène Boudin*, 32: 'Les pastels de l'époque Baudelaire faisaient espérer une vision lyrique du monde, des couchants de feu, des ciels d'orage, des éclairs de lune.' Some of these pastels could be thought of as the painterly counterpart of the 'poem' of sunset in 'De la couleur' (423).

[15] For example, *Landscape with Harvesters* (1826), reproduced from a private collection by Patrick Noon, *Richard Parkes Bonington, 'On the Pleasure of Painting'* (New Haven: Yale Center for British Art, 1991), 196.

[16] Gustave Cahen, *Eugène Boudin: sa vie, son œuvre* (Paris: Fleury, 1900), 113.

embourg ceiling, he thinks that Delacroix has revealed himself 'sous un aspect tout nouveau', adding in delight and surprise, 'Delacroix paysagiste!', as if the master had not already distinguished himself in the genre. However, what he says about the ceiling is of crucial importance for our understanding of his attitude to landscape in general:

Il est impossible d'exprimer avec de la prose tout le calme bienheureux qu'elle respire, et la profonde harmonie qui nage dans cette atmosphère. Cela fait penser aux pages les plus verdoyantes du *Télémaque*, et rend tous les souvenirs que l'esprit a emportés des récits élyséens. Le paysage, qui néanmoins n'est qu'un accessoire, est, au point de vue où je me plaçais tout à l'heure,— l'universalité des grands maîtres,—une chose des plus importantes. Ce paysage circulaire, qui embrasse un espace énorme, est peint avec l'aplomb d'un peintre d'histoire, et la finesse et l'amour d'un paysagiste. Des bouquets de lauriers, des ombrages considérables le coupent harmonieusement; des nappes de soleil doux et uniforme dorment sur les gazons; des montagnes bleues ou ceintes de bois font un horizon à souhait *pour le plaisir des yeux*. Quant au ciel, il est bleu et blanc, chose étonnante chez Delacroix; les nuages, délayés et tirés en sens divers comme une gaze qui se déchire, sont d'une grande légèreté; et cette voûte d'azur, profonde et lumineuse, fuit à une prodigieuse hauteur. Les aquarelles de Bonington sont moins transparentes. (p. 438)

Although the landscape is described in lyrical terms, it is clearly subordinate to the literary and narrative thrust of the painting. In Baudelaire's essentially conservative view, theme and subject-matter are never indifferent; landscape, no matter how stimulating, is secondary and most to be appreciated when it fulfils its function of being a correspondence of them, as for example in *Roméo et Juliette* or *L'Entrée des croisés à Constantinople*. The passage on the Luxembourg ceiling does much to explain Baudelaire's reservations about landscape painting; but more than that, it highlights what is astonishing and untypical in his sudden enthusiasm for Boudin's pastels.

The chapter ends on a pirouette and a preference for theatre décor over real landscapes, for the artificial over the natural, by now typical of the poet who had refused to be moved by 'des légumes sanctifiés'[17] or to believe that the soul of gods ever inhabited trees. However, if the conclusion fits the main burden of the *Salon*, it does not sit well with the exalted and lyrical lines on Boudin, who seems to survive the poet's strictures. Curiously, not long after his meeting with the young painter from Honfleur, his spontaneous enthusiasm is followed during

---

[17] See letter to Desnoyers, *Corr.* i. 248.

a train journey to Paris in the company of Courbet and Alexandre Schanne by an equally enthusiastic espousal of the artificial, intended no doubt to *épater* his companions to whom he is reported to have exclaimed:

Parlez-moi des ciels parisiens toujours changeants, qui rient et qui pleurent selon le vent et sans que jamais leurs alternances de chaleur et d'humidité puissent profiter à de stupides céréales [. . .] je vous dirai aussi que l'eau en liberté m'est insupportable; je la veux prisonnière, au carcan, dans les murs géométriques d'un quai. [. . .] Ma promenade préférée est la berge du canal de l'Ourcq.[18]

But it is not just the lyricism and the conviction of the passage on Boudin that lead one to feel that he survives the disenchantment with landscape painting. The year 1859 was the year of Baudelaire's great *Salon*; it was also the year in which many of the new poems for the second edition of *Les Fleurs du Mal* of 1861 were written, in particular the 'Tableaux parisiens', in which the emphasis falls increasingly upon the fleeting, the fragmentary, and the unstable. It could be argued that the poet's sudden admiration for Boudin can be explained by this new aspect in his thinking and that it marks a stage towards a new aesthetic in *Le Peintre de la vie moderne*, published in 1863, but written probably in November 1859, a few months only after the encounter at Honfleur.

Baudelaire never again mentions Boudin, and their correspondence is silent, though some commentators have speculated that they remained in touch. It is not known if Baudelaire saw any of the famous oils of beach scenes at the fashionable resorts of Trouville and Deauville, which Boudin began to produce in 1862 on the advice of Isabey,[19] and were to establish his reputation. For the most part, the skyscapes in these paintings, for all their translucency and power to 'faire rêver', lack the colour and intensity of the earlier pastels, and it is not until such splendid and diminutive works as *Etude de ciel sur le bassin du commerce* and the truly magnificent *Défouisseurs de vers*,[20] in which spectral forms of ships and fishermen emerge from the barely diffentiated mass of sea, sand, and sky, that Boudin achieves in oil a similar effect. It is, then, by no means certain that the beach scenes would have won Baudelaire's wholehearted approval, though it seems

---

[18] Cahen, *Eugène Boudin*, 58.
[19] Hamilton, *Boudin at Trouville*, 18.
[20] In Musée des Beaux-Arts André Malraux, Le Havre.

likely that Boudin had some acquaintance with the poet's thoughts on modernity. Certainly, there would have been much in these paintings that, theoretically at least, Baudelaire might have welcomed: the modern world of steamboats, iron bridges, and bathing huts; the fashionable Parisians on the jetties, and above all the society ladies in their crinolines and long skirts, together with the trivial observations of the *flâneur*. Thanks in no small measure to Boudin and to such predecessors as Bonington and Corot, modernity extended to the way people began to look at the sea. As Duranty was to write in the *Salon de 1877*, 'la mer moderne, c'est-à-dire accommodée avec des pêcheurs, des barques, des ports, des parisiens sur des jetées ou près des cabines de bain, intéressa soudain les peintres qui, auparavant ne connaissaient que le naufrage, la tempête, l'abordage, l'incendie, la mer à drames et mélodrames'.[21] In addition, there is in Boudin's diminutive studies a kind of poetry of the ordinary that stems from the juxtaposition of the natural and the artificial, of the sea and skyscapes and the paltry world of human beings engrossed in their barely differentiated worlds. Amidst the fashionable *fourmilière*, it is not possible to identify with certainty the figure of the Empress Eugénie, whose prestigious name appears in the title of one of his most famous paintings. The figures are resolved into more or less amorphous shapes and, apart from the direction of their gaze, their attitudes and gestures are dictated not so much by the requirements of social intercourse as by the sunlight and the wind. It is permissible to read into the spectacle of his tiny, barely particularized figures crowded together, reminiscent of what Baudelaire called Meissonier's *puces*, against the vast expanse of space, a gentle and discreet satirical note which would have been to the poet's taste.

In this modern vision there is much that finds a parallel in Guys: fashion, *flânerie*, the evanescent. Guys's sketches of the Crimean War, with his explanations and instructions to the engravers at the *Illustrated London News* written into the scene itself, have the same provisional quality as Boudin's notes with the season, time of day, colours, and wind direction written on the paper. In addition, they share, paradoxically, a sense of structure, of being, to use the poet's oxymoron, 'des ébauches parfaites' (p. 700), presenting an irresistible invitation to the unfettered imagination. But in Boudin the modernity is a by-product and the reverie is directed away from the people

[21] Quoted in Manœuvre, *Eugène Boudin*, 196.

towards nature, or rather to those aspects such as sea and sky that indicate the infinite or some ideal beyond human beings. In Boudin the individual and his *légende*[22] are lost in the anonymous crowd, whereas Guys's drawings, so often satirical and grotesque in a way that Boudin's are not, give the impression of the figure's relationship with the group and what distinguishes it. Except in the Crimean drawings and the famous scene on the Champs-Elysées, Guys's groups are smaller, and a very high percentage of his drawings are of single figures. The reverie they give rise to is, in the broadest sense, 'moral', about people in the 'unreal' real world of war or of the capital, and their engagement in time and place. Guys's figures seem to surge forth from space, whereas in Boudin's diminutive oils they appear sucked back into it. Finally, one cannot help being struck by the joyous intoxication of Baudelaire's commentary on both of these 'minor' figures. With the page on Boudin, one has the impression of the exuberance of a new sensation or idea, which has broken free from the conservative mould of the poet's thinking, but has not yet been fully developed into a thought or integrated into a coherent aesthetic. In the identification of these unique and fleeting instants, there is a sense of a creative explosion, in which the critical sensibility has cast aside preconceptions to rejoice in an aesthetic *volupté* which has not yet been transformed into *connaissance*. In *Le Peintre de la vie moderne*, on the other hand, the discussion of Guys's works is preceded by five sections setting out a new critical position, the main features of which are modernity and the tenuous relationship between the eternal and the transitory. In the process, as we shall see, the *volupté* has to a large extent been transformed into *connaissance*,[23] without, however, the descriptions losing anything of their joyous expansiveness and exhilaration.

Where, however, Boudin most resembles Guys is not in these oil paintings, but when he employs a more modest medium—watercolour, wash, charcoal, pencil—to capture, again in 'des ébauches parfaites', the silhouetted posture of boatmen, figures on the beach or at market, or Breton peasants at work, beautifully reproduced in Laurent Manœuvre's edition of his *Dessins*. As Hamilton observes, one

---

[22] For a discussion of the notion of 'légende' in Guys, see below, pp. 217–18.

[23] To transform one's initial, sensual response to a work of art into a rational awareness of its means is for Baudelaire one of the main functions of criticism. See his essay on Wagner: 'Je résolus de m'informer du pourquoi, et de transformer ma volupté en connaissance' (786).

or two lines and washes of colour are all that is needed 'to sum up the tiredness of the horse resting with its cart, the patient watchfulness of the fishermen, the attentiveness of a woman selecting her purchases'.[24] But even here the differences are crucial. In Boudin the figures are kept at a distance from the viewer and what is conveyed is a mood or action as ephemeral as the surrounding atmosphere; whereas in Guys the figures leap out from a background which is for the most part neutral and undifferentiated to give us the sense, beyond the present instant, of the universal types to which ultimately they belong.

Meryon

Immediately after the page on Boudin, apparently impatient to turn to an art that includes human beings, Baudelaire regrets the absence in the Salon of 'le paysage des grandes villes', a genre he defines as 'la collection des grandeurs et des beautés qui résultent d'une puissante agglomération d'hommes et de monuments, le charme profond et compliqué d'une capitale âgée et vieillie dans les gloires et les tribulations de la vie' (p. 666). His imagination abandons the moving architecture of Boudin's skyscapes in favour of the solid stone constructions of the capital, and brings him to a consideration of the work of Charles Meryon, which he discovered around February 1959 when he asks Asselineau[25] to get from Houssaye, by hook or by crook, copies of his engravings of Paris. He meets him almost a year later, and in February 1860 informs Poulet-Malassis that Delâtre is prepared to publish an album of the engravings with accompanying prose and verse texts by Baudelaire himself: 'des rêveries de dix lignes, de vingt ou trente lignes, sur de belles gravures, les rêveries philosophiques d'un flâneur parisien'.[26] The project came to nothing, because Meryon, whose mental equilibrium was far from stable, would not agree to a text that was anything other than factual, with precise historical information about the buildings and monuments depicted. It is clear from his correspondence that Baudelaire was as much exasperated by this eccentric, this 'fou infortuné qui ne sait pas conduire ses affaires',[27] as

[24] *Boudin at Trouville*, 115.
[25] *Corr.* i. 551: 'Autre histoire: tâchez donc de *carotter* pour moi à Edouard Houssaye TOUTES les images de Meryon (vues de Paris), bonnes épreuves sur chine.'
[26] Ibid. 670.   [27] *Corr.* ii. 8.

he was enchanted by the finesse and power of his work. Their first encounter is not without piquancy, for Meryon asked Baudelaire if he had ever read the stories of a certain Edgar Poe, and if he believed that Poe really had existed and was not the creation of *'une société de littérateurs très habiles, très puissants et au courant de tout'*.[28] In particular, he was interested in *Murder in la rue Morgue* because, like the monkey in the story, he was convinced that he himself was guilty, but only morally, of murdering a woman and her daughter.

Baudelaire shared with Meryon a passionate interest in the Paris that was rapidly disappearing under Haussmann's vast transformations. 'Le Cygne' of 1859 evokes the disappearance in the creation of the new Carrousel of the houses in the Louvre that Balzac had described in *La Cousine Bette*. But the emphasis is not upon a self-indulgent nostalgia, but on the sense of impermanence, even of the most solid structures. Similarly, Baudelaire felt it was wrong to think of Meryon's engravings as showing *'le vieux Paris'*[29] and appealing only to an interest in the past. They were rather 'des points de vue poétiques de Paris, tel qu'il était avant les immenses démolitions et toutes les réparations ordonnées par L'Empereur', and indeed several of the twelve great views of the capital which were to make up the album showed a Paris that had already gone or was under threat: the Petit Pont, the tower in the rue de la Tixeranderie, the scaffolding in the arch of the Pont Notre-Dame, the Pompe Notre-Dame, the morgue, and the drawings of the cathedral itself before Viollet-le-Duc's addition of the spire. Clearly, it was not the new aggressive Paris of the Second Empire that appealed to Meryon, but the medieval, gothic Paris, celebrated by Victor Hugo in the chapter of *Notre-Dame de Paris* entitled 'Paris à vol d'oiseau'. Although Baudelaire's own imagination is modern and can hardly be said to smack of medievalism, it is not difficult to see what drew him to Meryon; for here is a Paris that is not just a 'fourmillante cité'[30] in which myriads of tiny, almost imperceptible figures can be seen going about their business, dwarfed by the massive buildings and monuments, but one which, through the skilful use of perspective and chiaroscuro, is poetic and 'pleine de rêves'. Although Meryon is said to have worked with a *camera lucida* for some of the scenes, and although his drawings show

[28] *Corr.* i. 655.

[29] See his letter to his mother of 4 March 1860 in *Corr.* ii. 4.

[30] See 'Les Sept Vieillards': 'Fourmillante cité, cité pleine de rêves, / Où le spectre en plein jour raccroche le passant!' (*Oc.* i. 87).

a meticulous concern for architectural precision and detail, there is nothing photographic about his work. On the contrary, a powerful imagination and temperament preside over it to create a Paris that is menacing and spectral, a nightmarish city, full of visions and hallucinations. What is odd, however, is that the initial pencil drawings, delicate and rapidly executed, reveal few of these qualities, but appear purely architectural and documentary. It is at the second stage, in the creation of the etching that the oneiric or nightmarish aspects begin to appear. Meryon excels in the use of all sorts of alienating and disquieting devices; the choice of a bizarre point of view, the exaggeration of perspective, the intensification of light and shade, the dramatic use of cloud formation or of smoke belching from chimneys, the strange and complex scaffolding supporting the buildings, the presence of crows and other threatening birds in great numbers around the dark, baleful monuments, and the use of deep, inky-black spaces to draw in the imagination of the spectator.

Le Petit Pont, depicting the bridge with the twin towers of Notre-Dame rising steeply above it and the other buildings, is among the most typical and perfect of his works. As Burty[31] has pointed out, the perspective is quite impossible, since the cathedral towers could not appear so imposing from the point of view of the artist at the level of the river. A similar effect is found in *La Pompe Notre-Dame*, of which Meryon wrote: 'the towers of "Notre Dame" stand slightly higher above the houses than they do in reality; but I consider these licences permissible since it is, so to speak, in this way that the mind works as soon as actual objects which have arrested its attention have disappeared from sight'.[32] He has deliberately dramatized *Le Petit Pont* by increasing unnaturally the height of the towers which stand out all the more massively and menacingly[33] over the scene as they appear in heavy black, while the buildings in front are lit up, apart from their roofs, by a sunlight which, strangely, does not fall on the cathedral. As in many of his other etchings, the light does not come from a natural source, but is dictated by the aesthetic demands of the scene, which appears less as a real place than an artificial or theatrical creation. In

---

[31] Quoted in Richard S. Schneiderman, ed. *The Catalogue raisonné of the Prints of Charles Meryon* (London: Garton & Co., 1990), 33.

[32] Ibid. 52.

[33] Meryon's exaggeration of perspective serves to make the architecture more threatening, whereas with other artists the intention is often merely to enliven, dramatize or make it more majestic.

11. Meryon, *Le Petit Pont*

other words the function of the lighting is not mimetic or subservient to the demands of realism.[34] At the level of the river, an *enfilade* of

[34] M. S. in *Charles Meryon, Paris um 1850* (Frankfurt, 1975), 21, describes Meryon's use of light thus: 'Es schildert weder Tag noch Nacht, noch Sonne oder Mond, sondern dient als künstliche Beleuchtung einer Szenerie, die sie kalt und scharf gliedert oder in tiefen Schatten versinken lässt.'

dark, mysterious arches extends from left to right of the picture, cut across by the three taller arches of the bridge itself, which casts a dark shadow upon the river and an even more mysterious and disquieting sphinx-like shadow on the building, a shadow which Meryon said he noticed only after the etching was finished and which he declared was unintended.[35] As with *L'Arche du pont Notre-Dame*, one has the impression less of the Seine in nineteenth-century Paris as of the Styx, the river of death itself, flowing into the portals of the underworld. Similarly, the windows in the buildings do not seem to belong to a human world of passion or aspiration. Unlike those in Baudelaire's 'Les Fenêtres',[36] one cannot say of them: 'dans ce trou noir ou lumineux vit la vie, rêve la vie, souffre la vie'. On the contrary, reminiscent of Hugo's 'affreux soleil noir d'où rayonne la nuit',[37] or of the empty socket, 'vaste, noire et sans fond',[38] that Nerval's Christ finds in his vain search for the eye of God, they suggest the impossible reverie of a positive source of negation and absence. The building appears as a kind of Argos with a multitude of black, empty, unseeing eyes, heedless of the ant-like activity of the humans swarming on the shore or crowded into their tiny craft on the river. The effect is similar in *La Tour de l'Horloge*, though in the eighth state rays of light are made to come from two windows on the façade. But once again, since there is no natural source of the light which is so strong as to be surreal, the effect is not to soften or humanize, but to alienate and disturb. It resembles nothing so much as Hugo's illustration of 'la maison visionnée' of *Les Travailleurs de la mer*.[39]

The parallel with Hugo is not strained. Baudelaire himself thinks Hugo would appreciate Meryon's prints as a worthy representation of the Paris he had described in 'A l'arc de triomphe'[40] as a gloomy Isis (p. 667). Knowing that Delâtre intended to give Hugo a copy of the

---

[35] For an insight into the workings of Meryon's crazed mind, see *Corr.* i. 655: 'Il m'a fait remarquer, dans une autre de ses planches, que l'ombre portée par une des maçonneries du *Pont-Neuf* [Baudelaire is mistaken here] sur la muraille latérale du quai représentait exactement le profil d'un sphinx,—que cela avait été, de sa part, tout à fait involontaire, et qu'il n'avait remarqué cette singularité que plus tard, en se rappelant que ce dessin avait été fait peu de temps avant le coup d'Etat. Or le Prince est l'être actuel qui, par ses actes et son visage, ressemble le plus à un *sphinx*.'

[36] Here I regret to have to disagree with Rémi Labrusse's otherwise convincing article on 'Baudelaire et Meryon' in *L'Année Baudelaire*, 1 (1995), 99–132 (see in particular p. 116).

[37] *Les Contemplations*, 'Ce que dit la bouche d'ombre'.

[38] *Les Chimères*, 'Le Christ aux oliviers', II.

[39] Reproduced in Brombert, *Victor Hugo and the Visionary Novel*, plate 15.

[40] From *Les Voix intérieures*.

Vues de Paris, Baudelaire sends him the relevant passage from the 1859 *Salon*, to which Hugo responds enthusiastically: 'Ce qu'il fait est superbe. Ses planches vivent, rayonnent et pensent.'[41] Elsewhere, in terms equally applicable to his own drawings, which incidentally Baudelaire genuinely admired,[42] he talks of 'le souffle de l'Immensité' [qui] traverse l'œuvre de M. Méryon et fait de ses eaux-fortes plus que des tableaux—des visions'.[43]

The best-known and most reproduced of Méryon's views of the capital, *Le Stryge*, is also the most satanic and grotesque. It shows a gargoyle high on the north tower of Notre-Dame, facing westwards over the rooftops of the city, its depravedly misshapen head held in its hands, two horns on its head, and wings folded on its back. The figure is based on an addition by Viollet-le-Duc to the north tower of the cathedral, with this difference that in Méryon its tongue is made to hang out obscenely from its gaping mouth. The point of view is not, however, that of the Stryge, but of the artist, supposedly looking towards the Tour Saint-Jacques and the north of the city. As is Méryon's wont, the perspectives are exaggerated, particularly through the elongation of the elevations of the houses and of the tower itself, which is made to appear higher than the gargoyle. Large birds wheel round the top of the tower in the middle distance, while in the foreground the loathsome bodies of four large black crows crowd in a narrower circle under the stare of the grotesque like an incarnation of its evil thoughts. In ancient legends, a stryge was a kind of vampire, half-woman, half-dog, that wandered at night in search of human beings whose blood it would drink. Originally, Méryon called the figure *La Vigie*, but in the fourth state of the engraving he added a macaronic couplet (he admitted to his father that he did not know how to count syllables) that makes it a personification of Luxuria or Lust:

> Insatiable vampire l'éternelle Luxure
> Sur la Grande Cité convoite sa pâture.

This allegorical figure has a strong Baudelairean resonance, and the poet may well have had *Le Stryge* in mind in composing his 'Epilogue' for the second edition of *Les Fleurs du Mal*, the first lines of which give a similar view of the capital under the aegis of a satanic power.[44] For all

---

[41] *Lettres à Baudelaire*, 191.
[42] Baudelaire praises 'la magnifique imagination qui coule dans les dessins de Victor Hugo, comme le mystère dans le ciel' (668).
[43] Letter of 1860 quoted by Philippe Burty in 'L'Œuvre de Charles Méryon', *La Gazette des Beaux-Arts*, xiv (June 1863), 522.
[44] *Oc.* i. 191.

12. Meryon, *Le Stryge*

that, the etching has a distinctly gothic and Hugolian appearance which, together with its overt representation of the personal phantasms that ultimately destroyed Meryon's mind, detaches it from Baudelaire whose preoccupations are much broader in scope. Other works show even more clearly the quirky, fantastic and untransmissible obsessions of Meryon's peculiarly active but blocked imagination: the bizarre figures clinging like insects to the Collège Montaigne in *Saint-Etienne-du-mont*; the man climbing a rope in *L'Arche du pont Notre-Dame*; the extraordinary beasts that haunt the air in *Le Ministère de la Marine*, the third state of which shows in a piece of surreal private symbolism Meryon's naval sword, a gift from his father, enigmatically placed in the middle of la rue Royale; the anthropomorphic clouds in some of his less well-known drawings;[45] the balloon Speranza in *Le Pont-au-change*, borne on the wind in an extravagant but transparent piece of symbolism towards le Palais de Justice, and the equally astonishing birds of prey which replaced the balloon in later versions and which, as Baudelaire pointed out,[46] were implausible in a Parisian sky. The disorder of the artist's mind and the tension between form and meaning are perhaps best illustrated by *Tourelle, rue de l'Ecole de médecine*, which he considered his masterpiece. It shows the house in which Charlotte Corday assassinated Marat. In early states allegorical figures in the sky, seen only by roofers on a building opposite, represent Truth, Justice, and oppressed Innocence. At the sight of Truth shimmering in a supernatural light, Justice swoons and her balance and sword slip out of her hands. 'La maison, dite de Marat' bears in some states the sign 'CABAT', clearly an engraver's inversion, which, however, Meryon decides to keep to show his disapproval of the immoderate use made of a plant responsible for exhausting 'the finances of a great number of individuals'.[47]

Not all Meryon's works are so flawed, and Baudelaire must surely have reacted positively to the splendid images of *L'Abside de Notre-Dame*, *Le Pont Notre-Dame*, *Le Petit Pont*, and *La Pompe Notre-Dame*, as the following passage indicates:

[45] See Schneiderman, *Catalogue*, 175, and some states of *Le Ministère de la Marine* and *Le Pont-au-change*.

[46] *Corr.* i. 655: Meryon countered Baudelaire's objection by claiming that 'cela n'était pas dénué de fondement, puisque *ces gens-là* (le gouvernement de l'empereur) avaient souvent lâché des aigles pour étudier les présages suivant le rite,—et que cela avait été imprimé dans le journaux, même dans *Le Moniteur*.'

[47] See Schneiderman, *Catalogue*, 136.

J'ai rarement vu représentée avec plus de poésie la solennité naturelle d'une ville immense. Les majestés de la pierre accumulée, les clochers *montrant du doigt le ciel*, les obélisques de l'industrie vomissant contre le firmament leurs coalitions de fumée,[48] les prodigieux échafaudages des monuments en réparation, appliquant sur le corps solide de l'architecture leur architecture à jour d'une beauté si paradoxale, le ciel tumultueux, chargé de colère et de rancune, la profondeur des perspectives augmentée par la pensée de tous les drames qui y sont contenus, aucun des éléments complexes dont se compose le douloureux et glorieux décor de la civilisation n'était oublié. (p. 666)

He may even have viewed sympathetically the blackly humorous addition to a later version of *La Morgue*, with its diminutive cadaver *repêché* from the Seine, of a sign on one of the buildings on the right reading in a macabre allusion to the guillotine, 'Sabra./ Dentiste/ du/ Peuple', and on the left of another sign 'Hôtel des trois balances meublé'; the ironic presence of the lilliputian funeral procession on the Pont-au-change beneath the balloon of Hope, or the shape of the shadow on *Le Petit Pont*, which without the artist's intention had taken on the shape of a sphinx. Such elements would have fitted in well with the commentaries Baudelaire had envisaged for the engravings, 'méditations poétiques en prose', or 'rêveries philosophiques d'un flâneur parisien',[49] which clearly were to have been inspired by a similar aesthetic to that of *Le Spleen de Paris*. But in the final analysis the preponderance in Meryon of an individual and gratuitous fantasy[50] and the absence of real human beings with whom the spectator of the picture can identify himself, seriously limit the appeal of these splendidly executed engravings. Meryon's barely perceptible figures seem to belong to an insect species rather than to the human race, and if in many of the drawings they appear in pullulating numbers, one has less the impression of the vibrant intensity and 'sexuality' of Baudelaire's crowds than of a swarm or anthill. Dwarfed by the massive and ominous architecture, devoid of the dress, gestures, heroism, or pathos of modern life, they act as a block to the imagination and to memory, and

---

[48] These factory chimneys may well be an early sign of modernity in art, but they have little of the suggestive power of those of Laforgue in 'L'Hiver qui vient', Huysmans in ch. V of *En ménage*, or of some Impressionist painters.

[49] *Corr.* i. 670; ii. 8.

[50] Although sympathetic to Philippe Junod's view ('Voir et Savoir ou de l'ambiguité de la critique', *Etudes de lettres*, sér. iv, 3 (Apr.–June 1980), 1–41) that one should not seek to explain the engravings by Meryon's mental illness, I do feel that their impact is often diminished by his private obsessions.

provide, ironically, little stimulus for a mind whose enthusiasm for solitude and the absence of human beings proved to be as fleeting as Boudin's skyscapes. Meryon's images are most unlike any of the great poems of 'Tableaux parisiens' or *Le Spleen de Paris*—'Le Cygne', 'Les Sept Vieillards', 'Les Veuves', 'Les Yeux des pauvres', or even 'Les Fenêtres'. If Baudelaire ever thought that Meryon had any of the qualities of the painter of modern life he was looking for, he must soon have realized that these sombre engravings were a blind alley, a mere parenthesis in his aesthetic thinking, which was to receive a much greater creative impetus from the drawings and watercolours of Constantin Guys.

Constantin Guys

In *Le Peintre de la vie moderne*, Baudelaire turns his attention, as he had in the essays on laughter and caricature, to a minor art form. The *Salon de 1859* had dwelt almost exclusively on the high art of the oil on canvas with historical, cultural, or religious subjects, but here he turns to those minor figures whose genius resides in 'la beauté particulière, la beauté de circonstance et le trait de mœurs' (p. 683). The favour found by Debucourt and the Saint-Aubin brothers has, he claims, done much to mitigate the exclusive preoccupation with the great names of painting, allowing them and many others a place in 'le dictionnaire des artistes dignes d'être étudiés' (p. 683). Though he mentions no specific works by Debucourt, Baudelaire is likely to have known *Promenade publique*, the engravings of le Palais Royal and the famous gaming house of Frascati, which figures in 'Les Petites Vieilles'. Though again no specific works are mentioned, he is also likely to have been attracted above all to Gabriel de Saint-Aubin,[51] that eccentric *flâneur* and compulsive draughtsman, who so resembled Guys that one might consider him his eighteenth-century double. If, in spite of a certain rigidity of execution, Debucourt catches well the manners of his time, there is in many of Gabriel de Saint-Aubin's works (*Jeune Femme montant en carrosse*, *La Réunion du boulevard*, *La*

---

[51] Of the Saint-Aubin family, it was Gabriel (1724–80) who was most likely to appeal to Baudelaire. Like Guys, he too was 'fou de dessin', the creator of hundreds of rapid sketches of contemporary Paris life, bearing very often such notes as 'fait en marchant', 'fait au lit', 'vue du Palais Bourbon, 4 7bre, à 8 heures du soir', and showing street scenes, public gardens, buildings, shops, *guinguettes*, clubs, auctions, bailiffs, and even an execution.

Saisie par l'huissier, Spectacles de Tuileries, for example) a movement and spontaneity that seem to deny the contemporary dress of his figures and endow them with a nineteenth-century air of immediacy and modernity. However, in the first two chapters of *Le Peintre de la vie moderne* it is not the past that concerns Baudelaire. Typically, he uses it merely to justify his interest in the present and the depiction of contemporary manners. Since man shows his idea of the beautiful in his attire, gestures, and even his features, the engravings of fashion at the time of the Revolution and the Consulate, for example, reveal beyond their bizarreness 'la morale et l'esthétique du temps' (p. 684). Similarly, the contemporary 'croquis de mœurs' is not a superficial genre, but gives access to an understanding of the modern age. The artist who depicts modern manners may be working in a minor genre, he is none the less endowed with genius, though this genius may be of a mixed nature, since it comprises a considerable element of 'esprit littéraire'. The modern era can boast such monuments as Gavarni and Daumier, whose works have been described as complementing *La Comédie humaine*. To them can be added Devéria, Maurin, Numa, Tassaert, Lami, Trimolet, and Traviès. The painter of manners is in varying degrees all or several of the following: observer, *flâneur*, philosopher, *moraliste*, poet, or novelist; but however he is characterized, he has to be distinguished from the 'peintre des choses éternelles [. . .] des choses héroïques ou religieuses' (p. 687). The reference to heroic subjects is highly significant, indicating that in the essay on Guys Baudelaire's preoccupation is no longer with a Balzacian heroism, but with the manners and particularities of modern life.

Le Peintre de la vie moderne is a homage to Guys, but of a peculiar kind, very different from the essays on Delacroix. Guys, that 'ouragan de modestie',[52] as Baudelaire called him, had wished to remain anonymous and is referred to throughout simply as M. G. Five of the thirteen sections are devoted to general aesthetic considerations, and from chapter 8 to the end the discussion focuses on Guys's themes and types, but again in general terms, with few references to specific or identifiable drawings. It is only in 'Les Annales de la guerre' and 'Pompes et solennités' that, having completed the theoretical introduction, Baudelaire names particular works and comments on their salient features. It seems appropriate to begin with a consideration of the drawings of the Crimean War, and deal with the

---

[52] *Corr.* i. 639.

theoretical considerations as they arise in relationship to individual works.

The wood engravings of the war in the *Illustrated London News* would on their own give a poor idea of Guys's talent as an artist. There is such a discrepancy between the flatness and lack of drama of the prints and Baudelaire's enthusiastic commentary, that one might be inclined to suspect him of using an artist of mediocre merit to set off his own greater imagination and creativity. The engravings were not, of course, the work of Guys, but were done in the offices of the *Illustrated London News* from sketches sent from the Middle East and the Crimea, where he was war correspondent for the journal. Unfortunately, many of the originals were destroyed by the engravers or lost in the subsequent bombing of the building in 1941.[53] The engravings are not, however, without interest, as they provide a convenient and instructive point of departure for an understanding of Guys's art. By comparing them with the drawings that *have* survived, it is possible to gain insight into his originality. It springs immediately to the eye that the engravers have made the drawings more like photographs, by flattening the perspective, filling in minor detail, and removing much of the drama and movement from the scenes: in short, by imposing a bland and documentary realism upon a highly imaginative and on occasions disturbing visual experience.

Here are two examples not directly mentioned by Baudelaire. The *Illustrated London News* of 17 March 1855 contains an engraving entitled *Turks Conveying the Sick to Balaclava*.[54] It is intended to convey, in the words of the artist himself, 'une des visions les plus déchirantes', that of seeing these unfortunate brothers in arms carried on the shoulders of their comrades, who often have to pay dearly for their compassion and may never return to camp. On the whole the engravers have caught well the pathos of the scene, but the effect is mild compared to that of the original drawing, in which the soldiers bearing their wounded comrades on their hunched backs are portrayed dramatically in black ink as massive grotesque shapes, greatcoat upon greatcoat. The emphasis is on their posture and awkward movement, whereas in the engraving there is an effort to particularize the figures in the foreground and give them individual expressions. The exhausted soldier on the left staring disconsolately at the ground, which he no doubt sees as his final resting-place, is portrayed in the drawing as an anonymous object, a shapeless bundle of clothing and equipment which has

[53] Pierre Duflo, *Constantin Guys* (Paris: Arnaud Seydoux, 1988), 52.
[54] Pls. 7, 8.

lost all but a distant semblance of a human being. The dying horse occupying the middle ground in the engraving is placed significantly on the same level as the soldier, while crowding the sky in a manner worthy of Meryon an enormous flight of black birds, barely perceptible in the engraving, where they have only a decorative function, menacingly invades the scene, hungry for their prey. Of this sombre work, Grappe wrote:[55] 'Le jour où il peignit le convoi des blessés dans les Balkans, dominé par le grand vol sinistre et tournoyant des corbeaux, il accomplit une œuvre admirable, puissante et large. Il quitta l'anecdote et atteignit au plus grand art.' But the technical device that most distinguishes the drawing from the engraving is the foreshortening of the perspective and the way the figures, instead of being set back at a safe distance, are made to surge forth from the space of the picture, creating the effect of an assault upon the spectator's eye and an invasion of his mental and emotional space. This effect is so frequent in Guys as to be fundamental to his technique and vision. In many of his drawings it is through the manipulation of perspective and the suddenness of the foregrounding that the sense of the bizarre is pushed to the point of the surreal, so that they take on a dreamlike or even nightmarish quality, as we become aware of what Baudelaire enthusiastically calls the figures' 'explosion lumineuse dans l'espace' (p. 700).

A more tranquil but no less eloquent example is *Lord Raglan's Headquarters at Balaclava*.[56] In the engraving the presentation of space and perspective is geometric and without intensity. The elevations and proportions of the buildings are presented objectively; the houses and tents on the hill on the right obediently conform to the laws of perspective and do not violate the 'lignes de fuite'. The trees on either side of the picture and the mast of the ship that separates them stand at the same height, while all sorts of details are added, and the individual figures, including the oxen on the right, are clearly delineated amid the crowd of which they none the less form a part. Everything is clearly visible, with no uncertainties, and no spur to the imagination. By contrast, the sketch is dramatic, bizarre, and even humorous. What immediately strikes the eye is the looming presence of the five trees in the background, which, rising in an inky blackness, seem disproportionate in height and mass. Like the building on the left, whose

---

[55] Georges Grappe, 'Constantin Guys', *l'Art et le beau*, 4ᵉ année, vol. i, 1907, 34.
[56] Pl. 9.

dark elevations and 'lignes de fuite' towards the ship are greatly exaggerated, they dwarf both the human activity in the foreground and the ship itself in the background, which seems strangely to rise out of the land rather than the sea, creating a kind of visual metaphor reminiscent of Elstir's *Port de Carquethuit* in *A la recherche du temps perdu.*[57] The hill on the right, with its chaotically scattered houses, rises more abruptly than in the print, while the slender horses and riders in the foreground, barely outlined and lacking arm, leg, or hoof, are merely suggested by a few rapid strokes. The humorous elements are relegated to the extreme left and right of the scene in the snooty posture of the camels and the hyperbolic ox with a head like a lion, with a human expression, both perplexed and good-natured.

This sense of exaggeration and of the bizarre is often very powerful, as in the astonishing watercolour (Pl. 10), which must count among the finest of his production, showing Captain Ponsonby and Guys himself riding on donkeys, preceded by their negro runner, arm and baton dramatically outstretched to prepare their way through the streets of Alexandria. Here is how Guys describes the event:

Surgissant de la grand-place d'Alexandrie, nous prîmes, le capitaine Ponsonby et moi, la rue principale, précédés d'un grand nègre athlétique, une sorte de Mercure. Il portait une longue chemise sans manches, son seul vêtement, et brandissait un lourd bâton au-dessus de sa tête comme un avertissement aux passants et aux cavaliers venant en sens opposé qu'ils aient à dégager devant nous le chemin. Nous étions escortés d'une tribu de gamins habillés de même façon que le nègre, certains noirs, d'autres olive; ils fouettaient nos pauvres petits ânes avec une énergie si impitoyable que je souhaitais vraiment l'intervention de quelque membre de la Société protectrice des animaux. Un jeune garçon de mine éveillée, d'allure gracieuse, nous précède à dos d'âne, servant d'interprète, se retournant continuellement vers nous, expliquant tout ce qu'il voit, que cela nous intéresse ou non, successivement en cinq ou six langues.[58]

Apart from two minarets in the background, the architecture could belong to any part of France, Spain, or Italy, the exoticism and strangeness being in the use of perspective and the posture and movement of the figures. A touch of local colour is rendered by three Arabs, barely outlined, sitting smoking on the square on the left margin of the picture, but the viewer's eye is immediately drawn to the negro and riders in the centre. What fascinates above all is the sense of movement

---

[57] Proust, *A la recherche du temps perdu*, ii. 192.
[58] Duflo, *Constantin Guys*, 328.

given by these figures and the bizarre interrelationship of the forms;
the elongated figures of Guys and Ponsonby perched on the bravely
trotting donkeys, the much smaller figure of the interpreter/guide in
front turned three-quarters in their direction to engage their attention,
the diminutive boys, totally out of perspective, running behind and
alongside the main group with raised whips, and most astonishing of
all, the magnificent, hugely magnified black runner, right of centre of
the picture, in full flight, poised upon his arched right foot and leaning
forward with his baton at arm's-length above his head, looking indeed
like some kind of Oriental or African messenger of the gods. To the
right, and forming by way of a contrast, an almost separate self-
contained picture in stronger colours, a group of three Arab women,
one behind the other, in full Oriental garb, surges voluminously into
the foreground in a manner similar to the Turkish woman with a
parasol in a picture known to have belonged to Baudelaire's mother,[59]
and progresses through the streets, heedless of the passage of the
prestigious Europeans.

What characterizes these drawings is the element of surprise, nowhere more noticeable than in two of Guys's most extraordinary
works, *A travers les Balkans* and *Par les Balkans*, which I mention to
give an idea of the range of his style and technique. Unlike the other
Crimean works, their documentary function is minimal in the first and
non-existent in the second, which is no doubt why the engraving based
on them bears only a remote resemblance to the originals.[60] The first,
in ink and watercolour, shows three riders and two packhorses, followed by what could be two officers, also on horseback, making their
way through snow along a track in dimly sketched and featureless
mountains. The impression is of open space, with only a hint of the
difficult conditions and terrain. In the second, which may be a preparatory study for the first, the stylization has been pushed to the
limits of the figurative, as in a Japanese wash. As with Giacometti's
sculptures or some Zen drawings, one has the sense less of the figures
surging forth from space than of space threatening them, denying their
presence.

Baudelaire must have been aware of these features of Guys's art, but
strangely, says almost nothing about them apart from their explosive
effect. In the three pages on 'Les Annales de la guerre' he is content to
allude to a host of drawings, picking out particular aspects of the scene:

[59] Duflo, *Constantin Guys*, 79.
[60] Ibid. 160–2.

the coffee-drinking and long hookah-like pipes at Omer-Pacha's, the bizarre Kurdish troops, the Bashi-bazouks with their Hungarian or Polish officers, the robust figure of Canrobert looking over the sinister battlefield at Inkerman 'taken on the spot', the artist himself amid the dead at Inkerman with his horse sniffing at the bodies, Achmet-Pacha receiving two European officers, the field ambulances and wounded, the hospital at Péra, the camels, Tartars, and munitions, together with all the heteroclite impedimenta and clutter of war. Even the historic Charge of the Light Brigade is mentioned only for its speed, the smoke from the artillery, and the landscape blocked by the green hills at the head of the valley.

Two scenes, however, are made to stand out from the others, and are given more than a fleeting reference. Both are 'religious' pictures and provide a contrast with the violence and hurly-burly of battle. Again Baudelaire picks out few features, concentrating on the picturesque or the sense of disproportion. In one, easily identified as *Divine Service on Sunday Morning before Balaclava*,[61] he mentions only the central figure of the priest, reading the Bible on a lectern improvised from three drums in front of the diverse English regiments, with the kilted Scottish soldiers standing out picturesquely. There is no mention of the tents and Oriental troops in the background, or the sense of space and exile created by the landscape rising dramatically into the high mountains and plunging into the distance in a way which might be thought reminiscent of Delacroix's great poem of exile, *Ovide chez les Scythes*.

The other religious drawing, to which Baudelaire devotes a whole paragraph, is *Consecration of a Burial Ground at Scutari by the Bishop of Gibraltar*.[62] 'Le caractère pittoresque de la scène, qui consiste dans le contraste de la nature orientale environnante avec les attitudes et les uniformes occidentaux des assistants, est rendu d'une manière saisissante, suggestive et grosse de rêveries' (p. 701). He evokes the officers with their 'airs ineffaçables de *gentlemen*, résolus et discrets', the Anglican priests looking like *huissiers* or *agents de change*, but does not say what the suggestive quality of the scene is, leaving it to the imagination of the reader or spectator. In addition to the juxtaposition of East and West, there is an impression of depth and space which emphasizes the isolation and vulnerability of the little group, on the water's edge, with Constantinople, its mosques and minarets in the

[61] Ibid. 294.
[62] Pl. 11.

background. Beyond that, for those acquainted with Baudelaire's mental universe, this depiction of exile finds an analogue in his poetry, so that these soldiers in a foreign land, standing impassively before the coffins of their fallen comrades (which Baudelaire does not mention and which, curiously, are barely present in the engraving, while in the drawing they form two ominous rows on the left), appear to join those other *dépaysés* in front of danger, failure, illness, and death: 'la négresse, amaigrie et phtisique' of 'Le Cygne' and those who 'tettent la Douleur comme une bonne louve'. From this modest drawing memory sounds 'à plein souffle du cor', as we are made to think of the 'matelots oubliés dans une île, / Aux captifs, aux vaincus! [. . .] à bien d'autres encor!'

The section on 'Pompes et solennités' has much in common with the one on the war. Baudelaire alludes to various sights that had struck the artist's eye in the East, in Greece, and in Paris, giving the impression that he himself is going through an album, picking out for the reader characteristic or memorable features. In one sentence just short of a page long, in a 'telegram' style conveying a host of haphazard perceptions, he lists the festivals at Bairan, the ceremonies in front of the mosques, the obese Turkish civil servants, 'véritables caricatures de décadence' astride their horses labouring under their weight, the carriages with oriental women peeping out of the windows through their veils, the contrasting attractions of women of different nationalities in their exotic dresses, and most intriguing of all, the frenetic dancing of the heavily made-up tumblers of the 'troisième sexe' with their flowing robes, convulsive and hysterical gestures, and long hair floating down their backs (p. 704).

Guys's genius in conveying the solemnity of official occasions is exemplified by *La Fête commémorative de l'indépendance dans la cathédrale d'Athènes.*[63] Baudelaire draws attention to the individuality of the diminutive figures, the 'portraits' of the king and queen, the patriarch with his tiny eyes behind green spectacles, and, most curious of all because of the 'bizarrerie de sa physionomie', a German lady attached to the service of the queen. He notes the strangeness of the Orthodox Church, the national dress, and, especially, the immense space of the cathedral and the manipulation of perspective. Guys has executed this drawing of a solemn occasion not coldly, as some artists do as a lucrative *corvée*, 'mais avec toute l'ardeur d'un homme épris

[63] Duflo, *Constantin Guys*, 169.

d'espace, de perspective, de lumière faisant nappe ou explosion, et s'accrochant en gouttes ou en étincelles aux aspérités des uniformes et des toilettes de cour' (p. 705).

Baudelaire's admiration for *La Loge de l'Empereur*[64] (Pl. 12) is similarly motivated by the representation of space:

Une surtout de ces aquarelles m'a ébloui par son caractère magique. Sur le bord d'une loge d'une richesse lourde et princière, l'Impératrice apparaît dans une attitude tranquille et reposée; l'Empereur se penche légèrement comme pour mieux voir le théâtre; au-dessous, deux cent-gardes, debout, dans une immobilité militaire et presque hiératique, reçoivent sur leur brillant uniforme les éclaboussures de la rampe. Derrière la bande de feu, dans l'atmosphère idéale de la scène, les comédiens chantent, déclament, gesticulent harmonieusement; de l'autre côté s'étend un abîme de lumière vague, un espace circulaire encombré de figures humaines à tous les étages: c'est le lustre et le public. (p. 706)

In Baudelaire's commentary on these two drawings, those familiar with his other works will recognize a recurring theme and obsession: 'La Vie antérieure' with its 'vastes portiques', or 'Le Balcon' and 'La Chevelure' in which the intimate space of the alcove is infused with a powerful sense of depth. Similarly, under the influence of 'les paradis artificiels' or in certain almost supernatural states of mind, space is transformed and 'la profondeur de la vie'[65] appears magnified beyond our normal perception. The scene in the Athens cathedral is not just some strange exotic event in a far country; it has its place within the already existing structures of Baudelaire's imaginary universe, where it encounters a series of thematic analogues. Likewise, the Emperor's box denotes more than a fashionable moment when the imperial family has graced a public event; it is part of a continuing obsession with spatial depth and the way in which theatre lighting can change life into dream, and the real into the ideal.[66] No doubt the guards' posture and magnificent uniforms transform them into hieratic figures; but one can see also that the role of the light from the stage is not just to add

---

[64] Musée national, Compiègne.

[65] *Oc.* i. 659: 'Dans certains états de l'âme presque surnaturels, la profondeur de la vie se révèle tout entière dans le spectacle, si ordinaire qu'il soit, qu'on a sous les yeux. Il en devient le symbole.'

[66] Cf ibid. 682: 'Ce que j'ai toujours trouvé de plus beau dans un théâtre, dans mon enfance et encore maintenant, c'est *le lustre*—un bel objet lumineux, cristallin, compliqué, circulaire et symétrique. [. . .] Après tout, le lustre m'a toujours paru l'acteur principal, vu à travers le gros bout ou le petit bout de la lorgnette.'

sparkle but to endow them with depth, just as, in 'L'Invitation au voyage', the 'meubles luisants / Polis par les ans' are valued not merely for their shiny surface but for the depth of time, memory, and emotion that their sheen connotes. Similarly, the function of the military figures goes beyond that of guarding the Emperor; through the magic of the light from the stage, their physical presence has become an invitation to reverie on pomp and ceremony, on military and imperial splendour, on the transfiguration of the banal world of everyday perceptions, and the evocation of the prestige and permanence of a higher, essential, reality. The same criterion that Baudelaire applied to the works of the great painters ('il m'arrivera souvent d'apprécier un tableau uniquement par la somme d'idées ou de rêveries qu'il apportera dans mon esprit' (p. 579)) can thus be applied also to Guys's less exalted art, and if one needed any excuse for drawing the *Burial Ground at Scutari* or *Divine Service before Balaclava* into Baudelaire's own poetic universe, such a procedure finds justification in the critical practice of the poet himself.

These drawings are typical of Guys's production, and the technique is more or less the same as in his urban scenes and 'études de mœurs'. When one has taken into account the broader 'canvas', the larger topographical features and the landscape of a vast theatre of war, it is clear that they share the same qualities of drama, perspective, bizarreness, exaggeration, explosion, but with this difference: in the Crimea Guys is a war correspondent, a reporter, intent on conveying to his London readers the truth about the war and giving as broad a view of it as possible: the battlefields of Balaclava and Inkerman, the harsh conditions, the dead and wounded, the officers and generals, the regiments of the diverse nations, the disciplinary beatings, and so on. By a host of rapid fragments and throwaway observations, often with his comments and explanations intruding well into the space of the drawing, he seems to be bent on creating a narrative, and on reaching a panoramic, overall view of the war. It is for that reason that Baudelaire writes of the war drawings as of a 'poème fait de mille croquis, si vaste et si compliqué' (p. 702), and confidently asserts that 'nul journal, nul récit écrit, nul livre, n'exprime aussi bien, dans tous ses détails douloureux et dans sa sinistre ampleur, cette grande épopée de la guerre de Crimée' (p. 701). It is clear that for him the expressions 'poem' and 'epic' contain a strong element of totality and synthesis.

But in Paris Guys is no longer a war correspondent; he is 'l'homme des foules'. Like the poet of *Le Spleen de Paris*, he has espoused the crowd, 'accrochant sa pensée rapsodique à chaque accident de sa flânerie',[67] and by 'rapsodique' Baudelaire means 'un train de pensées suggéré et commandé par le monde extérieur et le hasard des circonstances'.[68] The creation of the drawings of the capital is of necessity haphazard, the continuing production of a frantic energy and creativity always at the call of outside stimuli, the creation of a 'moi' so joyously and extraordinarily active, so 'vaporized',[69] so 'insatiable du *non-moi*' (p. 692), that it loses itself in the diverse objects of its observation. This is no narcissistic self, engrossed in the contemplation of its own feelings and destiny. Far from living like the dandy before a mirror, the *artiste-flâneur* is a prince who has made the world his domain, who rejoices in passing incognito, and who himself becomes the mirror or kaleidoscope, reflecting and rearranging what is happening around him. He has none of the blasé cynicism of the dandy, engrossed in his own person. His openness of spirit, akin to what Gide was later to call *disponibilité*, makes him infinitely receptive, and at the same time transparently selfless and entire in his love of all that is visible and tangible in the outside world. In order to attain such an 'objectivity', he must possess the elusive art of being *'sincère sans ridicule'* (p. 691). He must also have the heightened sensitivity of the convalescent and the child's ability to see the world 'en *nouveauté*' and be 'toujours *ivre*'. In 'Mœsta et errabunda' Baudelaire had celebrated 'le vert paradis des amours enfantines' with nostalgia and longing, but here, in *Le Peintre*, he gives an original turn to the Romantic myth of the child, spelling out for the first time the link between artistic vision and that of the child, and stating his conviction that inspiration and genius are nothing more than childhood rediscovered by an act of will, whereby the artist is endowed with a childlike wonder before the world, together with the solid nerves and powerful mental constitution of the adult.

The emphasis in *Le Peintre de la vie moderne* falls also on the fecundity of the creative act and the proliferation of the stimuli. It has often been remarked that Baudelaire's vocabulary of the crowd is distinctly erotic, as is indicated by the use of the words *épouser* and *jouissance* and by the way the artist is referred to as the 'amoureux de la vie universelle' and compared to the lover of the gentle sex (p. 692). In the prose poem 'Les

---

[67] *Corr.* ii. 583.
[68] See *Oc.* i. 428.
[69] Ibid. 676: 'De la vaporisation et de la centralisation du *Moi*. Tout est là.'

Foules' what men call love is said to be vastly inferior compared to that ineffable orgy, 'cette sainte prostitution de l'âme qui se donne tout entière, poésie et charité, à l'imprévu qui se montre, à l'inconnu qui passe', and the 'ribote de vitalité' of the same poem finds a parallel in *Le Peintre* in the chaotic *pêle-mêle* in the streets, which in turn is echoed in a 'tantôt [. . .] tantôt' sentence structure, and in, for example, the nominal construction of the following passage: 'Un régiment passe, qui va peut-être au bout du monde, jetant dans l'air des boulevards ses fanfares entraînantes et légères comme l'espérance [. . .] Harnachements, scintillements, musique, regards décidés, moustaches lourdes et sérieuses, tout cela entre pêle-mêle en lui' (p. 693).

The dominant faculty of this truly cosmopolitan[70] *artiste-flâneur* is his curiosity: 'Ainsi il va, il court, il cherche' (p. 694), as if engaged in a desperate ambition to observe and record everything, to capture, exhaust, and subjugate the inexhaustible. As for Poe's Auguste Bedloe, who takes his daily dose of opium before his morning walk, the merest object or perception, the trembling of a leaf or the humming of a bee, is endowed with a heightened interest, as he experiences 'tout un monde d'inspirations, une procession magnifique et bigarrée de pensées désordonnées et rhapsodiques'.[71] This intoxicating and hallucinated state, in which the onrush of thought becomes '*infiniment plus* accéléré et plus *rhapsodique*', can be so intense that reason is enslaved, a mere 'épave à la merci de tous les courants'. Similarly, for the *flâneur* immersed in the crowd and impelled constantly towards the future and the new, the ordering power of reason seems to have little or no part. There is no question of imposing coherence on these random perceptions, no question of acceding to a synthetic view, and indeed Guys seems very far from seeking it. Curiously, this role has been passed from the artist to the critic, who yet again becomes involved in a creative act, and it is Baudelaire the essayist who, in the chapters on the dandy,[72] soldier, woman, and carriages, gives a synthetic portrait of each type. An excellent example would be the passage on 'l'amour

---

[70] Baudelaire sees the 'grâce divine du cosmopolitisme' (576) and curiosity as the 'point de départ' of Guys's genius (689).

[71] Ibid. 428.

[72] In spite of his own protestations (712), it is in 'Le Dandy' that Baudelaire appears at his most digressive, further removed from Guys, whom he seems to use much more as a pretext, than in the other chapters. Here, Guys is merely the point of departure for the poet's views, whereas in 'Le Militaire' and 'Les Femmes et les filles' one senses that particular works by Guys are embedded in the text. For an excellent study of the dandy, see Françoise Coblence, *Le Dandysme: obligation d'incertitude* (Paris: Presses Universitaires de France, 1988).

interlope' in 'Les Femmes et les filles', or on the kinds of soldier
Baudelaire identifies after some introductory moral reflections on their
'insouciance martiale' and simplicity of mind and behaviour:

Aucun type militaire n'y manque, et tous sont saisis avec une espèce de joie
enthousiaste: le vieil officier d'infanterie, sérieux et triste, affligeant son cheval
de son obésité; le joli officier d'état-major, pincé dans sa taille, se dandinant
des épaules, se penchant sans timidité sur le fauteuil des dames, et qui, vu de
dos, fait penser aux insectes les plus sveltes et les plus élégants; le zouave
et le tirailleur, qui portent dans leur allure un caractère excessif d'audace
et d'indépendance, et comme un sentiment plus vif de responsabilité
personnelle; la désinvolture agile et gaie de la cavalerie légère; la physionomie
vaguement professorale et académique des corps spéciaux, comme l'artillerie
et le génie, souvent confirmée par l'appareil peu guerrier des lunettes: aucun
de ces modèles, aucune de ces nuances ne sont négligés, et tous sont resumés,
définis avec le même amour et le même esprit. (p. 708)

Baudelaire is no mere *flâneur* of Guys's works, content to pick out
those which strike him forcibly. What he has done here is twofold.
First, from the haphazard and disparate individual studies, he has
transformed his 'volupté en connaissance' (p. 786) by defining each of
the various types of soldier. Second, he has given a panoramic overview or synthetic portrait of the essence 'soldier' in a way not dissimilar to the 'poem' which is made of the totality of the sketches of the
Crimean War. To the joy of immersing oneself in the proliferating
observations of the crowd and fixing them on paper has been added the
intellectual joy of imposing order and permanence on the random and
the evanescent. The essayist, who had identified himself with the artist
and espoused his point of view, has doubled as philosopher and
brought the anarchy of experience under the disciplining structures of
the intellect. As Baudelaire himself elegantly states at the end of *Le
Poème du hachisch*, 'Conclure, c'est fermer un cercle.'[73] In the case of
Le Peintre de la vie moderne he has encompassed the darting 'lignes
brisées' of Guys's work within the synthesizing circle of his own
thought.

As with Delacroix and the other artists Baudelaire favours, memory
is an essential factor in Guys's art. Although some of the Crimean
drawings were done on the spot, and though theoretically they do not
conform to the fundamental requirement of being produced from
memory, they do not appear to be any different in technique from his

[73] *Oc.* i. 440.

other works. Like Boudin's sketches with time of day, weather, and wind conditions added in pencil, they often have written into the space of the drawing explanations and instructions to the engravers. They emit as a consequence a powerful sense of improvisation and immediacy; like Guys's other works they have something both ingenuous and *barbare* which proves Guys's attachment to the authenticity of the original impression. But Baudelaire extends the meaning of *barbarie* beyond this kind of fidelity, to a vision which is synthetic and abbreviative, one which, like Corot's, seizes immediately and from the outset the structure, the physiognomy, and the principal characteristics of a scene or of an object, sometimes with an exaggeration that activates the imagination: 'et l'imagination du spectateur, subissant à son tour cette mnémonique si despotique, voit avec netteté l'impression produite par les choses sur l'esprit de M. G. Le spectateur est ici le traducteur d'une traduction toujours claire et enivrante' (p. 698). Because of this powerful structure, the Crimean drawings possess one of the essential qualities for an appeal to the spectator's memory. Furthermore, since Guys has avoided the photographic realism that delights in the myriad trivia of circumstantial detail, it is *as if* he had done all the drawings from memory, universalizing and in a sense idealizing the scenes and once again making them available to the memory of the spectator. Thanks to his abbreviated vision and the rapidity of the drawing, it is *as if* Guys had memorized the scenes as he perceived them, *as if* perception, memory, and execution were not discrete and successive stages but immediate and inseparable elements of the creation of the work. Although, then, the Crimean drawings are quite different in subject-matter from his urban works, and although some were done 'on the spot', the techniques and above all the effect on the spectator are virtually identical.

Memory is, as in Delacroix, the springboard of suggestiveness. Furthermore, Guys's method of drawing is similar to Delacroix's, but taken to an extreme of *dénuement*: 'M. G. commence par de légères indications au crayon, qui ne marquent guère que la place que les objets doivent tenir dans l'espace. Les plans principaux sont indiqués ensuite par des teintes au lavis, des masses vaguement, légèrement colorées d'abord, mais reprises plus tard et chargées successivement de couleurs plus intenses' (p. 699). With a typically arresting oxymoron, Baudelaire claims that what is thus created is a kind of 'ébauche, si vous voulez, mais ébauche parfaite' (p. 700). Here again, we might think of Boudin's pastels or remind ourselves that Delacroix himself was praised or blamed, depending on whether the critic was a partisan of colourists or draughtsmen, for producing mere *ébauches* instead of finished works. Guys has pushed this unfinished quality to an extreme. His indeed is a 'minimalist' art, with figures left incomplete, horses whose legs are not all there, faces almost totally deprived of features or expression, and a wilful blurring of background. What we have in most of his drawings is an art of gesture, so important in Baudelaire's art criticism that he repeatedly draws attention to it in Delacroix[74] and in the caricaturists, and even in his appreciation of actors such as Philibert Rouvière, or Frédéric Lemaître, whose 'sculptural' acting is mentioned in 'L'Art mnémonique' (p. 699). The drawings portray often little more than a posture, an attitude of the arm, leg, or head, which suggest depth of feeling, or reveal shallowness and insensitivity, as in the passage from La Bruyère quoted in 'Les Femmes et les filles': 'Il y a dans quelques femmes une grandeur artificielle attachée au mouvement des yeux, à un air de tête, aux façons de marcher, et qui ne va pas plus loin' (p. 720). Whatever its suggestive magic, it is a fleeting moment caught like an *instantané*, and it is left to the spectator to complete the shape or gesture that has been barely outlined or suggested. Such an art produces in the spectator the shock of the bizarre or the charm of the new, together with a sense of the rightness of the shapes, outlines, and gestures, which are then equated to an experience of *déjà vu*. By what is only the semblance of a paradox, this art of the instant is not limited to the one dimension of time, but like all great art, is inseparable from the workings of memory and recognition.

It is at this point perhaps that we can see more clearly how to apply to Guys Baudelaire's theory of modernity, and more particularly of the transitory and the eternal, developed in the opening chapters of the essay. Readers of the *Salon de 1846* will find themselves on familiar ground, and indeed Baudelaire admits that he has several times explained these things (p. 686). Beauty, he asserts, is always and inevitably of a double composition, the necessary consequence of the duality of mankind: 'Le beau est fait d'un élément éternel, invariable, dont la quantité est excessivement difficile à déterminer, et d'un

---

[74] Cf. the following passage in *L'Œuvre et la vie d'Eugène Delacroix*: 'Ce mérite très particulier et tout nouveau de M. Delacroix, qui lui a permis d'exprimer, simplement avec le contour, le geste de l'homme, si violent qu'il soit, et avec la couleur ce qu'on pourrait appeler l'atmosphère du drame humain' (745).

élément relatif, circonstantiel, qui sera, si l'on veut, tour à tour ou tout ensemble, l'époque, la mode, la morale, la passion' (p. 685). It is clear how Delacroix's art conforms to this definition, since in *Ovide chez les Scythes*, for example, or even *Les Femmes d'Alger*, it combines a modern Romantic sensibility with an impatient and tormented spirituality, with an 'aspiration vers l'infini' (p. 421). But how exactly does it apply to Guys, who is 'tyrannisé par la circonstance' (p. 697), whose modernity resides in his fidelity to 'le transitoire, le fugitif, le contingent' (p. 695), and whose representations of the present, like those of other 'peintres de mœurs', give pleasure because of its 'qualité essentielle de présent'? (p. 684). It is easy to see what in Guys corresponds to the transitory, but what is eternal in this evanescent art is more difficult to define. Baudelaire goes only some way towards helping the reader in this dilemma, and even then one senses a slippage in the terms and a blurring of the issue. For example, he talks of the artist as 'le peintre de la circonstance et de tout ce qu'elle suggère d'éternel' (p. 687), whose task it is (and the two phrases seem to be in apposition) to 'dégager de la mode ce qu'elle peut contenir de poétique dans l'historique, de tirer l'éternel du transitoire' (p. 694). On the next page he declares that if the modern is to be made worthy of taking its place as 'antiquity', 'il faut que la beauté mystérieuse que la vie humaine y met involontairement en ait été extraite'. It would appear, then, that the eternal element is linked not just to the idea of recognition but also to the eminently Baudelairean notions of suggestion, poetry, and mystery. In its depiction of space, *La Loge del'Empereur* found an analogue in Baudelaire's own mental universe; but at the end of his commentary the poet-critic sums up his reaction by defining the picture as 'le lustre et le public', reaching beyond what was evanescent and transitory to the permanent and unchanging essence of 'le lustre'. The contingent and cicumstantial give on to the essential and eternal. The use of the substantives 'le lustre' and 'le public' finds a parallel in a magnificent passage in *Le Poème du hachisch*, where, having evoked the transformation of colour, time, and space in certain intoxicated states, Baudelaire describes how our arid grammar itself becomes poetic, 'quelque chose comme une sorcellerie évocatoire; les mots ressuscitent revêtus de chair et d'os, *le substantif, dans sa majesté substantielle*'.[75] Adopting Baudelaire's idiom, we could say that the 'magie suggestive' and 'sorcellerie évocatoire' of Guys's drawings reside in a

---

[75] *Oc.* i. 431, my emphasis.

'substantialization' of the fleeting and the transitory, whether it be of scenes, as with *La Loge*, or of individual figures whose particularity of posture or gesture points at the same time to the eternal type to which they belong.[76]

Here, of course, the parallel with Delacroix's great paintings must be abandoned; for the cultural dimension is absent from these drawings of modern urban life, which in comparison appear limited to the instant. So much of Delacroix, with its heroic and noble subject-matter, takes us into the depths of our literary, historical, and cultural past, but with Guys things are very different. There is no sense of a source, of historical depth, or of intertextual resonance, whether in the positive manner of Delacroix or the negative and ironic manner of Manet. In addition, what is conveyed is almost nothing at all. No narrative element is made explicit. The figures stand before our gaze, anonymous and in a context where very little appears to be happening. If there is a caption (in the majority of cases supplied by museum cataloguers), it is usually a tautology, not a means of entry into the work. Contrast *La Barque de Dante*, *Ovide chez les Scythes*, *La Mort de Sardanapale*, or even the *Consecration of a Burial Ground at Scutari* with what one most often finds: *Mounted Soldiers*, *Family out Walking*, *Three Women in a Bar*, *Carriage in the Bois de Boulogne*. Such drawings are no doubt an invitation to memory and recognition, but because of their minimalism they require of the spectator an increased creative and imaginative response. Before Guys's drawings, more clearly than before the works of any other artist of the time, we can understand why it was that for Baudelaire memory and imagination were so indivisibly linked: 'La véritable mémoire, considérée sous un point de vue philosophique, ne consiste, je pense, que dans une imagination très vive, facile à émouvoir' (p. 470). These drawings invite the spectator to fill the gaps, to create a story or narrative, possibly a moral lesson, a personality, a *legend*, from a gesture, attitude, bearing, or movement, which is why Baudelaire defines the art of this painter of modern life as 'cette traduction *légendaire* de la vie extérieure' (p. 698).

If there is a parallel with Baudelaire's poetry here, it is not so much with the great poems of 'Tableaux parisiens' ('Le Cygne','Le Jeu', 'Danse macabre', or 'Crépuscule du matin') as some critics have

---

[76] Jean-Paul Dubray, *Constantin Guys* (Paris: Editions Rieder, 1930), 28 sees Guys as 'un portraitiste de types'.

claimed,[77] as with the kind of descriptive vignette in some of the prose poems: the 'beau monsieur ganté, verni, cruellement cravaté et emprisonné dans des habits tout neufs' of 'Un plaisant'; 'les yeux des pauvres' agog before the bright lights and the vulgar décor of the sparkling new café where history and mythology have been 'mises au service de la goinfrerie'; the sudden explosive appearance of Mademoiselle Bistouri, 'une grande fille, robuste, aux yeux très ouverts, légèrement fardée, les cheveux flottant au vent avec les brides de son bonnet'; above all, the old woman of 'Les Fenêtres', 'mûre, ridée déjà, pauvre, toujours penchée sur quelque chose, et qui ne sort jamais. Avec son visage, avec son vêtement, avec son geste, avec presque rien, j'ai refait l'histoire de cette femme, ou plutôt sa *légende* [my emphasis], et quelquefois je me la raconte à moi-même en pleurant.'

What Guys invites the spectator to exploit is not so much the 'reality' of his figures as their legendary quality: in a word, their virtuality. They are merely the point of departure of a creative process, the burden of which has been transferred away from the artist. Here it is truer than perhaps with any other artist of Baudelaire's time that 'la poésie d'un tableau doit être faite par le spectateur' (p. 9). Many of his drawings concern the elegant ephemera of fashionable life, a family out walking or ladies and gentlemen in carriages or on horseback, and the spectator is invited to interpret a gesture or posture, and to create from them a story or a life. It is a stirring paradox that this essentially fleeting and evanescent art should be the one which makes the most urgent and compelling appeal to memory and to the projective and creative powers of the imagination.

The verse poem of Baudelaire's which conforms more than any other to this new aesthetic of modernity is 'A une passante', the relevant aspects of which are the following: as with most of the 'Tableaux parisiens', the point of departure is not in the mind of the poet, but in the outside world, in the passing of the woman in the street amid the deafening hubbub of the crowd; the description of the woman is miminal, reduced to her gesture of lifting the hem of her skirt to reveal her statuesque leg, and to the enigmatic radiance of her eyes; the figure of the woman, an aristocratic widow, is highly sexualized; her fleeting presence suggests her history or legend which is projected into the future as a virtual love that can

---

[77] See Gustave Geoffroy, *Constantin Guys: l'historien du second Empire* (Paris: Crès, 1920), 88, and F. W. Leakey, *Baudelaire: Collected Essays, 1953–88* (Cambridge: Cambridge University Press, 1990), 106.

never be realized; and finally, because of this very virtuality, the poem appears as a fragment.

In the light of all this, it would not be easy to define accurately the mental universe of Guys, what Proust would have called 'ce monde de la pensée de Guys',[78] because it lacks precision and coherence. Of course, his themes and obsessions are plain to see, and Baudelaire has no difficulty in identifying them in the chapters on women, dandies, carriages, and so on, so that at first sight at least a *thématique* of Guys's world should not appear to elude the critic. But the problem is that the drawings, presenting as they do merely a starting point for the imagination, appear initially as empty spaces. In a much more dramatic and radical way than with other great artists, they break loose from their creator to become integrated into the world of the spectator who, like the poet-critic himself, has to flesh out a personality, create a past and a destiny, and subject the random and the proliferating to the discipline and categories of the mind. Because his works are so malleable, such a study of Guys, whose point of departure is almost nothing at all, would involve not so much an act of identification of critic with artist, as an appropriation of the artist by the spectator-critic and the imposition of a replacement mental universe. To make the point more forcibly, one might contrast the malleability of Guys's works with the strong sense of definition and resistance of caricature; for no matter how active the spectator's participation in the scene, his interpretation and response are more restricted and directed by the message the caricaturist wishes to convey. If the spectator were free to make his own interpretation, the caricaturist would have failed in what he set out to do, and his enterprise would be pointless. If the spectator were to see the person or thing caricatured as noble and praiseworthy, the joke would then fall on the caricaturist, in much the same way as it falls on the ironist who has the misfortune to be believed.

For all that, what Baudelaire presents in *Le Peintre de la vie moderne* is, for the most part, a confident and even affirmative art, an art which in addition has a moral dimension, whether it shows the realities and suffering of the Crimean War, or leads to speculation on the life of the social types it outlines. Its suggestiveness and the reveries it engenders in no way preclude it from being an art that evinces a strong sense of the real and of contemporary society. Even the drawings of fashion are far from being purely decorative pieces of art for its own sake; for they too point to a human destiny behind the elegant frivolities of attire and

---

[78] Marcel Proust, *Contre Sainte-Beuve* (Paris: Gallimard, 1971), 255.

adornment. In this sense they are most unlike Manet's works of the same period, being devoid of that irony and self-referentiality that are the essential ingredients of what might be called Manet's aesthetic agnosticism. What makes Baudelaire's account of Guys's drawings such a fulfilling and joyous experience is then, to sum up, that it reflects the quasi-sexual vitality of the artist, the confidence of a critical mind which achieves stability and synthesis amid proliferation, and that it makes an appeal to the creative imagination of the reader to provide the story or legend of the figures depicted.

But there are other drawings of bars, whorehouses, and street scenes which have nothing joyous about them and which are more deeply disturbing and baleful than anything Guys produced in his long career. His later years in particular are almost exclusively given to such images, as to a sick obsession. Gone are the radiant watercolours of his earlier work, replaced by sombre grey washes in which spectral figures play out the sordid rituals of 'l'amour interlope'. Clearly, Baudelaire had seen some of Guys's earlier treatments of such themes; for he mentions in 'Les Femmes et les filles' the atmosphere in which 'l'alcool et le tabac ont mêlé leurs vapeurs, la maigreur enflammée de la phtisie ou les rondeurs de l'adiposité, cette hideuse santé de la fainéantise', the grotesque and satanic 'Madame', and the smoke-filled chaos in which 's'agitent et se convulsent des nymphes macabres et des poupées vivantes dont l'œil enfantin laisse échapper une clarté sinistre' (p. 721). In such places, one finds 'rien que le vice inévitable, c'est-à-dire le regard du démon embusqué dans les ténèbres [. . .] la beauté particulière du mal, le beau dans l'horrible' (p. 722). He insists on the moral fecundity of these images and the suggestions they engender: 'Elles sont grosses de suggestions, mais de suggestions cruelles, âpres, que ma plume, bien qu'accoutumée à lutter contre les représentations plastiques, n'a peut-être traduites qu'insuffisamment.' As before the hyperbolic and convulsive laughter of Pierrot in the English pantomime,[79] as before the 'monstres hideux' of 'Les Sept Vieillards', the poet, 'Blessé par le mystère et par l'absurdité', seems here to sense a threat to reason and language, which appear to abdicate, inadequate to their task. And these figures are all the more bizarre, astonishing, unreal, and 'shocking' (Guys's aesthetic, like Baudelaire's, is indeed an 'esthétique du choc'), since, unlike those of the Crimean War where the alienation is in a sense relative stemming from

---

[79] 'Avec une plume tout cela est pâle et glacé. Comment la plume pourrait-elle rivaliser avec la pantomime?' (540).

their involvement in the extreme situation of war in a distant land, *their* alienation within the false security of an allegedly familiar urban environment can by comparison be said to be total, absolute.

Such drawings represent only a small part of Guys's production at that time, which no doubt explains why Baudelaire is careful not to exaggerate their importance in relation to his other works. In any case, we are still dealing with the relatively confident Baudelaire of 1859, since the essay was written in November of that year, though not published until 1863. By emphasizing and developing the structure of the first edition, the 1861 edition of *Les Fleurs du Mal* can be said to make an act of faith in the poet's ability to dominate and synthesize experience. But with *Le Spleen de Paris*, things become very different. We know that at a certain moment, in 1861, to be exact, he had thought of the title *La Lueur et la fumée, Poème* [singular], *en prose*.[80] The title is, however, inappropriate, because 'Poème' implies epic, implies synthesis, as when he had talked of Guys's 'grande épopée de la guerre de Crimée' as 'ce poème fait de mille croquis, si vaste et si compliqué' (pp. 701, 702). *Le Spleen de Paris*, which Baudelaire perhaps once thought might form a *Poème*, falls hopelessly into a world of endless proliferation and repetition, of which the poet had had some premonition in 'Tableaux parisiens'. Another title, which he had also contemplated, would have served him better, *Les 66*[81] (the number of the beast in the Apocalypse), or *Les 666*, or *Les 6666*, for in *Le Spleen de Paris* the One has 'chuté', like God in the *Journaux intimes*,[82] into number, into an imperfection which can only repeat itself endlessly to infinity, the negative counterpart of the absolute. There is an obscene fecundity in the ugly, whereas the sublime tends towards oneness. In spite of its shifting ironies, 'Les Foules', first published in 1861, had celebrated the exuberant and selfless espousal of the other, only to degenerate two years later in 'Les Fenêtres', with the poet's self-mocking protest, 'Qu'importe ce que peut-être la réalité placée hors de moi, si elle m'a aidé à vivre, à sentir que je suis et ce que je suis?', into the derisory spectacle of the *flâneur* turned Narcissus. Heaven/hell, God/Satan, Idéal/Spleen, 'extase de la vie/horreur de la vie', so many collapsing and telescoping opposites, to which can be added 'flâneur'/Narcissus, each condemned to a time made of the endless repetition

[80] *Corr.* ii. 197.
[81] *Oc.* i. 365.
[82] Ibid. 688. The positive side of Baudelaire's 'arithmetic' imagination can be found in *Le Poème du hachisch* (*Oc.* i. 419) and *Fusées* (649).

of the same. To conclude, it would appear that Guys's evolution, and the drawings of his last years support this view, follows a similar curve to Baudelaire's, and that after the joyous immersion in metamorphosis and number came the obsession with an eternity of damnation, as if each one of these proliferating images represented a horrific vision, a negative *ecstasis* before the endlessly repeated spectacle of 'l'immortel péché'.

6

Manet

FOR A long time Manet has presented a problem to students of Baudelaire. Why is it that, in spite of the modernity of his thinking and poetic output and of an increasingly close friendship from 1862 onwards, Baudelaire remains so reticent and apparently half-hearted about this most revolutionary of contemporary painters, whose theory and painterly practice have so much in common with his own in poetry? The relative silence of their correspondence and the poverty of the documentation make the problem even more intractable, and push the critic into speculation in order to find a key to the enigma. Initially at least, it seems paradoxical that Baudelaire did not recognize in Manet the painter of modern life so fervently hoped for in the last sentences of the *Salon* of 1845?

Au vent qui soufflera demain nul ne tend l'oreille; et pourtant l'héroïsme *de la vie moderne* nous entoure et nous presse. [. . .] Celui-là sera le *peintre*, le vrai peintre, qui saura arracher à la vie actuelle son côté épique, et nous faire voir et comprendre, avec de la couleur et du dessin, combien nous sommes grands et poétiques dans nos cravates et nos bottes vernies. (p. 407)

In the *Salon* of 1846 Baudelaire had seen Delacroix as the leader of the modern school and equated modern art to Romanticism; yet he ends that same *Salon* with a strong appeal for a different kind of art, rooted in modern times in a way that Delacroix's was not; for although Delacroix's art was modern in sensibility, colour and outline, it was not in subject matter. As a result some commentators have gone so far as to interpret the last paragraph of the *Salon* as an appeal to Delacroix to modernize his painting and to clothe his subjects in 'le frac funèbre et convulsionné que nous endossons tous' (p. 496). Here Baudelaire hopes for an art with an epic heroism about it, with heroes not from the *Iliad* but from *La Comédie humaine*—Vautrin, Rastignac, Birotteau— and sees in Balzac himself 'le plus héroïque, le plus singulier, le plus romantique et le plus poétique parmi tous les personnages que vous avez tirés de votre sein!' What he envisages is clearly something quite different from anything Delacroix had produced up to that point. Even *La Liberté guidant le peuple* could not be said to conform to this new demand, since the modernity of the figures—students, artisans, soldiers, bourgeois in top hat and frock coat—is engulfed by the allegorical figure of Freedom and the Romanticism of Revolution.

Many reasons have been put forward to explain, or explain away, Baudelaire's failure to recognize Manet as the painter of modern life: he was already acquainted with Guys and his work, and the composition of *Le Peintre de la vie moderne* may date from as early as November 1859 (it was sent to *Le Constitutionnel* in August 1860), with the result that Guys had in a sense got in first, before Manet had begun to produce his more characteristic work. Pichois emphasizes that 'quand Baudelaire est près de sombrer dans la paralysie [in March 1866, although he had felt '*le vent de l'aile de l'imbécillité* [1] as early as 23 January 1862], Manet n'en est qu'au numéro 68 de son œuvre picturale, qui en comptera presque sept cents' (p. 1258). It may be that Baudelaire thought his friend, who was some eleven years younger, was still only on the threshold of his career and not yet fully in command of his art. It could also be argued that his increasingly poor health, his diminishing creativity, and his absence in Brussels from April 1864 kept him both detached and remote from Manet's production. Finally, it has been suggested that if he did not intervene at the time of the uproar caused by *Le Déjeuner sur l'herbe* and *Olympia*, it was not out of indifference or incomprehension, as some critics have thought, but because as a writer of *Salons* he had made it a rule never to comment on the works of *refusés*.[2] For those sombre and blithe spirits who attach importance to famous last words a last-ditch recuperation is perhaps vouchsafed by the aphasic Baudelaire's cry at his clinic (p. 1258) shortly before his death, 'Manet, Manet!', taken as a tardy but enthusiastic recognition of his friend's genius.

Whatever one may think of such speculations, and however one may wish to nuance the 'terrible' letter of 11 May 1865 in which he accuses Manet of being but the first in the decrepitude of his art, there is little doubt from his few but flattering remarks in *Peintres et aquafortistes* that Baudelaire held a high opinion of Manet's *Guitariste* (1860) and at least some of his other Spanish paintings: 'M. Manet est l'auteur du

---

[1] *Oc.* i. 668.

[2] Pierre-Georges Castex, *Baudelaire critique d'art* (Paris: SEDES, 1969), 75: 'Comme il s'était fait un principe de ne jamais parler des refusés en rendant compte des *Salons*, il ne put, en 1859, signaler son *Buveur d'absinthe*.'

Guitariste, qui a produit une vive sensation au Salon dernier. On verra au prochain Salon plusieurs tableaux de lui empreints de la saveur espagnole la plus forte, et qui donnent à croire que le génie espagnol s'est réfugié en France' (p. 738). He goes on to mention Manet's vigorous taste for modern reality, and praise his lively and abundant imagination, 'cette imagination vive et ample, sensible, audacieuse, sans laquelle, il faut bien le dire, toutes les meilleures facultés ne sont que des serviteurs sans maîtres, des agents sans gouvernement'. This is high praise indeed, given that in the *Salon* of 1859 Baudelaire had elevated imagination to great heights, making of it 'la reine des facultés' without which genius in any activity is impossible. It is known that Delacroix, and even Ingres and Gautier, admired *Le Guitariste*. No doubt, like Gautier, Baudelaire appreciated the Spanishness of the dress and décor,[3] and possibly the way its realism was tempered by a discreet and 'Romantic' exoticism. One wonders also whether the poet for whom *'le beau est toujours bizarre'* (p. 578) was impressed by the strangeness this composition shares with several of Manet's early paintings, since the guitarist is, unintentionally, made to be left-handed and his leg seems to float in mid-air as if unsupported by the bench on which he is sitting.

Whether Baudelaire had a high regard for *Episode d'une course de taureaux* or was merely trying to help a colleague for whom he felt 'de l'amitié-passion',[4] he asks the director of the 1864 *Salon*, Philippe de Chennevières, to find a good place for it, together with *Le Christ aux anges* and two canvases by Fantin-Latour.[5] The picture did not please Manet, who excised from it *Le Torero mort*; nor did the bizarre perspective of the scene go without mocking comment from critics and caricaturists, Edmond About describing it as 'Un torero en bois tué par un rat',[6] while Callias in *L'Artiste* talks of a 'microscopic' bull: 'C'est la perspective, direz-vous.—Mais non; car au troisième plan, contre les gradins du cirque, les *toreros* représentent une taille raisonnable et semblent rire de ce petit taureau, qu'ils pourraient écraser sous les talons de leurs escarpins.'[7] Whether such a pictorial

---

[3] Gautier, *Abécédaire du Salon de 1861* (Paris: Dentu, 1861), 264–5: 'Caramba! voilà un *Guitarero* qui ne vient pas de l'Opéra-Comique, et qui ferait mauvaise figure sur une lithographie de romance; mais Vélasquez le saluerait d'un petit clignement d'œil amical, et Goya lui demanderait du feu pour allumer son papelito.'

[4] Claude Pichois and Jean Ziegler, *Baudelaire* (Paris: Julliard, 1987), 432.

[5] *Corr.* ii. 351.

[6] Edmond About, *Le Salon de 1864* (Paris, 1864), 157.

[7] *L'Artiste*, 1 June 1864, p. 241.

méprise was intended as part of a new and deliberately disconcerting aesthetic to shock the public out of conventional ways of looking at pictures, or whether it can be put down to artistic gaucheness or inexperience, the exotic and bizarre or alienating quality this painting shares with the *Guitariste* might well have appealed to Baudelaire.

The woman dressed as *majo* (1862) is much more problematic. One must suppose that, since Baudelaire owned it for a time, it held some appeal for him, with its humorous cat and yellow ball of wool, and its deliberately ironic bow in the direction of Goya's *Maja desnuda*, which he was known to have admired greatly. But the painting has none of the eroticism and suggestiveness of Goya's troubling masterpiece. Manet's Spanish works of this early period appear either as highly competent *exercices de style* in the manner of Murillo, Velásquez, or Goya but with very little that is *sui generis* or suggestive and able to 'faire rêver', or they appear as a puzzle or enigma. This enigmatic quality is nowhere more evident than in another 'transvestite' painting of the same year, Victorine as *espada*, which evokes nothing of the drama of the bullfight, but the paradox of the female matador. Here again the dressing of the woman as a man has none of the erotic charge of similar figures in the art and literature of the period, in Tassaert's extraordinary lithograph, *Ne fais pas donc la cruelle!*[8] for example (p. 444), or in the masculine get-ups of La Débardeuse and Rosanette in *L'Education sentimentale*. It cannot be made to equate to the typically Baudelairean allure of the 'femme qui veut toujours faire l'homme, signe de grande dépravation' (p. 74), of which Madame de Merteuil of *Les Liaisons dangereuses*, and to a lesser degree Emma Bovary, are the most formidable and heroic examples. This may be because the figure of the *espada* is all colour and gesture and because, as Thoré-Bürger felt, something of the personality of the figure is missing, and the head ought to have been painted with 'plus d'accent et de profondeur'.[9] The result, at all events, is that the eye and mind of the spectator are constantly diverted from meaning, narrative, value, or reverie to the balance of the composition for its own sake. What may have been disappointing or even disquieting about the painting was that it appeared to celebrate nothing beyond itself. Such 'agnosticism' in art could have appeared depressing or inexplicable to the poet who be-

---

[8] Reproduced by J. Mayne in Charles Baudelaire, *Art in Paris 1845–1862*, plate 17.
[9] Théophile Thoré, *Salons de W. Bürger 1861–1868* (Paris: Renouard, 1870), i. 424–5.

lieved that all great art should be endowed with naivety and have faith. In 1851 he had condemned Art for Art's sake to an inevitable sterility, since it excluded 'la morale, et souvent même la passion' (p. 26), and in *L'Ecole païenne* of the following year he had denounced the excessive preoccupation of modern art with technique and *métier* as a devouring canker (p. 48).

In these circumstances it would be difficult to imagine him reacting to many of Manet's early Spanish paintings with any degree of enthusiasm. True, he admired the 'merveilleux portrait' of *Lola de Valence* (Pl. 13) for which he wrote a mediocre quatrain, considered scandalous because of the erotic undertones of the expression *bijou* since Diderot's outspoken novel, *Les Bijoux indiscrets*:

> Entre tant de beautés que partout on peut voir,
> Je comprends bien, amis, que le désir balance;
> Mais on voit scintiller en Lola de Valence
> Le charme inattendu d'un bijou rose et noir.

In a note in *Les Epaves* he tries to dispel any obscene intention, claiming that the poet had simply meant that 'une beauté, d'un caractère à la fois ténébreux et folâtre, faisait rêver à l'association du *rose* et du *noir*'.[10] No doubt he admired it for the Spanish exoticism it shared with the *Guitariste*, and which he may have encouraged, and possibly also for the somewhat muscular and masculine attractiveness of the dancer. Perhaps, in spite of his protest of good intentions, he was even grateful for the opportunity to associate pink and black in such a provocative manner. Zola, aware of possibly forcing the text, sides for once with Baudelaire in his interpretation of Manet and takes the *paratonnerre* at its face value, stating: 'Il est parfaitement vrai que *Lola de Valence* est un bijou rose et noir; le peintre ne procède déja plus que par taches, et son Espagnole est peinte largement, par vives oppositions; la toile entière est couverte de deux teintes.'[11] He thus gives some support to Baudelaire's protestation that the appeal of the canvas is in the interplay of its two principal colours; but for all that there is something full-square and abrupt, one might even say staccato, about the portrait and its subject,[12] and we are certainly far from the kind of reverie that Delacroix's reds and greens aroused in the poet in the

---

[10] *Oc.* i. 168.

[11] Emile Zola, *Ecrits sur l'art* (Paris: Gallimard, 1991), 157.

[12] Robert Rey in *Manet* (Paris: Flammarion, 1966), 51 identifies the weaknesses of the painting: 'Le visage est esquissé par de larges cernes bruns qui donnent mal l'impression du modelé et de la profondeur. Le bras droit est sans densité, la jambe gauche est escamotée

famous quatrain of 'Les Phares'. We are equally far from the supernatural reverie that such a 'theatrical' subject might be thought to
invite. It is as if, by placing his dancer *behind* the curtain, Manet had
deliberately refused to exploit the appeal to the imagination afforded
by a figure on a stage. Lola stands behind the curtain, which has on the
right of the picture a small gap through which are glimpsed figures
from the 'real' theatre, so that, as with *La Musique aux Tuileries* and
Le Balcon, we are aware of a self-conscious reversal of the normal
point of view. Here is the actress on her stage, but a stage that
has been deprived of its function and of its theatricality.[13] There is
no manipulation of light and shade, no transformation of space to
make her appear to surge out of a magical depth. On the contrary, the
impression is of horizontality; in his 'realism' Manet seems to flatten
and demythologize his subject, denying it its poetic and 'illusory'
potential. The contrast with the theatrical evocations of Nerval in *Les
Filles du feu* with his unapproachable actresses, or his description of
Adrienne in the midst of the round of girls in the Valois forest,[14] or
indeed with Baudelaire himself in 'L'Irréparable', could not be more
pronounced:

—J'ai vu parfois, au fond d'un théâtre banal
   Qu'enflammait l'orchestre sonore,
Une fée allumer dans un ciel infernal
   Une miraculeuse aurore;
J'ai vu parfois au fond d'un théâtre banal

Un être, qui n'était que lumière, or et gaze,
   Terrasser l'énorme Satan [. . .].

Finally, *Lola de Valence* has little if anything of the appeal to
memory and the contained sensuality of that most intimate of all
Delacroix's paintings, *Les Femmes d'Alger*, which combines a quasi-
religious melancholy with 'je ne sais quel haut parfum de mauvais lieu
qui nous guide assez vite vers les limbes insondés de la tristesse'

dans une pénombre; elle repose sur un pied sans vie. Les pompons de laine rouge qui
garnissent la robe ne sont que des pastilles.'

[13] In this respect it is very different from Courbet's *La Signora Adela Guerrero, danseuse
espagnole* of 1851 with which it has, however, certain affinities. See Faunce and Nochlin,
Courbet Reconsidered, 110.

[14] See *Sylvie* in Nerval, *Œuvres*, i. 241: 'Indifférent au spectacle de la salle, celui du théâtre
ne m'arrêtait guère, excepté lorsqu'à la seconde ou à la troisième scène d'un maussade chef-
d'œuvre d'alors, une apparition bien connue illuminait l'espace vide, rendant la vie d'un
souffle et d'un mot à ces vaines figures qui m'entouraient.' See also the description of
Adrienne, 245.

(p. 440). There is nothing here that corresponds to 'l'*âme* dans ses belles heures' (p. 637) in *Ovide chez les Scythes*, where the look and the languid, *feminine* posture of the Latin poet, the depth of the lake and of the landscape, together with the intense blue of the distant mountains, as in a landscape by Poussin or by Claude, combine to suggest a reverie of exile and longing. Such a painting represents a moment of lyrical flight in which the inner being seeks to attain a higher region (p. 164); but in Manet the lyrical élan seems stillborn, the supernatural never leaves the ground in this least suggestive of arts. We have no hint of 'l'expansion des choses infinies' of 'Correspondances'. On the contrary, the painting is increasingly self-contained to the point that reverie is blocked, and interpretation becomes more hazardous, problematic, even superfluous.

It is unclear which of Manet's portraits were known to Baudelaire and whether he expressed any opinion of them. The portrait of the artist's parents which hangs in the Musée d'Orsay was much criticized at the time, not least for the apparent lack of communication between the figures. The painting evinces coldness or indifference, which may have been intended, and can be thought typical of Manet's production generally in its unwillingness or inability to capture the dynamics of the relationship between people. His figures, portraits or not, often appear juxtaposed, with little of the powerful and passionate interaction so striking in Delacroix, in *Romeo et Juliette*, for example. This can of course be explained by Manet's realism and his sense of the isolation of human beings locked in their own world. It could indeed be argued that the poetry of his work lies precisely in the depiction of a solitude that has gone beyond melancholy to the point of being accepted as inevitable, as part of a reality in which the tension of desire has been broken. We do not even know what Baudelaire thought of the extraordinary portrait of Jeanne Duval of 1862, in which the wooden, clumsy and doll-like figure of his mistress, her beauty faded and her expression hardened and masculine, is almost engulfed in a hyperbolically voluminous and quite inappropriate summer dress, with its broad violet and white stripes. Some critics have suggested the influence of Guys, and that the portrait resembles nothing so much as an enlarged drawing, watercolour or gouache by the painter of modern life,[15] whose celebration of the fashionable crinoline and the way it enhances the natural contours of the female form is amply

---

[15] P. G. Konody, *The Painter of Victorian Life* (London: Geoffrey Holmes, 1930), 10.

demonstrated in innumerable drawings. But the problem with that theory is that if Jeanne's dress is indeed a crinoline, it is so exaggerated in form and volume as to be a kind of anti-crinoline, a parody or caricature of elegance, nearer to Daumier than to Guys. The painting is decidedly odd, being not just a send-up of the dress, but also, and much more radically, a send-up of portrait painting. It is a portrait in which the subject has been all but lost, a non- or anti-portrait to match the dress which it ridicules rather than celebrates. Whether or not Baudelaire had seen any of these paintings, he would not have recognized the quality he required of portrait painting, 'la reconstruction idéale des individus' (p. 412), which he admired in Ingres, in the portraits of Monsieur Bertin and Madame d'Houssonville. In the *Salon* of 1846 he had placed Ingres firmly in the historical school along with David, but had gone on to doubt whether good portraits can be painted by artists who are not colourists:

Il faut savoir baigner une tête dans les molles vapeurs d'une chaude atmosphère, ou la faire sortir des profondeurs d'un crépuscule. Ici, l'imagination a une plus grande part, et cependant, comme il arrive souvent que le roman est plus vrai que l'histoire, il arrive aussi qu'un modèle est plus clairement exprimé par le pinceau abondant et facile d'un coloriste que par le crayon d'un dessinateur. (p. 464)

In this light Manet's early portraits[16] at least appear to fail on two counts: first, they are not sufficiently Romantic or intense, and second, they share with his other paintings, for all the brightness of the colours used, the qualities of the draughtsman rather than of the colourist. One critic indeed has suggested that in this respect Manet would have been an *Ingriste* rather than a follower of Delacroix,[17] while others have stressed that he was incapable of painting from memory, being on occasion forced to use photographs in the absence of his subject.[18] If there is substance in these allegations, then Baudelaire's judgement is unlikely to have been other than negative.

It is widely accepted that Manet's *Acteur tragique* is one of his finest works. It is a portrait of the famous Romantic actor Philibert Rouvière,

---

[16] Manet's *chef-d'œuvre* as a portrait painter was of course his magnificent study of Mallarmé (1876), which has no trace of *Ingrisme*.

[17] Jens Thiis, 'Manet et Baudelaire. Quelques considérations sur le Romantisme et le Naturalisme', *Etudes d'Art* (Algiers, 1945), i. 11.

[18] Manet himself admitted his fear of having to paint without a model: 'Quand je commence quelque chose, je tremble en pensant que le modèle me fera défaut, que je ne le reverrai plus aussi souvent que je voudrais le revoir' (Antonin Proust, *Edouard Manet Souvenirs* (Caen: L'Échoppe, 1988), 90).

which Manet called *L'Acteur tragique* because Rouvière died before
it was completed, and possibly because, as Charles Moffett suggests,
he 'hoped the image would succeed as a painting with a broader
significance than a portrait of a specific individual'.[19] In a letter to
Baudelaire, he writes that another (less praiseworthy) reason for the
change of title was to deflect the criticism of those people who would
not find it a good likeness.[20] The painting seems to owe something to
Velásquez's portrait of Pablillos de Valladolid which Manet had seen
in Madrid, but David Solkin has suggested that by painting him in the
role of Hamlet, Manet also intended a homage to Delacroix on whose
lithographs of Hamlet Rouvière had modelled himself. Solkin thinks
that 'in stylistic terms, the *'hommage'* element can perhaps be seen in
the very blackness of *L'Acteur tragique*, which in contemporary eyes
may have recalled Delacroix's celebrated *Hamlet* lithographs as well as
Velásquez'.[21] Solkin contrasts Manet's Rouvière with Geoffroy's etching, which appeared with Baudelaire's essay on the actor in *L'Artiste*
in December 1859, and in which he appears as a 'self-assured man of
anger and of action', while in Manet's painting 'he is no longer the
determined avenger. Instead we see a character assailed by doubts, left
helpless and defeated by life and by his own mind.' Whereas Geoffroy
sees the actor playing his role, Manet sees Rouvière and Hamlet
'essentially as one', and sensing the presence of death. In the posture
of the tragic figure, Solkin sees an allusion to the tragedy of an 'unsuccessful career and an early death'. Manet's figure certainly appears
downcast and full of self-questioning; but one wonders what Solkin's
biographical interpretation brings to the painting, especially as it
seems at variance with Manet's intention of universalizing the subject
and making it more a type than a particular person. Though very
different from the Delacroix lithographs, it does have, in addition
to the blackness, a feature in common with *Hamlet et le cadavre de
Polonius*, since in both pictures Hamlet's sword lies on the ground at
his feet. In the Delacroix, having used his sword to good effect, the
prince holds back the curtain with a calm and ironic indifference,
revealing the dead Polonius lying with his insignia of office almost
mingling with his old man's beard. The caption reads: 'Vraiment ce

[19] *Manet 1832–83*, catalogue of the exhibition at the Metropolitan Museum of New York,
(New York: Harry N. Abrams, 1983), 232.

[20] See *Lettres à Baudelaire*, 239.

[21] David Solkin, 'Philibert Rouvière: E. Manet's *L'Acteur tragique*', *Burlington Magazine*,
cxvii (Nov. 1975), 709.

conseiller est maintenant bien silencieux, bien discret, bien grave, lui qui dans sa vie était le drôle le plus bavard du monde.'[22] In contrast, the Manet painting shows no identifiable scene, though the sword lying uselessly on the floor, Hamlet's downcast posture, and his curiously shaped and ominous shadow might be thought to allude to the 'to be or not to be' speech where conscience is said to make cowards of us all, where the native hue of resolution is 'sicklied o'er with the pale cast of thought', and great enterprises 'lose the name of action'.

At all events Manet's tragic actor is very different from the Rouvière described by Gautier and Champfleury,[23] and especially from the figure evoked by Baudelaire in his essay on the actor. The stasis of the painting is at variance with what Baudelaire, in an expression that recalls Delacroix and his 'draperies voltigeantes'(p. 434), says of the costumes which Rouvière chose for himself with the care of a painter: 'ses costumes voltigent et entourent harmonieusement sa personnalité' (p. 64). Rouvière, we are told, will leave the classics behind and, intoxicated with the heady atmosphere of the Romantics, will seek out, with typical Baudelairean duality, 'plus d'animalité et plus de spiritualité' (p. 62). Finally, and above all, he has 'cette grâce suprême, décisive,—l'énergie, l'intensité dans le geste, dans la parole et dans le regard' (p. 60). Manet, however, shows a Hamlet, defeated and perplexed, who has lost his 'heroic' intensity. Here, as in the portrait of his parents, it can be said that 'Manet ne peint que des solitudes.'[24] Furthermore, he has succeeded in raising his tragic actor to the status of a universal figure whose doubt and despair seem to extend beyond the particular circumstances of the interpretation of a role to pose the anguished and eternal philosophical question 'where now?' One step further and the philosophical agnosticism would call in question the validity of art itself, and one would pass from doubt to derision, as when moving from Daumier's magnificent drawing of Don Quixote as representative of the idealistic strand in Western art to Picasso's portrayal of the Don wilting under the midday sun, his lance

---

[22] Delteil, *Le Peintre-graveur illustré*, iii, plate 113.

[23] Of Rouvière Gautier writes in *Histoire de l'art dramatique en France depuis vingt-cinq ans* (Paris: Hetzel, 1859), v. 205: 'il a de l'étrangeté, de l'imprévu, quelque chose d'âpre et d'incisif. Peut-être se montre-t-il trop nerveux, trop désordonné, trop fou, et joue-t-il d'une manière trop constamment saccadée; plus de mollesse et de rêverie, aux endroits méditatifs, donnerait de la valeur aux moments d'impétuosité.' Champfleury writes of him as having 'puisé toute sa force dans son tempérament, dans son individualité, et dans une fréquentation assidue de la plus grande œuvre de Shakespeare' (*Contes d'automne* (Paris: Lecou, 1854), 221).

[24] Raymond Cogniat, *Manet* (Paris: Hazan, 1982), 21.

pointing downwards, his nag drooping motionless, with nowhere to go.

There is no reason to think Baudelaire would have disapproved of Manet's painting; he may even have appreciated it because of its homage to Delacroix's lithographs and because it showed a less energetic Hamlet, closer to the one Delacroix had depicted in *Hamlet et Horatio au cimetière* (1835) and in which, in Roger de Beauvoir's words, 'la tête du jeune prince est belle de réflexion et d'isolement'.[25] Baudelaire himself had described this Hamlet as 'tout délicat et pâlot, aux mains blanches et féminines, une nature exquise, mais molle, légèrement indécise, avec un œil presque atone', and there can be no doubt that he preferred Delacroix's interpretation to Rouvière's: 'Ce n'est pas là le *Hamlet* tel que nous l'a fait voir Rouvière, tout récemment [1847 in fact] encore et avec tant d'éclat, âcre, malheureux et violent, poussant l'inquiétude jusqu'à la turbulence. C'est bien la bizarrerie romantique du grand tragédien' (p. 593), and in the obituary notice in *La Petite Revue* of October 1865 there are further signs of a waning of Baudelaire's admiration for the actor whose Hamlet he describes as 'furibond, nerveux et pétulant' (p. 241). As a portrait *L'Acteur tragique* can hardly be said to be faithful to Rouvière and his Hamlet, nor was it intended to be. As a painting, however, and as an interpretation of Shakespeare, it is unlikely to have displeased a poet who, 'ombre d'Hamlet',[26] had for many reasons recognized himself in a figure that had appealed to the imagination of a whole romantic generation.

Manet produced two religious paintings: *Le Christ aux anges* and *Jésus insulté par les soldats*, both in 1864. Baudelaire recommended the first to Chennevières for the Salon, but oddly entitles it *Christ ressuscitant, assisté par les anges*,[27] oddly because most commentators had remarked on the cadaverous aspect of the figure, who in addition seemed to some to be dirty and unwashed. Zola, always keen to take an unBaudelairean view, was quite categorical that the painting did not suggest resurrection:

je retrouve là Edouard Manet tout entier, avec les partis pris de son œil et les audaces de sa main. On a dit que ce Christ n'était pas un Christ, et j'avoue que cela peut être; pour moi, c'est un cadavre peint en pleine lumière, avec franchise et vigueur; et même j'aime les anges du fond,

[25] Quoted in Johnson, *Paintings*, iii. 72.
[26] See 'La Béatrice', *Oc.* i. 116.   [27] *Corr.* ii. 351.

ces enfants aux grandes ailes bleues qui ont une étrangeté si douce et si élegante.[28]

And, indeed, it could be said that the gratuitous richness of the angels' brilliant blue wings and the elegant detachment of their expression seem rather to mock the cadaverous lividity of the central figure than to evoke a sense of pity or transcendence over death. Baudelaire's title suggests he did not see the picture in that way, though Thoré in *L'Indépendance belge* thought that Manet was pastiching El Greco furiously, 'sans doute en manière de sarcasme contre les amoureux transis de la peinture discrète et proprette'.[29] Baudelaire must surely have sensed the lack of spiritual uplift in a work he had examined closely, pointing out that the wound in Christ's side should be on the right, according to the Bible, and not on the left, where Manet had put it.[30] Manet did not heed the criticism and made no alteration to the painting nor to the watercolour and etching which came after, a conscious anomaly which Moffett convincingly suggests was 'intended to remind us that the paintings are cogently composed works of art, not merely illustrations of a given subject painted according to conventions and formulas taught by professors at the Ecole des Beaux-Arts'.[31] If this is the case, then it is indeed odd that Baudelaire did not respond to this intended *bizarrerie* and its significance. Once again, such artistic agnosticism and lack of spiritual intensity[32] might well have been incompatible with his own views. As for the other canvas of the same year, *Jésus insulté par les soldats*, it is unlikely that he ever saw it, though Manet had written complaining of the unfavourable reception of this last of his religious paintings;[33] but it is every bit as difficult to imagine Baudelaire being enthusiastic about this all-too-human Christ surrounded by three modern ruffians in clothes of disparate times and origins.

Of the three most modern of Manet's early paintings, *La Chanteuse des rues* (1862), *Le Philosophe* (1865), and *Le Buveur d'absinthe* (1858–9), Baudelaire mentions only the latter, which again is puzzling, as they all represent the kind of contemporary figure associated with his

[28] Zola, *Ecrits*, 159.
[29] E. Moreau-Nélaton, *Manet raconté par lui-même* (Paris: Laurens, 1926), i. 58.
[30] *Corr.* ii. 352: 'A propos, il paraît que décidément le coup de lance a été porté à droite. Il faudra donc que vous alliez changer la blessure de place, avant l'ouverture. Vérifiez donc la chose dans les quatre évangélistes. Et prenez garde de prêter à rire aux malveillants.'
[31] *Manet 1832—1883*, 203.
[32] Contrast Delacroix's *Pietà*.   [33] *Lettres à Baudelaire*, 232.

'Tableaux parisiens'. It is possible that he found *Le Philosophe* too derivative of Velásquez to be a genuine and naïve expression of Manet's temperament; it is also possible that he found the street singer too contrived and artificial to capture the fleeting moment which is said to have inspired it, when Manet caught sight of a singer emerging from a café in the rue Guyot and asked her to model for him.[34] Here again one can only speculate. There is, however, clear evidence that he was sceptical about *Le Buveur*, which is particularly surprising, since it was based on a contemporary rag-picker by the name of Collardet, and since a case can be made for a link with 'Le Vin de l'assassin' and the description of the drunken rag-picker in *Du vin et du hachisch*.[35] It does indeed seem odd that Baudelaire's attitude towards this pathetic figure, which Delacroix alone among the jury of 1859 had admired, and which seems to leap from the canvas with all the suddenness of an *instantané*, should have been so unenthusiastic and negative. According to Proust, on seeing the painting Baudelaire is reported to have encouraged Manet to be himself, 'la conclusion, c'est qu'il faut être soi-même', and when Manet protested that in *Le Buveur* he had been himself, he is said to have dismissed the matter with an unconvinced and repeated 'Euh!'[36] Perruchot thinks that Baudelaire realized that it could have served as an illustration to a poem from *Les Fleurs du Mal*; but had felt that, in spite of the subject's 'beaux yeux noirs, épais et sourds', Manet had still not freed himself from Couture: 'de surcroît, artificielle, forcée, la pose du personnage est presque une attitude de mélodrame'.[37] This is all the stranger as the painting bears witness

---

[34] See Antonin Proust, *Edouard Manet Souvenirs*, 28 for this incident. The strange shape of the street singer's eyebrows, which Mantz likened to two dark commas, has led some commentators to see a connection between the painting and 'Les Promesses d'un visage' whose 'pâle beauté' has 'sourcils surbaissés' (see *Oc.* i. 1143 and George Heard Hamilton, *Manet and his Critics* (New Haven and London: Yale University Press, 1986), 40). Baudelaire's outspoken *galanterie* is, however, of quite a different inspiration, and the parallel seems more than a little strained.

[35] See *Oc.* i. 381: 'Voici un homme chargé de ramasser les débris d'une journée de la capitale. Tout ce que la grande ville a rejeté, tout ce qu'elle a perdu, tout ce qu'elle a dédaigné, tout ce qu'elle a brisé, il le catalogue, il le collectionne. Il compulse les archives de la débauche, le capharnaüm des rebuts. [. . .] Le voici qui, à la clarté sombre des réverbères tourmentés par le vent de la nuit, remonte une des longues rues tortueuses et peuplées de petits ménages de la montagne Sainte-Geneviève. Il est revêtu de son *châle d'osier avec son numéro sept*. Il arrive hochant la tête et butant sur les pavés, comme les jeunes poètes qui passent toutes leurs journéés à errer et à chercher des rimes.'

[36] Antonin Proust, *Edouard Manet Souvenirs* 25.

[37] H. Perruchot, *Manet* (Paris: Hachette, 1959), 87. Moreau–Nélaton also believes that the painting 'descend en ligne directe de Couture' (*Manet raconté par lui-même*), 27.

to Manet's rejection of Couture and his historical approach, and as Couture himself had dismissed it as the work of a madman, and Manet as the real absinthe drinker.[38] More convincingly, Pierre Daix praises the painting, of which Manet was justly proud, for its novel and challenging use of perspective, proclaiming that it proves beyond doubt the mastery of his art:

Celle-ci [the figure of the drinker] est cernée, littéralement arrachée au fond, comme à son ombre. On découvre alors qu'il n'existe aucun cadre perspectif. Le rebord où le buveur est assis et où est posé son verre n'est enserré dans aucune ligne de fuite, c'est notre regard qui balaie un espace d'où le personnage sort à notre rencontre, le plan du tableau se confondant avec le plan de la paroi à laquelle il est accroché.[39]

If Daix is right rather than Perruchot, then it would appear again that, limiting his attention to its literary aspects, Baudelaire had failed to see what technically was new and stimulating in the work.

Although he himself figured in *La Musique aux Tuileries* (Pl. 14) along with Manet, Gautier, Astruc, and others, Baudelaire remains strangely silent about it. Some have suggested that he did not think highly of the painting, and certainly there must have been much about it which he would have disliked or by which he would have been left cold, in particular the lack of drama or social or psychological depth in this large canvas, in which objects, chairs, and so on are put in the foreground and take on as much importance as the figures, who, in spite of their prestige as artists or *mondains*, appear as a décor on an equal footing with the objects and the trees. Also, the men, clad in black, appear as columns among the equally black tree trunks. Here indeed is 'la vie moderne' (black coats, hats and patent-leather boots), but only as spectacle, with none of that heroism which he had hoped might radiate from *La Comédie humaine* to invigorate and rejuvenate the world of painting. What we find is leisure, indolence, elegance, ennui, presented like a theatre décor and with a strong sense of stasis, accentuated by the lack of gradation in the colour of the costumes and dresses. Technically, of course, the painting is very interesting, with the verticals of the top hats and trees contrasting with the horizontals of the chairs, women and children in the foreground, and, typically, there are some bizarre features, in particular the mask-like faces of the

[38] Antonin Proust, *Edouard Manet Souvenirs*, 23: 'Mon ami, il n'y a ici qu'un buveur d'absinthe, c'est le peintre qui a produit cette insanité.'
[39] Pierre Daix, *La Vie de peintre d'Edouard Manet* (Paris: Fayard, 1983), 56.

women, inspired possibly by Japanese art, and above all the paradoxical absence of the orchestra which gives the painting its name. But at all events here is modern life, but with neither depth nor heroism, a piece of Paris life, but without the intensity or 'supernaturalism' that Baudelaire required of such scenes.

This is eminently the art of Manet the *flâneur*, and it is known that he frequented the Tuileries often in Baudelaire's company, but there is no trace of that 'morale désagréable' which Baudelaire considered an essential ingredient in his prose poems. In 'Les Veuves' from *Le Spleen de Paris*, for example, which, like Manet's painting, evokes a crowd in a public garden and a concert 'dont la musique des régiments gratifie le peuple parisien', the poet, who is also a philosopher, avoids the 'turbulence dans le vide' that characterizes the joy of the rich and idle, and feels himself irresistibly drawn towards what is 'faible, ruiné, contristé, orphelin', towards 'les éclopés de la vie'. In the scenes he picks out, he is able to unravel a narrative, the countless legends of love deceived, unrecognized devotion, unrewarded efforts, hunger and cold humbly, silently, endured. Eventually his attention focuses upon the 'singulière vision' of a widow who stands out from the crowd, like an almost allegorical figure of solitude and despair. Such pathos is nowhere to be found in Manet, and one would be hard put to find in his paintings any of these Balzacian souls, 'armes chargées de volonté jusqu'à la gueule' (p. 120), whose obsessions and monomanias are equivalent to a search for some kind of absolute experience. Gone are the contrasting colours, the 'draperies voltigeantes', the blurred outlines and turbulent backgrounds of Delacroix, which the drama of the subject demanded. In the *Salon de 1846* Baudelaire had written that 'la vie parisienne est féconde en sujets poétiques et merveilleux. Le merveilleux nous enveloppe et nous abreuve comme l'atmosphère; mais nous ne le voyons pas' (p. 496). One suspects he thought that Manet did not either, and though he knew *La Musique* he said nothing in its defence when it was severely criticized. This was no doubt because the narrative, 'human' and moral possibilities of the scene have been sacrificed in favour of the unusual perspective and the bizarre, self-conscious paradox of the spectators providing the spectacle, as in later works which Baudelaire could not have known, such as *Le Balcon* of 1868 and *Bal masqué à l'opéra* of 1873. Here again there is a possible blindness on Baudelaire's part, whose notion of modernity appears limited to theme and moral message, and does not, at least in his assessment of contemporary painters, extend to the kind of self-referential art that bends back upon itself and whose message lies in its own techniques and means. *La Musique* is certainly a modern piece, but not in a Baudelairean sense, and Tabarant's explanation of the poet's indifference is surely right: 'elle venait trop tôt; elle dépassait son temps et n'était point comprise'.[40]

La Musique aux Tuileries has much in common with Guys's *Les Champs-Elysées*, which may indeed have inspired it. It too gives a sense of stillness and of a spectacle, with the seated women and the standing men. But the differences are crucial, and help explain why Baudelaire liked the one and remained silent about the other.[41] In Manet the figures merge into a more or less uniform crowd, dehumanized and turned into objects; whereas in Guys there is much more variety in the scene, with horses and carriages at different angles, and though some of the men appear excessively tall, there is no hint of an ironical comparison with the trees, which in any case are much less numerous and prominent. Furthermore, the rapidity of the drawing endows the stillness with a contained vitality and movement, while the 'rightness' of the attitudes and gestures suggests what is typical beyond the diverse individual presences, conveying ultimately the assurance and elegance of a privileged social class. One could find no better comment on this work than a passage from *Le Peintre de la vie moderne*: 'Les attitudes du riche lui sont familières; il sait, d'un trait de plume léger, avec une certitude qui n'est jamais en défaut, représenter la certitude de regard, de geste et de pose qui, chez les êtres privilégiés, est le résultat de la monotonie dans le bonheur' (p. 722).[42]

It is difficult to know what Baudelaire would have thought of *Le Balcon* (1868–9) (Pl. 15), assuredly one of Manet's greatest and most poetic, magical, and modern creations. It would be comforting to believe he would have appreciated the look and posture of the three figures, and especially to the wistful expression in the eyes of Berthe Morisot. But the Baudelaire of 1863 might have been perplexed by the lack of communication between the figures, by the paradox of the

---

[40] A. Tabarant, *Manet et ses œuvres* (Paris: Gallimard, 1947), 38.

[41] Lois Boe Hyslop is sensitive to the similarities between Manet's painting and Guys's drawing, but overlooks the differences ('Baudelaire and Manet: A Reappraisal' in *Baudelaire as a Love Poet and Other Essays* (University Park and London: Pennsylvania State University Press, 1969), 102.

[42] See Castex, *Baudelaire*, 72, who adds this passage to the reproduction of *Les Champs-Elysées*.

spectators looking out at us[43] and not at the scene from the balcony
while we are looking in at them, by the curious perspective which,
helped by the use of an aggressively bright green for the railing and
shutter, seems to abolish the depth between them, and by the novel
way of presenting a tripartite portrait, of Berthe, Fanny Claus, and
Antoine Guillemet. The picture shares with *La Musique aux Tuileries*
a self-consciousness in the depiction of elegant society. It has a similar
snapshot quality, but as Françoise Cachin suggests, a snapshot in
which the people look away at the wrong moment: 'something is
going to happen, or has just happened'.[44] What is original about
the painting is brought out when it is set against Goya's *Majas on a
Balcony*, which Manet certainly had in mind. But in order to
understand how it might have appeared to Baudelaire, it would perhaps be instructive to set it against his own treatment of the balcony
in 'Le Balcon' or 'Recueillement'. His balcony is an archetype
of the lofty site and can be related to a *thématique* of mountain
tops, promontories, and high towers. Specifically, in 'Le Balcon' it is
linked to the peace of sunset, communication between lovers, the
spiritualization of matter, an opening-up of physical and emotive
space, and a meditation on memory and resurrection. The final verse
reads:

> Ces serments, ces parfums, ces baisers infinis,
> Renaîtront-ils d'un gouffre interdit à nos sondes,
> Comme montent au ciel les soleils rajeunis
> Après s'être lavés au fond des mers profondes?
> — O serments! ô parfums! ô baisers infinis!

Similarly, in 'Recueillement', which antedates *La Musique aux
Tuileries* by less than a year, there is an equally poignant evocation of
the depths of time, space, and memory in the magnificent image of the
dead years leaning over 'les balcons du ciel, en robes surannées', and of
an allegorized 'Regret souriant' rising from the depth of the waters
which serve as a mirror. Baudelaire's balcony is then part of a
thematics of depth; Manet's, on the contrary, is a kind of non- or anti-
balcony, whose meaning is displaced into the enigmatic uncertainties
of the absent look of its three figures.

---

[43] Much has been written about the way that Manet's figures challenge the viewer by
their look, as in *Le Balcon*, *Le Déjeuner sur l'herbe*, and *Olympia*. See, for example, James
H. Rubin, *Manet's Silence and the Poetics of Bouquets* (London: Reaktion Books, 1994), 46–
57.
[44] *Manet 1832–1883*, 306.

It is doubtful whether Baudelaire would have praised Manet's imagination in these paintings, as he had in the *Guitariste*. Nor is he likely to have seen much of an appeal to memory. Indeed, it has been suggested by Lois Hyslop that, unlike Delacroix, Daumier and Guys, he did not draw from memory,[45] feeling impotent when deprived of his model and having recourse to photographs to compensate for the absence. If this is so, then the possibility of idealization is lost from the outset, and since such a painting does not proceed from memory, it cannot perforce speak to the memory of the spectator. It fails to meet yet again a requirement of all art according to Baudelaire, indeed the fundamental plank on which his literary and artistic aesthetic is based. In Manet the appeal to memory is strangely absent, or silenced. If it is there at all, it does not open on to the depth of the past, or project itself into the future with 'l'expansion des choses infinies', as in 'La Chevelure', nor does it give on to some kind of legendary *histoire*, as in 'Les Veuves' or in Guys. If, as they surely do, his pictures have the power to charm, it is because through the stasis and the monument-ality of the figures, together with the unfamiliar perspectives and viewpoints, we are constantly brought back to a fascinating and enig-matic present, to the presence of the figures themselves, as by a con-stantly stimulated but blocked affective memory which never yields its secret, but leaves us with the desire for meaning beyond these pres-ences, of which ultimately one can say only that they are there. It was Gaëtan Picon who saw more clearly perhaps than anyone that in modern painting we have 'a present simply present', 'without a hidden text', and that the image is 'no longer the illustration of a text'.[46] Although this is indeed increasingly so from the 1860s onwards, many of Manet's paintings seem none the less to contain fleeting intimations of meaning, which are perhaps nothing more than the illusory promise of what Flaubert called the 'virtualités secrètes'[47] of a scene. Such is perhaps the very modern poetry and the suggestive magic of Manet's work which, without pathos, without Romanticism, offers to memory and to the desire for meaning something not far removed from that hope without hope which Malraux saw at the heart of mankind, 'espoir de rien, attente'.[48]

[45] Lois Boe Hyslop, *Baudelaire: Man of his Time* (New Haven and London: Yale Univer-sity Press, 1980), 60.

[46] Gaëtan Picon, *The Birth of Modern Painting* (London: Tiger Books International, 1991), 45, 48.

[47] *L'Education sentimentale* (Paris: Conard, 1923), 470.

[48] André Malraux, *Œuvres complètes* (Paris: Gallimard, 1989), i. 742.

It is clear that, in spite of their frienship and the poet's influence on the early work of the painter, many differences separate the two men. It may be that when the downcast and embittered Manet complained of the hostile reception of *Olympia*, Baudelaire, in his reply from Brussels, was trying to strengthen his pride by mentioning the fortitude of Chateaubriand and Wagner in the face of similar adversity. The devastating statement, underlined in the letter, 'vous n'êtes que le premier dans la décrépitude de votre art',[49] has none the less the ring of a definitive and negative judgement, even when due allowance is made for 'premier', which is admittedly less offensive than 'dernier' would have been. To this must be added the almost equally damning remarks in a letter to Madame Paul Meurice about Manet's lack of temperament: 'Jamais il ne comblera absolument les lacunes de son tempérament',[50] temperament being the essential quality celebrated in the *Salon de 1846* that makes for the fatality of artistic genius. It is significant that Champfleury had similar misgivings, noticing that in the Salon the only truly new work was Manet's, adding, however, a sceptical note, 'mais il y a beaucoup de mais'.[51]

Of course Baudelaire's strictures on the decadence of modern art are a continuing theme in his criticism from 1846 onwards, and the point about decrepitude serves to set Manet in the context of a more or less universal decline. Without Delacroix the chain of history is broken, the great tradition has been lost and not replaced, small mindedness and puerility have replaced ardour and nobility in art, as in literature. Erudition, imagination, knowledge of the past, and 'l'amour du grand' are no longer to be found among contemporary painters whose intellectual level has singularly fallen (p. 745). He also subscribes to the traditional hierarchy of genres and sees in the increasing incidence and popularity of landscape painting a clear sign of debasement. The great painter will find an outlet for his genius in religious painting, leaving the minor genres for those who lack imagination, ambition, and temperament: 'l'homme d'imagination a dû généralement se produire dans la peinture religieuse et dans la fantaisie, tandis que la peinture dite de genre et le paysage devaient offrir en apparence de vastes ressources aux esprits paresseux et difficilement excitables' (p. 627). The decline of the *écoles* has also played a major part in this artistic decrepitude, and in place of the tradition, continuity, and cohesion they assured, we are left with the

---

[49] *Corr.* ii. 497.   [50] Ibid. 501.   [51] *Lettres à Baudelaire*, 86.

dangerous and unfruitful freedom and indiscipline of 'ouvriers émancipés'.

According to Rebeyrol, it was his fixation with Delacroix that made Baudelaire blind to the greatness of Daumier's paintings, to Courbet, and to Manet: 'le monde s'arrêtait pour lui au romantisme, ultime et suprême expression de l'art et de toute vie nouvelle ou moderne. Après, ne pouvaient plus commencer que les ténèbres et la mort.'[52] From 1846 onwards Baudelaire had confused modernism with Romanticism, and his artistic instinct, which of itself was sure and reliable, was obscured by the excessive importance he attached to moral ideas in art. In short, his ideas on art were distorted by his ideas on literature. One could add the absence of modelling in the *Déjeuner sur l'herbe*, revealing the somewhat livid body of the nude, and generally the lack of shading, the violent juxtaposition of colours, the lack of depth and perspective to draw the spectator into the work as with Rembrandt, the neutral backgrounds, and the importance of outline at the expense of the vibration of colour in many of the paintings. One thinks in this latter connection of *Le Fifre*, which reminded some contemporary critics of an *image d'Epinal* or of a cut-out; nothing could be further from that turbulence of a Delacroix canvas which, like nature itself, abhors a vacuum (p. 439). A further example would be the notorious *Olympia* (Pl. 16), about which Baudelaire was also silent, no doubt because he had never seen it, as indicated in a letter from Brussels in which he asks if there really is a cat in the picture.[53] Some have thought it a very Baudelairean work because of an alleged parallel with 'Les Bijoux', one of the six 'pièces condamnées' from the first edition of *Les Fleurs du Mal*. There are indeed certain points in common: the fact that the woman is naked but has kept on her jewels, her 'air vainqueur', and her eyes fixed upon the spectator, and it may be that Manet had the poem in mind at the time of painting. But 'Les Bijoux' is an extremely sensual poem, doing credit to the imagination and human frailty of its judges of 1857 who had it excised from the collection for being inimical to public morality. The woman tries various poses to arouse the poet and the description of her physical charms is explicit and voluptuous:

> Et son bras et sa jambe, et sa cuisse et ses reins,
> Polis comme de l'huile, onduleux comme un cygne,

---

[52] Philippe Rebeyrol, 'Baudelaire et Manet', *Les Temps modernes*, 48 (1949), 714.
[53] *Corr.* ii. 497.

Passaient devant mes yeux clairvoyants et sereins;
Et son ventre et ses seins, ces grappes de ma vigne,
S'avançaient, plus câlins que les Anges du mal.

In Manet's painting, on the other hand, the most sensual object is the satin of the bed on which Olympia is so starkly and incongruously placed. The squatness of the body and the limbs, the smallness of the head, the caricatural cat which provoked so much glee at the the time, and the hyperbolic bouquet which seems disproportionate to its narrative function, give to the painting a bizarre, ironic, possibly even comic quality, enhanced by its overt attempt at intertextual undermining. The position of Olympia's hand is the same as that of Titian's Venus of Urbino, but the gesture is not languid and graceful but awkward and full-square; and the little dog, symbol of fidelity, is replaced by the outrageous cat (a direct reference to Chardin's La Raie) with its arched back and rigid tail, indicating both hostility and unrestrained sexuality. One might think that such a painting would meet with Baudelaire's approval because of what separates it from Titian and because it has caught the attitude and look of a modern courtesan,[54] but it has also a negative intention or result, which is to show the impossible, fictive nature of idealizations of the female body and their incompatibility with a modern sensibility, so that a whole history of Venuses and Odalisques from Titian to Ingres seems to be called in question by Manet's ironic treatment of the subject. Moreover, it does not seem at all plausible, as some critics have sought to argue, that Olympia be recuperated into a context of meaning by some social message denouncing the ugliness and venality of illicit love. It is fundamentally a painting about painting, as it was possibly intended to be.

Similarly, Le Déjeuner sur l'herbe, which fulfils Manet's ambition to paint an open-air nude, treats ironically or sceptically the theme of the fête champêtre from Titian to Watteau and Fragonard. Le Déjeuner is every bit as difficult to recuperate as Olympia, though some have

---

[54] See his comment in Le Peintre de la vie moderne: 'Si un peintre patient et minutieux, mais d'une imagination médiocre, ayant à peindre une courtisane du temps présent, s'inspire (c'est le mot consacré) d'une courtisane de Titien ou de Raphaël, il est infiniment probable qu'il fera une œuvre fausse, ambiguë et obscure. L'étude d'un chef-d'œuvre de ce temps et de ce genre ne lui enseignera ni l'attitude, ni le regard, ni la grimace, ni l'aspect vital d'une de ces créatures que le dictionnaire de la mode a successivement classées sous les titres grossiers ou badins d'impures, de filles entretenues, de lorettes et de biches' (696). See also his comment on le nu in modern art (496).

sought to see it as a realist allegory of paradise lost.[55] Of course, it is always possible to read such an ironical work as regretting the thing it derides or sends up; but one is aware also in this painting of an absence of nostalgia or regret. There is no sense of grief or exile, that we are cut off from a world we have lost. Even the suggestion of an invitation to reverie in the background figure is blocked by the impression the painting gives of a theatre décor rather than a natural scene. There is little drama, tension, or stridency in this work, and if there is humour, it is wry, subdued, and deadpan. It is the discreet and playful irony of an artist who, far from rejuvenating a myth, has sought to impart a caricatural twist by literalizing it.

These points of fundamental difference might well seem convincing, but it is perhaps becoming clear that matters are not quite so simple, precisely because one could very easily take most, if not all of these points, turn them on their heads and make of them reasons why Baudelaire should have found in Manet a fellow spirit. Most important, Baudelaire himself is an adept practitioner of intertextual debunking, of what might be called a negative intertextuality whose function is to upset our expectations as readers by making of the text an ironic or subversive retort to another text, genre, or topos. A typical example would be 'Duellum' whose title and first lines indicate some armed conflict; but by a surprising about-turn the poem suddenly changes direction and theme in order to treat the ambiguities of love and hatred. There is a kind of double upset because of the discrepancy between the title and the content of the poem, and between the praise of love which one might have expected and the modern cynicism of the poet. A similar phenomenon is at work in poem XXIV of *Les Fleurs du Mal*:

> Je t'adore à l'égal de la voûte nocturne,
> O vase de tristesse, ô grande taciturne.

The reader thinks himself in the familiar terrain of love poetry, expecting the praise of the mysterious charms of the poet's mistress; but is soon disoriented by the description of the poet who '[s]'avance à l'attaque, et [je] grimpe aux assauts, / Comme après un cadavre un chœur de vermisseaux'. Similarly, 'Je te donne ces vers . . .' is situated immediately in the context of the gift of the poem practised by the

---

[55] Of the nudity of the figures Werner Hofmann writes: 'Sie verkörpert nicht mehr die Rückerinnerung des verlorenen Paradieses, nicht Ursprünglichkeit, sondern deren Verlust' (*Nana: Mythos und Wirklichkeit* (Cologne: Verlag M. DuMont Schauberg, 1973), 40).

Renaissance poets. The poet repays his Muse for inspiring him by the gift of immortality. 'Ronsard me célébrait du temps que j'étais belle' is no doubt the best-known example. But in the tercets of his sonnet, Baudelaire upsets our expectation and procedes not to bless his muse, but to curse her. And indeed nothing could be further from the Renaissance muses or even from those of Romanticism—think of 'Poète, prend ton luth, c'est moi ton Immortelle' of Musset's 'Nuit de mai'—than Baudelaire's 'Muse vénale' or 'Muse malade' whose hollow eyes, blue feet, shivering shoulders, madness, and anguish replace the health and innocence of the white muses of tradition. And to understand what was shocking about Baudelaire's interiors which he describes in the 'Spleen' poems and in 'Tableaux parisiens', one has only to think of Hugo's 'Regard jeté dans une mansarde' in *Les Rayons et les ombres*.[56] Both poets appear as voyeurs; but, while Hugo finds the chaste eye and limpid gaze of a poor but impeccably innocent young girl, Baudelaire uncovers what is sordid, impure, and unhealthy, the degeneration, anguish, and ugliness in the recesses of the modern capital.

Similarly, by putting 'Le Crépuscule du matin' and 'Le Crépuscule du soir' in a traditional context, one can see immediately how they must have appeared astonishing or shocking to the contemporary reader. Traditionally, the *aubade* celebrated the return to life and light after sleep and darkness, emphasizing freshness, health, and confidence in life. It might take the form of a call to action, inviting the poet's mistress to cast off sloth and respond to her lover's pleas. Similarly, the poem about sunset would celebrate the peace at the end of the day, and a sense of decline analogous to autumn in the cycle of seasons. It is an invitation to introspection and a quasi-religious meditation, while in the melancholy of the setting sun there is the promise of a resurrection and a return guaranteed by a cyclical conception of time. But in Baudelaire the innocent sloth of the mistress becomes 'les rêves malfaisants' of adolescents and the leaden stupor of the whores with open mouths; one finds also 'les pauvresses, traînant leurs seins maigres et froids', blowing into their frozen fingers, and, enveloping everything, the thick fog of Paris. And 'Le Crépuscule du soir', 'ami du criminel', offers an equally disquieting and baleful spectacle with 'les démons malsains dans l'atmosphère', prostitution, which 's'allume dans la rue', and crooks in cafés and gaming-houses.

[56] See also 'Dans l'alcôve sombre . . .', in *Les Feuilles d'automne*.

The effect of this ironic or critical intertextuality is not merely to highlight the originality of the poet's vision but to relativize it at the same time. By accentuating its literary character and appealing to the cultural memory of the reader, it causes the latter to doubt in some measure the seriousness of the enterprise and its ability to come to grips with a reality other than literary. So, by a supreme irony, this work which claimed above all to be a spiritual adventure, bearing witness to the exalted mission of art——'dans ce livre *atroce*, j'ai mis tout mon *cœur*, toute ma *tendresse*, toute ma *religion* (travestie), toute ma *haine*'[57]——appears among the first, if not to proclaim, then to suggest its own self-referentiality. In *Le Spleen de Paris* Baudelaire's pessimism and literary agnosticism deepen and the ambiguities become less delicate and nuanced as the stridency of the tone intensifies. Alongside the parody of nature Romanticism, of the lofty site from which the soul can take its flight in 'Le Gâteau', for example, we find in 'Les Projets' the poet's irony extending over a whole range of literary commonplaces from the aristocratic to the exotic and to the rustic dream, including even the conclusion of the poem, which seems to extol the wisdom of remaining within the four walls of a room and of undertaking the kind of journey favoured by Xavier de Maistre in his *Voyage autour de ma chambre*. But at the end nothing is celebrated and no values are made to emerge except that of stating the problematical nature of values. So the poem, by apparently concluding in favour of the virtual over the real, impacts upon itself and denies itself in a final pirouette, whereas a more conventional ending would hold or prolong a sense of resolution against the destructive action of time.[58]

Appropriately, the prose poem 'La Corde', dedicated originally to Manet, is perhaps the most striking and the most poignant instance of a work consumed and destroyed by its own irony. It is based on a true story concerning the suicide in the artist's studio of a boy, Alexandre, whom Manet had employed to clean his brushes and keep the place tidy. Most commentators have been content to interpret the piece as an example of the 'morale désagréable' the poet wished to draw from the haphazard encounters and experiences of his *flâneries* in the capital. Thus for Robert Kopp the poem demonstrates 'la perversité foncière—naturelle, selon Baudelaire—dont est capable

---

[57] *Corr.* ii. 610.

[58] See my *Baudelaire and 'Le Spleen de Paris'*, 75–6, 70–1 for commentaries on these prose poems.

une femme',[59] while F. W. J. Hemmings thinks its purpose is to show 'how unwise we are to make any assumptions whatsoever about human nature, or perhaps to illustrate how events continually upset our preconceived view of reality'.[60] On a superficial level, the poem can indeed be read as a *conte cruel* showing that even such a fundamental and natural instinct as mother love can be corrupted by the desire for financial gain, since it is not in order to have 'une horrible et chère relique' that the mother wishes to keep the rope with which her son hanged himself, but to sell pieces to the superstitious who believe that the hanged man's rope brings good luck.[61] From this perspective, the first paragraphs of the poem can be read as showing the painter as a generous and optimistic spirit with a naïve belief in the natural and instinctive goodness of mankind. But the briefest examination of his character and utterances reveals self-satisfaction, smugness and insensitivity:

Les illusions,—me disait mon ami,—sont aussi innombrables peut-être que les rapports des hommes entre eux, ou des hommes avec les choses. Et quand l'illusion disparaît, c'est-à-dire quand nous voyons l'être ou le fait tel qu'il existe en dehors de nous, nous éprouvons un bizarre sentiment, compliqué moitié de regret pour le fantôme disparu, moitié de surprise agréable devant la nouveauté, devant le fait réel. S'il existe un phénomène évident, trivial, toujours semblable, et d'une nature à laquelle il soit impossible de se tromper, c'est l'amour maternel. Il est aussi difficile de supposer une mère sans amour maternel qu'une lumière sans chaleur [. . .].

The didacticism and the philosophical pretension of these irrefutable axioms based on a somewhat 'abridged'[62] wisdom show clearly that the young painter, like all creators of maxims according to Baudelaire, has been unable to resist the temptation of giving himself the appearance of a wisdom at variance with his youth and inexperience,[63] while the image of heat and light smacks both of the cliché and the pious sentiment of the phrasemonger. All this is no doubt more or less inoffensive, but one becomes increasingly aware of less innocent

---

[59] Baudelaire, *Petits Poèmes en prose*, ed. Robert Kopp (Paris: José Corti, 1969), 305.

[60] F. W. J. Hemmings, *Baudelaire the Damned* (London: Hamish Hamilton, 1982), 191.

[61] A similar superstition can be found in Hardy's tale, *The Withered Arm*, where it is thought that by touching the neck of a hanged man one may be cured of an illness.

[62] Baudelaire describes Hugo thus: 'Il m'apparut comme un homme très doux, très puissant, toujours maître de lui-même, et appuyé sur une sagesse abrégée, faite de quelques axiomes irréfutables' (129–30). See also *Oc.* i. 671, where he prescribes for himself 'Une sagesse abrégée. Toilette, prière, travail.'

[63] See Ch. 3, n. 11.

characteristics, of insensibility and the aesthetic detachment of one who considers the world as a constantly renewed and amusing spectacle. As the story progresses, the painter's mentality appears more and more unpleasant. Proud of his fine district 'où de vastes espaces gazonnés séparent encore les bâtiments', he speaks smugly of his profession as painter which brings him to observe closely the faces and physiognomies which he comes across, 'et vous savez quelle jouissance nous tirons de cette faculté qui rend à nos yeux la vie plus vivante et plus significative que pour les autres hommes'. He goes on to relate how he used to dress up the little boy, whose 'drôlerie' amused him, in all sorts of costumes, making him pose as a bohemian, angel, or Cupid, making him carry 'le violon du vagabond, la Couronne d'Epines et les Clous de la Passion', and using him as an infinitely variable aesthetic object without the remotest awareness of his feelings or his real suffering. Even the horror he feels in front of the boy's dead body is tainted by his patronizing references to his 'petit bonhomme' and the 'espiègle compagnon de ma vie'. The tone of the poem is very subtle, and it is only on second reading or at least at the end of the piece that the reader becomes fully aware of the insensibility of the artist who at first had appeared only as glib. What are we to think of the 'surprise agréable devant la nouveauté, devant le fait réel' when we learn of the terrible fate of the boy and the macabre avarice of his mother? The objectivity and realism of the description and the absence of any expression of regret or responsibility (the suicide is caused by the boy's fear of being sent back to his parents for having stolen some of the painter's liqueurs) complete the charge against the artist, who is condemned by his own account.

The result is that the poem can be read as an ironical comment on the nature of art which can convey through the model the attraction of Eros and the Passion of Christ, but is unconscious of the suffering which literally stands before it. The beauty of Eros and the Passion of Christ are then by implication mere games, amusements, totally devoid of seriousness, for all their power to persuade and move. But the irony does not stop at the painter. We notice also that Baudelaire is at pains to endow him with qualities he himself shares: the painter, like Manet, resembles 'le rôdeur parisien', the disenchanted view of human nature is typically Baudelairean, and the various roles the little boy is allowed to play do not correspond to any known paintings of Manet's, but are carefully chosen to represent, as in the prose poem 'Les Vocations', fundamental aspects of Baudelaire's temperament.

It seems clear that he would not have drawn the painter to himself in this way with the sole aim of denouncing his art. It seems equally clear that what is being called in question is not so much the art of the painter as that of the poet himself, and that in 'La Corde' there is a kind of *mise en abyme* through which the poem gives rise to the same problems and is open to the same objections as the fictional paintings it evokes. After all, the paintings never existed, and Manet is known to have used Alexandre as a model only in the Murillo-like canvas *L'Enfant aux cerises* and the engravings of *Le Garçon au chien*. What does exist is Baudelaire's prose poem, composed and read shortly after the boy's death. The ultimate moral message appears to be that art, whether the painter's or the poet's, is unable to come to grips with reality, which it sidesteps or fails to recognize. Art is a lie, a simulacrum, a comedy, which appeals only to the eye of the spectator or ear of the reader without involving any genuine emotion, so that the problematics of the piece involve not only the artist as creator but also the reader who, if he is sensitive to poetry, enjoys a purely aesthetic thrill thanks to a real suffering. The real torment of the boy has become an aesthetic experience in Baudelaire's poem as much as in the hypothetical paintings, so that it is possible to read 'La Corde' as a moral and aesthetic indictment of itself. It appears, then, that in this deceptively straightforward piece Baudelaire is expressing his despair before what Proust called in a moment of agnosticism the illusory magic of literature,[64] and is asking the anguished question: what is the value of art if, in veiling the terrors of the abyss, it removes from men's eyes the contemplation of real suffering?

Further similarities and parallels between Baudelaire and Manet could no doubt be established, not least the creation of an art that appears fragmentary. The *Gitane à la cigarette* seems cut off by the frame, the portrait of Jeanne Duval seemed unfinished to contemporary viewers, as did *Les Hirondelles*, and in spite of its size *La Musique aux Tuileries* appears as a kind of fragment, as if something needed to be added to complete the significance of the scene. Another example would be the *Torero mort*,[65] which Manet deliberately cut out from the original and larger *Episode d'un combat de taureaux*. Similarly, some of Baudelaire's 'Tableaux parisiens', and in particular his prose poems, seem to be fragments of a larger work. David Scott has contrasted the

---

[64] *A la recherche du temps perdu*, iv. 301.
[65] Baudelaire defends this painting as not being derived from Velásquez (*Corr.* ii. 386).

great poem of 1859, 'Le Voyage', which provides the concluding and synthesizing statement to the spiritual journey which is *Les Fleurs du Mal* (1861 edition), with what he calls 'three altogether more oblique and fragmentary texts', 'Déjà!', 'Le Port', and 'Any where out of the world', and draws our attention to such *contes* or fragments of *conte* as 'La Corde', and to the conversational and digressive style of many of the prose poems.[66] It might be thought strange that the poet, who had developed a similar aesthetic of the fragment, which was to have a determining influence on the decadent aesthetic of the 1880s as defined by Bourget in his *Essais de psychologie contemporaine*,[67] did not espouse more enthusiastically works which were clearly marked by a similar modernity.

It was not to be, and as we have seen, it was Constantin Guys whom Baudelaire came to see as the painter of modern life. What he admired in Guys, however, was not the heroism of modern life but the manner in which the rapidity of execution, the drawing from memory and the consequent appeal to the memory and imagination of the spectator, the absence of context and minor detail, and finally the sense of movement and evanescence enabled these barely outlined sketches and *croquis* to pass from the real world to an 'ideal' world and to give a kind of permanence to the elegant ephemeralities of fashion and to the fleeting observations of the *flâneur*. One suspects that what more than anything else so impressed Baudelaire in Guys was the perfect adequacy of form to content. Such a subject-matter demanded the peculiar qualities of the minor arts of wash and water-colour, just as in order to be fully modern and capture the transient and discordant life of the capital in *Le Spleen de Paris*, Baudelaire moved from verse to prose. Lyricism and the 'beaux jours de l'esprit' demanded the high seriousness of verse, until the mould broke under the pressure of the modern in 'Tableaux parisiens', in which, by chaotically shifting the caesura and introducing the most daring and dramatic enjambements sometimes extending, as in 'Le Cygne', over several stanzas, Baudelaire is aware of having transgressed the

---

[66] Barbara Wright and David H. T. Scott, *Baudelaire: 'La Fanfarlo' and 'Le Spleen de Paris'* (London: Grant & Cutler, 1984), 66, 77.

[67] (Paris: Lemerre, 1890), i. 25. Bourget defines the decadent style as 'celui où l'unité du livre se décompose pour laisser la place à l'indépendance de la page, où la page se décompose pour laisser la place à l'indépendance de la phrase, et la phrase pour laisser la place à l'indépendance du mot'. Gide, on the other hand, maintains that classical perfection implies 'la soumission de l'individu, sa subordination, et celle du mot dans la phrase, de la phrase dans la page, de la page dans l'œuvre' (*Incidences* (Paris: Gallimard, 1924), 211).

limits assigned to poetry and to have pushed it to the confines of prose.[68]

Perhaps we have here an adequate explanation for Baudelaire's uncharacteristic silence about Manet: the oil on canvas, like the high lyricism and seriousness of *Les Fleurs du Mal*, is less suitable than the *croquis*, *ébauche*, watercolour, or lithograph to capture the fleeting and above all the bizarre, strident, and mocking aspects of modern life. It may have been that for one so convinced of the specificity of art forms the scandal of *La Musique aux Tuileries* lay in a sense of disproportion, since it was presented as 'une grande machine',[69] but without depth of meaning or narration. It is true also that Baudelaire's humour in *Le Spleen de Paris* is often violent and hysterical, whereas Manet's is gentler and more understated. But for all that, one suspects that in Baudelaire's view the irony, the hint of a tendency towards caricature, and the artistic agnosticism that Manet reveals in these paintings would have been more properly expressed through a different medium. Here, there is a possible parallel with Daumier, whose caricatures and lithographs Baudelaire fulsomely praises while remaining silent about his astonishing oil paintings. So, if my speculation has any force in it, we can understand that Baudelaire thought Manet to be but the first in the decrepitude of his art not just because it was symptomatic of a general decline, but because it testified to a mismatch between form or medium, and content.

[68] *Corr.* i. 583: 'je crains bien d'avoir simplement réussi à dépasser les limites assignées à la Poésie'.

[69] In *L'Œuvre et la vie d'Eugène Delacroix*, having placed his idol among Rubens, Raphael, Veronese, Lebrun and David, Baudelaire states that they have in common 'une espèce de fraternité ou de cousinage dérivant de leur amour du grand, du national, de l'immense et de l'universel, amour qui s'est toujours exprimé dans la peinture dite décorative ou dans les grandes *machines*' (743–4).

7

Language and Rhetoric

ONE OF the most striking, and frustrating, features of Baudelaire's art criticism is that it says very little about individual paintings. His comments rarely amount to more than half a page, and often to much less, and the length of the commentary is not always an indication of the extent of his appreciation. It is, for example, quite astonishing that he should say next to nothing about the extraordinary *Mort de Sardanapale* which, in his enthusiasm, he thought represented what was most typical and Romantic in Delacroix's production. In 1846 he had placed it among a series of paintings which seem to portray the celebration of some dolorous mystery, and in 1862 his enthusiasm remains undiminished as he exclaims 'Le *Sardanapale* revu, c'est la jeunesse retrouvée' (p. 734). The rest of his criticism is inexplicably silent about what is probably the painter's most extravagant work, the one which, more than any other, served to establish his reputation.

He is quite unlike Diderot, whose practice is to give an ordered description of a work, in the round, as it were. Baudelaire is much more allusive, picking out a gesture, an aspect he finds suggestive, or a material detail which seems to summarize the work. There is nothing comprehensive about his strategy,[1] nothing to help the reader form a mental picture of the whole. So we find, for example, brief outbursts of admiration, for the colour of *Le Sultan du Maroc*, the posture of Juliet whose neck in its vigorous movement resembles that of a cat being caressed, for the sky, sea, and fluttering flags in the Crusaders entering Constantinople, or the observation with respect to *L'Enlèvement de Rébecca* that, like nature itself, Delacroix's paintings abhor a vacuum. At their most elevated, as in the comments on Delacroix or in the elegiac opening paragraphs on sculpture in the

---

[1] The exception is his account of Haussoullier's *Fontaine de Jouvence* in the *Salon de 1845* (359), where he approaches the painting systematically, describing in turn left, right, and centre of the foreground, and then the middle and background.

Salon de 1859, with the allegorized figures of Melancholy and Mourning and the evocation of parks with ruins, fountains, and still ponds, Baudelaire's writings represent a discourse which is the critical counterpart of the high moments of lyricism in *Les Fleurs du Mal*, similarly dominated by echoes, analogies, and an invitation to memory and to reverie. The analogy may spring from some physical or technical aspect of the painting, or take the form of an association with another artist—Weber for *Les Femmes d'Alger*, Shakespeare for *Les Croisés*, Fénelon for the Luxembourg ceiling, or Chateaubriand for *Ovide chez les Scythes*. But whatever the trigger, the sublime has of necessity a vocabulary to match the seriousness and the dignity of its mission to express what is deepest and most spiritual in the human imagination.

But these 'ideal' moments are balanced by others of critical spleen or discordance in which the poet pours his contempt upon the paltry productions of time-serving hacks devoid of dedication or vision. The exuberance of his criticism is perceptible to the most somnolent reader, as it moves from lyricism and reverie to the most strident raillery. Like the prose poems of *Le Spleen de Paris*, it can pass without transition from the serene 'ondulations de la rêverie' to the most violent 'soubresauts de la conscience'. Think of his exclamations and expletives, his wilful and skilful obscenities, his references to the colour 'jaune et pisseuse' (p. 486) of Saint-Jean, the 'effroyables dysenteries' (p. 21) of Alexandre Dumas, the 'flueurs blanches' (p. 475) of aesthetic ladies who admire the paintings of his *bête noire* Ary Scheffer, his view that the works of Horace Vernet, which decorate whorehouses and palaces alike, are not paintings at all, but 'une masturbation agile et fréquente, une irritation de l'épiderme français' (p. 470).[2] One might like to think that his outrageous remarks about George Sand and Belgian women in the *Journaux intimes* and *Pauvre Belgique!* satisfied a need to air in private the pent-up anger and resentment of his miserable last years, but before such indiscretions, as before his evocation of eighteenth-century 'polissonneries' showing behind a half-open door 'le jeu d'une seringue entre les appas exagérés

---

[2] In *La Démocratie pacifique* of 7 May 1846, the Fourierist critic, Charles Brunier, criticized the *Salon* for its 'crudité de style' (p. 1293), a crudeness Baudelaire had found in Diderot, and no doubt wished to emulate. Cf. Diderot, *Salons*, iii. 242: 'Mon ami, si l'on vous présente un canevas de comédie ou de tragédie, faites quelques tours autour de l'homme et dites-lui, comme la fille de joie au président de Brosses: Cela est beau, sans contredit, mais où est le cu [*sic*]?'

d'une marquise' (p. 641), spelled out 'en toutes lettres' in the public medium of the *Salon*, one is obliged to appreciate at their true value not just the extravagance of a licentious imagination, but the recklessness of one for whom critical circumspection never tempered 'le plaisir aristocratique de déplaire'.[3] Alongside these, there are intentional lapses in linguistic register—Vernet 'est né *coiffé*' (p. 470), M. Sosthènes de La Rochefoucauld is made to opine that Delacroix, whose colours are too violent, should put 'un peu d'eau dans son vin' (p. 430), and the modern allegorical figure of *Fatuité* has been stuffed full of sophisms 'à gueule-que-veux-tu' (p. 618). These, together with his use of the slang of the art world (paintings are 'aimables', 'd'une crâne facture', 'd'une pâte solide', 'astiquées', or 'exécutées avec bonhomie'), and his neologisms ('articliers', 'factureurs', 'sculptiers', 'malingreux', 'sabouleux', 'razzias', 'délicatisant', 's'obtusant'), may appear relatively unadventurous, but they all contribute to the vitality and the irresistible appeal which his criticism has for the reader, even in more outspoken, modern times.

Baudelaire's genius can be said to reside in large part in the creation of simile and metaphor, and we have already sufficiently stressed their importance in his criticism and in *Les Fleurs du Mal*. But the image is an essential component not just of his lyricism and 'les beaux jours de l'esprit', but also of the bizarrerie of his poetic vision. It was Laforgue who first drew attention to his 'comparaisons énormes', his 'yankee' images, in which the inordinate distance between the two terms has the power at once to disconcert and to invigorate: the woman's bosom compared to 'une belle armoire', the eyes lit up like 'boutiques', the carcass with its legs in the air 'comme une femme lubrique', the angel whipping the suns, or the flesh of the lesbians clapping in the wind like an old flag. It is precisely these juxtapositions of the sublime and the grotesque, the forced and sudden coming-together of elevated sentiments and the humble objects of daily experience, which make for the power and the immediacy of his poetry. When he writes of night thickening like a partition or kisses fresh as watermelons, these are so many examples of the 'suggestive magic containing at once the object and subject, the world exterior to the artist and the artist himself' (p. 598); they are demonstrations of the way that the sublime and grotesque unite to create 'une mnémotechnie du beau', illustrating a fundamental truth of Baudelaire's aesthetic that, like Delacroix's

---

[3] *Oc.* i. 661.

painting or Guys's drawings, the poetic image proceeds from the memory of the artist, and also speaks to that of the reader or viewer, who has the impression not so much of being in front of something external to himself, but of recognizing a part of his own life, resuscitated through the working of the affective memory. The abstractions of anguish or the pursuit of pleasure are rendered present in and through images both humble and concrete, all the more powerfully as the discrepancy between the terms produces a shock sufficiently strong to jolt and activate the deeper layers of memory. Their bizarrerie creates a new world in which divergent objects and feelings from opposing poles of experience upset our habitual perceptions and give access to the surreal.

It is because of such successes that critics have emphasized the importance of the doctrine of analogies and correspondances. The 'ténébreuse et profonde unité, / Vaste comme la nuit et comme la clarté' has become for many the key image in his poetic universe, just as the relationship between the imagery and Baudelaire's metaphysics have for many readers transformed his poetic adventure into an eminently spiritual and religious quest. The transmutation of the mud of reality into the gold of poetry, the brightness of 'les beaux jours de l'esprit', and the coincidence of opposites by which each oxymoron is integrated into a total vision, are for many the essential characteristics of Baudelaire's lyricism. So it has been frequently stated that the poet is he who, through antithesis and oxymoron, passes from a tragic universe to a paradise, from duality to unity,[4] and that for some the thyrsus, 'amalgame tout-puissant et indivisible du génie',[5] is the most perfect Baudelairean symbol of poetic creation and beauty. But one must be careful. Not all images are resolved in unity and the coincidence of opposites. Since Lautréamont and the Surrealists we have grown used to oxymorons—and an oxymoron is merely an extreme form of the poetic image—which, far from indicating the resolution of opposites, leave the two terms in a simple juxtaposition, irreconcilable in their separation. These are ironic figures which seem to mock poetry and its ambitions at the same time as they celebrate them. In other words, they are a kind of 'anti-figure', like Breton's famous soluble fish. In such cases, the figure acts not so much as a poetic image but as humour and irony, which use similar means. According to Jean-

---

[4] Léon Cellier, 'D'une rhétorique profonde: Baudelaire et l'oxymoron', in *Parcours initiatiques* (Neuchâtel: La Baconnière, 1977).

[5] *Oc.* i. 336.

Paul Richter, wit is a disguised priest who weds every couple,[6] but it is most often an impossible or risible union, and it is precisely from the incompatibility of the couple that the humour and irony are born. In reading Baudelaire it is important to observe how his lyricism and supernaturalism are increasingly infected by bitterness, discordance, and irony. Nothing could be more elevated or reassuring than the unity in which analogy and correspondence are merged, but it is important to follow the evolution of his aesthetic through the bizarrerie of these 'yankee' images towards the most violent and grating disharmonies. It is in the 'Tableaux parisiens' and especially *Le Spleen de Paris* that this phenomenon is most in evidence, since the stridency and chaos of the modern capital city and the close alliance of supernaturalism and irony, these two fundamental literary qualities,[7] produce poems in which black humour, bitterness, and the most absurd 'soubresauts de la conscience' give to what has been called his 'esthétique du choc' its most disquieting expression.

That Baudelaire's genius in creating this kind of ironic imagery should be well in evidence in his art criticism, in particular in his *éreintages* and mockery of inferior or misguided artists, is only to be expected. The range is exceedingly wide, from the incongruous comparison and extravagant simile to the most absurd and hilarious extended metaphors. Thus, Samson is seen as a cross between Hercules and the Baron von Münchhausen (p. 361), Gérard as 'l'amphytrion qui veut plaire à tout le monde' (p. 411), Catlin as 'le cornac des sauvages' (p. 446), Papety as representing 'la queue ridicule de l'école impériale' (p. 477), and Ingres's works are dismissed in a biblical sideswipe: 'filles de la douleur, elles engendrent la douleur' (p. 460).[8] The frock coat is called 'la pelure du héros moderne' (p. 494), while enthusiasts of landscape are variously called herbivorous animals (p. 667) or 'flâneurs enthousiastes de la plaine et de la montagne' (p. 450). Poor colour prompts comparison with gaudy cafés, opera-houses or village scarves, and a kaleidoscope is pronounced preferable to the paintings of Díaz de la Peña since its modest role is to provide designs for shawls or carpets (p. 453). Culinary images can be used to grotesque effect, as in the prose poem, 'L'Invitation au voyage', where

---

[6] See Sigmund Freud, *Jokes and their Relation to the Unconscious* (Harmondsworth: Penguin, 1976), 41.

[7] *Oc.* i. 658.

[8] The veiled reference is to Genesis 3:16, where God says to Eve: 'J'augmenterai la souffrance de tes grossesses, tu enfanteras avec douleur.'

the cooking in the poet's ideal country, the analogue of his mistress's virtues, is said to be 'poétique, grasse et excitante à la fois', and where 'tout est riche, propre et luisant, comme une belle conscience, comme une magnifique batterie de cuisine'. Lehmann, for example, is accused of making eyes so big that the pupil swims in them 'comme une huître dans une soupière' (p. 461), and in a devastating drubbing of the once-esteemed Troyon it is claimed that this imitator of an imitator, generating his own imitators, is open to nothing new, reading nothing, not even *Le Parfait Cuisinier*, which could, however, have opened a less lucrative, but more illustrious career for one so versed in 'l'art des sauces, des patines, des glacis, des frottis, des jus, des ragoûts' (p. 613). Painting can be compared to a meal, more or less nourishing and appetising like 'les saucissons d'Arles, les piments, les anchois, l'aïoli', indigestible like 'bonbons et sucreries écœurantes' (p. 453), or taste-less and debilitating like 'le thé et le beurre esthétiques' (p. 466). The extravagant praise of Decamps is expressed in purely gastronomic terms: 'Les mets les plus appétissants, les drôleries cuisinées avec le plus de réflexion, les produits culinaires le plus âprement assaisonnés avaient moins de ragoût et de montant, exhalaient moins de volupté sauvage pour le nez et le palais d'un gourmand, que les tableaux de M. Decamps pour un amateur de peinture' (p. 449). At other times, the images serve merely to lend spice to the text and to bring out the flavour and the diversity of a painter, to bring home to the reader with an amusing parallel a point about great and minor painting, or simply to change tone at the end of an elevated passage, as when he makes fun of a young painter who had called Delacroix's magnificent *Pietà* at Saint-Denis-du-Saint-Sacrement 'peinture de cannibale': 'Cet hymne terrible de la douleur faisait sur sa classique imagination l'effet des vins redoutables de l'Anjou, de l'Auvergne ou du Rhin, sur un estomac accoutumé aux pâles violettes du Médoc' (p. 436).

On occasion the distance between the components of the image can be so great as to be surreal; for example, Peña's figures are said to resemble bundles of rags or arms and legs 'dispersés par l'explosion d'une locomotive' (p. 453), and unimaginative lovers of landscape, content with the world as it is, will not, we are told, 'pendre les citrouilles aux branches des chênes' (p. 450).[9] Among the most devastating *éreintages* are those in which an outlandish metaphor is

---

[9] But see also below, n. 23.

sustained over several lines, as when having derided Vidal for his
depiction of so-called modern women with insipid names like
Fatinitza, Stella, Vanessa, and Saison des roses, 'un tas de noms de
pommades', he goes on to say that in any case 'toutes ces afféteries
passeront comme des onguents rancis. Il suffit d'un rayon de soleil
pour en développer toute la puanteur' (p. 463). An intertextual allusion to the famous image of the black sun gives added bite to an already
mordant denunciation of the notion of progress: 'ce fanal obscur,
invention du philosophisme actuel, breveté sans garantie de la Nature
ou de la Divinité, cette lanterne jette des ténèbres sur tous les objets de
la connaissance' (p. 580); while a witty and punning fantasy brings the
Salon de 1859 to a close as he imagines the blessed letters of the word
fin in their black skins executing like tiny Ethiopian dancers 'la plus
aimable des danses de *caractère*' (p. 681).

Punning and wordplay enliven the text, at times wilfully and excru-
ciatingly debilitated, as in the prose poems: for example, Delacroix's
name as 'un motif de signe de croix' (p. 353) or as a rallying symbol,
the interchangeability of objects 'décolletés' or 'déculottés' (p. 372) in
an opera to compensate for the inadequacies of its music, the *cardinal*
faculty of imagination arousing ideas of purple (p. 623), or in an
obvious reference to Delacroix's much vaunted use of red and green
his 'fumées *rouges*' being treated 'd'une *verte* façon' by some fashionable chronicler whose mission hitherto had been to comment on ladies'
dresses at the latest ball at the Hôtel de Ville (p. 632). Baudelaire's
most innocent, and most impertinent, quips often involve the names of
his targets, as in the cases of Wattier suggesting Watteau, or of Liès
and Leys, whose paintings and names are so inseparable as to prompt
comparison with Castor and Pollux (p. 651), or Calame and Diday
(p. 393) thought to be the same artist, stricken like Giglio Fava in
La Princesse Brambilla (p. 542) with '*dualisme chronique*', until it was
discovered that he preferred the name of Calame on the days he was
painting well.

Baudelaire's mockery of the cultural clichés of his time can be every
bit as comprehensive and crushing as Flaubert's, from a throwaway
allusion to Granet's 'vieilleries gothiques et religieuses' (p. 364), to
Gleyre's women 'solfiant de la musique romantique dans un bateau'
(p. 372), Scheffer's interchangeable Christ and Faust, 'tous deux
semblables à un pianiste prêt à épancher sur les touches d'ivoire ses
tristesses incomprises' (p. 649), or Isabey's *Un intérieur d'alchimiste*
with its inevitable heteroclite contents to show off the artist's brio with

colour: 'Il y a toujours là-dedans des crocodiles, des oiseaux empaillés, de gros livres de maroquin, du feu dans des fournaux, et un vieux en robe de chambre,—c'est-à-dire une grande quantité de tons divers' (p. 382). The downright bad taste of some clichés provokes the most humiliating sarcasm, none more effectively or comically than a statue by Frémiet[10] called *Ourang-outang entraînant une femme au fond des bois* which had attracted Baudelaire's scorn to such an extent that, even though it had been rejected, he feels obliged to lambast it in the *Salon de 1859*. Why, he asks, an orang-utan and not a crocodile, tiger, or any other beast likely to devour a woman? The answer, of course, is that it is not a question of eating but of raping, giant apes having sometimes shown for women a human appetite: 'Voilà donc le moyen d'étonnement trouvé! "*Il* l'entraîne; saura-t-*elle* résister?" telle est la question que se fera tout le public féminin' (p. 675). (One must admit, however, that the irony loses much of its power when one realizes that the real title of the offending work is *Gorille femelle*, and that Baudelaire has had more regard to rhetoric than to fact.)[11]

Those whom he dubs the apes of sentiment are given hilarious treatment in the *Salons* of 1846 and 1859. They rely for effect upon the catalogue, where the title, however, never tells the subject of the painting but provides, in a horrendous mixture of sentiment and would-be wit, a kind of sentimental puzzle. What can one possibly expect from an egregious title like *Pauvre Fileuse!* if not a female caterpillar or silkworm squashed by a child?; and for *Aujourd'hui* and *Demain*, which depict a beautiful and evidently pampered young woman on a sumptuous bed, and the same person on a bed of straw, he suggests a white flag and a tricolour, or perhaps 'un député triomphant, et le même dégommé' (p. 476). Among other absurd titles, which attract his scorn and are dismissed as mere 'logogriffes', are *Monarchique, catholique et soldat* (p. 615) and *Jamais et Toujours* (p. 677); but his most preposterous fantasy concerns a masterpiece

---

[10] Frémiet receives another hilarious drubbing for his *Cheval de saltimbanque*, which figures, mysteriously, an owl on the horse's back and puppets attached to the saddle. Pretending that he has not read the catalogue, Baudelaire suggests that the work represents human intelligence carrying everywhere with it the idea of wisdom and the taste for folly. But the title does not cast light, and he finally hits on a more appropriate one: '*Cheval de saltimbanque, en l'absence du saltimbanque, qui est allé tirer les cartes et boire un coup dans un cabaret supposé du voisinage! Voilà le vrai titre!*' (676).

[11] See photograph in Wolfgang Drost, 'De la critique d'art baud :lairienne', *Baudelaire, Actes du colloque de Nice, Annales de la faculté des lettres et sciences humaines de Nice*, 4–5 (1968), 84.

entitled *Amour et Gibelotte*, which again, he has not seen, but which excites his appetite for madcap irrelevancies:

Je cherche à combiner intimement ces deux idées, l'idée de l'amour et l'idée d'un lapin dépouillé et arrangé en ragoût. Je ne puis vraiment pas supposer que l'imagination du peintre soit allée jusqu'à adapter un carquois, des ailes et un bandeau sur le cadavre d'un animal domestique; l'allégorie serait vraiment trop obscure. Je crois plutôt que le titre a été composé suivant la recette de *Misanthropie et Repentir*. Le vrai titre serait donc: *Personnes amoureuses mangeant une gibelotte*. Maintenant, sont-ils jeunes ou vieux, un ouvrier et une grisette, ou bien un invalide et une vagabonde sous une tonnelle poudreuse? Il faudrait avoir vu le tableau. (p. 614)

The moral of this kind of elucubration would appear to be that those so-called artists who live by wit will perish by it.

The school of the *pointus*, in which an excessive display of erudition is intended to conceal a pitiable lack of imagination, also attracts Baudelaire's scorn. His denunciation[12] is all the more savage as it comes immediately after the long purple passage on *Ovide chez les Scythes*. The devotees of this school, given to proverbs, puzzles, and the representation of the *vieux-neuf*, produce pale-tinted pastiches of the frescoes of Herculaneum which allows them to sidestep the difficulties of rich and solid painting. They fill their canvases with the bric-à-brac of antiquity and transpositions of the vulgarities of modern life into a classical context; 'Nous verrons donc des moutards antiques jouer à la balle antique et au cerceau antique, avec d'antiques poupées et d'antiques joujoux' (p. 637). Above all, we are told, in a passage reminiscent of Emma Bovary's monstrous wedding cake,[13] that 'L'Amour, l'inévitable Amour, l'immortel Cupidon des confiseurs, joue dans cette école un rôle dominateur et universel. Il est le président de cette république galante et minaudière' (p. 638). In the light of this, one can readily understand Baudelaire's objection to the presence of the cupid in Planet's otherwise admirable depiction of St Teresa (p. 371). So far, so clear, and his irony at such sugary and insipid depictions is transparent. But how seriously are we to take his statement that he would represent love as a mad horse devouring its master, or, in words that anticipate the prose poem 'Les Tentations', as a demon with eyes ringed by debauchery and insomnia, dragging clanking chains at its ankles, like a spectre or a galley-slave, shaking a phial of

---

[12] Cf. Daumier's *Histoire ancienne*.
[13] *Madame Bovary*, 39.

poison in one hand, and in the other a dagger dripping with the blood of its crime (p. 639)? Irony builds on irony,[14] and as in the poem, the gruesome, 'gothic' overstatement is clearly intentional, his critical strategy being to replace one *poncif* by another in order to underscore, by a double irony, what is laughable in such deformations of reality.

Baudelaire's absurd and extended developments are relieved by damning one-liners of often caustic wit and concision: Lépaulle always produces successful pictures when all he has to do is paint well and have a pretty model, 'c'est dire qu'il manque de goût et d'esprit'; 'M. Bigand le coloriste a fait un tableau tout brun—qui a l'air d'un conciliabule de gros sauvages'; Scheffer is 'un poète sentimental qui salit des toiles' (p. 413); Géricault has qualities which are almost original (p. 429); Baudelaire once thought Haffner a great artist full of poetry and inventiveness, 'mais il paraît que ce n'est qu'un peintre' (p. 454). The effect of such uncompromising judgements is greatly increased when, as in the *Salons*, several artists are dispatched one after the other in a negative run (p. 453). Anticlimax and damning through faint praise are frequent devices: the Leleux brothers' paintings are all 'très bien faits, très bien peints, et très monotones' (p. 383); Vernet as a portrait painter is inferior to Vernet as a painter of heroic subjects (p. 379); Béranger's pictures are said to be charming, like Meissonier's, which could not be more offensive, since we have read ten pages back that Meissonier executes his little figures (elswhere referred to as 'puces') excellently—'C'est un Flamand moins la fantaisie, le charme, la couleur et la naïvete—et la pipe!' (p. 387); Bard returns from time to time to his own manner 'qui est celle de tout le monde' (p. 479); and Fleury's will-power is praised in one passage, but so insistently that the virtue becomes a defect (p. 363). On occasion, Baudelaire's judgements take the form of well-crafted maxims, some of which are relatively unsurprising, such as 'un dessinateur est un coloriste manqué' (p. 458), or 'un éclectique n'est pas un homme' (p. 473), while others have the characteristic ingredients of surprise, mystery, or paradox associated with the author of *Le Spleen de Paris*: doubt is 'un Protée qui souvent s'ignore lui-même' (p. 477); fantasy is 'la première chose venue interprétée par le premier venu' (p. 645), and an imitator is 'un indiscret qui vend une surprise' (p. 454), which is both witty and cryptic.

[14] Here, Baudelaire seems consciously to be outdoing Diderot, who frequently describes how he would have painted the picture (see, for example, Diderot, *Salons*, iii. 154).

For all their irreverence and wit, the *Salons* of 1846 and 1859 have a strong theoretical structure, being dramatized by the notions of Romanticism and modernity in the one, and imagination in the other. No such intellectual framework exists, however, for the *Salon de 1845* which, as has often been observed, is much closer to the model of Diderot's *Salons*, first brought to the notice of the public in the same year (p. 1250). The element of argument and exposition is very reduced, even in the passages on Delacroix, Haussoullier, Corot, and modernity, and the *Salon* is dramatized in quite a different mannner. If the request of the director of the *Revue française* was that, in the *Salon de 1859*, Baudelaire should give 'quelque chose comme le récit d'une rapide promenade philosophique à travers les peintures' (p. 608), his own express intention in 1845 appears to have been to suggest a rapid *flânerie* (if that is not too much of a contradiction) among the paintings for the benefit of the casual visitor. In order to stimulate the latter and guide his reaction, the pace of the text is accelerated by constant recourse to exclamation: 'Approchons vite—car les Decamps allument la curiosité d'avance' (p. 361); 'Voilà un beau nom [Devéria], voilà un noble et vrai artiste à notre sens' (p. 364); 'Hélas! que faire de ces gros tableaux italiens?' (p. 367); 'Eh quoi! c'est là un tableau de M. Bigand!' (p. 370); and, in *Le Musée du Bazar Bonne-Nouvelle*,[15] 'Voici venir l'aimable Prud'hon' (p. 411), which is followed by further exclamations designed to convince by affirmation rather than by argument. The style is indeed to a large extent exclamatory rather than explanatory, reduced at times in its desire for immediate communication to the elliptic devices of the telegram (p. 372). The use, or rather the abuse, of suspension points and the *tiret* or dash (the latter is particularly noticeable in the two pages on Corot) springs from the same desire for immediacy, as does the practice of *enchaînement* from one artist to the next, very often with a characteristic or motif introduced by a constantly repeated and dismissive 'toujours',[16] or the damning 'on parle trop de, on parle aussi trop de . . .' The dominant impression is of movement, and although the *Salon* keeps to the classical division of chapters according to the various genres—historical subjects, portraits, genre painting, landscapes, drawings and en-

---

[15] Though characteristic of the *Salon de 1845*, this device is found in the later writings, for example: 'Voulez-vous contempler encore une fois, mais sous une autre forme, le contraire de la sculpture?' (674).

[16] See pp. 392–4, for example: 'Toujours des beffrois et des cathédrales très adroitement peints.'

gravings, sculpture—the reader has the impression of an almost haphazard promenade among the paintings, following the 'rhapsodic' and
haphazard notations of the critic.[17]

Occasionally, in the *Salon de 1845*, it is as if in his spontaneity
Baudelaire were asking a question which is not so much rhetorical as
directly addressed to the painter. Thus it seems that it is Huet who is
being asked if by any chance he is thinking of changing his style (p.
391), and Matout is invited to reflect on Haussoullier to understand
the advantages of being radical and absolute and never making conces-
sions (p. 375). In all the *Salons*, however, his constant technique is
to address the reader directly, whether to reproach the 'égoïstes
populaces' for neglecting the once-admired Achille Devéria whose
latest works are now widely thought to be naïve (p. 365), or whether,
much more frequently, to put the reader on his side by flattery or by
assuming his agreement in what otherwise might have been a controversial opinion. One of the most extraordinary moments in his art
criticism is his passionate denunciation of Vernet, when he suddenly
switches from the third to the first person, which is sustained over
three paragraphs, each beginning with 'Je hais': 'M. Horace Vernet est
un militaire qui fait de la peinture.—Je hais cet art improvisé au
roulement du tambour, ces toiles badigeonnées au galop, cette
peinture fabriquée à coups de pistolet, comme je hais l'armée, la force
armée, et tout ce qui traîne des armes bruyantes dans un lieu pacifique'
(p. 469). Baudelaire's contempt for Vernet was genuine, as no doubt
was his hatred of the military, deepened by his troubled relations with
his stepfather, General Aupick, though there had been no trace of
adverse criticism in his comments on David's or Gros's depictions
of Napoléon at St Bernard or at the battle of Eylau, which, on the
contrary, were said in *Le Musée classique du Bazar Bonne-Nouvelle* to
be poetic and grandiose (p. 410). However that may be, in the final
paragraph of the chapter the first-person subjective stance is abandoned, as the poet claims to be speaking not as an individual, but as the
mouthpiece of a new generation. To counter any accusation that his
drubbing is excessive and clumsy, he insists that beneath every sentence in the first-person singular there is concealed a plural, a '*nous,
nous* immense, *nous* silencieux et invisible,—*nous*, toute une génération nouvelle, ennemie de la guerre et des sottises nationales; une

---

[17] Baudelaire himself uses the term 'rhapsodic' to indicate, as with his prose poems or the
musings of a hashish-induced reverie, 'un train de pensées suggéré et commandé par le
monde extérieur et le hasard des circonstances' (*Oc.* i. 428). See also *Corr.* ii. 583.

génération pleine de santé, parce qu'elle est jeune, et qui pousse déjà à la queue, coudoie et fait ses trous,—sérieuse, railleuse et menaçante!' (p. 471). This, as Richard Burton rightly observes, is a truly remarkable sentence, one which 'for the first time, opens up the possibility of an "elsewhere" from which the Bourgeois Monarchy, its values, and supporters might be subjected to a systematic strategy of attack by and in the name of a *nous* immense" acting in unison'.[18] It stands in strong contrast to the wit and ambivalence of the *dédicace* to the bourgeois at the beginning of the *Salon*, and leaves them in no doubt about his antagonism to what they stand for. To that extent it is overtly a passionate political statement, all the more forceful as it takes the form of a threat. It is also a rallying call for the young generation, who, in practice, constitute the only public that can understand him and identify themselves with these exalted sentiments. Who among them could possibly be in favour of national idiocies, and who could afford not to be considered serious, scornful, and threatening? The outburst is a defiance of the bourgeois to be sure, but its compelling rhetoric serves also to validate what otherwise might have appeared a personal prejudice by claiming to speak in the name of a hidden, silent, and right-minded public. By claiming to speak in the name of that public, Baudelaire is at the same time enlisting its support, and seems intent on so doing independently of its attitude to art. In the central section he had set out the aesthetic reasons for denouncing Vernet, but in the concluding *nous* paragraph his earlier comments about colour, memory, and structure are forgotten as the emphasis returns to the anti-militarist and anti-nationalist sentiments of the beginning of the chapter.

The immediately preceding paragraph contains an anecdote about the German painter, Pierre de Cornélius, concerning an alleged meeting between the two painters in which Vernet is said to have overwhelmed him sycophantically with compliments, whereas in response Cornélius had merely congratulated the Frenchman drily on the amount of champagne he could drink without ill effect. The anecdote, which Baudelaire admits may be without foundation—'Vraie ou fausse, l'histoire a toute la vraisemblance poétique'—is intended to put the reader on the side of the quietly sardonic Cornélius and excite disdain for the vain and slow-witted Vernet. It is not just an aside or amusing filler, but has an important function in the strategy of the

---

[18] Richard D. E. Burton, *Baudelaire and the Second Republic: Writing and Revolution* (Oxford: Clarendon Press, 1991), 39.

chapter. It is clear that, for all its passion and venom, the *éreintage* is a carefully crafted piece of rhetoric: the central part was to discredit Vernet aesthetically, as the anecdote was to discredit him intellectually. The anti-militarist passages at the beginning and end carry the main burden of the attack, which is to discredit him politically. The *éreintage* complete, Baudelaire's strategy becomes evident: to destroy the reputation of Vernet, who for many was 'le représentant le plus complet de son siècle' (p. 471), the idol of the bourgeoisie and the *juste-milieu*, on three free-standing arguments, aesthetic, intellectual, and political.

Anecdotes do not always have such a negative function. They may simply serve as an innocent aside or as a curious irrelevancy before more fundamental issues are engaged, as on the opening page of *Le Musée classique du Bazar Bonne-Nouvelle*, where Baudelaire evokes the story of the starving musician who organizes a concert, the proceeds of which are appropriated by the *sabouleux*, or bogus poor who exploit such events. No comment is made, and the reader is invited to form his own opinion on such practices. On other occasions a more substantial point is given a concrete illustration, and a general truth about the nature of art is made all the more convincing and tangible for being associated with living persons in apparently real situations. One such anecdote concerns Balzac, whose massive authority and reputation serve to authenticate the poet's arguments, who reveals his strategy by asking in parenthesis who would not listen with respect to the smallest anecdotes concerning this man of genius. Balzac finds himself one day before a sad painting of a winter scene with peasants and their modest houses, from one of which rises a thin wisp of smoke. His enthusiasm and imagination are aroused, as he wonders what the peasants are doing and thinking in their dwellings, whether they have sorrows and if the harvests have been good. '*Ils ont sans doute des échéances à payer?*' The result is that the ideal critical method has been exemplified in the anecdote before being finally formulated in the subsequently often quoted sentence: 'Il m'arrivera souvent d'apprécier un tableau uniquement par la somme d'idées ou de rêveries qu'il apportera dans mon esprit' (p. 579).

Another anecdote, which Jacques Crépet has traced to Diderot (p. 1387), features a German peasant, synonym of naïvety, who approaches a painter to paint his portrait. He states exactly what he wishes: he is to be shown at the entrance to his farm in the large armchair which he inherited from his father, with his wife spinning and, in the background his daughters busying themselves with the preparation of his supper. His sons are to be seen in the avenue returning from the fields, and his grandchildren bringing back the carts laden with hay. The painter is enjoined not to forget the smoke from his pipe nuanced by the light of the setting sun, to be sure '*qu'on entende* les sons de l'Angelus', and to paint the peasant's '*air de satisfaction*' at looking at '*ma famille et ma richesse augmentée du labeur d'une journée*' (p. 613). The lesson is simple, that the naïve peasant has a better understanding of painting than fashionable artists, whose imagination had not been heightened, like the peasant's, by the love of his profession; and the tactic is both powerful and well established, involving a paradox to which the public can readily respond, whereby the norm is reversed by placing the truth with the apparently naïve, and error with the would-be sophisticates.[19]

Another device Baudelaire uses to incline the reader to his point of view is to modify well-known and easily recognizable quotations from famous writers and incorporate them into his own sentences, La Fontaine and Molière being among his favourite sources. For example, to emphasize his belief that watercolour is a minor art form that cannot match oil on canvas, he adapts the title of La Fontaine's fable, 'La Grenouille qui se veut faire aussi grosse que le boeuf':[20] 'L'aquarelle est réduite à son rôle modeste, et ne veut pas se faire aussi grosse que l'huile' (p. 440); and in order to set the excellence of Gustave Planche's criticism and his openness to modern art against the stupidity of journalists he dubs him 'un paysan du Danube' (p. 351), after the fable with that title in which the peasant's eloquence silences the arrogant and unfounded pride of the Romans.[21] The title of a painting by Hornung, '*Le plus têtu des trois n'est pas celui qu'on pense*', is used to demolish not just the perpetrator of the work, but Bard and Geffroy as well, under whose names Baudelaire drily comments 'Voir le précédent' (p. 388). The title of the painting is rashly based on a famous line, which every schoolboy must have known, from 'Le Meunier, son fils et

---

[19] Cf. his comments on the *épicier*, below, p. 274.
[20] *Fables*, I. 3.
[21] Ibid., XI. 7: 'Le Paysan du Danube'. Planche had been an early admirer of Delacroix, whom he had seen as a *phare* (see Ch. 2, n. 3) along with Gros et Géricault. In *Le Hibou philosophe*, however, Baudelaire criticizes his contempt for Romantic poetry. Gautier, in calling Courbet 'un paysan du Danube', is presumably highlighting his rusticity (quoted by Klaus Herding, *Courbet: To Venture Independence* (New Haven and London: Yale University Press, 1991), 189).

l'âne',[22] in which 'têtu' is replaced by 'âne', with the result that Baudelaire is able to suggest their asinine stupidity without actually using the word. At the same time the reader has the impression of complicitly sharing a joke with the writer to which the victims are denied access. Elsewhere, lovers of landscape, for all their big-heartedness, are said to be lacking in imagination, and so will not, we are told, go so far as to 'pendre les citrouilles aux branches des chênes' (p. 450). The phrase seems just another example of the extravagant image that has already been noticed, until one realizes that it is an allusion to another of La Fontaine's fables, 'Le Gland et la citrouille',[23] which tells of a villager who, finding God's creation illogical, wishes to replace the acorn on oak trees with the more appropriate pumpkin.

In another instance, having established the basic criterion of *naïveté* and the sincere expression of temperament, Baudelaire concludes that the critic also must do his duty with passion, wittily adapting Tartuffe's famous hypocritical excuse, 'pour être critique on n'est pas moins homme';[24] and in the *Salon de 1859*, by altering 'méchant' to 'mauvais' in a famous outburst by Alceste against the stylistic contortions of his age—'Le mauvais goût du siècle en cela me fait peur'[25]— Baudelaire contrives at one and the same time to mock the ridiculous prudishness of his own century and, punningly, to cast his scorn on the pretensions of a famous contemporary newspaper called *Le Siècle* (p. 653). Such allusions, like those to Hugo, Béranger, and other contemporary figures, would have been transparent to the reader with a modicum of culture, though others must have appeared hermetic to all but Baudelaire's most intimate inner circle. Few, if any, could have made sense of the conflated references in the *Salon de 1859* to a scene from Dumas's *La Tour de Nesle* and a chapter on Cazotte from Nerval's *Illuminés* (p. 617), or in *Exposition universelle (1855)* to Pierre Leroux's denunciation of Art for Art's sake in a philosophical poem, 'La Grève de Samarez' subsequently published in 1863 (p. 581).[26] These are perhaps to be seen as rare instances of his enthusiasm and erudition causing him to lose contact with his readers, and should be distinguished from other moments when his allusiveness in intentional, as when he wishes to sow in the reader's mind the idea that the absence of Delacroix from the Bazar Bonne-Nouvelle can be explained

---

[22] Ibid., III. 1.   [23] Ibid., IX. 4

[24] *Le Tartuffe*, III. iii, 'Ah! pour être dévot, je n'en suis pas moins homme.'

[25] *Le Misanthrope*, I. ii.   [26] See Cl. Pichois's notes pp. 1389, 1370.

by the conniving ingratitude of his mediocre co-pupil under Guérin, Cogniet (p. 414).

The critic who believes that criticism should be passionate and written from an exclusive point of view is naturally not afraid to express his opinions in the first person, not just because he thereby engages much more readily and 'sincerely' with his reader than in the detached and anonymous third person, but because paradoxically it implies, contrary to common belief, a greater modesty. The opening paragraph of the essay on Wagner makes this clear:

Ce *Je*, accusé injustement d'impertinence dans beaucoup de cas, implique cependant une grande modestie; il enferme l'écrivain dans les limites les plus strictes de la sincérité. En réduisant sa tâche, il la rend plus facile. Enfin, il n'est pas nécessaire d'être un probabiliste bien consommé pour acquérir la certitude que cette sincérité trouvera des amis parmi les lecteurs impartiaux; il y a évidemment quelques chances pour que le critique ingénu, en ne racontant que ses propres impressions, raconte aussi celles de quelques partisans inconnus. (p. 779)

But sometimes Baudelaire will begin in the first person and pass quickly to the third in order to universalize a subjective reaction. For example, in *Le Salon de 1846* his attention is drawn to Manzoni's, *La Rixe des mendiants*, whose poetic brutality far outdoes, he thinks, anything produced in Flemish orgies. But to convey his enthusiasm for the painting he affects to step outside himself by dramatizing the impressions of anyone passing in front of the picture and showing the stages whereby a final appreciation is reached. Thus a highly subjective and idiosyncratic process is given the appearance of objective certainty: 'Voici en six points les différentes impressions du passant devant ce tableau: 1° vive curiosité; 2° quelle horreur! 3° c'est mal peint, mais c'est d'une composition singulière et qui ne manque pas de charme; 4° ce n'est pas aussi mal peint qu'on le croirait d'abord; 5° revoyons donc ce tableau; 6° souvenir durable' (p. 451). It is precisely because of its apparent spontaneity that the passage carries conviction, seeming to mimic by its unpolished, 'telegram' style a thought in the process of formulation. The device is unique in Baudelaire, and the result so compelling that it is not impossible that Proust had it in mind in the famous brio performance of the painter in *Un amour de Swann*.[27]

A first-person voice can in practice have more than one tone, so that

---

[27] *A la recherche du temps perdu*, i. 250–1.

its sincerity can appear doubtful and even masquerade as its opposite. Nothing, of course, could be more genuine than Baudelaire's admiration for Delacroix, and we have no reason to doubt the serene joy that fills his heart when, in the fourth section of the *Salon de 1846*, he expounds the virtues of his hero among painters. But when he adds that he has chosen his newest quills, 'tant je veux être clair et limpide, et tant je me sens aise d'aborder mon sujet le plus cher et le plus sympathique' (p. 427), we are aware that an ironic tone has contaminated the text: the ritual choice of pens, the repeated 'tant', the 'literary' and somewhat archaic 'je me sens aise', and the literalness of his new-cut pens enabling his writing, not his handwriting, to be clear and limpid indicate a self-consciousness which no doubt stems from admiration itself, which, he says elsewhere,[28] is an embarrassing emotion, difficult to convey adequately. Admiration may indeed, as we all know, invite the charge of exaggeration or of seeking too assiduously to impose one's convictions on the reader. The passage reflects a typically Baudelairean *pudeur* and quirkiness, which contrive to gain the reader's confidence by a mock display of guileless veneration.

At other times the voice can be less discreet and innocent, as when, in 'la glorieuse analyse de cette belle Exposition' (p. 579), he promises to set aside all pedantry and erudition which seem to him in most cases puerile and unenlightening, and to forswear the jargon of studios which critics affect to show off at the expense of the artists themselves. It would be too easy, he claims, to expatiate subtly upon symmetrical or balanced composition, upon tonal equipoise, upon warmth and coldness of tone, and so on; but with a grandiloquent and ironically hyperbolic 'O vanité!', he prefers to speak in the name of feeling, morality, and pleasure, hoping that learned people without pedantry will find his (italicized) ignorance in good taste. The modesty is so blatantly false as to be immediately recognized as unalloyed arrogance, while the irony of the paragraph is all the more impudent, as we have witnessed elsewhere his own use of studio jargon to impress his readers, and his distrust of the excesses of sentiment. Other first-person passages take the form of digressions on a minor artist, which are not always easy to justify in the context. Such is the development on erotic art for which Tassaert's painting, and in particular his licentious 'transvestite' lithograph, *Ne fais donc pas la cruelle!*, which does not

---

[28] 'Je ne connais pas de sentiment plus embarrassant que l'admiration. Par la difficulté de s'exprimer convenablement, elle ressemble à l'amour' (103).

even figure in the Salon of 1846, are merely an excuse and a hardly convincing justification (p. 443).[29]

The voice of Baudelaire the critic can resemble nothing so much as that of the cuckoo which identifies the place where he is not. If the first person may be ambiguous, an anonymous third person buried in the text may reveal an authentic opinion. Most readers, however, will have little difficulty in recognizing Baudelaire in the 'homme imaginatif' who prefers the monsters of his fantasy to things as they appear in nature (p. 620), or in the cosmopolitan man of the world who goes to a far country and whose sympathetic openness creates in him 'un monde nouveau d'idées, monde qui fera partie intégrante de lui-même, et qui l'accompagnera, sous la forme de souvenirs, jusqu'à la mort' (p. 576). Nor, as with studio jargon, does Baudelaire fear to be in contradiction with ideas he has expressed previously, sometimes in the same work, if it allows him to meet the demands of the moment and to drive home a point. Take, for example, the spurious comparison of Delacroix and Hugo, which he thinks cannot be justified by the intrinsic characteristics of the two men, and is born of the current fad for finding pendants and analogues in the different arts, a practice which brings with it 'd'étranges bévues' (p. 430). This may be true, and the case in question perhaps lends force to the argument, but it is an argument, in the form of a generalization, which sits uneasily in the works of a critic who believes that analogy underlies all art and that the arts themselves, as he argues in the essay on Wagner, are interpenetrable. After all, he could quite simply have claimed that the analogy with Hugo was false. Are we then to believe that, when he makes parallels between Charlet or Gavarni and Balzac, he has changed his mind, or are we rather to think that in order to establish his hero as the undisputed head of Romanticism, he must not only belittle Hugo but also the kind of thinking by analogy that has brought him into such illustrious and unmerited company? Such inconsistencies are no doubt justified by a criticism which is required to be passionate, and which, more than anything, belongs not to the academic thesis but to the less objective and rigorous genre of journalism and the *Salon*. Inaccuracies and critical licence are perhaps excusable, when conviction does not require one to be prodigal with the truth.

An amusing instance closes, appropriately, the chapter on imagina-

---

[29] The chapter on Tassaert was probably to have been part of the book Baudelaire announced on the cover of the *Salon de 1845* (see *Curiosités esthétiques*, ed. J. Crépet (Paris: Conard, 1923), 450).

tion in the *Salon de 1859*. To prove his contention that imagination is a sure judge of excellence in art, he relates how he found himself in a railway carriage where a copy of *L'Indépendance belge* with an article by Dumas had been left on a seat. This is probably as near as you can get to the critical equivalent to stolen goods that have fallen off a lorry. Although clearly Dumas had no specialist knowlege of painting, no one could deny that, for all his stylistic laxity, this great figure of Romanticism was endowed with an exceptionally powerful imagination, which precisely enabled him to appreciate the great painters of the time according to their true merit, and thus confirm Baudelaire's own judgements and conviction that imagination is inseparable from 'l'esprit critique'. Without imagination, Baudelaire claims, Dumas would have written only nonsense, and he drives home his conclusion that 'l'imagination, grâce à sa nature suppléante, contient l'esprit critique' (p. 623). Of course, he says, doubters are free to resort to the time-worn objection that Dumas was not the author of his *Salon*;[30] which is possible since, as Pichois points out (p. 1392), he was known to use ghost writers. The other possibility, which is not mentioned, is that Baudelaire did not read the article and that the whole passage is a fabrication to lend a spurious authority to his argument. This turns out indeed to be the case, since Dumas makes no mention in the article of the Devérias, Poterlet, or Bonington, whom he is said to praise along with Delacroix and Boulanger, and since, far from proving that Troyon is lacking in genius, he covers him with praise, putting him on an equal footing with the great Delacroix himself. Baudelaire's tongue must have been firmly set in his cheek when, at the beginning of the passage, he alludes to the 'magnificent privileges' accorded to imagination, that essential faculty for artists and critics alike!

Inaccuracies and strategic half-truths, contradictions and inconsistencies, puns, extravagant images, and zany developments might all be thought to belong to the stock-in-trade of the literary journalist—were it not that Baudelaire is at pains from the beginning to distance himself from such a debased and biased form of discourse. He will, on the contrary, in 1845, be impartial (p. 351), which hardly fits with his practice in the rest of the *Salon* or in that of 1846 where he maintains that criticism should be 'partiale et politique'. His *Salon*, unlike newspaper journalism, will accede to greater heights of seriousness and pertinence than the 'guide-ânes qu'on nomme comptes rendus de

---

[30] Dumas's five articles in *L'Indépendance belge* were published later in the year as a separate volume.

Salons' (p. 351); but his beating of journalists with their own weapons is so manifestly in contradiction with his proclaimed intention that the reader is led to suspect the author is sending him up. Irony builds on irony, so that, like his other writings, Baudelaire's art criticism is distinctly subversive. His *Salons* of 1846 and 1859 in particular are remarkable for their trenchant and damning judgements, but above all for the extent to which they set out to subvert the very genre which they are supposed to exemplify. Like that of 1845, the *Salon* was expected to be an enlightened *flânerie* among the year's paintings in the company of an expert. But the *Salon de 1846* departs from convention to put forward an aesthetic programme drawing on the notes already in existence for Baudelaire's intended book on modern painting announced on the back cover of the 1845 *Salon*; and in 1859, confessing he has visited the Salon only once, he detaches himself almost completely from the paintings of the year in order to acquire the freedom to expatiate at will on realism and photography, on imagination and its governance. His characteristic strategy is to upset the reader's expectations, not to astonish gratuitously but as a systematic challenge to received opinion and practice. As with his verse and prose poetry, his originality is rarely confined to content alone, but extends to a radical rethinking and remodelling of the genre in which he is operating.

It is in 'Aux bourgeois' and 'Des écoles et des ouvriers' in the *Salon de 1846* that his penchant for mystification is at its most perplexing. Much ink has been spilled by commentators of diverse critical and political persuasions in trying to pin down stable interpretations of the two passages. I shall not attempt to do justice to the complexity and ingenuity of so great a volume of research, but limit myself to suggesting a different perspective on the issues involved. The shifting ironies of the extraordinary *dédicace* to the bourgeois, sustained throughout by a burlesque rhetoric based upon the abuse of maxims, an aggressive but faulty logic, and the hyperbolic geometricality of the argument, have inevitably attracted much comment, often of a very high quality. Ross Chambers, Richard Burton, David Kelley, and Annie Becq have subjected it to penetrating analyses, from which a clear consensus has emerged: that the mystification conceals a serious foundation, that the seemingly pro-bourgeois stance is 'simultaneously genuine and bogus',[31] and that, since the bourgeois can have had at most a limited

[31] Burton, *Baudelaire and the Second Republic*, 37.

understanding of art and the *Salon* itself, the text is caught in a historical contradiction between a real but inappropriate public and an inexistent ideal one.[32] It is perhaps precisely this tension and contradiction which explain why the vehemence and ferocity of his attacks on his *bêtes noires* are much more in evidence in this *Salon* than elsewhere. Baudelaire is more conscious here of the problem of whom to address than in any other of his writings on art, all of which, with this one exception, are addressed to an enlightened and sophisticated public, capable of accepting or at least understanding his views, however original and unconventional they may be. The intention and result were no doubt to *épater* his friends, and certainly to unsettle the bourgeois who must have been far from flattered, since one message of the *dédicace* at least emerges intact from the irony: that the bourgeois is ignorant of art and requires the instruction of enlightened criticism. The poet's distaste for his task is as evident as his *raillerie*, and he must have been perversely aware that his irony at the bourgeois' expense would alienate them every bit as much as his reference later in the text to the works of their idol, Vernet, as a masturbation of the national epidermis, and his relegation of the popular Ary Scheffer to the hospital of painting.

If the *dédicace* is both genuine and bogus, it participates not in the kind of irony which to be successful needs to be disbelieved, but in the kind which, like that of the Cretan liar paradox, is marked by an inner contradiction which effaces the boundaries between the true and the false, or rather which is both true and false at the same time. Such uncertainty in his attitude towards the bourgeois is short-lived in Baudelaire, whose impatience and scorn are unalloyed in his denunciation of the mercantile spirit in the essays on Poe, and in the *Salon de 1859* where he threatens to throw his *écritoire* at 'l'Ame de la Bourgeoisie' with a vigour they could not expect, for maintaining that imagination is unnecessary in art (p. 654). But in the 1840s his attitude is somewhat enigmatic and ambiguous, and it would be helpful to examine briefly his pronouncements in other texts of the same year. The *Conseils aux jeunes littérateurs* and *Le Musée classique du Bazar Bonne-Nouvelle* are marked by a spirit of realism and a desire to avoid the clichés and stereotypes of the time. In the first he reproaches young writers for complaining of their bad luck and of the success of mediocre talents like Eugène Sue and Paul Féval. The answer, he says,

[32] This is Ross Chambers's argument in 'Baudelaire et la pratique de la dédicace', *Saggi e ricerche di letteratura francese*, xxiv (1985), 121–40.

is to show more talent, more originality and more power, 'et vous n'aurez plus le droit de médire du *bourgeois*, car le *bourgeois* sera avec vous' (p. 14). His aim is to strengthen their resolve, but what also emerges is an ambivalence concerning the taste of the bourgeois who at one and the same time are impressed by mediocrity and capable of recognizing true originality. A similar ambivalence is found in the last paragraph of the *Musée classique*, where Baudelaire rails against the *artiste-bourgeois* who complains about the bad taste of the bourgeois and their inability to understand what is great and beautiful. But the bourgeois, having no scientific or technical knowledge, goes where he is pushed by the voice of the *artiste-bourgeois*. Left to himself, the *épicier* would be capable of understanding great art and carry Delacroix in triumph. The passage ends in a burlesque vein, leaving the reader with a greater sense of disparagement of the *artistes-bourgeois* than belief in the instinctive judgement of the *épicier*. But for all that, in addition to the poet's dislike of the bourgeois artists' facile judgements on art and the public, there is in both passages more than a suggestion that, in spite of his bad taste, all is not lost for the bourgeois who can and will respond to great art. This hope is based on an optimistic view that human beings are capable of understanding their culture, naïvely, if their minds have not been corrupted by the *poncifs* of fashion, the superficiality of the *juste-milieu*, or the kind of art which falsifies the conditions of life. Left to himself, the man of good will, oblivious of the voice of the bourgeois artist, will be open to the appeal of a work and reach an authentic response to it. What, then, can be said to emerge from these early texts, as indeed from the introduction to the 1845 *Salon*, is a typical impatience with the received ideas of middle-class artists and an ambivalent attitude towards the bourgeois consumer, but above all a realistic assessment of the position of art in contemporary society, and a recognition that if it is to survive there must be some engagement with the public which is there.[33]

In the *dédicace* of 1846 the bourgeois artists have been replaced by the 'aristocrates de la pensée' and 'accapareurs des choses spirituelles', that is to say critics, members of Salon juries, professors or other distributors of praise and blame, and the ambivalence towards the bourgeois public is complicated by the addition of a sustained and unrelenting irony which must have bewildered the contemporary

---

[33] This realism, tinged with irony and condescension, is evident in the following passage from the 1845 *Salon*: 'En second lieu le bourgeois—puisque bourgeois il y a—est fort respectable; car il faut plaire à ceux aux frais de qui l'on veut vivre' (352).

reader as much as his modern counterpart, though for different reasons. The uncertainty stems from the conduct of the argument, the maxims, false deductions, and non-sequiturs, and the irony of repetition. But the main problem of the text is in the citational and intertextual irony that pervades it. The first three paragraphs in particular are a farrago of buried allusions to Pascal, Saint-Simon and Fourier. 'Vous êtes la majorité,—nombre et intelligence;—donc vous êtes la force,—qui est la justice.' According to Pascal's famous *pensée*,[34] force and justice should go together; for justice without force is impotence, and force without justice is tyranny. But such is the world that 'ne pouvant faire que ce qui est juste fût fort, on a fait que ce qui est fort fût juste'—which is exactly what Baudelaire is implying. The power of the bourgeois is no doubt a fact, but its legitimation lies in the power that its majority gives it, not in its inherent justice. Force need not be balanced or legitimated by justice; since by definition might is right. The mystification is, if I may put it so, clear from the outset, and the flattery of the bourgeois two-faced.

It may be objected that Baudelaire himself equates force with justice, in *Conseils aux jeunes littérateurs*: 'rien n'est vrai que la force, qui est la justice suprême'. But the context is quite different, since, as in 'Des écoles et des ouvriers' where he is making a similar point, Baudelaire is talking here of the privilege of artistic genius, whereas in the *dédicace* he is talking about politics and social structures. So Baudelaire's irony in the *dédicace* is transparent, or would be transparent but for the word 'intelligence' which casts a veil over it. Not only is the flattery excessive and out of character, but the paragraph seems askew and its aggressive logic bizarre. 'Intelligence' seems to have been slipped in parenthetically as a not very convincing flattery, because if the flattery had been genuine, the logic would have been different: it would have asserted that political power based upon a majority plus intelligence equals justice. But it does no such thing. It posits power based upon a majority, adds intelligence which it then appears to discount in equating tautologically majority with force, to which is added the platitudinous 'qui est la justice'. In a word, the 'logic' equates majority to force and justice, and the rapid appearance and apparent discounting of 'intelligence' reveal the intentional bad faith of the writer which is confirmed when the argument is repeated in the fourth paragraph but without the intrusion of 'intelligence':

[34] Lafuma 103, Brunschvicg 298.

'Vous possédez le gouvernement de la cité, et cela est juste, car vous êtes la force.'

The second paragraph compounds the irony and mystification by what would probably have been recognized by most readers at the time as veiled references to Saint-Simon's *Catéchisme des industriels* of which the following is the clear and essential intertext:

Les industriels composent plus des $24/25^{es}$ de la nation; ainsi ils possèdent la supériorité sous le rapport de la force physique. Ce sont eux qui produisent toutes les richesses; ainsi ils possèdent la force pécuniaire. Ils possèdent la supériorité sous le rapport de l'intelligence, car ce sont leurs combinaisons qui contribuent le plus directement à la prospérité publique.[35]

Saint-Simon comes to the inevitable conclusion that the *industriels* should pass from being the class of the governed to that of the *gouvernants*. Baudelaire's irony would not be lost on the bourgeois reader, who knows that his majority in the chamber, based on a restricted franchise, does not represent *le pays réel*, which for Saint-Simon means the *industriels*, defined in the broadest manner as any producer, from cultivator to blacksmith to shoemaker. But Baudelaire's address is to the bourgeois, not to the *industriels*, thus making the majority purely parliamentary and emasculating Saint-Simon's radical view that the reign of the bourgeois should come to an end.[36] This is not his only editing sleight of hand; for behind the second paragraph with its gobbledegook of *savants* becoming property-owners and vice versa, there lurks another crucial Saint-Simonien intertext, *L'Artiste, le Savant et l'Industriel*, a dialogue which ends with the hope that the arts, sciences, and industry, 'cette grande trinité', will unite to produce the complete well-being to which society legitimately aspires. Here Baudelaire 'edits' by replacing *industriels* by *propriétaires*, the class Saint-Simon thought should be extended to include the *prolétaires* who, since the sale of the *domaines nationaux*, have proved themselves capable landowners.[37] The bourgeois might well have been grateful for the flattery and the reassurance buried in

[35] *Œuvres de Claude-Henri de Saint-Simon*, 6 vols. (Paris: Anthropos, 1966), iv. 13 (reprint of *Œuvres de Saint-Simon et Enfantin*, ed. E. Dentu, 1869).

[36] 'Aujourd'hui, la nation n'est plus partagée qu'en deux classes: les bourgeois, qui ont fait la révolution et qui l'ont dirigée dans leur intérêt, ont anéanti le privilège exclusif des nobles d'exploiter la fortune publique; ils se sont fait admettre dans la classe des gouvernants, de manière que les industriels doivent aujourd'hui payer les nobles et les bourgeois' (ibid. 8). Saint-Simon's attitude towards the bourgeoisie had been more tolerant in an earlier stage of his career (see *Lettres d'un habitant de Genève*, *Oc.* i).

[37] Ibid. v. 117.

the *dédicace*; their right to rule is incontrovertible and no one is going to challenge it for being built on unsound, unjust foundations. But of course the tampering with the intertexts by this poet/critic/artist who is supposedly on their side reveals the spoof and his unreliability, with the result that if the bourgeois, having dropped his guard, is temporarily flattered, he is also unsettled and ill at ease.

The irony is far from simple; it is indeed double in the reference to *force* and *intelligence*; for these, combined with *amour*, form the grand synthesis in the Saint-Simonian religion of the future, the 'jour radieux' and the 'harmonie suprême' of the *dédicace*. Force and intelligence are the domain respectively of the *industriel* and the *savant*, the function of love being to provide an educative impact without which the other two would be incomplete and meaningless. It is the domain of the arts and involves the development of sentiment. Though Baudelaire does not mention love, it is of course embedded in the text, in the injunction to the bourgeois to be 'aptes à sentir la beauté', and not least in his own status as artist-critic exercising his *sacerdoce*[38] and educating his public.

The assertion that the bourgeois could live three days without bread (how would they know?) but not without poetry is also made tongue in cheek, going as it does against common sense and common experience.[39] Those among them who say the opposite are mistaken; 'ils ne se connaissent pas',[40] which, if it is a nod in the direction of Pascal, adds a very different view of the constitution of the self from any utopian one. It is, however, this latter which punctuates the rest of the *dédicace* in the references to 'l'exercice des cinq sens', 'l'équilibre naturel de l'idéal' of mind and belly, the 'équilibre des forces' of the soul of the bourgeois, and finally in 'l'équilibre de toutes les parties' of their being. Clearly, Baudelaire is pointing to utopian notions of the harmony of the human being in the perfect society where Pascalian *misère* will have been set aside. The irony lies in the fourfold repetition of 'équilibre', in the primacy of the physical over the spiritual, and the suggestion that art is a commodity to be enjoyed, an investment with excellent returns: 'Si vous récupérez la quantité de jouissances nécessaire pour rétablir l'équilibre de toutes les parties de votre être, vous êtes heureux, repus et bienveillants, comme la société sera repue,

---

[38] Baudelaire's impatience with the Saint-Simonien role of the artist as some form of lay priest is evident in the *Salon de 1859* in the passage on Millet (661). See also p. 183.

[39] It appears, somewhat less ironically, in *Conseils aux jeunes littérateurs* (19).

[40] Pascal, Lafuma 72, Brunschvicg 66: 'Il faut se connaître soi-même.'

heureuse et bienveillante, quand elle aura trouvé son équilibre général et absolu.' This is of course a send-up of the Fourierist view that happiness lies in the satisfaction of the senses and the consequent experience of fulfilment and harmony. What, restrospectively, adds piquancy to the passage is that the vocabulary is almost identical to the description of 'les amants des prostituées' in 'Les Plaintes d'un Icare' as 'heureux, dispos et repus'.[41] It cannot be claimed that the *dédicace* is referring to the poem, since the latter dates from 1862. What can be argued, however, is that in writing the poem Baudelaire was thinking back to the *dédicace* as he sought to express his disgust at the obscene, self-satisfied equilibrium of the pimp.

The irony is pervasive, mocking the intertexts from which it springs as well as the bourgeois, and presenting a *reductio ad absurdum* of utopian optimism, as if Baudelaire were saying 'that'll be the day'. For my part, I cannot see in what way the *dédicace* is Fourierist or utopian, as has been claimed; for to take the allusions to Saint-Simon seriously or to detect genuine Fourierist intimations of the *harmonien* society and the healing process of art would be to underestimate Baudelaire's deferential impudence towards the bourgeoisie and to deprive his *dédicace* of the overpowering thrust of its citational irony.[42] What does, however, survive the irony and the mystification is the poet's recognition of the beneficial influence of the *grande bourgeoisie* in the institution of museums in the Monarchie de Juillet, together with his realism in accepting, however reluctantly, the importance of the bourgeois public for the future of art. The reception of the *dédicace* is difficult to evaluate. It is a mirror, in the form of a eulogy in the second person, which both deforms and tells the truth. As such, it is unflattering, most unlike the mirrors in the essay on Gautier: 'Comme Paris aime surtout parler de Paris, la foule se complaît dans les miroirs où elle se voit' (p. 119). The poet is unlikely to have made new converts from the class he is overtly addressing, but his other audience, his circle of artists and friends, would have enjoyed the wit, the impertinence, the verbal and intertextual gymnastics, and sniggered in delight—unless they too were made to feel uncomfortable by the references to *accapareurs* and pharisees.

[41] 'Dispos' replaces its synonym, 'bienveillants', because of the demands of the octosyllabic line.
[42] Kelley, *Salon de 1846*, 37, rightly sees in the 'jour radieux' something analogous to the Saint-Simonian and Fourierist idea 'selon laquelle l'histoire se divise en époques "subversives" et "harmoniques", ou "critiques" et "organiques"'; but he does not appear to think that the idea is subverted by the irony.

'Des écoles et des ouvriers' is another part of the *Salon* which has caused much speculation on Baudelaire's political views, in particular his alleged anti-republicanism in the famous opening paragraph where he applauds the 'sergent de ville', 'municipal de mon cœur', for beating the republican, hater of roses and perfumes, fanatical lover of tools, sworn enemy of Watteau and Raphael, butcher of Venus and Apollo. David Kelley thinks that it is in this chapter that the poet allows his social ideas to appear with the least reticence and without irony;[43] Gretchen van Slyke argues that it is the socialist critique of individualism and private property, associated with Leroux, that is behind Baudelaire's hatred of bourgeois and republicans;[44] and Hartmut Stenzel is categorical that 'Il s'agit là en premier lieu d'une critique de l'individualisme qui résulte de l'organisation marchande de la société bourgeoise', and stresses the link between his aesthetic and political ideas.[45] But the question of Baudelaire's political position seems misdirected, not least because the style of the opening paragraph is diametrically opposed to the expository seriousness of the rest of the chapter. The elements of irony are plain enough to see: the curiosity of the bourgeois *flâneur* is more likely to be checked by circumspection than allow him to stray into a riot, and yet it is stated, wryly, that he has often found himself in such a position; the true army is said to be that of the *sergent de ville*, 'gardien du sommeil public', indicating that for all his love of national grandeur and military glory after the manner of Vernet, the bourgeois's first priority is his own safety from the enemy within; his shallow aestheticism is, to say the least, vulgar, conservative, and uninformed, undelivered from the Greeks and the Romans, and with no hint of the 'morale du siècle' as found in Delacroix, or of the heroism of modern life called for at the end of the *Salons* of 1845 and 1846; finally, the discrepancy between the exquisite sensibility of the bourgeois and his hysterical violence against the undisciplined anarchy of the republican, combined with the poet's concurrence in such grotesque views, serves to put the passage on a level of gross farce. If Baudelaire is to share the bourgeois' hatred of the republican, he would also have to share their other

---

[43] Ibid. 45, and 'Deux aspects du *Salon de 1846* de Baudelaire: la dédicace aux Bourgeois et la Couleur', *Forum for Modern Language Studies* 5/4 (Oct. 1969), 338.

[44] Gretchen van Slyke, 'Riot and Revolution in the *Salon de 1846*', *French Forum*, 10/3 (Sept. 1985).

[45] Hartmut Stenzel, 'Les écrivains et l'évolution idéologique de la petite bourgeoisie dans les années 1840: le cas de Baudelaire', *Romantisme*, 17–18 (1987), 86.

preposterous views, which of course would be an absurd reading of the passage, and the poor man would once again be caught in the lamentable position of the ironist who is believed. Manifestly this is not the case; he is using a rhetorical trick, old but perennial, which is to have the bourgeois articulate their cherished and unavowed prejudices and reveal their inanity, rather than the mealy-mouthed utterances which normally conceal their sentiments.

Baudelaire's strategy is to base his argument upon a simple comparison which is rendered all the more forceful and immediate by the brevity of a single sentence: 'Ainsi, les philosophes et les critiques doivent-ils impitoyablement crosser les singes *artistiques*, ouvriers émancipés, qui haïssent la force et la souveraineté du génie.' Just as x, so y; just as the republican who is a disruptive and anarchic force in the body politic, and who into the bargain is the enemy of beauty, cannot be tolerated, so also the undisciplined artist is seen as a pernicious presence in the world of art. The thesis of the chapter is aesthetic, not political, its message being that the decline of the schools has led to a corresponding decline in the art of the time. *Naïveté*, faith, and genius are incompatible with total freedom and can only work within a continuing tradition, 'la grande chaîne de l'histoire', which, without Delacroix, would break and crumble to the ground. Some commentators have perhaps been too quick to read a political meaning into such statements as 'Et comme aujourd'hui chacun veut régner, personne ne sait se gouverner', without sufficient regard to the context of art in which the poet has firmly anchored them. Such a procedure could only be justified if it were *already* clear that his views on the republican were in fact the same as those of the bourgeois, and not just a rhetorical device. Whatever his opinion of republicans, socialists, or Fourierists, which in 1846 was probably tinged with more than a little scepticism, his strategy is to drive home in his own style a truth about the state of contemporary art which will appear all the more acceptable to the bourgeois as it is seen to exist in parallel to, and as it were as a consequence of, their own deeply-held convictions—expressed in the parodic language of a lampoon. In other words, Baudelaire is using the bourgeois' hatred of the republican to convince them of his point about art. To identify *his* political views in this extravagant and ironic charade would be, at best, ill-advised; at worst it might involve the risk of a fruitless, and possibly humourless, wild goose-chase.

Much also has been made of Baudelaire's references to the idea of progress in the *Salon de 1846* in an effort to identify ideological leanings in his thinking. In Kelley's words, they represent 'un accent peu baudelairien'[46] in the *Salon*, incompatible with the poet's well-known denunciation of the idea of progress, whether material or moral, and his contention that true progress could reside only in the diminution of original sin. But this, it is argued, is the position of the depoliticized Baudelaire of after the *coup d'état*, the admirer of Maistre and Poe; whereas the Baudelaire of 1846 is tinged with a belief in progress, just as his social thinking leaned towards Fourier and his attitude towards nature was more optimistic and harmonious. The argument might be appealing were it not that in *De l'essence du rire*, the composition of which is contemporaneous with the *Salon*,[47] he explains laughter by the Fall and man's dual nature. He would appear, then, to be in contradiction with himself, believing at about the same time both in progress and original sin, exercising no doubt the right he claimed for all men to contradict themselves.[48]

Progress is mentioned twice, in chapters two and four. Having established that Romanticism is the most recent expression of the beautiful and that there are as many notions of the beautiful as there are ways of seeking happiness, he declares that the philosophy of progress explains this aesthetic relativism (p. 421), there being not one absolute ideal but as many as there are ways of understanding ethics, love, and religion. Romanticism resides in a conception analogous to 'la morale du siècle'. The indication is that, as such, it represents a progress on past conceptions; but the problem is to understand in what way the notion of progress affects the argument, and to see its relevance. If the *morale* of an age is different from that of preceding ages, and beauty is relative, not absolute, what need is there of an idea of progress, since it is the difference that counts? The 'philosophy of progress' has explained nothing at all, and the use of the expression appears odd or ill chosen.

The requirement that in order to express 'la morale du siècle' the modern artist should get to know those aspects of nature and human situations unknown to or disregarded by artists in the past, does little to advance or clarify the argument, serving only to elaborate on the ways in which a modern view might differ from a previous one. If of course a modern artist is more knowledgeable and more aware than his

---

[46] *Salon de 1846*, 9.   [47] See Ch. 3.

[48] 'Parmi l'énumération nombreuse des *droits de l'homme* que la sagesse du XIXe siècle recommence si souvent et si complaisamment, deux assez importants ont été oubliés, qui sont le droit de se contredire et le droit de *s'en aller*' (306). See also *Oc.* i. 709.

predecessors, if he has grown in judgement and understanding, then one could say there has been progress, but this would not involve a philosophy of progress. If in 'aspects of nature and human situations' Baudelaire is thought to include awareness of the human condition and the different situations in which it is played out, an interpretation justified by the spirituality and aspiration towards the infinite in his definition of Romanticism, rooted, as we have seen, in the notion of human duality, a similar objection can be made. The human condition is, in broad terms, invariable, but the situations are not. What, in that case, he would seem to be saying is that progress lies in an increased awareness of that condition. If that is so, there is no contradiction with his subsequent rejection of the idea of progess, since what is involved is an increasing appreciation of what is fundamental in mankind, a sense of imperfection and a striving towards a beyond—upon which, after all, his aesthetic and his view of the function of art are predicated. An increased awareness of the aspiration towards the infinite may well mark a progress on more blithe views of the human condition, but since it is grounded in human imperfection, it is of necessity incompatible with a belief in progress as such, or in a serial sense. A belief in human perfectibility may be replaced by its opposite, an acceptance of original sin. Such a move can be seen as a progress, but, here again, it excludes of necessity a philosophy of progress.

The second incidence of 'progress' occurs some twenty pages later where it is stated that Delacroix is the latest expression of progress in art (p. 441), because of the entirely new and modern quality of his painting which is gesture, rivalled only outside his art in the acting of his great contemporaries, Lemaître and Macready. The context is vital; for in the preceding paragraph Baudelaire argues that each great master has his own realm and prerogative: Raphael form, Rubens and Veronese colour, Rubens and Michelangelo imagination in draughtsmanship, Rembrandt drama. To the extent that he achieves sublimity of gesture, Delacroix is the latest expression of progress in art: 'Héritier de la grande tradition, c'est-à-dire de l'ampleur, de la noblesse et de la pompe dans la composition, et digne successeur des vieux maîtres, il a de plus qu'eux la maîtrise de la douleur, la passion, le geste!' Take away Delacroix and 'la grande chaîne de l'histoire est rompue et s'écoule à terre'. The association of the idea of progress with the chain of history adds clarification and goes a very considerable way towards ironing out possible contradictions.

The image of the chain with its implied emphasis on tradition recurs elsewhere in his art criticism. It is embedded in his lament in the last chapter of the *Salon* that 'la grande tradition s'est perdue, et que la nouvelle n'est pas faite' (p. 493), and much more significantly, it reappears at the end of the *Exposition universelle (1855)* in his great panegyric of Delacroix whose future glory and place among the great are assured. Posterity will say that he united in his art qualities found variously in Rembrandt, Rubens, Lebrun, and Veronese,

mais qu'il eut aussi une qualité *sui generis*, indéfinissable et définissant la partie mélancolique et ardente du siècle, quelque chose de tout à fait nouveau, qui a fait de lui un artiste unique, sans générateur, sans précédent, probablement sans successeur, un anneau si précieux qu'il n'en est point de rechange, et qu'en le supprimant, si une pareille chose était possible, on supprimerait un monde d'idées et de sensations, on ferait une lacune trop grande dans la chaîne historique. (p. 597)

The two passages are in essence almost identical, the only difference being that in 1846 the chain is linked to the idea of progress, and in 1855 it appears after a chapter containing an outspoken diatribe against the whole idea of progress which he sees as the invention of present-day *philosophisme*. In the domain of morality, belief in progress leads to fatalism, irresponsibility, the diminution of will-power and of freedom. This does not mean to say, however, that Baudelaire accords no value to the word. If this year an artist produces a work which gives evidence of greater knowledge or imaginative force than last year, then of course there has been progress. Similarly, if foodstuffs are cheaper and better today than yesterday, again there has been progress.[49] But more importantly: 'Si une nation entend aujourd'hui la question morale dans un sens plus délicat qu'on ne l'entendait dans le siècle précédent, il y a progrès; cela est clair' (p. 580). But that is essentially what in 1846 he said was explained by the philosophy of progress. It emerges that there is no fundamental difference between 1846 and 1855, and that the latter serves only to clarify the imprecise formulation of the former. What he is now refuting, and what he never intended to convey, is the idea of progress as a

---

[49] Baudelaire's hesitations in the use of 'progress' span his career: in the *Salon de 1845* he claims Delacroix to be 'dans une voie de progrès sans cesse renaissante' (354) in colour and harmony; in 1855 he looks in vain for 'des échantillons de progrès', concluding that the painter had been great from his earliest works (590); and in 1863 he declares that Delacroix 'ne connaît pas la décadence; il ne montre que le progrès' (752). In 1855 he intends to analyse 'les éléments de progrès' in the French school (583), and in 1859 he declares that poetry and progress are 'deux ambitieux qui se haïssent d'une haine instinctive' (618).

continuing series, for which there can be absolutely no guarantee. Applied to works of imagination, it is an absurdity; for each artist is alone, without ancestors or descendants, and every flourishing is spontaneous, individual, self-contained.

The image of the chain is not, however, thereby rendered inoperative; what it indicates is not a chain of progression but a linking of the greatest moments of painterly expression in the tradition of Western art. It is significant that each time the chain appears, Baudelaire mentions not just the link that is Delacroix, but his other great heroes of the past, Rembrandt, Rubens, Lebrun, Veronese, and the *phares*[50] celebrated in the poem of that name, which, interestingly, he quotes towards the end of the article. True, he quotes only the quatrain on Delacroix, and that in the context of the painter's mental world. But the mention of beacons in the context of chains is far from gratuitous, the two being more or less interchangeable; for what are beacons if not links in a chain of light? They connote continuity, but at the highest level, and are in turn linked with the image of the 'cri répété par mille sentinelles', the 'ordre renvoyé par mille porte-voix', and the 'appel de chasseurs perdus dans les grands bois' of the same poem. If the chains of the article can be said to celebrate genius in painting, the beacons of the poem celebrate in addition mankind's eternal dissatisfaction with its condition and the aspiration towards a higher order of things. The shift is from the painterly to the metaphysical, both of which were of course fundamental elements in the definition of Romanticism in the *Salon* of 1846.

What Baudelaire is saying in 1855 is essentially the same as in 1846.[51] The uncertainty in the *Salon* lies in the use of the word 'progress', which adds nothing but confusion to what without it would have been pellucidly clear. It may be that in 1855 Baudelaire was reproaching himself (and others) for applying the notion of progress to the arts and that the *Exposition universelle* marks a rift with 1846 on this count. An alternative reading and, I suggest, a more plausible one, is that in the *Salon* he was using 'progress' to emphasize the mobility and dynamism of relativism against the static conception of absolute, normative art, and not so much out of philosophical conviction, but as a catch-phrase, a rhetorical device to capture the goodwill of the bourgeois by speaking their language and reflecting

---

[50] See Ch. 2, n. 3.
[51] This interpretation would be strengthened if, as some have thought possible, the initial composition of 'Les Phares', in some form or another, was as early as 1845 or 1846.

their beliefs, just as he had done in the famous *dédicace* and in the chapter on schools and workers, but without the citational or mystifying irony.

The argument that the *Salon de 1846* presents a synthesis of Baudelaire's thinking at the time,[52] extending beyond his aesthetic and moral views to include a social philosophy, is based upon too little or too uncertain evidence to be reliable. As we have seen, it involves taking the social and political aspects of the *dédicace* and 'Des écoles et des ouvriers' seriously, deeming them to have escaped the poet's irony unscathed and depriving them of their rhetorical thrust. Supporting evidence has been sought from sources outside the *Salon*, in particular in *Conseils aux jeunes littérateurs*, of which the following is a crucial passage:

Je fais la part des mille circonstances qui enveloppent la volonté humaine, et qui ont elles-mêmes leurs causes légitimes; elles sont une circonférence dans laquelle est enfermée la volonté; mais cette circonférence est mouvante, vivante, tournoyante, et change tous les jours, toutes les minutes, toutes les secondes son cercle et son centre. Ainsi, entraînées par elles, toutes les volontés humaines qui y sont cloîtrées varient à chaque instant leur jeu réciproque, et c'est ce qui constitue la liberté. (p. 14)

Kelley's comment on this passage is central to his argument concerning the poet's view of a balanced and harmonious society: 'Vouloir donner libre cours aux désirs de l'individu, sans prendre garde à la volonté commune, exige un effort volontaire qui risque de détruire l'équilibre des forces intérieures, et entraîne immanquablement la dislocation de l'ensemble.'[53] But this interpretation seems far removed from the context of the *Conseils* which concerns young artists who blame their lack of success on *le guignon*, or bad luck. The poet's advice is that they should show more strength of will and character, that they should quadruple their force until they have as much as those who succeed, instead of passively accepting things as they are. His image of the circumference is easily understood; each human being has limits upon his freedom, but these limits are not fixed, so that one can extend one's area of freedom by pushing back the extent to which other people and circumstances encroach upon us. There is, then, an interplay between freedom and necessity in what seems an eminently common-sensical attitude towards a very old problem; but there is no

[52] Asselineau was surely right to see it as 'un livre de haute esthétique' (1294).
[53] *Salon de 1846*, 12.

mention here of the danger of upsetting the harmony of society. Indeed, one finds the exact opposite, the duty of the talented individual to widen the area in which his willpower operates, and devil take the hindmost, or as the text itself says, '*vae victis!* car rien n'est vrai que la force, qui est la justice suprême'. If there is any echo from contemporary thinking here, once again it is the Balzac of *Louis Lambert* and the theory of will-power who comes to mind rather than any proponent of a *harmonien* view of society. But Kelley links the passage directly to the beating of the republican by the 'gardien du sommeil public', to support his interpretation of 'Des écoles et des ouvriers' as the most comprehensive expression of the poet's social ideas. There *is* a link between the two texts, not in the promotion of a harmonious society, but in the 'whiff of cultural fascism'[54] which comes with the poet's glorification of the artist of genius who alone has the right to govern.

Much has been made of Baudelaire's rejection of systems in 1855:

J'ai essayé plus d'une fois, comme tous mes amis, de m'enfermer dans un système pour y prêcher à mon aise. Mais un système est une espèce de damnation qui nous pousse à une abjuration perpétuelle; [. . .] Et toujours un produit spontané, inattendu, de la vitalité universelle venait donner un démenti à ma science enfantine, fille déplorable de l'utopie. (p. 577)

Commentators have read this as a disavowal of 1846, and an admission that it had been tainted by utopian thinking. But there are grounds to doubt this: first, 'plus d'une fois' (not 'une fois' as one critic has read it) is a characteristic phrase of Baudelaire's,[55] loosely added for emphasis, and second, because 1846 contains in fact several contradictions, as does his thought scattered in the various writings of that year. Felix Leakey and David Kelley have done much to clarify the evolution of the poet's thinking and have exposed the defects of previous interpretations. What they have written about harmony in man and nature has replaced the previous monolithic view of Baudelaire with a more subtle and complex one. But it is important not to lose sight of the contradictions: his utterances on nature are ambivalent, sometimes favourable, sometimes hostile; his attitude to religion and religious paintings is hardly compatible with a view of integration into the

---

[54] See p. 6 n. 10.
[55] Of Delacroix's paintings he writes: 'J'ai essayé plus d'une fois, moi-même, de dresser cet énorme catalogue' (743). See also p. 758, and p. 760: 'Il m'est arrivé plus d'une fois, en le regardant, de rêver des anciens souverains du Mexique.'

harmony of the natural world; and his 'optimism' jars with his belief in the 'accident d'une chute ancienne'. Given these contradictions, one must be wary of importing ideas or statements from contemporary works without regard to their context and place in the overall economy and strategy of the argument. His production at the time is varied in genre, tone, purpose, and the audience being addressed. Is it legitimate, for example, to take from a review of Ménard's *Prométhée délivré* statements about the cult of Nature, Diderot, and pantheism as if they applied to Baudelaire himself? The review considered as a review and not as a depository of embedded beliefs is unambiguous: having made cruel fun of Ménard's atheism and stressed the aridity of the work, Baudelaire is suggesting that the cult of Nature, 'cet unique ornement de l'athéisme' (p. 11), would have given it some relief and made it more poetically attractive. There are no grounds in the review for believing that the critic is an atheist or lover of nature. Similarly, one should be wary of supporting an argument about the unity of opposites with passages taken from the overtly teasing and impertinent *Choix de maximes consolantes sur l'amour*, especially when laced with so many unsettling exclamation marks; 'd'une si grande coquine la grande Nature seule sait ce qu'elle veut faire. Bonheur et raison suprêmes! absolu! *résultante* des contraires! Ormuz et Arimane, vous êtes le même!'[56] Can we be sure enough of the poet's seriousness to find support here for an argument about 'contraire et contradiction' and an underlying moral unity in diversity? In 1846 Baudelaire is a mere twenty-five years old, at the outset of his career. It would indeed have been extraordinary if a 'paresseux nerveux', whose reading was disparate and unsystematic, who gleaned his ideas from a great diversity of contemporary writing, a young mind having something of the *touche-à-tout* and the magpie, should have achieved so early and almost at one go, a coherent philosophy of man, art, and nature. Neither his thinking nor his rhetoric are rigorously systematic; his arguments often proceed by a series of memorable assertions; and his mind is prompted by enthusiasms, sudden intuitions, and instinctive likes and dislikes. The contradictions and inconsistencies are to be expected, and far from being a fault are the distinctive virtue of a restless, questing and spontaneous intellect in tune, as he himself implied, with 'la vitalité universelle'.

There is no one text that synthesizes Baudelaire's thinking. The

[56] *Oc.* i. 550.

Salon de 1859 is a mature reflection, free of the instabilities and contradictions of 1846, but it concerns the principles of high art, of sculpture and the oil on canvas. The aesthetic ideas it propounds are broadly analogous to those that inform *Les Fleurs du Mal*, of which it can be considered the critical counterpart. *Le Spleen de Paris*, on the contrary, which exemplifies the 'minor' genre of the 'petit poème en prose', is much more closely linked in conception to the essays on laughter and caricature, and to *Le Peintre de la vie moderne*, though it accedes to levels of disillusionment that these texts seem only to prefigure. To enter fully into Baudelaire's mental universe, it is important to read his criticism in the light of his poetic practice and appreciate the extent to which they complement each other, ranging as they do over a great diversity of subject matter, and from the heights of 'les beaux jours de l'esprit' to the most poignant questioning of the validity of art and the function of the artist.

Bibliography

ABOUT, EDMOND, *Le Salon de 1864* (Paris, 1864).

ALEXANDRE, ARSÈNE, *L'Art du rire et de la caricature* (Paris, 1892).

BACHELARD, GASTON, *L'Air et les songes* (Paris: José Corti, 1950).

BAKHTIN, MIKHAIL, *Rabelais and his World* (Bloomington: Indiana University Press, 1984).

BALZAC, HONORÉ DE, *La Comédie humaine*; vol. x (Paris: Gallimard, 1950).

BARRÈS, MAURICE, *Le Mystère en pleine lumière*, in *L'Œuvre de Maurice Barrès*, vol. xii (Paris: Club de l' Honnête Homme, 1967).

BARTHES, ROLAND, *L'Aventure sémiologique* (Paris: Seuil, 1985).

BAUDELAIRE, CHARLES, *Curiosités esthétiques*, ed. J. Crépet (Paris: Conard, 1923).

——*Baudelaire: documents iconographiques*, ed. Claude Pichois and F. Ruchon (Geneva: Cailler, 1960).

——*Curiosités esthétiques: L'Art romantique*, ed. H. Lemaître (Paris: Garnier, 1962).

——*The Painter of Modern Life and Other Essays*, ed. Jonathan Mayne (London: Phaidon, 1964).

——*Art in Paris 1845–1862*, ed. Jonathan Mayne (Oxford: Phaidon, 1965).

——*Baudelaire*, exhibition at Petit Palais, 1968–69 (Paris: Réunion des Musées Nationaux, 1968).

——*Petits Poèmes en prose*, ed. Robert Kopp (Paris: José Corti, 1969).

——*Correspondance*, ed. Claude Pichois, 2 vols. (Paris: Gallimard, 1973).

——*Salon de 1846*, ed. David Kelley (Oxford: Clarendon Press, 1975).

——*Œuvres complètes*, ed. Claude Pichois, 2 vols. (Paris: Gallimard, 1975, 1976).

BECQ, ANNIE, 'Baudelaire et "l'Amour de l'art": la dédicace "aux bourgeois" du *Salon de 1846*', *Romantisme*, 17–18 (1977).

BENJAMIN, WALTER, *Charles Baudelaire: A Lyric Poet in the Era of High Capitalism* (London: NLB, 1973).

——*Paris Capitale du XIXe siècle: Le Livre des passages* (Paris: Editions du Cerf, 1993).

BERGSON, HENRI, *Le Rire* ([1924] Paris: Presses Universitaires de France, 1956).

BERNARDIN DE SAINT-PIERRE, HENRI, *Paul et Virginie* (Paris: Garnier-Flammarion, 1966).

BIDERMANN, JACOB, *Philemon Martyr* (Cologne: Hegner, 1960).

BLANC, CHARLES, *La Peinture* (Grammaire des arts du dessin) (Paris: Renouard, 1886).

BLANCHOT, MAURICE, *La Part du feu* (Paris: Gallimard, 1949).

BONAVENTURA, *Die Nachtwachen* (Edinburgh: Edinburgh University Press, 1972).

BOSSUET, JACQUES-BÉNIGNE, *Maximes et réflexions sur la comédie* ([1694] Paris: Eugène Belin, 1881).

BOURGET, PAUL, *Essais de psychologie contemporaine* (Paris: Lemerre, 1890), vol. i.

BOWNESS, ALAN, 'Courbet and Baudelaire', *La Gazette des Beaux-Arts*, 90 (Dec. 1977).

BRETON, ANDRÉ, *Œuvres complètes*, 2 vols. (Paris: Gallimard, 1988).

BROMBERT, VICTOR, *Victor Hugo and the Visionary Novel* (Cambridge, Mass.: Harvard University Press, 1984).

BUGLIANI, IVANNA, *Baudelaire: L'Armonia e la discordanza* (Rome: Bulzoni, 1980).

BURTON, RICHARD D. E., *Baudelaire and the Second Republic: Writing and Revolution* (Oxford: Clarendon Press, 1991).

BURTY, PHILIPPE, 'L'Œuvre de Charles Meryon', *La Gazette des Beaux-Arts*, xiv (June 1863).

BYRON, GEORGE GORDON LORD, *The Complete Poetical Works*, ed. J. J. McGann and B. Weller, vol. vi (Oxford: Clarendon Press, 1991).

CAHEN, GUSTAVE, *Eugène Boudin: Sa vie, son œuvre* (Paris: Fleury, 1900).

CALLIAS, HECTOR DE, *L'Artiste* (1 June 1864).

CASTEX, PIERRE-GEORGES, *Baudelaire critique d'art* (Paris: SEDES, 1969).

CELLIER, LÉON, 'D'une rhétorique profonde: Baudelaire et l'oxymoron', in *Parcours initiatiques* (Neuchâtel: La Baconnière, 1977).

CHAMBERS, ROSS, 'Baudelaire et la pratique de la dédicace', *Saggi e ricerche di letteratura francese*, xxiv (1985).

CHAMPFLEURY [JULES HUSSON], *Contes d'automne* (Paris: Lecou, 1854).

——*Histoire de la caricature moderne* (Paris: Dentu, 1872).

——*Son Regard et celui de Baudelaire*, textes choisis et présentés par Geneviève et Jean Lacambre (Paris: Hermann, 1990).

CHATEAUBRIAND, FRANÇOIS-RENÉ DE, *Œuvres romanesques et voyages*, 2 vols. (Paris: Gallimard, 1969).

——*Essai sur les révolutions: Génie du christianisme* (Paris: Gallimard, 1978).

CLAPTON, GEORGE, 'Lavater, Gall, et Baudelaire', *Revue de littérature comparée*, xiii (1933).

CLARK, T. J., *The Absolute Bourgeois* (London: Thames & Hudson, 1973).

——*Image of the People* (London: Thames and Hudson, 1973).

——*The Painting of Modern Life* (London: Thames & Hudson, 1984).

COBLENCE, FRANÇOISE, *Le Dandysme: obligation d'incertitude* (Paris: Presses Universitaires de France, 1988).

COGNIAT, RAYMOND, *Manet* (Paris: Hazan, 1982).

COMPAGNON, A., *Les Cinq Paradoxes de la Modernité* (Paris: Seuil, 1990).

CONSTANT, BENJAMIN, *Œuvres* (Paris: Gallimard, 1957).

CURTIUS, QUINTUS, *History of Alexander*, ed. J. C. Rolfe (London: Heinemann, 1946).

DAGUERRE DE HUREAUX, ALAIN, *Delacroix* (Paris: Hazan, 1993).

DAIX, PIERRE, *Delacroix le libérateur* (Paris: Club des Amis du Livre progressiste, 1963).

—— *La Vie de peintre d'Edouard Manet* (Paris: Fayard, 1983).

DELACROIX, EUGÈNE, *Œuvres littéraires*, 2 vols. (Paris: Crès, 1923).

—— *Correspondance générale d'Eugène Delacroix*, ed. André Jubin (Paris: Plon, 1938).

—— *Journal 1822–1863* (Paris: Plon, 1981).

—— *Delacroix, Le Voyage au Maroc*, catalogue of the exhibition at the Institut du monde arabe (Paris: Flammarion, 1994).

DELÉCLUZE, E. J., *Salon de 1824* (Paris, 1824).

DELTEIL, LOYS, *Le Peintre-graveur illustré*, 32 vols. (New York: Da Capo Press, 1969).

DESCARTES, RENÉ, *Œuvres et lettres* (Paris: Gallimard, 1953).

DIDEROT, DENIS, *Salons*, ed. Jean Seznec (Oxford: Clarendon Press, 4 vols., 2nd edn., 1975–83).

DIODORUS OF SICILY, ed. C. H. Oldfather (London: Heinemann, 1933).

DROST, WOLFGANG, 'De la critique d'art baudelairienne', *Baudelaire, Actes du colloque de Nice, Annales de la faculté des lettres et sciences humaines de Nice*, 4–5 (1968).

DUBRAY, JEAN-PAUL, *Constantin Guys* (Paris: Editions Rieder, 1930).

DUFLO, PIERRE, *Constantin Guys* (Paris: Arnaud Seydoux, 1988).

DUMUR, GUY, *Delacroix romantique* (Paris: Mercure de France, 1973).

ESCHOLIER, RAYMOND, *Eugène Delacroix* (Paris: Cercle d'Art, 1963).

FAIRLIE, ALISON, *Imagination and Language* (Cambridge: Cambridge University Press, 1981).

FARWELL, BEATRICE, 'Sources for Delacroix's *Death of Sardanapalus*', *The Art Bulletin*, xl (1958).

FAUNCE, SARAH, and NOCHLIN, LINDA, *Courbet Reconsidered* (New Haven and London: Yale University Press, 1988).

FERRAN, ANDRÉ, *L'Esthétique de Baudelaire* (Paris: Hachette, 1933).

FLAUBERT, GUSTAVE, *L'Education sentimentale* (Paris: Conard, 1923).

—— *Par les champs et par les grèves* (Paris: Conard, 1927).

—— *Madame Bovary* (Paris: Conard, 1930).

—— *Correspondance*, 3 vols. (Paris: Gallimard, 1973–91).

FREUD, SIGMUND, *Jokes and their Relation to the Unconscious* (Harmondsworth: Penguin, 1976).

FRIED, MICHAEL, *Courbet's Realism* (Chicago and London: University of Chicago Press, 1990).

FRIED, MICHAEL, *Manet's Modernism or, The Face of Painting in the 1860s* (Chicago and London: University of Chicago Press, 1996).

GAUTIER, THÉOPHILE, *Histoire de l'art dramatique en France depuis vingt-cinq ans* (Paris: Hetzel, 1859).

——*Salon* (Paris, 1859).

——*Abécédaire du Salon de 1861* (Paris: Dentu, 1861).

——*Portraits contemporains* (Paris: Charpentier, 1874).

——*Voyage en Espagne* (Paris: Charpentier, 1879).

——*Ecrivains et artistes romantiques* (Paris: Tallandier, 1929).

GEOFFROY, GUSTAVE, *Constantin Guys: l'Historien du second Empire* (Paris: Crès, 1920).

GIDE, ANDRÉ, *Incidences* (Paris: Gallimard, 1924).

GILLOT, HUBERT, *E. Delacroix* (Paris: Belles Lettres, 1928).

GONCOURT, EDMOND AND JULES DE, *Gavarni: l'Homme et l'œuvre* (Paris: Fasquelle, 1925).

GOYA, FRANCISO DE, *Goya: The Complete Etchings and Lithographs* (New York: Prestel, 1995).

GRANDVILLE, J. J., *Un autre monde* (Paris, 1844).

——*L'Œuvre graphique complète de Grandville*, 2 vols. (Paris: Arthur Hubschmid, 1975).

GRAPPE, GEORGES, 'Constantin Guys', *L'Art et le beau*, 4ᶜ année, vol. i (1907).

HAMBLY, PETER, 'Idéologie et poésie: notes sur Baudelaire et ses contemporains', *Australian Journal of French Studies*, 16/2 (1979).

HAMILTON, GEORGE HEARD, *Manet and his Critics* (New Haven and London: Yale University Press, 1986).

HAMILTON, VIVIEN, *Boudin at Trouville* (London: John Murray, 1992).

HANNOOSH, MICHELE, *Baudelaire and Caricature: From the Comic to an Art of Modernity* (University Park: Pennsylvania State University Press, 1992).

——*Painting and the* Journal *of Eugène Delacroix* (Princeton: Princeton University Press, 1995).

HAUSSARD, P., 'Le Christ au sépulcre', *Le National* (10 Nov. 1844).

HEMMINGS, F. W. J., *Baudelaire the Damned* (London: Hamish Hamilton, 1982).

HERDING, KLAUS, *Courbet: To Venture Independence* (New Haven and London: Yale University Press, 1991).

HIDDLESTON, J. A., *Essai sur Laforgue et les 'Derniers Vers'* (Lexington: French Forum Publications, 1980).

——'"Fusée", Maxim and Commonplace', *Modern Language Review* (July 1985).

——*Baudelaire and 'Le Spleen de Paris'* (Oxford: Clarendon Press, 1987).

——'Les Poèmes en prose de Baudelaire et la caricature', *Romantisme*, 74 (1991).

HOBBES, THOMAS, *Leviathan*, ed. R. Tuck (Cambridge: Cambridge University Press, 1991).

HOFFMANN, E. T. A., *The Golden Pot and other Tales*, trans. Ritchie Robertson (Oxford: Oxford University Press, 1992).

HOFMANN, WERNER, *Nana: Mythos und Wirklichkeit* (Cologne: Verlag M. DuMont Schauberg, 1973).

HORACE, *Odes*.

HORNER, LUCIE, *Baudelaire critique de Delacroix* (Geneva: Droz, 1956).

HOWELLS, BERNARD, *Baudelaire: Individualism, Dandyism and the Philosophy of History* (Oxford: Legenda, 1996).

HUET, RENÉ-PAUL, *Paul Huet* (Paris: Laurens, 1911).

HUGO, CHARLES, *Victor Hugo en Zélande* (Paris: Lévy, 1868).

HUGO, VICTOR, *Théâtre complet*, 2 vols. (Paris: Gallimard, 1963).

——*Œuvres dramatiques et critiques complètes* (Paris: Pauvert, 1963).

——*L'Homme qui rit* (Paris: Flammarion, 1982).

HYSLOP, LOIS BOE, *Baudelaire as a Love Poet and Other Essays* (University Park and London: Pennsylvania State University Press, 1969).

——*Baudelaire: Man of his Time* (New Haven: Yale University, Press, 1980).

JOHNSON, LEE, *The Paintings of Eugène Delacroix: A Critical Catalogue*, 6 vols. (Oxford: Clarendon Press, 1981–9).

JOHNSON, SAMUEL, *The Rambler*.

JOUBERT, LAURENT, *Traité du ris* (Paris: 1579).

JUNOD, PHILIPPE, 'Voir et Savoir ou de l'ambiguité de la critique', *Etudes de lettres*, série iv, 3 (Apr.–June 1980).

KANT, EMMANUEL, *Critique of Judgement* (Oxford: Clarendon Press, 1986).

KELLEY, DAVID, 'Deux aspects du *Salon de 1846* de Baudelaire: la dédicace aux Bourgeois et la couleur', *Forum for Modern Language Studies*, 5/4 (Oct. 1969).

——'L'Art: l'harmonie du beau et de l'utile', *Romantisme*, 5 (1973).

KNYFF, GILBERT DE, *Eugène Boudin raconté par lui-même* (Paris: Meyer, 1976).

KÖHLER, INGEBORG, *Baudelaire et Hoffmann* (Uppsala: Studia Romanica Uppsaliensia, 1979).

KONODY, P. G., *The Painter of Victorian Life* (London: Geoffrey Holmes, 1930).

LABRUSSE, RÉMI, 'Baudelaire et Meryon', *L'Année Baudelaire* 1, (1995).

LA BRUYÈRE, JEAN DE, *Les Caractères*, ed. R. Garapon (Paris: Garnier, 1962).

LA FONTAINE, JEAN DE, *Fables*.

LAMMENAIS, FÉLICITÉ DE, *De l'art et du beau* (Paris: Garnier, 1872).

——*Esquisse d'une philosophie* (Paris, 1840).

LA ROCHEFOUCAULD, FRANÇOIS DE, *Maximes*.

LEAKEY, F. W., 'Baudelaire: The Poet as Moralist', in *Studies in Modern French Literature presented to P. Mansell Jones* (Manchester: Manchester University Press, 1961).

——*Baudelaire and Nature* (Manchester: Manchester University Press, 1969).

LEAKEY, F. W., *Baudelaire, Collected Essays, 1953–1988* (Cambridge: Cambridge University Press, 1990).

LEMOINE, PASCALE, *Eugène Boudin: roi des ciels* (Lausanne: Bibliothèque des Arts, 1981).

LLOYD, ROSEMARY, *Baudelaire et Hoffmann: affinités et influences* (Cambridge: Cambridge University Press, 1979).

MACCHIA, GIOVANNI, *Baudelaire critico* (Milan: Rizzoli, 1988).

MCWILLIAM, NEIL, *Dreams of Happiness: Social Art and the French Left, 1830–1850* (Princeton: Princeton University Press, 1993).

MAIGRON, LOUIS, *Le Romantisme et les mœurs* (Paris: Champion, 1919).

MALRAUX, ANDRÉ, *Les Voix du silence* (Paris: NRF, 1951).

——*Œuvres complètes*, i. (Paris: Gallimard, 1989).

MAN, PAUL DE, *Blindness and Insight*, 2nd edn. (London: Methuen, 1983).

MANET, EDOUARD, *Manet 1832–1883*, catalogue of the exhibition at the Metropolitan Museum of New York (New York: Harry N. Abrams, 1983).

MANŒUVRE, LAURENT, *Boudin et la Normandie* (Paris: Editions Anthèse, 1991).

——*Eugène Boudin: dessins* (Arcueil: Editions Anthèse, 1991).

MATURIN, CHARLES, *Melmoth the Wanderer* (Harmondsworth: Penguin, 1977).

MAURON, CHARLES, *Le Dernier Baudelaire* (Paris: José Corti, 1966).

——'Le rire baudelairien', *Europe* (Apr.–May 1967).

MAY, GITA, *Diderot et Baudelaire: critiques d'art* (Paris and Geneva: Minard/Droz, 1957).

MERYON, CHARLES, *Charles Meryon, Paris um 1850* (Frankfurt: Städelsches Kunstinstitut, 1975).

MILLET, JEAN-FRANÇOIS, *Jean-François Millet* (London: Haywood Gallery, 1976).

MOLIÉRE, *Œuvres complètes*, 2 vols. (Paris: Gallimard, 1956).

MOSS, ARMAND, *Baudelaire et Delacroix* (Paris: Nizet, 1973).

MOREAU-NÉLATON, E., *Manet raconté par lui-même* (Paris: Laurens, 1926).

MRAS, GEORGE P., *Eugène Delacroix's Theory of Art* (Princeton: Princeton University Press, 1966).

NERVAL, GÉRARD DE, *Œuvres*, vol. i (Paris: Gallimard, 1974).

NOON, PATRICK, *Richard Parkes Bonington: 'On the Pleasure of Painting'* (New Haven: Yale Center for British Art, 1991).

ŒHLER, DOLF, *Pariser Bilder I (1830–1848): Antibourgeoise Asthetik bei Baudelaire, Daumier und Heine* (Frankfurt: Suhrkamp, 1979).

OVID, *Tristia: Epistulae ex ponto* (London: Heinemann, 1988).

——*Metamorphoses.*

PASCAL, BLAISE, *Pensées*, Brunschvicg and Lafuma.

——*Les Provinciales*, ed. H. F. Stewart (Manchester: Manchester University Press, 1920).

PATTY, JAMES, 'Baudelaire and Bossuet on Laughter', *Publications of the Modern Language Association of America*, 80 (Sept. 1965).

PERRUCHOT, HENRI, *Manet* (Paris: Hachette, 1959).

PICHOIS, CLAUDE, *Baudelaire: études et témoignages* (Neuchâtel: La Baconnière, 1976).

——(ed.) *Lettres à Baudelaire* (Neuchâtel: La Baconnière, 1973).

—— and ZIEGLER, JEAN, *Baudelaire* (Paris: Julliard, 1987).

PICON, GAËTAN, *The Birth of Modern Painting* (London: Tiger Books International, 1991).

PLANCHE, GUSTAVE, *Etudes sur l'école française*, 2 vols. (Paris: Michel Lévy, 1855).

POINSINET DE SIVRY, LOUIS, *Traité des causes physiques et morales du rire* ([1768] Exeter: Exeter University Publications, 1986).

POULET, GEORGES, *La Conscience critique* (Paris: José Corti, 1971).

PRÉVOST, JEAN, *Baudelaire* (Paris: Mercure de France, 1953).

PROUST, ANTONIN, *Edouard Manet Souvenirs* (Caen: L'Echoppe, 1988).

PROUST, MARCEL, *Contre Sainte-Beuve* (Paris: Gallimard, 1971).

——*A la recherche du temps perdu*, 4 vols. (Paris: Gallimard, 1987).

QUINTILIAN, *Institutio oratoria*.

RACINE, JEAN, *Théâtre complet* (Paris: Garnier, 1980).

RASER, TIMOTHY, *A Poetics of Art Criticism: The Case of Baudelaire*, North Carolina Studies in the Romance Languages and Literatures (Chapel Hill: University of North Carolina Press, 1989).

REBEYROL, PHILIPPE, 'Baudelaire et Manet', *Les Temps modernes*, 48 (October 1949).

REY, ROBERT, *Manet* (Paris: Flammarion, 1966).

RIMBAUD, ARTHUR, *Œuvres complètes* (Paris: Gallimard, 1972).

ROGER-MARX, CLAUDE, *Eugène Boudin* (Paris: Crès, 1927).

ROY, DENIS-PRUDENT, *Traité médico-phylosophique sur le rire* (Paris: Crochard, 1814).

RUBIN, JAMES H., *Manet's Silence and the Poetics of Bouquets* (London: Reaktion Books, 1994).

RUFF, M. A., *L'Esprit du mal et l'esthétique baudelairienne* (Paris: Armand Colin, 1955).

SAHLBERG, OSKAR, *Baudelaire und seine Muse auf dem Weg zur Revolution* (Frankfurt: Suhrkamp, 1980).

SAINTE-BEUVE, CHARLES-AUGUSTIN, *Nouveaux Lundis* (Paris: Michel Lévy, 1886).

——*Volupté* (Paris: Gallimard, 1986).

SAINT-SIMON, CLAUDE-HENRI DE, *Œuvres* (Paris: Anthropos, 1966) (reprint of *Œuvres de Saint-Simon et Enfantin*, ed. E. Dentu, 1868–76).

SAND, GEORGE, *Correspondance*, ed. Georges Lubin, vol. ii (Paris: Garnier, 1964–90).

SCHMIT, ROBERT, *Eugène Boudin 1824–1898* (Paris: Schmit, 1973).

SCHNEIDERMAN, RICHARD S. ed. *The Catalogue raisonné of the Prints of Charles Meryon* (London: Garton & Co., 1990).

SCOTT, SIR WALTER, *Ivanhoe* (Edinburgh: T. C. & E. C. Jack, n.d.).

SCUDO, PAUL, *Philosophie du rire* (Paris: Poirée, 1840).

SLYKE, GRETCHEN VAN, 'Riot and Revolution in the *Salon de 1846*', *French Forum*, 10/3 (Sept. 1985).

SOLKIN, DAVID, 'Philibert Rouvière: E. Manet's *L'Acteur tragique*', *Burlington Magazine*, cxvii (Nov. 1975).

SPECTOR, J., *Delacroix: The Death of Sardanapalus* (London: Allen Lane, 1974).

STAROBINSKI, JEAN, *Portrait de l'artiste en saltimbanque* (Geneva: Skira, 1970).

STENDHAL, *Racine et Shakespeare* (Paris: Le Divan, 1928).

——*Histoire de la peinture en Italie* (Paris: Le Divan, 1929).

——*Molière, Shakespeare: La Comédie et le rire* (Paris: Le Divan 1929).

——*Le Rouge et le Noir* (Paris: Garnier, 1973).

——*La Chartreuse de Parme* (Paris: Garnier, 1973).

STENZEL, HARTMUT, *Der historische Ort Baudelaires* (Munich: Fink, 1980).

——'Les écrivains et l'évolution idéologique de la petite bourgeoisie dans les années 1840: le cas de Baudelaire', *Romantisme*, 17–18 (1987).

TABARANT, A., *Manet et ses œuvres* (Paris: Gallimard, 1947).

THIIS, JENS, 'Manet et Baudelaire. Quelques considérations sur le Romantisme et le Naturalisme', *Etudes d'Art*, i. (Algiers, 1945).

THORÉ, THÉOPHILE, *Salons de W. Bürger 1861–1868* (Paris: Renouard, 1870).

TOURNEUX, MAURICE, *Eugène Delacroix devant ses contemporains* (Paris: Jules Rouam, 1886).

TRAPP, F. A., *The Attainment of Delacroix* (Baltimore and London: Johns Hopkins University Press, 1971).

VIGNY, ALFRED DE, *Œuvres complètes*, 2 vols. (Paris: Gallimard, 1986).

VORAGINE, JACQUES DE, *La Légende dorée*, ed. Teodor de Wyzewa (Paris: Perrin et Cie, 1925).

WRIGHT, BARBARA, and SCOTT, DAVID H. T., *Baudelaire: 'La Fanfarlo' and 'Le Spleen de Paris'* (London: Grant and Cutler, 1984).

WRIGLEY, RICHARD, *The Origins of French Art Criticism* (Oxford: Clarendon Press, 1993).

ZOLA, EMILE, *Ecrits sur l'art* (Paris: Gallimard, 1991).

Index

Printed in the United Kingdom
by Lightning Source UK Ltd.
1005